DARK HORSE

A Biography of Wendell Willkie

ALSO BY STEVE NEAL

The Eisenhowers: Reluctant Dynasty

Tom McCall: Maverick (with Tom McCall)

Steve Neal

DARK HORSE

A Biography of Wendell Willkie

DOUBLEDAY & COMPANY, INC.
GARDEN CITY, NEW YORK
1984

Library of Congress Cataloging in Publication Data

Neal, Steve, 1949–
Dark Horse.

Bibliography.
Includes index.
1. Willkie, Wendell L. (Wendell Lewis), 1892–1944.
2. United States–Politics and government–1933–1945.
3. Politicians–United States–Biography. I. Title.
E748.W7N43 1984 973.917'092'4 [B]

ISBN: 0-385-18439-5
Library of Congress Card Catalog Number 83-1977

Printed in the United States of America

First Edition

CONTENTS

CONTENTS

INTRODUCTION

Wendell L. Willkie never held a public office, yet he nearly became President of the United States. A registered Democrat until the fall of 1939, he captured the Republican party's most coveted nomination less than a year later. More than any other private citizen, Willkie would unite his country against the menace of Nazi Germany and Imperial Japan. Without him, the United States would have entered World War II bitterly divided. Largely because of Willkie, Americans entered the war with a common purpose.

"It is impossible to think of a career like that of Wendell Willkie in Europe," said British scholar Harold Laski, "save as the outcome of the breakdown in a social system." In the spring of 1940, it took nothing less than the collapse of European democracy to make possible Willkie's spectacular political breakthrough. With revivalist oratory, he had been warning his countrymen for months about the danger of a Hitler-controlled Europe. Front-running Republican contenders Thomas Dewey, Robert Taft, and Arthur Vandenberg insisted the world war wasn't a national concern since two oceans protected the United States from the aggressors. Shortly before the GOP convened in Philadelphia, Hitler's armies swallowed Denmark, Norway, the Low Countries, and France. Pointing out that Britain would be the next Nazi target, Willkie called for American military assistance short of direct intervention.

In a time for heroes, Willkie was a man of the hour. The Hoosier who spoke with such passionate conviction struck millions of Americans as fresh and appealing. "He touched something fundamental in the hearts of our people," said Dwight D. Eisenhower. Willkie's forthright views on the war gained him the active support of powerful newspaper and magazine publishers who used their news columns to promote his long-shot candidacy. At the 1940 Republican National Convention, this remarkable publicity buildup and the "We Want Willkie" fervor of the galleries combined to make him the presidential nominee of his adopted party.

Almost overnight Willkie moved the Republican party out of its hidebound isolationism and sent a message to the world that Americans stood together against Axis aggression. Franklin D. Roosevelt, though concerned about him as a formidable opponent, called Willkie's nomination a "godsend" because it finally brought national unity. Walter Lippmann later wrote, "Second only to the Battle of Britain, the sudden rise and nomination of Willkie was the decisive event, perhaps providential, which made it possible to rally the free world when it was almost conquered. Under any other leadership but his, the Republican party would in 1940 have turned its back on Great Britain, causing all who still resisted Hitler to feel that they were abandoned."

Broad-shouldered and handsome, slightly overweight, Willkie stood an inch over six feet and weighed 220 pounds. His thick, dark hair was usually tousled. Though he wore freshly pressed suits, his clothes soon looked as if they had been slept in. His mind was quick, alert, endlessly curious. He was a man of driving energy and compelling force.

Nearly everyone who met him was captivated. "Few Americans have had so powerful a magnetism," said historian Bernard De Voto. Henry Luce termed him "a force of nature." Stanley Walker of the New York *Herald Tribune* wrote, "In any gathering, he is about as anonymous and inconspicuous as a buffalo bull in a herd of cattle." Oren Root, the young lawyer who organized the Willkie clubs, called him "a meteor of unusual brilliance." John Gunther remembered him as "one of the most lovable, most gallant, most zealous, and most forward-looking Americans of this–or any–time." Few persons were neutral about Willkie. Alice Roosevelt Longworth acidly remarked that he had "sprung from the grass roots of the country clubs of America." Harold Ickes dubbed him "the simple, barefoot boy from Wall Street." Right-wing industrialist Edgar M. Queeny described him as "America's leading ingrate." Lord Halifax found him

to be "a rough and uninhibited frontiersman." Not even Willkie's political adversaries could fully resist his charm. "He's grass-roots stuff," declared FDR. "His sincerity comes through with terrific impact."

As the Republican standard-bearer, he waged the most energetic campaign of any presidential candidate since Teddy Roosevelt. By the end, his voice was reduced to a hoarse whisper. The same factors that had compelled his nomination worked against his election, for FDR was the political beneficiary of the worsening international situation. Though losing what turned out to be the closest presidential race in a generation, Willkie received more votes than any previous Republican candidate, setting a record that would not be eclipsed until Eisenhower's 1952 landslide. "Willkie earned a permanent place for himself in American history," wrote Henry Steele Commager, "that of a statesman who understood the sound principles of American party politics, and who removed foreign policy from the realm of party controversy and furthered national unity in this most delicate and important field."

Following his defeat, Willkie grew in stature. While failing to win the presidency, he left a more lasting impression than many of the men who did. His wartime collaboration with FDR included special missions to London during the Blitz and later to the Middle East, Russia, and China. On the home front, he became the conscience of American politics, speaking out against isolationism, imperialism, and the persecution of minorities. In the process, he alienated the power elite of the GOP, which blocked his attempted comeback in 1944. Within a few months, the nation was stunned to learn of his death at the age of fifty-two. "Willkie placed principles above compromise and expediency," Adlai E. Stevenson later observed. "It was this kind of selflessness following so closely on the disappointment of political defeat that has kept and will always keep Wendell Willkie's memory alive for all Americans."

In memory of William H. Jones and Aldo Beckman, newspapermen and friends who exemplified the best of their profession. And also for Tom McCall of Oregon, who was a free spirit in the Willkie tradition.

DARK HORSE

A Biography of Wendell Willkie

CHAPTER ONE

ELWOOD

On a sweltering August afternoon in 1940, Wendell Lewis Willkie returned to his boyhood home of Elwood, in north central Indiana, and accepted the Republican presidential nomination. What was said to be the greatest crowd in American political history—nearly 200,000 persons—had converged on the small town for Willkie's day. Although he now lived in New York and had been gone from Indiana for twenty years, Willkie still spoke in a word-slurring Hoosier twang and often noted that his roots were in the American heartland.

Some local residents held against Willkie the fact that he and his five brothers and sisters had moved away. But, in truth, Elwood was the kind of small midwestern town which the most ambitious young people left following their graduation from high school. Once a prosperous community, the Elwood of 1940 was an industrial graveyard. A large percentage of the local population was receiving state and federal relief. A tin mill had closed in December of 1937, and the last of the big glass plants shut down in 1938. Weeds and hollyhocks had sprung up around the huge factories that were now abandoned and turning to rust.

During Willkie's youth, Elwood had been a booming industrial center. With the discovery of natural gas, the population jumped from two thousand to more than thirteen thousand in the early 1890s. In 1892, the year of Willkie's birth, Governor William McKinley of Ohio came to town and dedicated what was called the nation's largest tinplate plant. Elwood's overnight prosperity attracted other entrepreneurs, and within a short time it numbered among its business establishments forty poolrooms and whorehouses. His father led a campaign to wipe out the town's red-light district and shut down its saloons. The Willkie family was viewed with awe by the people of Elwood. Herman Willkie organized the local school system and raised funds for a town library. He was also considered Elwood's best trial lawyer. His wife, Henrietta, the first woman to be admitted to the Indiana bar, was his law partner.

All of the Willkie children were brought up to succeed. His parents encouraged his early interest in literature and history. Herman Willkie woke his children each morning by shouting literary quotations up the stairs. He owned the largest private library in town—more than six thousand books—and Wendell went through Alger and Henty, Shakespeare, Thackeray, Scott, and Dickens. In the evenings, Herman read aloud to the children for more than an hour and sometimes had them interpret Shakespearean roles. Wendell's favorite was King Lear. He observed years later that his brothers and sisters had been reared in "a constant atmosphere of reading and discussion."

He was born Lewis Wendell Willkie on February 18, 1892, the fourth of six children, in the parlor of his parents' house on the corner of South A and Nineteenth streets. From the start, other members of the family addressed him as "Wen" rather than Lewis. There was intense competition among the Willkie siblings, and they often argued about their reading and nearly everything else. Years later, Wendell said that he learned how to debate at the family dinner table in an effort to hold his own with his brothers and sisters.

Henrietta Willkie was the dominant personality in the household. To her children, she seemed stern and aloof, a woman who commanded respect more than affection. Yet it was from her that Wendell inherited his passion for success. She kept rigid rules and demanded achievement from her children, who later characterized her as "a woman driven by an indomitable will." As a working mother, she hired a housekeeper to take care of the children and prepare meals. Henrietta hated to cook, although she enjoyed canning fruits and making berry jam. She won prizes for crochet, painted china, and played the piano. She was unsentimental, had a quick mind, and, something of a nonconformist, was the first woman in Elwood to smoke cigarettes.

Before going into law practice, Herman had been superintendent of schools in Elwood and replaced the old-fashioned one-room school system with a progressive grade system that resulted in the construction of new schools. He invested heavily in real estate during Elwood's boom period and built more than two hundred homes and a downtown commercial building. When he turned to the law, Herman was known as a reformer and people's advocate. In an age when there were no workmen's compensation laws, he often brought personal injury suits for blue-collar clients. He was one of the few lawyers in Indiana who refused to carry a free railroad pass.

Born in Prussia in 1857, Herman Willkie came to Indiana with his family at the age of four. His father had been among the university students who took part in the 1848 German revolution against the autocratic monarchy. One of Herman's earliest memories was being beaten by a Prussian officer who, while watching the household, had stumbled over him as he played. In raising his own children, Herman often spoke of the incident as an example of Old World militarism and its brutality. Henrietta's family, too, had been among the German liberals who had fled their homeland as a direct result of their participation in revolutionary disturbances.

It was from his father that Wendell derived his fascination with politics and an early commitment to liberalism. One of Madison County's leading Democrats, Herman once supported a Socialist party candidate for mayor and campaigned actively for William Jennings Bryan in the 1896 presidential election. Wendell said later that he first became aware of politics that fall, when he was four years old, because it was the main topic of conversation at home. His father took him to a torchlight parade for Bryan in late October. The Willkie brothers had a sidewalk fight with the McCarl brothers, who were Republicans, over the outcome of the presidential race. Although the Willkies won their fight, Bryan was defeated by Republican William McKinley. Four years later Bryan regained the Democratic presidential nomination and was an overnight guest at the Willkie house during his swing through Indiana. At the age of eight, Wendell met his political hero, and he would always remember the excitement of that evening. As he matured, Wendell shifted his allegiance from Bryan to Robert La Follette, Wisconsin's great progressive leader, and Woodrow Wilson, the public man he admired above all others.

In campaign speeches, Wendell asserted that he had grown up "the hard, not the soft way." In fact, he grew up in comfortable surroundings. While not wealthy, the Willkies were financially secure. In 1900 they moved into a new three-story house on the more fashionable north side of town. With a broad lawn and shaded by soft maple trees, it was the sort of home that might have served as the setting for one of Booth Tarkington's richly evocative stories of Indiana life.

All of the Willkie children were required to work. While still in grade school, Wendell drove a cow to pasture on the northern outskirts of town in the morning and brought it back each night. One summer he sorted spoiled vegetables from the good produce at a neighborhood grocery store. Another summer he worked for a junk dealer. He helped his older brother Robert distribute handbills and patent medicine samples for a Cleveland advertising agency. For another summer, he drove a horse-drawn delivery wagon for a bakery from four in the morning until dusk and traded bread for eggs when some of the farmers could not afford to pay cash.

Entering Elwood High School in January of 1906, Wendell was a tall, gangling fourteen-year-old who was considered bright but less interested in his studies than having a good time. During his first semester, he and several friends climbed the town's highest gas tank and painted their class numerals in six-foot-high letters. One night he stole the physiology class skeleton and hung it from a nearby tree. He was caught painting graffiti on the school sidewalk and suspended from school. "Every boy who was worth a damn was at one time or another suspended from our school," Robert Willkie recalled years later.

That summer Willkie's parents sent him to Culver Military Academy, partly because they thought he needed some discipline and also because Wendell had begun to develop a slight stoop, which Herman hoped the Culver instructors might help correct. For Wendell, it was an emotionally wrenching period. A group of older cadets subjected him to frequent hazing and, when he fought back, taunted him even more. Homesick and frustrated, he often wept in his room. But there were also bright moments. Wendell learned how to swim and operate a sailboat.

On returning to Elwood, Wendell showed more enthusiasm for his studies and his grades improved considerably. One of the reasons for this radical change was Wendell's determination not to be sent back to Culver. But another factor was his youthful new teacher, Philip Carleton Bing, who came to Elwood after receiving a master's degree at the University of Chicago. "That boy wasn't worth a damn until his second year in high school," Calvin Sizelove, a Willkie classmate, said years later. "It was a little redheaded Irishman, Professor Pat Bing, that fixed that boy up. He started preaching to Wendell to get to work and that kid went to town."

Although he played on the football team his sophomore year, Wendell was uncoordinated and spent most of his time on the bench. In such a competitive family, Wendell's failure at sports was a keen disappointment. His brothers, larger and better coordinated, were among the school's athletic heroes. Edward, the youngest, would go on to become an All-American football lineman for Navy and an Olympic wrestler.

Wendell managed to outshine his brothers in another field. He became the star performer on the school's debate team, which was coached by Bing. In three years of competition, he finished on the losing side only once, failing to convince a panel of small-town judges that immigration should not be restricted in the United States. Willkie did not hesitate to challenge his teachers in the classroom and sometimes got into trouble with disciplinary authorities for questioning a teacher's facts and interpretation.

It was in high school that Willkie's personality began to emerge. He was more purposeful and ambitious than his brothers. His brother Robert said that Wendell was "less of a nonconformist than the rest of us." Wendell told another of his brothers that it was important to be clever and to consider the likes and dislikes of other people. He was chosen president of Beta Phi Sigma, the school's most elite fraternity, but resigned his membership when a sorority blackballed his girlfriend because she was the daughter of immigrants. Wendell organized an antifraternity club called the King of Beasts that held its own social functions. One of the most popular students at Elwood High, Willkie was elected class president in his senior year.

His most time-consuming activity during his school years was his courtship of Gwyneth Harry, a black-haired Welsh girl with fair skin and dark blue eyes. Although he had been attracted to several girls, she was his first serious romantic interest and the person for whom he quit the fraternity. When he was with her, he took pains to be on his best behavior and discontinued his habit of swearing. In order to spend Sundays with her, Willkie stopped going to the Methodist

Church, where his father taught Sunday school, and joined the Episcopal Church, where she sang in the choir.

In the summer of 1908, Wendell worked as an assistant catcher in Elwood's largest tinplate factory. His job was to guide white-hot steel ingots from a revolving steel cylinder back to the roller, who would repeat the process until the metal sheets were the right thickness. Willkie said later that the sweltering heat and fumes had been almost unbearable, and he considered it a major accomplishment that he lasted the entire summer.

The following summer Wendell took the train to South Dakota. His friend Paul Harmon was working as a restaurant cashier in Aberdeen and arranged for him to get a job as a dishwasher. The restaurant's owner soon moved Willkie out of the kitchen and had him running a tent hotel. Thousands of acres had recently been made available for homesteading in the area and pioneers descended on the pioneer town thicker than flies on raw meat. The owner, hoping to capitalize on the population boom, bought an old, faded circus tent and offered Willkie 30 per cent of the profits. They filled the tent with wooden bunks and straw mattresses, then charged homesteaders 50 cents a night. When business got slow, Willkie went out and dragged in half-conscious derelicts. After saving nearly $300, Willkie grew tired of running a flophouse and decided to move elsewhere.

He hopped a freight train to Powell, Wyoming, and spent all his money on a machine that made cement bricks. He had been told that scores of buildings were to be going up and his machine would help him get a piece of the local construction market. Unhappily enough, it was impossible to find any cement in Powell and his investment was worthless.

Willkie took another westbound freight train and got off in Montana, where he worked in a wheat field until his back was injured by a falling load of hay. While he liked working on the farm, he decided to move on when the farmer suggested he might have the neighboring farm for marrying his daughter. Wendell made his way to Yellowstone National Park and got a job as driver of a six-horse stagecoach for tourists. On his first trip, he ran the horses off the road, flipped over the stagecoach, and gave his passengers the scare of their lives. Remarkably, no one got hurt. But the manager of the stagecoach line saw the accident and fired Willkie on the spot.

In August of 1909, Wendell returned to Elwood and found his father in the middle of a three-month strike by the tinplate workers. The elder Willkie represented the Amalgamated Association of Iron, Steel, and Tin Plate Workers, which had called the strike in resistance to management efforts to institute an open-shop policy. The striking workers forced twenty-six mills to shut down, and the companies fought back by bringing in strikebreakers from Pennsylvania. One night as they were walking near the local train depot, Herman and Wendell were roughed up by strikebreaking thugs. When his father was struck in the temple, Wendell rushed and tackled one of the assailants. By the time Elwood police broke up the fight, both of the Willkies were bruised and bloody. The two men who attacked them later pleaded guilty to charges of assault and battery. When management sought a court injunction against the union, Herman Willkie blocked it in federal district court. He made Wendell his junior law clerk and took him to all meetings and conferences relating to the strike.

Herman took Wendell with him to Chicago for a meeting with Clarence Darrow, the nation's most renowned trial lawyer. The tinplate workers wanted Darrow to take over the case. Darrow said that he would defend the union for $20,000 and $1,000 a day in the courtroom. "There is nothing unethical in being adequately compensated for advocating a cause in which you deeply believe," Darrow told the seventeen-year-old Willkie.

The union's strike funds, however, were nearly depleted, and union officials told Darrow that they could not afford him. Herman Willkie took the case for $25 a day. Though he won the union's suit, it was a hollow victory, because the strike went on for so long that many workers returned to the plants and management succeeded in breaking the union.

Wendell now hoped to follow his father into law practice. In his final semester at Elwood High School, he received perfect grades for the first time. On January 28, 1910, he graduated from high school. A few days later, he enrolled at Indiana University.

CHAPTER TWO

REBEL WITH A CAUSE

In his four years at Indiana University, Lewis Wendell Willkie was known as a campus radical. "Any man who is not something of a Socialist before he is forty has no heart," he observed years later. "Any man who is still a Socialist after he is forty has no head." Wearing a red turtleneck sweater, Willkie denounced Bloomington's elite fraternities, called for the abolition of all inheritances, and challenged the faculty's rigid conservatism. During this period, the university's president, William Low Bryan, lectured football players on the virtues of platonic love, disapproved of student dissent, and was especially upset about an irreverent magazine called *Bogus,* to which Willkie and his brothers were contributors.

Bloomington, then as now, was a peaceful, tree-shaded college town set amid tumbling hills and lush green foliage. Five blocks east of the courthouse square was the heavily wooded campus of Indiana University with its broad, well-manicured lawns, ivy-covered brick buildings, and large Gothic structures with forbidding limestone walls. In later years, Indiana University would acquire a formidable national reputation, but in Willkie's student years it was still a parochial midwestern school, full of native students and native faculty. Wendell lived with his older brothers, Robert and Fred, and his sister Julia in a frame house at 523 East Third Street, which was within walking distance of the campus.

While not completely self-supporting as college students, the four Willkies had part-time jobs and their earnings were turned in to a family pool. Julia, a graduate student, taught at the local high school.

Robert, in law school, also was a part-time schoolteacher. The undergraduates, Fred and Wendell, waited on tables and took various other jobs.

The house on Third Street became a popular gathering place for a group of Indiana University students who shared Willkie's liberal political views. Wendell had discovered the writings of Karl Marx and, as a result, had become absorbed with socialism. After reading Marx's *Das Kapital,* he studied John Spargo's *History of Socialism* and Herbert Spencer's essay "The Coming Slavery." He approached the dean of the economics department and suggested that a course on socialism be included in the fall curriculum. When the dean expressed doubt that students would sign up for such a course, Willkie pledged to recruit ten others for the class. With some difficulty, he reached his quota–and, in the process, gained a reputation as leader of the campus socialist movement. In fact, Willkie was a liberal Democrat and had been a precinct worker for the party in Elwood.

Willkie became someone to be reckoned with in campus politics. By tradition, the most socially prominent fraternities dominated student elections. Willkie persuaded Paul Harmon, his friend from the South Dakota trip, to seek the presidency of the sophomore class. Though Harmon was considered an underdog, Willkie forged an alliance among the independents and fraternities that had been left off the official slate. With the Greek vote splitting, Harmon won the class presidency and Willkie earned considerable recognition as a political strategist.

His next target was the Indiana Union, the organization that controlled the student center, sponsored lectures and concerts, and governed all campus activities. For years, its directors had been chosen by the interfraternity leadership. Willkie supported an opposition slate headed by Paul McNutt, a maverick member of Beta Theta Pi, who later became governor of Indiana. With Willkie delivering the independents, McNutt won. As his reward, Willkie was named to the commission that rewrote the union's constitution.

When he switched from kingmaker to candidate, Wendell was less successful. In the spring of 1912, he sought to become manager of the university's yearbook, which would have given him a salary as well as prestige. Since it was expected to be a close vote, Willkie went to Indianapolis and obtained the proxies of thirty-six medical students who were members of the class. At the class meeting, Earl

Stroup, campaign manager for Willkie's opponent, waved a stack of papers and announced that the proxies had been revoked by the same students. Jolted, Wendell moved to have his proxies withdrawn and his motion quickly passed. By a vote of 129 to 91, Willkie was defeated. He later found out that Stroup had been bluffing and that the papers in his hand were blank. If Willkie had not folded so easily, he would have been within three votes of winning his only bid for student office.

The defeat, however, was little more than a temporary setback, for Willkie had lost none of his driving ambition. He was appointed to the student council's executive committee as well as the board of the Jackson Club, a Democratic organization on the campus. In April of 1912, he served as chairman of the Pennsylvania delegation at the Jackson Club's mock Democratic convention and worked the floor for Governor Woodrow Wilson of New Jersey, his favorite presidential candidate.

By his senior year, Willkie, while still a liberal, had moderated his views and was an influential member of the campus establishment. Wendell said that it was possible to get more accomplished by cooperating with the power elite on the campus.

Another reason for Willkie's changing attitude was the influence of Gwyneth Harry. Throughout his undergraduate years, Wendell continued dating Gwyneth, who attended Butler University in Indianapolis. Although they cared for each other, they also were becoming aware of strong differences in personality and temperament. Gwyneth lectured Wendell about his unkempt appearance and lack of tact. Willkie stubbornly resisted her suggestions, just as she refused to follow his blunt advice. Once, at a Butler University party, Wendell told Gwyneth that he didn't want her dancing because it was too intimate. What really bothered him, though, was that he felt awkward on the dance floor. While he was extremely open, Willkie was also extremely shy and self-conscious. Gwyneth told him she wouldn't give up something which she enjoyed. And despite Wendell's outspoken criticism of fraternities and sororities, Gwyneth joined Kappa Alpha Theta and began pressuring him to get into a fraternity at Bloomington. "The fact that he did not belong caused some embarrassment when he visited me at Butler," she wrote years later. Gwyneth felt that a social fraternity "would give him the polish he lacked."

Several houses were interested in pledging Willkie, and Gwyneth told his high school friend George De Hority that she would urge him to join Beta Theta Pi. When Willkie balked at the idea, she threatened to end their relationship. "If I don't join Beta, I'll lose my girl," Willkie told his roommate. Willkie did not call her bluff. In his final term, he accepted the bid from the Beta house and sent Gwyneth his fraternity pin with this note: "I have dedicated my life to you. In thee I have put my trust; let me never be confounded."

Despite his strong principles, Willkie's decision to join a fraternity provided an early indication that he was willing to bend them when there were personal considerations. Although Willkie told his roommate that his choice had been emotionally wrenching, his passion for Gwyneth outweighed his objections to the fraternity system.

With a B-plus grade point average, Willkie graduated in June of 1913. He planned to attend law school in Bloomington but decided to take at least a year off and earn enough money to finance the additional studies. Dr. James Albert Woodburn, dean of the history department, recommended him for a teaching slot in Coffeyville, Kansas. A few weeks later, the school board offered him a position as high school history teacher and Willkie accepted.

A small community in southeastern Kansas near the Oklahoma border, Coffeyville was best known as the place where the legendary Dalton Gang had made its last stand while attempting to rob two local banks. Robert and Grattan Dalton had been killed and their brother Emmett severely wounded during the Coffeyville raid. It had also been the jumping-off place for the great Oklahoma land rush when what had previously been Indian Territory was opened for settlement.

Willkie was a remarkable teacher who made history come vividly alive to his students. "The battle of the Marne is puny to me," a former student wrote him years later, "because I can never forget your description of England's defeat of the Spanish Armada." In Willkie's civics class, he encouraged his students to take an interest in world affairs and told them that England had the most perfect system of government. He also organized the school debate club, and when schools of neighboring towns failed to come up with teams, his students were matched against debate clubs of local farmers. Willkie had his class debate the proposition that American Presidents should be elected for a six-year term and ineligible for reelection.

Outside the classroom, Willkie coached the men's and women's basketball teams and a track squad that went undefeated in dual meet competition. His most embarrassing moment as a coach was taking his basketball team into Bartlesville, Oklahoma, only to make the discovery that Coffeyville had been booked for a football game. Though Willkie acknowledged that he should have checked out details beforehand, he talked Oklahoma officials into paying his team's travel expenses in spite of the fact that they didn't have enough men to field a football team.

After deciding to spend another year in Coffeyville, Willkie resigned in early November of 1914 when his brother Fred offered him a better-paying job as a lab worker in Puerto Rico. Although he loved teaching and would always talk about returning to it someday, Willkie's main ambition was to become a lawyer. "I knew that I could not be really independent," he said later, "unless I made good money."

To prepare for his job as a laboratory assistant, Willkie took a month's chemistry course at Oberlin College. In January of 1915, he sailed to San Juan and was met by his brother. The Willkies took a train along the eastern coastline to the village of Fajardo, where Fred was head chemist with a sugar company. Wendell's job, it turned out, was to check the sucrose content of hundreds of samples taken at different intervals during the refining process. He found it boring and tedious, but it paid well.

From his earliest days on the island, Willkie was struck by its wretched poverty, the misery and suffering of its people. One afternoon Willkie went horseback riding with a wealthy plantation owner. Suddenly, an emaciated native crawled out of the sugar cane, where he had been hiding for several days following a workers' revolt. Without hesitation, the owner hacked the worker with a machete, nearly dismembering an arm, then continued riding. The owner brushed aside Willkie's suggestion that they "help that poor devil." It was a scene that Willkie would always remember. In a 1978 interview, Gardner Cowles said that Willkie once told him that incident had resulted in his commitment to social justice. "Wendell said that from then on, he was determined to work for a better balance with a social conscience," said Cowles. "If he ever got into a position of influence, he wanted to make a difference."

In the fall of 1915, Willkie returned to Bloomington and resumed

his law studies, working with an intensity that allowed little time for outside activities. He developed a study plan in which he and three classmates went through a different book every night. Most of his study time was spent in the basement clubroom of Phi Delta Phi, the honorary law fraternity. After six years, Wendell and Gwyneth had broken off their relationship. The long months of separation had brought both of them to the realization that the magic of their high school romance had faded. Even so, both found it painful when they decided to stop seeing each other, and Gwyneth hinted to friends that she had been genuinely hurt by his growing indifference.

Willkie's hard work produced results. He won a forty-three-volume legal encyclopedia given annually to Indiana's top law student. In addition, he took the Moot Court Prize and the award for the school's best thesis. He was also elected class orator, which gave him a prominent role in graduation ceremonies. By tradition, the student speaker delivered a bland, upbeat address aimed to please his elders.

Always the maverick, Willkie had other ideas. His oration stunned the faculty and gray eminences of the Indiana Supreme Court. In a free-swinging assault on the state's constitution, Willkie called for the state to enact tougher regulations on banking and business. He then made some biting comments about the law school and its methods. President Bryan called it the most radical speech he had ever heard, and it created a sensation on the campus. For two days, the law school delayed awarding a degree to its top student. Finally, Dean Enoch Hogate summoned Willkie to his office, where he was reprimanded but still given his diploma.

In his first courtroom appearance, Willkie went up against his father. Although set to join the family law firm, Wendell agreed to prosecute an arson case so that his brother Robert, deputy county prosecutor, could leave town. For three hours, Wendell made his arguments to the jury. Since he had no witnesses, Wendell's evidence was shaky at best. Herman Willkie's summation of the case took only a few seconds. "I believe my son will be a very great lawyer," said the elder Willkie. "He can make so much out of so little."

Wendell lost the verdict.

CHAPTER THREE

ADVENTURES OF A YOUNG MAN

Willkie would not stay in Elwood for long. On April 2, 1917, President Wilson asked Congress to declare war on Germany, and, on the same day, Willkie enlisted in the United States Army. Although of German ancestry, he had strongly favored the Allied powers and American intervention, because "we Willkies inherited a hatred of everything Prussian."

For Willkie's generation, the Great War would become the central event in the shaping of its political philosophies and perceptions of the world. Franklin Delano Roosevelt, thirty-five years old and Assistant Secretary of the Navy, had vigorously pressed for U.S. intervention and tried in vain to resign his position and join the fighting. Captain Dwight D. Eisenhower, twenty-six years old, newly assigned to the 57th Infantry as regimental supply officer, had also requested combat duty but was destined to spend most of the war as a tank instructor. Harry Truman, thirty-three years old, a Missouri National Guard sergeant, would become commander of an artillery unit on the Western Front.

In May of 1917, Lewis Wendell Willkie, twenty-five years old, was among those reporting to Army Officers Training Camp at Fort Benjamin Harrison near Indianapolis. Eight weeks later he was commissioned as a first lieutenant. An army clerk, filling out the forms, reversed Willkie's first and middle names. Willkie, whose friends had always called him "Wen" or Wendell, made no effort to correct the clerk's error because he felt it would involve too much red tape. From then on, he went by Wendell L. Willkie.[1]

In August, Willkie took a special course on infantry tactics at Harvard University, then, much to his disappointment, was transferred to the 325th Artillery Regiment at Camp Zachary Taylor near Louisville. While his infantry buddies were sailing for Europe, Willkie was moving to another training camp. One of the reasons he disliked camp so much was that he had no sense of rhythm and had trouble keeping in step.

At the time, he was dating Edith Wilk, an attractive, slender, soft-spoken librarian from Rushville, Indiana. They had met two years earlier when Willkie was an usher and Miss Wilk a bridesmaid in the wedding of George De Hority and Louise Mauzy. Wendell commented that it would be easy to change her name from Wilk to Willkie and later arranged for her appointment as Elwood's town librarian, confiding to his mother that he had found the woman he planned to marry. Late in 1917, he proposed and she accepted. Their wedding was scheduled for January 12, 1918.

As chance would have it, Willkie got stranded in one of the heaviest blizzards in southern Indiana's history and arrived in Rushville two days late. Edith's bridal bouquet of white orchids and lilies of the valley, which he had brought from Louisville, was badly wilted. The Willkies were married in the big brown Victorian house in which Edith had grown up. Most of their guests bundled up in overcoats, because the furnace had gone out during the snowstorm. The next day Edith and Wendell returned to Camp Taylor and moved into a Louisville apartment.

In the spring of 1918, Willkie was ordered to take further artillery instruction at Fort Sill, Oklahoma. Soon after he got there, another officer made him a fifty-dollar bet that he didn't have the nerve to jump from a balloon. Willkie, who had never been in a balloon, accepted the wager with the hope that the commanding officer would refuse to grant permission for him to attempt it. But he gave Willkie a parachute and told him to go ahead. An instructor took the balloon to an altitude of about 1,500 feet and Willkie made his sky dive, landed safely, and collected the money. When a friend asked him why he had done something so reckless, Willkie replied, "If you are going into war, you can't be a coward."[2]

On September 9, Willkie departed for overseas service on the British ship *Canada*. By the time his regiment landed at Le Havre, the war was nearly over. They went by train to Camp De Souge and received orders to proceed to the Western Front. Before they made it, the armistice had been announced. Though celebrating the Allied triumph, Willkie regretted that the war had ended before he had heard shots fired in anger.

Over the next few months, he frequently served as defense counsel in court-martial cases for young soldiers who had gone AWOL. "I voluntarily defended boys, mostly from my own regiment, who, the fighting being over, relaxed their respect for some of the military regulations and saw no reason why they should not slip off now and then for a night in Paris," Willkie later wrote. "This activity won for me no recommendation of promotion. On the contrary, my immediate superior suggested that on account of it, I was a nuisance and should be demoted."[3]

Willkie had, in fact, been recommended for promotion to captain, and, while it was approved, the official papers never came and he was discharged as a first lieutenant. As a man who dealt with life in both realistic and imaginative ways, Willkie did not forgive this slight. But he more than made up for it, giving himself the promotion. In his own eyes, he was a captain and never ceased being one. Willkie's biographical sketches stated that he returned from France with the rank of captain. And on the rare occasions he wore a uniform, Willkie sported a bright pair of captain's bars.[4]

On his return to Indiana, Willkie gave serious thought to the possibility of a political career. Local Democratic leaders offered the returning war veteran their party's nomination for Congress from Indiana's eighth district. His chief sponsor was Dale Crittenberger, an Anderson newspaper editor who was then the most influential Democrat in Madison County. Congressman Albert Vestal, the forty-four-year-old Republican incumbent, then in his second term, was considered vulnerable to an attractive challenger. Willkie strongly leaned toward making the race. Before making up his mind, though, he sought the advice of Indianapolis Democratic boss Frank C. Dailey, an old family friend. Dailey acknowledged that Willkie might well upset Vestal in 1920, but said that it would be difficult to retain the seat in the traditionally Republican district. Dailey said that if Willkie ran and lost it would be damaging to his law practice and suggested that his long-term prospects in politics and the law would be much greater in a growing industrial area. Dailey suggested Akron, Ohio, and offered to help him get a job there. Willkie reluctantly took himself out of the running for Congress. As it turned out, Vestal handily won re-election a year later and remained in Congress until his death in 1932.

One of Willkie's favorite professors at Indiana University, Ernest H. Lindley, who had since been named president of the University of Idaho, offered him a position on Idaho's law faculty. Willkie liked the idea and said later that he would probably have taken the job except for the fact that his salary would not have begun until fall term.

Herman Willkie was interested in having both Wendell and Robert as law partners, but their mother, Henrietta, said they should seek greater opportunities and strongly opposed taking them back into the family firm. In a letter applying to the Firestone Tire and Rubber Company, Wendell said he wanted to make the move to Akron because of his "conviction that the future of a lawyer in a town of 10,000 is very much limited" and his "great desire to become connected with the legal department of a corporation such as you represent." Dailey, who had contacts at Firestone, also wrote him a recommendation. Willkie was soon hired as head of Firestone's employee legal department. In this position, he looked after the personal legal problems of Firestone workers, offered advice, and drafted wills.

In May of 1919, Willkie settled in Akron. In the booming rubber capital, lodging was tough to find, it was not uncommon for boardinghouses to have three men in a room, shared by nine men sleeping in eight-hour shifts. Chicken coops were transformed into lodging for factory workers. On his first night in town, he slept in an overstuffed chair in a hotel hallway. Eventually, Willkie managed to rent a room in a house on South Balch Street.

It would be fully seven months until Edith would join her husband. At the time, she was pregnant and chose to remain in Indiana until the baby came. Soon after the birth of their son, Philip, the Willkies were living together again. In their first months in Akron, they shared an apartment on Rhodes Avenue with another young couple. Later, they moved into a house at 80 Beck Avenue.

Bored with his mundane duties at Firestone, Willkie was eager to move into private law practice. Harvey Firestone, acknowledging the young man's talent, tried to keep him by offering to double his $5,000 salary. While the money was tempting, Edith told her husband that his long-term potential was better in private practice than with a huge corporation. "Wendell Willkie, you take your name on the letterhead and let the salary go," she told him. "The money doesn't matter now. Just make your name important." On December 31, 1920, Willkie resigned from Firestone and became a junior partner in the well-established Akron firm of Mather and Nesbitt. As Willkie left, Firestone told him that he would "never amount to much" because he was a Democrat.

Willkie soon gained a reputation as one of the city's top lawyers. Within five years, he was elected president of the Akron Bar Association. "I did get on well enough at the bar to keep me busy night and day, to accumulate a modest competence, and to win the respect of my fellow practitioners," he later recalled. "I represented all sorts and conditions of people—individuals, corporations and partnerships, involving every kind of problem—all those types of business that a lawyer in general practice in a city of 200,000 normally handles."[5]

In oral argument, he was logical, factual, and capable of pulling surprises. Some of his tactics became part of Akron folklore. By repeating a hostile judge's words to the jury, Willkie demonstrated judicial bias and had a case thrown out of court. On another occasion, he got a little girl to admit that she had been coached on what to say by the opposing lawyer and thereby won the case. Willkie also blocked a lawsuit against one of his clients by Harvey Firestone, his former employer.[6]

He became the law firm's specialist on utilities. By his own estimate, Willkie spent a fourth of his time representing the Northern Ohio Power and Light Company. He also served as counsel for such blue-chip clients as the Erie Railroad and the Ohio State Bank and Trust Company. In Columbus, he frequently testified before the Public Utilities Commission and negotiated rate increases and additional franchises for his clients. He was particularly effective in dealing with state legislators.

Without holding political office, he became one of Akron's best-known figures in the 1920s. At the age of thirty-three, Willkie was elected president of the Akron Bar Association. As commander of the Summit County American Legion post, he was the leading spokesman in the area for World War I veterans. During the 1921 recession, he converted Legion offices into unemployment centers for veterans. As a leader of the Akron Democratic Club, he was in frequent contact with Ohio's most prominent Democrats. In 1920 he gave the speech introducing Governor James M. Cox, the Democratic presidential nominee, at a local rally. In 1922 he was a key strategist in the re-election drive of Congressman Martin L. Davey. In 1924 Willkie was elected as a delegate to the Democratic National Convention in New York.

In April of 1924, Willkie wrote to former Secretary of War Newton D. Baker and offered his assistance in the League of Nations floor fight at the convention. President Wilson had died in February, and Baker, his adviser and confidant, was now the leading advocate for American entry into the League. "As aside from my loyalty to Governor Cox," wrote Willkie, "the principal reason I am going to the convention is to do what little I can to have the Democratic party pledge itself into the entrance of the United States into the League of Nations. I notice by press dispatches that you intend to insist upon such a plank in the national Democratic platform.

"My personal feeling about the United States' entrance in the League of Nations," Willkie went on, "almost reaches the point of religious conviction and I was wondering whether you could suggest anything that I might do between now and the date of the convention which might help toward getting the convention to adopt such a plank in its platform."[7]

A few days later Baker designated Willkie as one of his lieutenants on the convention floor. With his flair for revivalist oratory, Willkie had delivered hundreds of pro-League speeches at schoolhouses, county fairs, and street corners. Once when he was introduced as a guest of the Akron Rotary Club, Willkie stunned its membership by making a rip-roaring speech on the League of Nations.

While the controversy over the League of Nations seems dated to people who have grown accustomed to political debate over how to avoid thermonuclear holocaust, the struggle over American membership in the world peace organization stirred great passions. Indeed, it was one of the most critical ideological debates in the nation's history, one which foreshadowed the battle between isolationism and internationalism that would be the dominant issue in Willkie's political career.

On June 24, 1924, the Democratic party gathered at the old Madison Square Garden, a Moorish castle designed by Stanford White, for what would be the longest and most bitterly fought of all conventions. Because of the party's two-thirds rule, the leading presidential contenders, William Gibbs McAdoo and Alfred E. Smith, were headed for an epic deadlock. Willkie, for the moment, was much more concerned with the battle over the League than with the nomination. Their chances of getting a pro-League vote looked dim even though Wilson remained popular and a banner with the former President's portrait was the backdrop for the convention podium. A great many politicians who had been ardent supporters of the League thought it was a dead issue. "I shall never forget those early morning hours when Baker, physically a slight man, would return exhausted to his room to tell us—ardent, young and uninitiated in the obduracy of mentally set politicians—of his battles in the [Resolutions] Committee and to get fresh stimulation from our naive and infectious belief that so just a cause, so ably advocated, could not lose," Willkie recalled years later. "We heard him try out idea after idea, expression after expression, and were thrilled when he found anything of merit in one of our suggestions."[8]

Baker's appearance before the convention provided its most exciting moment. Earlier, the Resolutions Committee had rejected immediate entrance into the League in favor of a mild recommendation for a national referendum on the League. Undaunted, Baker drafted a minority report and made an emotional appeal to the delegates in which he evoked memories of American soldiers dying on the battlefields of Europe and Wilson's dream of a permanent peace.

The former War Secretary's remarks touched off a thunderous ovation. From the floor to the galleries, the applause was deafening. Many in the audience wept as they cheered. "I saw hard, stern men of the Western plains cry," Willkie recalled. Baker returned to the platform and the organist struck up "Onward Christian Soldiers." Willkie thought it had been "not only the greatest speech in the country but the greatest speech in the world."

For all his eloquence, though, Baker failed to change more than a few votes. By more than two to one, his pro-League resolution was voted down. "He lost," Willkie said, "because we who were his lieutenants were no match for the experienced convention manipulators in the practical business of lining up delegate votes."[9] In later years, Willkie suggested that the defection of Franklin D. Roosevelt had been a major factor in the outcome. In truth, FDR had supported the League after it was no longer politically fashionable to do so. Baker's resolution was doomed because of the combined opposition of big city and midwestern Democratic machines.

No sooner had this struggle ended than Willkie plunged into another emotional battle. He vigorously supported a resolution condemning the Ku Klux Klan. At the time, the "Invisible Empire" represented a powerful bloc in the Democratic party. The *New Republic* reported in November of 1923 that the Klan was a dominant influence in the politics of Indiana, Ohio, Texas, Oklahoma, Maine, Connecticut, and New Jersey. Back in Indiana, Herman Willkie had actively campaigned against the Klan. At the convention, the Klan had the votes to thwart the resolution that would have put the Democratic party on record against it.[10]

"The Klan fight was very bitter," Willkie told the Akron *Beacon-Journal*. "The fact that the resolution was defeated by only one vote means the Klan was absolutely exposed. They didn't gain anything by keeping the name of the Klan out of the plank. It got just as much publicity. I consider that there was an absolute repudiation of the Klan by this convention."[11]

In the presidential balloting, Willkie voted for Governor Smith. The Akron Klan, which opposed Smith because of his Catholicism, sent Willkie a telegram asking when he had "joined the payroll of the Pope." Willkie shot back, "The Klan can go to hell." For nine days, the convention deadlocked between Smith and McAdoo until both withdrew their candidacies and Wall Street lawyer John W. Davis was chosen on the 103rd ballot.

What happened at the convention made Willkie start organizing against the Klan. In 1924 the Ohio Klan was reported to have a membership of 400,000, which was the largest in the nation. In Akron, where most rubber workers had flocked from the hills of the Deep South and border states, the Invisible Empire claimed 50,000 followers, and it controlled city hall and a majority of the school board. With energy and gusto, Willkie organized a citizens' committee in June of 1925 for the stated purpose of breaking the Klan's influence over Akron's public school system. "Sometimes in a crisis there is a doubt as to the course to be pursued," said Willkie. "But I do not believe that any honest citizen has any doubt what to do in this case. This man Hanan [Akron Klan leader] has thrown down the challenge he controls this city. Let me take it up and fight it out."[12]

Willkie's committee nominated its own slate of candidates for the school board. He raised funds for the anti-Klan candidates and actively campaigned for them. And, in November, three of the four members of the slate were elected. It was widely recognized as the beginning of the end of Klan influence in Akron. A series of internal feuds further weakened the local Klan, and its leadership was dealt a major blow when a dissident faction made public the Akron chapter's financial records.

In his years in Akron, Willkie was in frequent demand as a public speaker. He made speeches before the Rotary Club, the Knights of Columbus, the Kiwanis Club, and the Akron Real Estate Board. He portrayed Lincoln in an Independence Day pageant. His speeches indicate that Willkie was still an outspoken progressive. The local newspaper dubbed him "the Bill Borah of Akron," comparing his oratory to the renowned Idaho senator. Attacking special-interest groups, Willkie told a local audience that constitutional democracy had been "changed to indirect democracy by the influence of blocs and organizations." In foreign policy, Willkie spoke out against war. "I do not care whether peace comes through leagues, courts, international agreements or otherwise," he said. "I only ask that the children of today be so educated to the futility of war that peace will come in the next generation." John S. Knight, then the young editor of the Akron *Beacon-Journal,* recalled in 1978 that Willkie "had a booming voice, waved his arms a great deal, and was indeed an impressive figure of a man."[13]

Although Akron's prosperity was directly tied to the automobile industry, Willkie did not own a car. His brothers explained later that he was never interested in mechanical things and tended to be a careless driver. Years earlier, while driving his brother Robert's 1911 Overland, Wendell let go of the steering wheel and gestured with his hands during a conversation with Edward Willkie and the car flipped over when he lost control. Wendell was unharmed, but his younger brother was pinned underneath the car, and he struggled to push the gravel away from Edward's face so that he wouldn't suffocate. "It was the one time I ever saw him really scared," Robert told Ellsworth Barnard years later. Before going into the Army, Wendell owned a Ford but sold it and never bought another automobile.[14]

Youthful in appearance, Willkie was a powerfully built, handsome man, full of energy and self-confidence. A member of an

Akron country club, he found golf dull and often sat on a bench by the eighteenth green and joked with his friends as they returned to the clubhouse weary and perspiring from several rounds. Willkie also abandoned bridge as too boring. What he enjoyed most were good arguments with well-informed friends. In the field of American history, he was a voracious reader. He chain-smoked cigarettes and never carried a watch. Edith set the household clocks several minutes ahead so that he wouldn't be late for appointments. He paid little attention to clothes, and his suits were always rumpled. Willkie hated shopping for clothes, and his wife would have him order three suits when she finally got him to the store. Edith would throw away his hats when they became shabby and put a new one in the closet.

It was during their years in Akron that Wendell began spending less time at home and devoting more of his energies to his career and political activities. He also became less than attentive in remembering anniversaries and birthdays. When Mrs. Willkie asked if he could shorten his long work schedule, he replied, "I won't be a clock watcher." Years later, she lamented, "I don't feel as if Wendell and I ever had time to play in our lives." Willkie's brothers later confided that they felt he had been somewhat negligent in his parental responsibilities. Wendell was, however, very much concerned with Philip's development and complained privately that Edith was overprotective.

Though Willkie accumulated a modest fortune during his ten years in Akron, he cared little for the social status that came with his wealth. The Willkies attended the smaller of Akron's two Episcopal churches. And when a friend suggested that they ought to attend the larger and more socially prominent church, Wendell told him off. He was unimpressed on another occasion, when William F. O'Neil, a General Tire and Rubber Company executive, invited him to a dinner party for the purpose of meeting some of Akron's wealthy elite. "I'll come to your house any time you want," Willkie replied, "but I don't want to meet your rich friends."[15]

Willkie's work in the utility field had brought him to the attention of the Northern Ohio Power and Light Company's parent holding company in New York. In the summer of 1929, utility tycoon Bernard Capen Cobb invited him to move to New York at a starting salary of $36,000 as the law partner of Judge John Weadcock in representing his newly formed holding company, Commonwealth and Southern. Cobb had dissolved his three midwestern and southern utility holding companies and merged their eleven operating companies into a giant holding company. Willkie asked for several days to consider the offer.

Willkie confided his doubts to John S. Knight. The Akron newspaperman told Willkie that it was an offer he could hardly refuse. If it didn't work out, Knight suggested that Willkie could return to Akron and seek the fourteenth district congressional seat that had formerly been held by the editor's father.[16] He also sought the advice of his college roommate, Maurice Bluhm, then a Chicago railroad executive. Bluhm urged him to make the move.

In the end, Willkie decided to accept Cobb's offer. At several farewell dinners, he confided to friends that leaving Akron had been his most painful decision. "I thought I was fixed for life," he said later. "I wanted to stay right there."[17] More than any other decision of Willkie's career, going to New York would change his life and move him into position for national prominence.

CHAPTER FOUR

COMMONWEALTH AND SOUTHERN

The Willkies arrived in New York on October 1, 1929, just four weeks before the Great Crash. At first, he felt uncomfortable in the big city. Sitting in the back seat of a taxicab with a friend, Willkie noted that in Akron he couldn't take a walk without meeting a friend; then, pointing at the crowded Manhattan sidewalks, he blurted out, "My god, there isn't a soul here I know."

Within a short time, however, Willkie found himself captivated by the great city. He enjoyed the prestige of working near Wall Street, the world's greatest financial center and marketplace. A chain reader of newspapers, he subscribed to a dozen local papers. He was also a devoted fan of the Broadway theater. "Living in New York is a great experience," he told David Lilienthal. "I wouldn't live anywhere else. It is the most exciting, stimulating, satisfying spot in the world. I can't get enough of it."[1]

Wendell and Edith obtained a seven-room apartment overlooking Central Park at 1010 Fifth Avenue. Their neighbors reported that the Willkies were thoughtful, cordial, and tolerant but, most of all, people who valued their privacy. Geoffrey T. Hellman, a *New Yorker* writer who lived in the adjacent sixth-floor apartment, estimated that in eleven years, his contacts with Willkie were limited to four or five brief conversations on the elevator landing they shared. In the tradition of rural Indiana, the Willkies never locked their apartment door.[2]

At Commonwealth and Southern, Willkie rose quickly, impressing his superiors as quick-witted, articulate, and resourceful. Cobb soon promoted him over fifty junior executives and designated him as the heir apparent. The scion of an old New England family, Cobb was a pioneer of the utility industry. He built, acquired, and consolidated gas and electrical properties, and his crowning achievement was the 1929 merger of 165 companies into the nation's largest utility holding company.

Willkie's role with Cobb dealt mostly with the nuances of utility law. "My work for Commonwealth and Southern, before I became its president," he wrote years later, "was almost exclusively in supervising litigation of the operating companies of the system. I was out of New York, for the most part, helping lawyers in the field with their most important briefs and in the trial of what we, at least, deemed our most important litigation."[3]

Soon after coming to New York, Willkie had his first and, it would turn out, only encounter with Samuel Insull, the Chicago public-utility tycoon who symbolized the industry's prosperity and corruption. A short, stocky fireplug of a man, Insull, then seventy, was at the peak of his authority. At a conference of utility executives, Willkie sat in the audience as Insull denounced critics of big business as dangerous radicals and suggested that they should be silenced in some fashion.

When asked for his views, Willkie, thirty-seven years old and still a liberal Democrat, said that Insull was mistaken. Everyone had a right to be heard, he retorted, including the industry's opposition. A hushed, tense silence followed Willkie's comments. Insull said curtly, "Mr. Willkie, when you are older, you will know more."[4]

A few months later the ambitious Willkie sounded almost like Insull when he spoke before midwestern utility executives in French Lick, Indiana, and denounced the industry's "insidious" and "unintelligent" critics. In the same speech, Willkie asserted that government efforts to get into the power business would be unconstitutional.

Early in 1940, Willkie referred to "the money-mad period of the Twenties" when "the heads of some of our corporations forgot their primary function. Instead of attending to the duties of management they began playing with corporate structures as with a child's building blocks, becoming promoters rather than businessmen." In a speech to Toledo businessmen, he said, "You have sat in Board rooms, as I have done, and heard businessmen talk about putting pressure on this man or this newspaper, or this or that group, so that opposition would be eliminated." Rather than using such crude and, more often than not, counterproductive tactics, Willkie argued that businessmen should be running their corporations "in a way that would be sound for the worker, the consumer and the investor."[5]

In the summer of 1932, Willkie went to the Democratic National Convention in Chicago as an assistant floor manager for Newton D. Baker's presidential campaign. Oddly enough, Willkie's law office was across the street from the New York law offices of Franklin Delano Roosevelt, and both firms represented private utilities. But Willkie remained loyal to Baker, still the country's leading advocate of U.S. leadership in international affairs. Like Willkie, Baker had grown more conservative. His law firm represented such clients as J. P. Morgan & Co. and he had recently urged the shutdown of a municipal power plant in Cleveland.

It was one of the most significant and bitterly fought conventions in the nation's history, a fierce struggle among FDR, Al Smith, Baker, and House Speaker John Nance Garner. Baker's hopes were pegged to a stalemate between Roosevelt and Smith. "We moved on Chicago and, while assisting in the efforts to produce a deadlock between the two, worked feverishly for second-choice votes for the leader who almost alone through the dark isolationist Twenties had fought consistently for world cooperation," Willkie wrote years later.[6]

For three ballots, Roosevelt held the lead but could not muster the required two-thirds majority. The anti-FDR coalition appeared to be gaining strength and a deadlock seemed imminent. Roosevelt telephoned Baker and offered his support in the event of a stalemate. FDR's forces, though, struck a deal with publisher William Randolph Hearst that swung the ninety votes of Texas and California into their column and sealed the nomination. Though disappointed by the outcome, Willkie backed Roosevelt in the general election and contributed $150 to his campaign.

On January 24, 1933, Willkie became president of Commonwealth and Southern. At forty-one, he was the youngest president of a major utility system. Within the week, Hitler would be named Chancellor of Germany. In five weeks, Franklin D. Roosevelt would take the presidential oath from Chief Justice Charles Evans Hughes. Robert A. Taft, just defeated for reelection to the Ohio state senate, had returned to his Cincinnati law practice. Thomas E. Dewey, thirty years old, was finishing out his term as assistant U.S. attorney for the southern district of New York.

Willkie faced a formidable challenge. The effects of the Great Depression spread throughout American business, and the utilities had been hit hard. In three years, Commonwealth and Southern's gross earnings had dropped nearly $40 million and its dividends had plunged from 70 cents to 1 cent per share. The Depression blighted household and industrial consumption of electric power, and the condition was expected to worsen.

In an effort to attract new consumers, Willkie hired more than five hundred salesmen and launched a campaign to sell electrical appliances. He also introduced what became known as the "objective rate," in which customers received a bonus for using more electricity. If a household used $3.50 worth of electricity, it received an extra third of that amount at no charge. Over the next six years, the amount of household electricity sold by C&S doubled and rates were slashed 50 per cent.

Willkie became chief executive officer of Commonwealth and Southern on June 20, 1934, when Cobb retired as chairman, and immediately proved that he had different ideas about management than his predecessor. Until then, the C&S board had been dominated by men of finance. Willkie promptly removed four directors not involved in utility operations, including two executives with the powerful banking firm of Bonbright and Company. He replaced them with representatives from the operating power companies. In another policy change, Willkie stopped the practice of awarding stock bonuses to C&S lawyers. He fired lawyers in seven states who owned Commonwealth and Southern stock, some of whom had been paid off for not opposing the company's subsidiaries in court.[7]

From the beginning of the Roosevelt presidency, Willkie was among the New Deal's outspoken critics. He first shouted his opposition in April of 1933 following FDR's proposal to build the Tennessee Valley Authority. Of all the programs introduced by Roosevelt in his dramatic first hundred days, the TVA was the boldest and most controversial–a plan for the development of America's fifth largest river–the Tennessee–that held the promise of inexpensive electric power, flood control, soil conservation, and better living conditions for the poverty-stricken southeastern United States.

On April 14, 1933, Willkie told the House Military Affairs Committee that the TVA legislation threatened the destruction of $400 million in Commonwealth and Southern securities. "I have not much at stake in this except my position, and that does not amount to anything," he said, "but I do feel a great urge as a trustee for these security holders."

In his testimony, Willkie conceded that the public held his industry in low esteem. He then grinned, adding, "I know you gentlemen will not take this amiss; but, frankly, I think Congress is in the same boat with us. It is not very popular."[8]

Although he succeeded in getting the House of Representatives to place restrictions on the TVA transmission lines, the Senate removed the restrictions and passed TVA by an overwhelming vote. The President asserted that there should be no limits on the government's authority to produce hydroelectric power. Willkie had lost the first round.

FDR named thirty-four-year-old David E. Lilienthal as the TVA's chief negotiator with Commonwealth and Southern for the purchase of its holdings in the Tennessee Valley. Lilienthal, like Willkie, had grown up in Indiana. After attending DePauw University, he went to Harvard Law School and became a protégé of the legendary Felix Frankfurter. Lilienthal earned a national reputation as Wisconsin's public service commissioner for writing its utility laws, which were soon adopted by a half dozen other states. In his view, the term "private utility" was a contradiction, for the nation's energy resources belonged to the people.

In October of 1933, Willkie and Lilienthal met for the first time over lunch at Washington's exclusive Cosmos Club. Willkie offered to "take all your power off your hands" for $500,000 and warned that Lilienthal ought to accept this proposition before TVA's budget was slashed. He suggested, too, that Lilienthal might damage his future career by taking a hard line against Commonwealth and Southern. Lilienthal, who had given up a lucrative law practice for public service, was unmoved by this argument. Even so, he wrote later that Willkie's "cocksuredness" had left him "somewhat overwhelmed" and "pretty badly scared."[9]

Three months later, Willkie and Lilienthal reached a short-term agreement. Commonwealth and Southern would sell its properties in Mississippi, northern Alabama, and eastern Tennessee, and TVA would not compete with its systems in other areas. And, until the Norris Dam was completed, Commonwealth and Southern retained the lion's share of the region's market.

Before the agreement could be put into effect, a group of stockholders in the Alabama Power Company filed suit to prevent the Commonwealth and Southern subsidiary from transferring its properties to TVA. Willkie heatedly denied charges that he had initiated the lawsuit. "An absolute and unqualified falsehood," Willkie told White House Press Secretary Stephen Early. It was later revealed that the counsel for the stockholders had been paid $50,000 from the Edison Electric Institute, of which Willkie was a director.

President Roosevelt served notice that TVA might be duplicated throughout the nation if the private utilities were not more cooperative.

On December 13, 1934, Willkie met Roosevelt in the Oval Office. "I am glad to meet you, Mr. Willkie," said FDR. "I am one of your customers." Willkie replied, "We give you good service, don't we?" While their talk was friendly, nothing was resolved. Willkie wired his wife: "Charm greatly exaggerated. I did not tell him what you think of him." Roosevelt told reporters that he had outdebated his guest, but wrote Willkie, "I hope you give as little credence to the many statements you hear about me as I do to the many statements I hear about what you say and do."[10]

By now, FDR had decided that breaking up the holding companies would be the only fail-safe method of ending fraud and corruption in the utilities field. In his January 4, 1935 State of the Union message, Roosevelt urged the "abolition of the evil of holding companies." By their pattern of disregard for both the consumer and their operating companies, many of the holding companies had forced the Administration to take strong action.

Willkie returned to the White House on January 24, 1935, and listened as FDR explained his position. "During most of this time, Willkie said nothing," reported Lilienthal, "but I could see he was getting hotter and hotter." Then, in frustration, he pulled his glasses out of his coat pocket and pointed them at FDR, saying, "If you will give us a federal incorporation law, we can get rid of the holding companies." The President jutted his chin and told Willkie that he was determined to wipe out holding companies. "Do I understand then," said Willkie, "that any further efforts to avoid the breaking up of utility holding companies are futile?" Nodding, FDR said, "It is futile."[11]

In the spring of 1935, Willkie won recognition as an articulate voice of American business in leading the fight against FDR's "death-sentence" for holding companies. It was true, he conceded, that some holding companies had exploited their stockholders and operating companies. "No radical public-ownership advocate hates half as much as I do the men who profited from engineering services rendered to their companies and who acquired property only to put it on the books at excessive values," he declared. Willkie claimed that utilities had learned from past mistakes and had eliminated unethical practices. As a compromise, Willkie suggested that Congress extend the Securities and Exchange Act to utility companies. The administration rejected anything less than the "death-sentence."

Willkie, choosing not to attack FDR directly, concentrated his fire on Thomas Corcoran and Benjamin Cohen, the brilliant and energetic Frankfurter protégés who had written the holding-company legislation. "Mr. Corcoran and Mr. Cohen have the advantage of fresh minds on the subject because they have never been in, or had any experience in the utility or banking or investment banking or any other type of business," Willkie told a congressional committee.

In the Senate, the "death-sentence" passed by a single vote. Willkie launched another propaganda campaign and shifted his attention to the more conservative House of Representatives. In speeches and newspaper advertisements, Willkie called on the American public to send Congress the message that holding companies should be permitted to stay in business. The grass-roots response was impressive—more than 800,000 letters and telegrams were delivered to congressmen in the last two weeks of June.

On July 1, 1935, the House rejected the "death-sentence" by seventy votes. The next day it passed the holding-company bill without the controversial provision.

Willkie's legislative triumph over FDR was soon tainted, however, by revelations that the public opposition to the measure had been manufactured by the utility lobby. Although Willkie was not implicated in the scandal, a congressional investigation produced admissions from utility officials that many of the telegrams had been secretly funded with names copied from telephone books. Texas

Congressman Sam Rayburn called it "the richest and most ruthless lobby Congress has ever known."

President Roosevelt, taking full advantage of the public outcry against the utility lobby, got the House to approve a revised bill that would dissolve the major holding companies within three years. "I have only one possible regret," said Willkie. "If by spending more money legitimately, the Commonwealth and Southern could have prevented this destructive act from being passed, then I am very sorry that I did not authorize such additional expenditure."

CHAPTER FIVE

NEW DEAL CRITIC

One of the reasons Willkie had been guardedly optimistic about an ultimate victory over the TVA was his conviction that Franklin D. Roosevelt would be defeated for a second term. With a Republican in the White House, Willkie felt that Commonwealth and Southern would regain its power monopoly in the Southeast. In the fall of 1936, the *Literary Digest* poll reported that Alf M. Landon was running well ahead of FDR. Willkie confided to Lilienthal that it would be a tight contest in which Ohio would provide Landon's margin of victory. Lilienthal, too, viewed Landon as the likely winner.[1]

The Democratic Roosevelt, however, scored a landslide as he swept all but two of the forty-eight states. In the face of FDR's mandate, Willkie knew that his battle was lost. The President's public-power allies urged him to go for the kill. Senator Norris of Nebraska, denouncing Commonwealth and Southern as "an outfit who would destroy you in a minute if it had the power," told Roosevelt to capitalize on the momentum of his re-election and take a harder line against the private utilities.[2]

Throughout 1936, Willkie attempted to stay on friendly terms with FDR. "I want you to know that I feel the problem should be settled by agreement," he wrote Roosevelt on May 21, "and I am of the opinion that you, and you alone, are the one person who has the power to bring such a settlement about."[3]

In September of 1936, Roosevelt summoned Willkie to the White House for a conference that resulted in a three-month extension of the TVA contract with Commonwealth and Southern. As a compromise settlement, the President suggested the pooling of transmission facilities between the TVA and private utilities. Willkie said that such a plan would be acceptable if the utilities retained their metropolitan markets, but the President said this would be unconstitutional for it denied cities the option of building their own power plants. "The trouble with cooperating with you fellows," FDR told Willkie, "is that you don't play the game."[4]

Despite their differences, Willkie hailed Roosevelt's power conference as an act of political statesmanship and expressed the hope that negotiations might continue. On December 22, 1936, a federal district court granted Willkie's operating companies an injunction against TVA and prohibited it from entering into any new contracts for six months. A month later the President broke off his talks with Willkie on the grounds that the injunction represented a breach of faith.

Roosevelt and Willkie did not confer again until November 23, 1937. After a ninety-minute session in the Oval Office, Willkie was tight-lipped and cautious in meeting reporters. FDR, though, boasted at a press conference that he had kept Willkie on the defensive. The President depicted him as indecisive and bumbling, adding that Willkie had given him a memorandum which he hadn't bothered to read.[5]

Willkie, hurt and angered that FDR had gone public with their private talk, gave a copy of his memorandum to Associated Press. The document revealed that Willkie had made a series of proposals to FDR for ending the five-year war between the Administration and private utilities. He recommended modification of the Public Utility Act, so as to eliminate all intermediate holding companies within three years, but to permit existing holding companies to remain in business on the provision that any future acquisition of property be subject to the approval of the Securities and Exchange Commission or the Federal Power Commission. He also called for TVA to sell power at a price arrived at under the cost-accounting methods set for private utilities by the Federal Power Commission. A New York *Times* editorial said that Willkie had offered "sensible and realistic terms for the settlement of a long-continuing controversy which has been costly to the country."

In an effort to bring his cause before a national audience, Willkie wrote articles for such publications as *Life,* the *Saturday Evening Post, Forbes,* and the New York *Times.* He was the subject of an adulatory profile treatment in the May 1937 issue of *Fortune*. Before it went to press, managing editor Eric Hodgins sent the manuscript to Willkie and invited him to make any changes he wished. The piece was so complimentary that Willkie made few suggestions to improve it. *Fortune* compared Willkie to Robert E. Lee as "nobler than his cause" and described him as a Jeffersonian liberal. Edward Weeks, editor of the *Atlantic,* commissioned Willkie to write a defense of industry against New Deal attacks. "By common consent," Weeks wrote Willkie, "you were regarded as the authority best equipped to speak for the private ownership of utilities."[6]

Willkie's "Political Power," which appeared in the August 1937 issue of *Atlantic,* recounted the history of his dispute with the TVA and his arguments against public power. "I believe that the utility companies would have been neglecting their duty if they had failed to resort to the courts to protect their property," he wrote. "But I am under no delusion as to the value of litigation."[7]

On January 3, 1938, he was dealt a major blow when the Supreme Court rejected a suit by the Alabama Power Company for injunctions against federal loans and grants for construction of municipal power plants. The TVA had been given undisputed authority to build power plants in competition with private companies. "The decision is unfortunate from the standpoint of the utility," Willkie conceded, "but the Supreme Court has spoken and it is the last word."

Willkie proposed that the sale of private utilities in the Tennessee Valley be determined by three outside arbitrators named by the President, the Supreme Court, and the utility industry. Lilienthal rebuffed this suggestion and announced that TVA would negotiate with Willkie for the generation and transmission systems of Commonwealth and Southern companies as well as the distribution lines.

For nearly a year, Willkie and Lilienthal made little progress in their talks. Willkie was asking $94 million and Lilienthal was offering $55 million. To break the deadlock, Willkie offered to sell at a price set by the Securities and Exchange Commission.

In December of 1938, he wrote Lilienthal, "We should be willing to surrender our personal prejudices on behalf of the simplest and quickest method of settling a controversy which has puzzled the American people and been a handicap to American industry for nearly five years."[8]

SEC Chairman William O. Douglas, however, would have nothing to do with Willkie's proposal. In his memoirs, Douglas recalled that Willkie often dropped in to see him at the SEC: "I would always politely rise as he entered and offer him a chair. He never would take my proffered seat; instead he would walk across the room, pull up a chair, sit down with his back to me, put his feet on the window sill, and bellow at me. What interested me most was that he kept his hat on–better to show his contempt. His approach was indeed juvenile. But it happened over and over again; so I knew it was a studied effort probably to make me lose my head and say indiscreet things."[9]

On January 30, 1939, the Supreme Court struck down the challenge to TVA's constitutionality. "The utilities have exhausted their legal remedies in seeking to protect their properties from the Tennessee Valley Authority," Willkie said somberly.

As the negotiations continued, Lilienthal became ill with undulant fever caused by drinking unpasteurized milk and was replaced by youthful assistants Julius Krug and Joseph Swidler. On February 1, they met in Willkie's New York office and reached final terms. Willkie agreed to sell Commonwealth and Southern's facilities for $78,600,000. He said that the most gratifying part of the agreement was that TVA had promised to keep Commonwealth and Southern's employees in power-related jobs. He declared, "We accept the inevitable with good spirit and are selling our properties at as good a price as we can get the government to pay."

In an elaborate ceremony, he presented the Commonwealth and Southern deeds to Lilienthal at the First National City Bank of New York. When Lilienthal gave him the check, Willkie grinned for the newsreel cameras and said, "Dave, this is sure a lot of money for a couple of Indiana farmers to be kicking around."

Willkie had driven a hard bargain. "At the SEC," said Douglas, "we always thought Willkie outsmarted David Lilienthal." Though losing his power struggle with the New Deal, Willkie had achieved national stature. Indeed, a few prominent political commentators were already touting him as a presidential dark horse. In a July 1939 *Time* magazine cover article, it was said that he had plenty of fight left in him and happened to be "the only businessman in the U.S. who is ever mentioned as a presidential possibility."[10]

CHAPTER SIX

A LOVE IN SHADOW

From the start, Edith Wilk's friends had been apprehensive about her marriage to Wendell L. Willkie. Apart from their youthful romance, they had little in common. Edith, whom he called Billie, was soft-spoken, shy, and home-oriented. Wendell was restless, politically outspoken, and full of driving energy. She had good taste in clothes and he wore rumpled suits. He was extroverted and she was reclusive. "Sometimes I think I could successfully be a hermit," Billie once told an interviewer. In the summer of 1940, when the Willkies attended a Broadway play, she became noticeably uncomfortable as the audience rose and cheered her husband. "If I go to the theater again," she said, "I'm going alone."[1]

Once their romance had faded, it became an empty marriage. Since leaving Indiana, Wendell had grown a great deal and Billie was still the small-town girl. Because they were such different people with different needs, Willkie was compelled to look outside his marriage for intellectual challenge and stimulation. Following their move to New York, Willkie would spend up to six months a year on the road for Commonwealth and Southern. While the passion had gone out of their marriage and Willkie was attracted to other women, he still felt affection for Billie and was determined not to hurt her. He took Billie and their son on annual vacations to such places as Bermuda, Europe, and the Chicago World's Fair. When her father suffered financial reverses in the Great Depression, Willkie bought a farm in Rushville and let him manage it. He also bought a commercial building for his mother-in-law, because he thought it was "more dignified for a woman of her age to have her own independent income."[2]

Willkie eventually bought five farms covering nearly fourteen hundred acres on the outskirts of Rushville. With Billie and Philip, he spent the Christmas season in Indiana. "I had the good fortune to marry a sane Indiana girl with a rare quality to bear with a restless and altogether unsatisfactory husband," he wrote an old friend in December of 1937.[3]

Despite her husband's wandering eye, Billie remained devoted to him and her life-style was more than comfortable. "I can find more pleasure in walking down the street with him than in anything else I know," she said. When she got lonely, Billie would often walk across the street from their apartment building and spend the afternoon at the Metropolitan Museum of Art. "You couldn't help but admire her," said William L. Shirer. "She was probably terribly hurt. But she wasn't going to ruin his career."[4]

Willkie was a ladies' man and he looked for romantic flings. Women found him handsome and full of vitality. "Physically he is greatly superior to the impression given by his photographs," observed his friend Rebecca West. "They make him look big but soft and blowsy. Actually, he has the well-organized bulkiness of a healthy bear, and singularly brilliant eyes."[5] Raoul de Roussy de Sales, who met Willkie at a dinner party given by Hamilton Fish Armstrong, wrote, "I understand a little better his charm for women: a lock of his hair carelessly falls over his forehead, the eyes which can take on an expression of reverie, the very masculine looks, the good health and a certain warmth of the generous good fellow—all this can be pleasing."[6]

Willkie's associates linked him with a variety of women ranging from secretaries to movie stars. "Willkie likes to play with a lot of women and is quite catholic in his tastes," Harold Ickes wrote privately. Gardner Cowles, Willkie's close friend, said, "He was not at all discreet. I thought it was careless and stupid." Willkie, though, told friends that his personal life was his own concern.[7]

Late in 1937, he met Irita Van Doren, book editor of the New York *Herald Tribune* and one of the nation's most influential literary figures. A year older than Willkie, she was a radiant personality, a charming, witty, articulate woman with a soft southern accent. "She was not pretty, but she was beautiful," said William L. Shirer. "She was a southern woman with impeccable southern manners." Ickes described her as "the kind of woman that I like–good to look at, physically well set up, but intelligent."[8] Van Doren inspired remarkable loyalty and respect from the New York literati. "Among the kind-hearted editors I have known she was by far the kindest," said Malcolm Cowley. "Young ambitious people wanted to write for her." Hiram Haydn, editor of the *American Scholar,* added, "Her graciousness was unmistakably innate, not simply bred. It came from some well of sweetness deep within her. She bloomed rosily with affection."[9]

In Willkie's judgment, Van Doren was the most intelligent and captivating person he had ever known. "Before they met," said Marcia Davenport, "he was just a big businessman. She brought him into a world where his intellect was stimulated." Willkie told her, "You can't imagine what limited intellectual interests businessmen have."[10] She sensed, though, that he was different than other industrialists and soon brought him into her charmed circle. Van Doren presided over a literary salon that included some of the most noted writers of the age. Among those who gathered under her roof were Carl Sandburg, Rebecca West, Virginia Woolf, John Erskine, André Maurois, James Thurber, Sinclair Lewis, Dorothy Thompson, Hugh Walpole, Stephen Vincent Benét, and Mark Van Doren. Irita Van Doren's close friends included such gifted foreign correspondents as Vincent Sheean, Joseph Barnes, William L. Shirer, and John Gunther. "Irita opened enormous doors to Willkie and he loved it," said Kenneth McCormick, who was then a rising editor at Doubleday.[11]

From childhood, Irita had been brilliant and creative. She was born in Birmingham, Alabama, in 1891, and her unusual name was coined from "Ida" and "Marguerite." When she was four, her family moved to Tallahassee, Florida, where her father owned a sawmill. Five years later he was shot and killed by a discharged worker, and Irita's mother gave music lessons and sold preserves and jellies to support the family. At the precocious age of seventeen, Irita graduated from Florida State College for Women and edited the college literary magazine. She then embarked for New York and studied literature at Columbia University. While working on her doctorate, she taught part-time at Hunter College. She married another graduate student, Carl Van Doren, who went on to become a well-known critic and Pulitzer Prize-winning historian. They bought a farm in

West Cornwall, Connecticut, where they spent weekends and the summer. The Van Dorens had three daughters and, in the early years of their marriage, Irita assisted her husband in researching his books. Politically liberal, she joined the editorial staff of the *Nation* in 1919 and within four years was promoted to literary editor. Then, in 1924, her friend Stuart P. Sherman was named book editor of the New York *Herald Tribune,* accepting the post on the condition that she come along as his chief assistant. Sherman concentrated his efforts on a weekly column and Van Doren edited Books. When he died in 1926, Van Doren succeeded him and would remain the *Herald Tribune*'s literary editor for thirty-seven years.

Van Doren quickly established her reputation and was widely recognized as a major asset to the *Herald Tribune.* She hired distinguished writers as visiting critics, initiated a national best-seller list, and gave representation to books of all tastes and opinions. "She had great skill and charm," said her associate John Hutchens, "and she also had a vein of iron." Hutchens recalled that Van Doren did not hesitate to call a book publisher's bluff when he threatened to discontinue advertising in the *Herald Tribune* in retaliation for an unfavorable review.[12] Working with a much smaller staff than that at the rival *Times,* she built a literary supplement that was considered at least the equal of its crosstown rival.

While Van Doren's career prospered, her marriage had gone sour. In 1935 she and Carl were divorced after twenty-three years of marriage. One of the initial ties between Wendell and Irita was a mutual interest in southern history. Before they knew each other, Willkie had sent her the galleys of a romantic, oversized Civil War novel. The author was the thirty-six-year-old wife of the advertising manager of the Georgia Power Company, a Commonwealth and Southern subsidiary. Her name was Margaret Mitchell. The novel was called *Gone With the Wind.*

Later, he confided to Van Doren that he had long thought about writing his own Civil War novel or an economic history of the antebellum South. Other projects that he sought her advice about were a study of American family dynasties and a book on lost men of American history. He had already written some material on Alabama secessionist William Lowndes Yancey, whom Willkie considered the true father of the Confederacy.

Van Doren was the granddaughter of Confederate General William Brooks, who had been another of Willkie's favorite historical characters. In the summer of 1938, Wendell sifted through dusty archives in Alabama and South Carolina to verify her claim that Brooks had owned three hundred slaves. On discovering that the number had actually been seventeen, he wired Van Doren: "As I certainly do not wish to dispute the accuracy of a lady's statement, I wired my investigator to go positively no further."[13]

By this time, Wendell and Irita had fallen in love. Willkie became completely devoted to her and would never waver in his feelings. "Irita directed Wendell's immense energy and broadened and deepened him," Shirer said. Van Doren taught him how to pronounce words which he had read but never heard used in conversation. She carefully selected and put aside newly published books and articles for him to read. He took great satisfaction in reviewing two works of English history for Books. She assisted him in his magazine articles and speeches, and her efforts brought new polish and vigor to his literary style. One of her daughters told Willkie that his first sentence of a book review was "lousy" but assured him that "when Mother gets through with it all will be okay."[14]

Hosting the *Herald Tribune*'s popular Book and Author luncheons made Van Doren among the newspaper's most visible personalities. After attending one of these programs, Willkie wrote her: "The artistry with which you made even some of us commonplace stuffed shirts at the head table seem interesting was perfection itself."

In longhand, he copied Walter Scott's tribute to Jane Austen and enclosed it: "That young lady has a talent for describing the involvements, feeling and characters of ordinary life which to me is the most wonderful I have ever met with. The big bow-wow I can do myself like anyone going but the exquisite touch which renders commonplace things and characters interesting from the truth of description and sentiment is denied me." Willkie added, "I enjoyed very much re-reading this tribute to Jane Austen. I have always been a devotee of her works and have reveled vicariously in Scott's compliment to her. But more pleasing by far it gave me a way of saying how good I thought you were—you who I admire inordinately and love excessively."[15]

Gradually, Wendell began spending weekends at Van Doren's farmhouse in West Cornwall. He would either take a taxi from his office in Lower Manhattan or a commuter train and be met at the nearby station by Van Doren or her daughters. Her country home was lighted by kerosene lamps. On learning that the local power company had denied her request to have electric service installed, Willkie immediately pulled the right strings and had a power line constructed just for the farm. After Willkie received a TVA check for $44.9 million, he went to West Cornwall and showed it to the Van Dorens. In the summer of 1939, Wendell and Irita spent a week at Dorothy Thompson's Vermont farm. A few days later, Willkie shipped the *Herald Tribune* columnist a sparkling electric refrigerator to replace her ancient icebox.[16]

While on the road, Willkie telephoned Van Doren nearly every day and sent frequent telegrams, referring to himself as an "Indiana buccaneer" and Van Doren as "a proud daughter of the old South" and "New York's leading intellectual." He joshed about her liberal friends. "You certainly are a sweet thing to send such an attractive and what I believe will be interesting book to a 33rd degree member of the power trust," he wrote in an undated letter. "Don't tell any of your old friends on *The Nation* that you did such an indecent act. You will be dishonored and hung/wrong? if you do. I shall read it over the weekend and when you let me buy you that drink I will tell you about it and other things."[17]

With her encouragement, he began thinking more and more in political terms. Barnes said that she challenged him to work out his own positions on major issues and to have greater confidence in himself as a political thinker and writer. Van Doren, said Barnes, was largely responsible for Willkie's "acceptance of himself as a potential leader with original and important ideas."[18]

A close friend and confidante of Helen Rogers Reid and her husband, Ogden, publishers of the *Herald Tribune,* Van Doren's influence at the newspaper went far beyond her own department. For many years she served as a member of the *Herald Tribune* board of directors. "Helen Reid sought her advice constantly on all kinds of problems," said a former *Herald Tribune* colleague. It was through Van Doren that Willkie developed his close ties with the Reids, who would become among his earliest and most influential political sponsors. Willkie and Van Doren frequently were dinner guests at the Reid home, although on some occasions when political figures or outsiders were to be present, he would bring his wife. "I could never figure it out," said a friend. "Sometimes he'd be there with Mrs. Willkie. But most of the time he'd be there with Irita."

Willkie and Van Doren discussed marriage, but Wendell could not bring himself to ask Billie for a divorce. It was not a matter of keeping their family together. By now, Philip was attending Princeton University and no longer living at home. "Wendell was very sentimental," said a close friend. "He didn't feel that you could discard someone just because you'd grown beyond them."[19]

Van Doren never pressured Willkie to get a divorce. "At the time, I thought Mother might be getting the short end of the stick," said her daughter Barbara Klaw. "But that wasn't the case. She was wise enough to know that she had everything except the title. They were endlessly and happily in love. Two people couldn't have been more attracted to each other." Joseph Alsop, who once dined with Willkie and Van Doren, observed, "They were very much like a married couple." Gardner Cowles said, "He was totally devoted to her."[20]

Another reason that Willkie may have been reluctant to seek a divorce was that he knew it would be politically damaging. A generation later the divorce and remarriage of Nelson Rockefeller would ruin his bid for the GOP presidential nomination. "Wendell was realistic about politics," said Marcia Davenport. "In those times, a political candidate could not possibly have anything like a divorce. No step was to be taken that would impinge on their marriage."[21]

Although Van Doren had been among the first to suggest that Willkie had a political future, she also recognized that a national campaign would force changes in their relationship. "Irita knew that if Wendell would be elected that things would be much different," said Marcia Davenport. "It might have been impossible to meet except under the most exaggerated secrecy. This would have all been painful to Irita." Even so, Van Doren encouraged Willkie's presidential aspirations. And when he decided to become a candidate in 1940, she told him that he should keep his distance from her and make the most of his opportunity. Willkie's advisers agreed that she should remain in the background.

Willkie resented the hypocrisy of politics and believed his private life was his own. He took chances that other political figures wouldn't take. Two friends were jolted when Willkie told them that he was scheduling a press conference at Van Doren's apartment. "Everybody knows about us—all the newspapermen in New York," he told his friends. "If somebody should come along to threaten or embarrass me about Irita, I would say, 'Go right ahead. There is not a reporter in New York who doesn't know about her.' "[22]

Van Doren was private and discreet about the affair. John K. Hutchens, who worked with her for many years, noted that she never discussed Willkie in the office. By contrast, Willkie told his associates about the relationship. "Wendell told me, rather explicitly, how close," Lilienthal wrote in his journal. The TVA director said he found their friendship "touching and beautiful."[23]

The press conference went on as scheduled. And their relationship was never hinted at in the public prints during the 1940 campaign. Franklin D. Roosevelt, though, had learned of their affair and told Ickes that Willkie had shown poor political judgment. At the time, FDR's own extramarital dalliances were a closely-guarded secret, but he was hardly in a position to make a campaign issue of Willkie's private life.[24]

In the summer of 1940, Willkie asked Marquis Childs what the gossip was about him in Washington. Without hesitation, Childs replied, "They say you have a mistress with whom you live much of the time." Poker-faced, Willkie asked the St. Louis *Post-Dispatch* political writer who the woman was supposed to be. "They say it's Irita Van Doren," said Childs. Willkie told him that they were nothing more than "good friends" and that she was one of his advisers. That fall, on the campaign train, Willkie jovially taunted Childs in telling a group of newspaper colleagues that the columnist had accused him of having five mistresses.

At the Philadelphia convention, Van Doren watched Willkie's nomination from a remote spot in the balcony. "I've lost him forever," she reportedly told a friend as she left the auditorium.[25] Willkie, however, assured her that they would resume their relationship once the campaign was over. "Cheer up and good luck," he wired from a western campaign stop. "You have pulled off triumphantly much worse situations than this."[26]

CHAPTER SEVEN

THE LONG SHOT

On the night of January 6, 1938, Wendell L. Willkie debated one of the New Deal's brightest stars, Robert H. Jackson, on "America's Town Meeting of the Air," a popular weekly radio program. Jackson, Assistant U.S. Attorney General, was rated a strong possibility for the 1940 Democratic presidential nomination. It was well known that FDR supported him for the New York governorship. Willkie, forty-five years old and largely unknown outside of the business community, was making his first appearance before a national audience.

During the program, Jackson asserted that big business had been responsible for the Great Depression. Willkie countered that it was time to stop analyzing the past and begin reviving the nation's economy. In his concluding remarks, Willkie called for reconciliation between the New Deal and American industry. Jackson committed something of a gaffe in suggesting that fairness wasn't a consideration in shaping New Deal policies.[1]

Most political observers gave Willkie the edge on points. General Hugh S. Johnson wrote in his column that Willkie had made "a perfect monkey" of Jackson. Raymond Moley, former FDR brain truster, wrote that Jackson had held his own in the opening exchange, but "in the rough-and-tumble that followed, Willkie so utterly outclassed him that the Jackson build-up dissolved into the elements from which it came."[2] The White House persuaded Governor Herbert Lehman to seek re-election, while Jackson's candidacy was scratched. FDR later named Jackson to the Supreme Court.

In a letter to his former law partner, Willkie confided, "Jackson, like most of the fellows who get connected with the federal government, has been subjected to an entirely false build-up as to ability. He is a very nice fellow. He practiced law at Jamestown, New York and as I understand, with some degree of success. If he practiced in Akron he would be about half way up the bar."[3]

Willkie's winning performance against Jackson provoked the first discussions about him as a presidential possibility. Samuel F. Pryor, Republican National Committeeman from Connecticut and one of his party's most influential leaders, now listed Willkie as a ranking contender. University of Chicago economist Mary Gilson wrote Willkie that she supported him for the presidency. Herbert Bayard Swope, former editor of the New York *World,* wrote Willkie that he had been plainspoken and courageous.[4]

Two months later, Willkie took on another New Deal heavyweight, Felix Frankfurter, in an informal debate at the Harvard Club of New York. For three hours, they argued over the Roosevelt administration's policies before a hushed audience of lawyers and bankers. At one point, Willkie charged that Frankfurter's former students—Corcoran, Cohen, and Lilienthal—were subverting the constitution. The next morning, Willkie wrote Frankfurter, noting that it had been "one of the most fascinating evenings I have had in years" and saying he hoped his remarks had not been offensive. Frankfurter replied, "We met in the simple, direct way in which two Americans should meet who have a common concern about great public issues, even though they may view them on the basis of different experiences and are preoccupied with different interests. I see no point to talk unless it is forthright."[5]

Meanwhile, Willkie gave no clues that he was giving much thought to switching parties. At a New York *Herald Tribune* Forum in October 1938, he referred to "the Democratic Party of which, incidentally, I am a member." Indeed, he had served until recently as a member of the New York County Democratic Committee. In the 1938 elections, he backed Democratic Governor Herbert Lehman over youthful GOP challenger Thomas E. Dewey.

As early as 1937, a *Fortune* editor had suggested that Willkie might be of presidential stature. When staff writer John Knox Jessup profiled Willkie in the May issue, he rejected the editor's idea as too improbable. By the winter of 1939, Arthur Krock of the New York *Times* proposed Willkie as his long-shot candidate. "If he is a Republican, you can't wholly count on Willkie," Krock wrote on February 22. "But he'll have to go down as the darkest horse in the stable. 1940 will be a little early to bring out a utilities man. But if anyone like that can be put over, I'd watch Willkie. He still has his haircuts country style."[6]

On March 3, 1939, the *Herald Tribune* published a letter on its editorial page that urged Willkie's nomination in 1940. What made the letter noteworthy was its author, G. Vernor Rogers, former general manager of the old New York *Tribune* and the brother of the *Herald Tribune*'s Helen Rogers Reid. The Rogers letter gave the first hint that Willkie had potentially strong support from the Eastern Establishment press.[7]

At about the same time, the *Saturday Evening Post* published Alva Johnston's "The Man Who Talked Back," a Willkie puff piece that triggered hundreds of letters urging him to seek the presidency.

Willkie, still insisting that he wasn't a candidate, responded to many of the letters. "The suggestion which you make about my running for president has been humorously made by others," he wrote to J. G. Baldwin of Atlanta. "Really, from my standpoint, it cannot constitute more than a joke. I do not think that the American people would even consider the election of a utility executive with an office in the precincts of Wall Street for constable, not alone president." In another letter, he added, "Believe me, I do not have the slightest political ambitions."[8]

Much to his surprise, Willkie's disavowals of candidacy did not end the speculation. On May 22, 1939, David Lawrence wrote in his syndicated column, "What the Republicans really want is a man who understands the economic situation, who has had some experience with the large mechanism called business and who is broad-gauged enough to deal with political factors as well. . . . In Wendell Willkie, the Republicans would have an independent Democrat with a business ability and a leadership capacity which would fit the pattern that nine out of ten Republicans really want but do not venture to ask for."

In a handwritten note written in early June, Willkie told Lawrence: "I have refrained from writing you heretofore in appreciation of that article you wrote about me for fear that I would seem a bit too sentimental in my thanks. I am utterly devoid, I believe, of political ambition but no man could be honest and at the same time indifferent to the suggestion from one such as you that he was qualified to lead the country in these times. I hope you all the luck in the world and for myself that no one takes your suggestion seriously."[9]

Despite his efforts, Willkie was being taken seriously by a small but growing number of influential political writers. And with the conclusion of the TVA deal in late July, he suddenly became more receptive to the idea of getting into politics. Now that Commonwealth and Southern had sold its major properties, Willkie was looking for something else to do. Among his most attractive options was a senior partnership in the Wall Street law firm of Miller, Owen, Otis, and Bailly. Former New York Governor Nathan Miller was retiring from the firm and wanted Willkie to succeed him. In a frank discussion at the former governor's apartment in the Hotel Pierre, Miller told Willkie: "Wendell, you and I know that the businessmen of America, if they had a free choice, would make you President. You know and I know that there just isn't a chance of this. But you are a public figure anyway and the place for you to be a good one is at the bar. We want you to come back to the practice of law."[10] Willkie was interested in Miller's offer but said he didn't know if he was ready to return to the law.

He was growing increasingly confident of his political potential. By the summer of 1939, he was openly suggesting that he might run for the presidency.

Willkie dropped broad hints in the July 31, 1939 *Time* cover article that he would like nothing more than a chance to have Franklin Delano Roosevelt one-on-one in the 1940 general election. "The New Deal is going to be on trial again," said Willkie. "President Roosevelt is its ablest spokesman and in a Democratic country it deserves an able advocate. I hope he runs. Then we can debate it to everybody's satisfaction. It will be a great discussion."[11]

Early in August, Willkie took part in a discussion group sponsored by *Fortune* magazine, another *Time-Life* publication. Its managing editor, Russell W. Davenport, said later that Willkie "took the whole group by storm" and "put into words that day the things that I had been thinking for years." At the end of the meeting, Davenport told Willkie that he should seek the presidency and volunteered his help in the campaign. Willkie indicated that he would like to discuss the matter further and Davenport invited him for a weekend at his summer house in Connecticut. Later, Davenport told his wife Marcia, "I've met the man who ought to be the next President of the United States." Asked whether the White House was Willkie's idea or his, Davenport said, "It's spontaneous. You see him and you know it."[12]

Over the next year, Davenport would be the central figure in Willkie's campaign, his chief strategist, speechwriter, and alter ego. "I think of Willkie as a force of nature. I think of Davenport as a force of spirit," *Time* publisher Henry R. Luce later wrote. "When the two met, the chemical reaction produced an event of political history."

When Davenport became managing editor in 1937, *Fortune* was a slick, glossy business magazine that reflected Luce's conservative biases. Davenport gave it a more liberal editorial direction, publishing articles which urged détente in the bitter warfare between American business and the New Deal. He also led campaigns for cancer research and safer air travel. Friendly with many labor leaders and such New Dealers as Corcoran and Harry Hopkins, Davenport also had good relations with top industrialists and had talked of writing a series of novels with businessmen as protagonists. His *Fortune* colleague John Knox Jessup said, "Willkie was exactly the hero Davenport had been looking for: the American businessman at his candid, articulate best, large-minded, earthy, brave, wholly committed to a bigger and better America and a bolder and more confident foreign policy."[13]

Before launching the Willkie campaign, Davenport had never been involved in politics, although he had a keen understanding of public affairs and had long wanted to take a more active role. "Davenport was haunted," said Jessup, "by the conviction that he had a special mission on this earth." At about the time he met Willkie, Davenport had just completed the first chapter of what he hoped would be a mind-bending book on American democracy. After listening to Willkie, he abandoned the project in favor of the 1940 presidential race.

In background and temperament, Russell W. Davenport was more poet than political strategist. Tall, slender, and darkly handsome, he had just turned forty years old when he met Willkie. As a youngster, Davenport had a severe attack of pneumonia which permanently impaired his hearing, and he still wore a hearing aid. A native of Pennsylvania, he attended the Thacher School at Ojai, California, which, his wife suggested, had helped make him fresher and more unorthodox than contemporaries who went to traditional Eastern prep schools. At seventeen, Davenport enlisted in the American Field Service and drove an ambulance on the Western Front. Assigned to a French division, he was cited for bravery under fire and twice received the Croix de Guerre. He went to Yale University after the war. Davenport edited the literary magazine, organized the Liberal Club, and won the school fencing championship. On graduating in 1923, he worked briefly as a researcher for *Time,* then later was among the gifted young American writers who moved to Paris. Though not part of their circle, he knew Hemingway, Fitzgerald, and Gertrude Stein. Davenport wrote a novel, *Through Traffic,* and an epic poem, *California Spring,* which took six years to write.

Davenport's work habits were legendary. At *Fortune,* he sometimes rewrote the magazine on deadline. Late at night, he would continue working by drinking quarts of black coffee. The large doses of caffeine often gave him stomach cramps and he carried a bottle of antacid medicine. Like many writers, he was absentminded. Davenport once left a finished book manuscript in the back seat of a New York taxicab and never recovered it. He later wrote a book-length poem, *My Country,* and *The Dignity of Man,* in which he set forth his political philosophy.

On the weekend of August 19, 1939, the Willkies stayed with the Davenports at Great Marsh, their country home on Saugatuck Harbor. In preparation for the visit, the Davenports obtained weekend golf passes from a nearby country club, patched up their own tennis court, scheduled bridge and poker games with neighbors, brought in some of their best wines from the city, and planned gourmet meals. Willkie, however, showed little interest in social chitchat, card games, or outdoor sports. He pulled Davenport aside, and they went out to the front porch for what would become a two-day marathon conversation on politics, foreign affairs, and each other's ideas. Others were excluded from the discussion. Davenport's wife, Marcia, a staff writer for the *New Yorker* and author of an acclaimed biography of Mozart, reported that Willkie "noticed my appearance only to the extent of a smile and a nod." Mrs. Davenport said that her husband and Willkie discovered an "intellectual and temperamental affinity like the anvil and the hammer, between which the forged iron takes form."[14]

Sitting in a wicker armchair, Willkie rested one leg over an arm of the chair. He loosened his tie, took off his jacket, and ran his hand through his hair. Willkie smoked cigarettes incessantly, and the ashes fell across his shirt and he tossed the butts on the porch. As Willkie spoke, Davenport took notes.[15] Although still a registered Democrat, Willkie knew that his only hope for the presidency was to become a Republican. Even though President Roosevelt was hedging about his plans for a third term, Willkie fully expected him to be the nominee. As a Republican, Willkie recognized that he had serious problems. Not only was he still a registered Democrat, but a former member of Tammany Hall's executive committee and a contributor to FDR's 1932 campaign. As a public-utility tycoon and Wall Street lawyer, he had the image of a big-money wheeler-dealer. The fact that he had never held public office was considered a liability. With the notable exception of military heroes U. S. Grant and John Frémont, an outsider had never captured the Republican presidential nomination. Yet for all these drawbacks, they decided to undertake a campaign.

Willkie and Davenport were in agreement that his long-shot hopes were pegged to a convention deadlock. They would not enter the spring presidential primaries, which were expensive, politically risky, and had been of negligible value to such past winners as William E. Borah and Hiram Johnson. At the time, the Wisconsin, Nebraska, and Oregon primaries were the Republican battlegrounds. In the summer of 1939, Willkie did not have the staff or budget to start a national effort. Davenport recommended that he seek exposure outside of conventional political forums as a means of capitalizing on his position as an outsider and, at the same time, building name recognition. Willkie stepped up his speaking schedule and became an even more prolific contributor to national magazines and newspapers.

In foreign policy, Willkie and Davenport were both interventionists, and on that weekend they talked of moving the Republican party from its diehard isolationism. Willkie had supported FDR's efforts to revise the Neutrality Act in July so that the United States might aid European democracies against Nazi aggression. The leading Republican contenders helped defeat Roosevelt on this measure. Later in August, Hitler signed a nonaggression pact with the Soviet Union. And on September 1, Nazi Germany invaded Poland in the opening round of World War II in Europe. Finally, in November, FDR overcame congressional opposition and amended the arms embargo provision of the Neutrality Act. In the months ahead, Willkie would speak out with increasing frequency on the European war and American vulnerability. The war transformed Willkie from a big-business critic of the New Deal into a champion of freedom. And it gave his candidacy new purpose.

For the remainder of 1939, Willkie kept in constant touch with Davenport. Each week the Davenports brought together small groups of businessmen, journalists, and political figures for informal dinners with Willkie at their fashionable East Side apartment. The chain-smoking Willkie paid little attention to the multiple ashtrays that surrounded him, and his ashes littered the rug and furniture. "He made the most unholy mess," Mrs. Davenport said years later, but she also found Willkie "a personality to charm a bird from a tree–if he wanted to."[16]

Time publisher Henry Luce and his wife, playwright and editor Clare Boothe Luce were dinner guests at the Davenport home over the weekend. Mrs. Luce said that she recalled Willkie asking her husband if he thought Thomas E. Dewey or Robert A. Taft had a chance against FDR. Luce said he was doubtful. Willkie said that the nation needed an experienced businessman and administrator "like you, Harry" as its next President. Mrs. Luce told Willkie that he should "know better than to think that any businessmen can get nominated and elected President of the United States" in the midst of the Depression. Luce kicked his wife under the table. When they were driving home, Mrs. Luce said, "On the way over here you told me that Wendell Willkie was a great guy. Now you know yourself, he must be an absolute fool to sit there and try to persuade you to run for President." Luce had a ready answer. "Wendell Willkie doesn't want me to be President. He wants to be President himself. All that talk about a successful businessman was just his way of opening the conversation."[17]

Early in the fall, Willkie had been approached about the campaign by Charlton MacVeagh, a publishing executive and former chief assistant to Republican National Chairman John D. M. Hamilton. "Russ Davenport is doing something along those lines," said Willkie. "Why don't the two of you get together?" Davenport promptly tapped MacVeagh as Willkie's political director. Only thirty-eight years old, MacVeagh had played a major role in Alf M. Landon's 1936 GOP presidential campaign and knew Republican stalwarts in nearly every state. Until MacVeagh came along, Mrs. Davenport told author Jane Dick, "Nobody had the thinnest idea how you organized the votes of delegates or how you reached delegates in a political convention." The Davenports installed a battery of telephones in their apartment and MacVeagh went to work contacting prospective delegates on Willkie's behalf. "The telephones multiplied like flies and almost drove me mad," Mrs. Davenport recalled. "Every time I turned around another telephone had been installed."[18]

Samuel Pryor, Connecticut's Republican boss, quietly had moved into Willkie's corner. Originally, Pryor supported Dewey and had also backed his home-state ally, Governor Raymond Baldwin, as a favorite son. On May 2, 1939, he invited Willkie and Baldwin to take part in ceremonies commemorating the two hundredth anniversary of Christ Church in Greenwich. The governor spoke in platitudes. Willkie, by contrast, warned about the rise of totalitarianism in Europe. "Hitler and others cannot dim the bright light that made this country the great country that it is which permits us to hold this meeting," he declared. Pryor settled on Willkie as his presidential candidate and began promoting Baldwin for vice-president.[19]

Willkie had dinner with Alfred E. Smith and former President Hoover in the early fall at the home of Raoul Desvernine, a prominent New York lawyer. Willkie no doubt mentioned that he had been a Smith delegate at the turbulent Democratic National Convention of 1924. At sixty-six, the Happy Warrior said that he was too old for any more active politics and proposed that Willkie pick up the mantle of old-fashioned Democratic liberalism. Smith, who had broken with FDR after the 1932 election, had supported Landon in 1936. Raymond Moley, another dinner guest that night, shortly afterward speculated in his *Newsweek* column about Willkie's possible candidacy.[20]

There was still much skepticism about whether Willkie would be a factor in the 1940 Republican campaign. Frank Altschul, head of the international banking firm of Lazard Frères and former vice-chairman of the Republican National Finance Committee, had been recruited by MacVeagh to raise money for Willkie. In September, Altschul brought up Willkie during a conversation with Kenneth F. Simpson, Republican National Committeeman from New York. Simpson, who was feuding with Dewey and looking for another candidate, said Willkie was the silliest idea he had heard. "So I am supposed to go back to the clubhouse and tell the boys that we will all have to pull together now to get the nomination for Wendell Willkie," snorted Simpson. "They'll ask me, 'Willkie, who's Willkie?' And I'll tell them he's the President of the Commonwealth and Southern. The next question will be, 'Where does that railroad go to?' And I will explain that it isn't a railroad, it's a public utility holding company. Then they will look at me sadly and say, 'Ken, we always have thought you were a little erratic, but now we know you are just plain crazy.' And that," concluded Simpson, "would be without my even getting to mention that he's a Democrat."[21]

Without fanfare, Willkie registered as a Republican a few weeks prior to the November election. "Well, I've done it," he told Mrs. Willkie, who had been urging him to make the switch. Willkie saw no reason to issue a press release or make a public statement. And, oddly enough, none of his advisers seized the opportunity. More than thirty years later, a liberal Republican, John V. Lindsay, would get his face splashed across the covers of national magazines for becoming a Democrat in preparation for his 1972 presidential bid.

On November 21, 1939, General Hugh S. Johnson, former New Deal administrator who was then a popular syndicated columnist, told the New York Bond Club that Willkie "would make a powerful candidate and, if elected, a great president."

Willkie, in Atlanta on corporate business, was asked by reporters for his reaction. "In view of the speed with which the government is taking over my business, I'll probably have to be looking around for a new job," he quipped. "General Johnson's is the best offer I've had so far."

At the end of the year, Willkie found himself under increased pressure from some advisers to make his candidacy official. "When we do this it'd better be the right time," he told Pryor. "Otherwise, they'll build up enough mud pies to throw at me. You probably wouldn't even want to know me. If they think I'm getting close to Roosevelt, the smears will come out. Let's hold off until the last minute."[22]

Referring to the "presidential talk" in a December 1, 1939 letter to Krock, Willkie wrote: "I would not go through the pretense of saying that if a major party nominated me for President on a platform in which I believed that I would decline the nomination. By the same token, I would not accept a nomination on a platform in which I did not believe.

"Now, please understand me–I have no illusions that any party is going to nominate me. I merely make the above statement, in view of the talk, in order to preserve my intellectual integrity. I am tremendously interested in the principles both economic and political which are to guide us in the next few years. I hope that the parties draw the issues clearly and that they are each represented by a candidate who fully believes in what he is advocating."[23]

Willkie, however, fervently wanted the nomination of his adopted party and was less than impressed with his leading Republican rivals, Senator Arthur Vandenberg and Thomas E. Dewey. In a letter to Gardner Cowles, Willkie suggested that he found himself forced to run after making fruitless efforts to get the GOP front-runners to take a more realistic view of the Nazi threat. "I saw Arthur Vandenberg and Bob Taft, both of whom I know very well and like very much, and urged them to take the position outlined in my article. I was wholly unsuccessful in convincing them," wrote Willkie. "I then saw Eugene Meyer of the Washington *Post* and talked to him about persuading Mr. Dewey about taking such a position. It was only after failure to convince those gentlemen that I decided."[24]

CHAPTER EIGHT

HATS IN THE RING

On January 16, 1940, the New York *Sun* reported that Wendell L. Willkie had switched his registration to Republican. The *Sun* added that "something like a whispered Willkie-for-President movement" was already underway. Although he was still denying reports about his candidacy, the fact that Willkie leaked his new party affiliation was evidence that he was running.[1]

Two weeks later, speaking at the College of Wooster in northeastern Ohio, Willkie dropped all pretense that he wasn't interested in politics, saying publicly for the first time that he would accept his adopted party's nomination. "No man in middle life and in good health could do otherwise," he said. "But I couldn't go out and seek delegates and make two-sided statements. I value my independence. That's what I've been fighting for all these years."

At the beginning of 1940, there were plenty of Republicans who were more than eager to seek the presidency. GOP leaders had every reason to be optimistic about their chances of recapturing the White House in November. Despite FDR's bold social programs and massive spending, the nation had not fully recovered from the Great Depression. Nearly 10 million workers were still unemployed. And the national debt had reached $36.7 billion. All of these factors worked against the Democrats. According to the polls, FDR appeared to be the only Democrat who could win. Even so, those same polls indicated that a majority of Americans were against a third term.

In March, *Time* magazine concluded, "The shift toward the GOP is now so marked that nothing short of a Rooseveltian miracle can save the election for the Democrats."

Republican fortunes had been on the rebound since the 1938 off-year elections in which they gained eighty-one seats in the House of Representatives, eight in the Senate, and thirteen governorships. On election night, a half-dozen fresh Republican faces were projected on the national scene, including New York's racket-busting district attorney, Thomas E. Dewey, Ohio's Senator Robert A. Taft, and governors Harold E. Stassen of Minnesota, John W. Bricker of Ohio, Leverett Saltonstall of Massachusetts, and Charles A. Sprague of Oregon. "The Republican Party wants and needs new names, new ideas, new blood," Senator Arthur H. Vandenberg wrote in his diary soon after the 1938 elections. "I have carried the flag through the lean years, so it is a great relief to me to have the Gallup Poll bring forward some new names. Nothing could have been more detrimental to the Republican Party than to have persisted in the bankruptcy of presidential names which have been evident for the past two years when the only ones standing forward in the Gallup Poll were Hoover, Landon, and myself. It has been a pathetic confession of weakness."[2]

Vandenberg, however, remained the early favorite for the 1940 Republican presidential nomination. The plump, hardworking Michigan senator held a commanding lead over the GOP field in a December 1939 *Newsweek* poll. Vandenberg was also rated the most likely Republican nominee in a national survey of newspaper editors. Democratic National Chairman James A. Farley, too, predicted that Vandenberg would emerge as the Republican candidate.

At the age of fifty-six, Arthur Hendrick Vandenberg looked like a *New Yorker* cartoonist's version of a U.S. senator. He brushed his thinning gray hair across a high-domed head, smoked long black cigars, and wore white suits. An old-fashioned orator, the Michigan senator often came across as an overblown windbag. His friend Dean Acheson acknowledged, "Vandenberg would often be carried away by the hyperbole of his own rotund phrases." Before coming to the Senate, Vandenberg had been editor of the Grand Rapids *Herald*. In his editorial columns, he denounced Sinclair Lewis for mocking flag-waving, churchgoing, small-town society. He wrote Horatio Alger-type stories for national magazines and a song about silent-movie queen Bebe Daniels called "Bebe, Be Mine" that became a popular hit. In political philosophy, Vandenberg was a Hamiltonian conservative. He had written three books about Alexander Hamilton, including one entitled *Hamilton: The Greatest American.* Vandenberg confided that his biggest ambition in the Senate was to build a Hamilton monument on the banks of the Potomac that would dwarf the Lincoln and Washington monuments.

On May 29, 1939, Vandenberg declared his availability for the nomination in a letter to Michigan political allies. "Words fail to express my gratitude for this expression of confidence," he wrote. "I shall hope to proceed with whatever responsibilities lie ahead in a manner that may justify these generous opinions." Vandenberg, attempting to capitalize on the third-term issue, pledged that he would serve only one term so that his administration would be "free of all incentive but the one job of saving America."

Like other midwestern isolationists, Vandenberg's eyes seemed blind to the rising threat of Adolf Hitler. A month after the Nazi armies had crushed Poland, the Michigan senator claimed, "This so-called war is nothing but about twenty-five people and propaganda." Vandenberg assured American mothers: "I will never vote to send your sons to war." Throughout 1939, he fought FDR's efforts to amend the Neutrality Act. "Repealing the arms embargo probably won't get us into war," he said. "But it's like taking the first drink of whiskey. After a while, you're drunk." Early in 1940, Willkie met with Vandenberg and told him bluntly that it would be nothing less than a disaster for Republicans to nominate a candidate holding his foreign-policy views. Willkie felt that an isolationist nominee would be overwhelmingly defeated because the American public would consider him out of touch with world events.

In domestic affairs, Vandenberg had been a moderate conservative. He supported many of the New Deal's social welfare programs and had, in fact, been the principal sponsor of the Federal Deposit Insurance Act. In January 1940, he published a magazine article called "The New Deal Must Be Salvaged" in which he endorsed FDR's reform measures but made the argument that they could be better administered by a Republican chief executive.

Vandenberg's major shortcoming as GOP front-runner was that he lacked nerve. He did nothing to dispel those doubts in announcing plans to seek re-election to the Senate at the same time he was making a national campaign. In 1936 he did not enhance his popularity

with Republican professionals by rejecting the vice-presidential nomination on the grounds that Landon was a certain loser. Four years later he demonstrated a lack of zeal in sidestepping the New England primaries. "Why should I kill myself to carry Vermont?" asked the Michigan senator.

His presidential strategy rested on a two-hundred-delegate base from the Midwest and Far West. And he chose the familiar turf of Wisconsin and Nebraska as the key primary battlegrounds. In February of 1940, Vandenberg made appearances in Wisconsin and Illinois, then formally launched his campaign at a Lincoln Day dinner in Minnesota.

By this time, thirty-seven-year-old Thomas E. Dewey of New York had established himself as Vandenberg's principal challenger. Interior Secretary Harold Ickes joked that Dewey had "thrown his diaper into the ring." In spite of his youth, Dewey was a formidable candidate. During the 1930s, he had won the nation's admiration as New York's dogged and industrious district attorney. In tabloid headlines, he was known as the "racket-buster." Among his trophies were Tammany Hall boss James J. Hines and such notorious mobsters as Charles "Lucky" Luciano, Jack "Legs" Diamond, and "Dutch" Schultz [Arthur Flegenheimer]. Underworld kingpin Louis Lepke [Buchalter] surrendered to columnist Walter Winchell and J. Edgar Hoover so that he would be tried in a federal court and not have to face Dewey. As district attorney, Dewey won all but one of the seventy-three cases he brought to court. Novels and comic books were published about Deweyesque prosecutors. A Dewey character, Walter Abel, starred in a 1938 film, *Racket Busters*. And CBS radio introduced a Dewey-inspired weekly series called "Gangbusters" that became a popular thriller. In 1938 he ran for governor and came within one percentage point of unseating the durable Herbert Lehman. On the strength of his near miss and his growing national reputation, Dewey was suddenly boomed as a presidential contender.

Even before he ran for the governorship, Dewey had been looking toward a presidential bid in 1940. Early in 1939, he began soliciting the support of Republican leaders. *Life* portrayed him as the "Number One Glamour Boy of the GOP." In the summer of 1939, Dewey's private polls showed him leading President Roosevelt by a substantial margin. By the end of the year, Dewey and FDR were locked in a virtual dead heat in the Gallup poll. Dewey wasn't at all modest about his chances in 1940. "Don't you realize that Franklin Roosevelt is the easiest man in the world for me to beat?" he told a New York *Daily News* reporter who suggested that FDR would be a tough opponent.[3]

Dewey was not a particularly likable young man. It was frequently alleged that he cared more about his public image than obtaining justice. He showed little concern for civil liberties. His office made extensive use of illegal wiretapping and unauthorized grand jury subpoenas. It was not unusual for Dewey's witnesses to be held in "protective custody" for months. In one case, an innocent man spent twenty years in prison. "Tom is a very self-confident young man who has never indicated willingness to give any credit for anything to anybody else if he happened to be in the picture in any way," grumbled S. Burton Heath, a New York *World-Telegram* reporter who had supplied Dewey with key evidence in several cases.

In his brief political career, Dewey had already managed to rub a great many people the wrong way. He was stiff, humorless, and overbearing. The wife of a New York GOP leader said he was a man you really had to know well to dislike. On an early 1940 campaign swing, Dewey was late in reaching the back platform of his train and a local politician filled time by talking to the crowd; the district attorney was indignant. "I won't have other people making capital for themselves out of crowds that have come to hear me," he snapped.

Dewey was attracting bigger crowds than any Republican since Teddy Roosevelt. In February he whistle-stopped across the country in his own campaign train, making ninety-four speeches. In South Dakota schoolchildren were given a holiday to get a glimpse of the crime-busting district attorney. In Oregon twenty-seven thousand applicants for tickets to Dewey's Lincoln Day address were turned away. "One big jump which Thomas E. Dewey has on all the other Presidential candidates, except Franklin D. Roosevelt," *Life* magazine declared, "is that he is a national celebrity in his own right, fully as famed in every notch and hamlet of the land as Clark Gable, Henry Ford, Charles A. Lindbergh, Joe Louis or Joe DiMaggio."

With his waxworks mustache, bland features, and medium height, Dewey feared that in personal appearances he would seem smaller than life. One of his aides made certain that taller men were kept at a distance. Alice Roosevelt Longworth would later observe that Dewey reminded her of the groom on the wedding cake. Sensitive about his public image, Dewey irked newspaper photographers by prohibiting unposed pictures.

Dewey's campaign was off to the fastest start of the year. He had put together a superb organization headed by J. Russell Sprague, Long Island GOP leader, and Ruth Hanna McCormick Simms, former Illinois congresswoman and the daughter of the legendary Mark Hanna. Dewey had an around-the-clock staff of speech writers, secretaries, and pollsters. George Gallup let Dewey have two men from his organization to set up a national organization to conduct public opinion surveys. Whenever Dewey wanted to issue a statement, he had the pollsters determine whether it would be politically smart. It followed then that Dewey, like the overwhelming majority of Americans, was a staunch isolationist. He also favored a balanced budget and a two-ocean Navy. If the pollsters got a negative response, Dewey either revised the statement or scrapped it altogether. He spoke in platitudes and hedged on controversial issues.

In March Dewey stumped Wisconsin while Vandenberg, still the favorite, stayed in Washington and said loftily that his "Senate duties" were too pressing for him to campaign. The New York *Times* reported that Vandenberg was a solid three-to-two favorite. Two days before the primary election, however, Dewey's private polls showed him winning by 62 per cent. Dewey poor-mouthed his chances to political reporters. On April 2, Dewey trounced Vandenberg by more than two-to-one in Wisconsin. A week later Dewey proved that this was no fluke by defeating the Michigan senator by a smaller margin in Nebraska. Dewey had cut Vandenberg down to size and, in the process, replaced him as the Republican front-runner.

Following those primaries, Senator Robert Alphonso Taft of Ohio was perceived as the most likely Republican alternative if Dewey stumbled. Taft, the son of a former President of the United States and Chief Justice of the Supreme Court, had perhaps the best-known name in the GOP. Four years earlier, Taft had been Ohio's favorite-son presidential candidate at the Republican Convention. On his election to the Senate in 1938, Taft became a political force in his own right. He had already earned the respect of Senate colleagues and was on his way to becoming the most influential senator of his generation. At fifty, Taft was a man of intelligence, calm, and quiet reserve. Tall, large-framed, and balding, he wore old-fashioned rimless glasses and in appearance and demeanor seemed professorial.

He had, in fact, been a brilliant scholar and graduated first in his class at both Yale University and Harvard Law School. He lacked the personal warmth of his father, William Howard Taft. In personality and temperament, Taft resembled his strong-willed mother, Helen Herron Taft. Like her, he appeared solemn and aloof and did not laugh easily. It was said that Helen Taft had pushed her reluctant husband into the White House against his better instincts. She did not have to push her son, who wanted very much to be President.[4]

In June 1939, Taft met with his advisers and began planning his presidential campaign. That same month, under pressure from Taft's camp, Ohio's ambitious governor, John W. Bricker, took himself out of the presidential race. Taft's son, Robert A. Taft, Jr., said later that in exchange for Bricker's support, his father agreed to back the governor for the presidency in 1944. With Bricker out of the running, Taft controlled Ohio's Republican machinery and was assured of bloc support at the national convention.

Taft was pursuing an insider's strategy. He avoided the primaries on the theory that the nomination would be determined by a network of party professionals and power brokers. The Ohio senator had convinced a great many GOP leaders that he was their best choice for his father's old job.

An outspoken critic of the New Deal, Taft was the most conservative Republican contender. He had fought to reduce federal spending and had voted against the extension of Social Security. Taft hated war and there were elements of pacifism in his isolationism. In many ways, Taft was his own worst enemy. Speaking in Iowa, he denounced federal farm loans on the same day that the administration made $70 million available to Iowa farmers. He offended blue-collar workers by crossing a year-old picket line in Kansas City. In an ill-advised effort to look like a sportsman, Taft permitted himself to be photographed in a blue serge suit holding a long-dead turkey that someone else had shot. *Time* called it the silliest political picture since Calvin Coolidge wore an Indian bonnet. *Life* dubbed Taft "the Dagwood Bumstead of American politics."

Another powerful senator, Charles Linza McNary of Oregon, had also announced his candidacy for the GOP presidential nomination. As Senate Minority Leader, McNary was the highest-ranking Republican officeholder in the land. He was more highly regarded by President Roosevelt than anyone in the field. Indeed, FDR confided to

Harold Ickes that if he could have a Republican running mate on a wartime "unity" ticket, his first choice would be his good friend, Charley McNary.

One of the last great western progressives, McNary still lived on his family's pioneer homestead. As a young justice on the Oregon Supreme Court, he had written landmark opinions on workmen's compensation and the eight-hour workday. An urbane, thoughtful, cultivated man, McNary had been in the Senate since 1917. During the 1920s, he gained national prominence as author of the McNary-Haugen Bill, which sought to provide relief for American farmers by subsidizing the sale of surplus crops abroad. McNary's plan was the forerunner of FDR's bold New Deal measures and it struck conservative presidents Coolidge and Hoover as downright radical. Hoover, who had known McNary since they were young boys growing up together in Salem, Oregon, attempted to block his selection as Senate Republican Leader.

McNary and Roosevelt had a warm and cordial relationship. The Oregon Republican supported FDR's monumental social legislation. And the President reciprocated by giving McNary the massive Bonneville Dam on the Columbia River, which provided cheap public power for the Pacific Northwest. The wily McNary was, at the same time, an effective opposition leader. In 1937 he forged the coalition between Republicans and Democratic conservatives that blocked FDR's "court-packing" plan.

Though less strident in his isolationism than Vandenberg and Borah, McNary firmly opposed U.S. intervention in the European war. Following Germany's invasion of Poland, McNary wrote privately, "We have no business in becoming involved in the European mess that has been going on for a thousand years."

With the exception of his home state, McNary did not enter the primaries. His hopes, too, were pegged to a deadlocked convention. "I am not an active candidate and if I were it would react to our disadvantage," he wrote Oregon GOP Chairman Kern Crandall. "I know the great outlay necessary to promote an active candidacy, the tremendous outlay necessary to promote an aggressive candidacy. We have not such resources, nor would I want them employed in that direction if we did. In my opinion our prospects are brighter under an unobtrusive program. All the candidates are friendly, and really it is only by last will and testament that we can assume the state of heirship. At all times I am conscious of the many hurdles that lie between."[5]

For a short time in the spring, McNary appeared to be the favorite liberal dark horse. It was whispered that Landon, House Minority Leader Joseph Martin, and New York GOP National Committeeman Kenneth Simpson were working on his behalf. Their dream ticket, *Time* reported, would be headed by McNary with New York Mayor Fiorello La Guardia as his running mate. "As McNary's backers see it," wrote Richard L. Neuberger in *Life*, "the Republicans will make decisive gains in the industrial East regardless of whom they nominate. The election will be decided in the Corn Belt and the Far West. Who among the Republicans would have as good a chance in these areas as McNary?" What made the McNary scenario implausible was the Oregon senator's reluctance to seek delegates from other parts of the country.

Meanwhile, Herbert Hoover maneuvered to bring about a convention deadlock as his last hope of regaining the White House. In preparation for his comeback, he spent more than $100,000 of his own fortune and organized small groups of party activists into groups called Hoover "Circles," which had eighty-five thousand members by the end of 1939. Two national committeemen, R. B. Creager of Texas and Harrison Spangler of Iowa, were supporting him. In October he met with advisers in New York and discussed whether he should formally announce. It was decided that Hoover would be more formidable as an unannounced candidate, but he was running hard. One month later he spent a week in Chicago with friends and political allies and assessed his prospects. To help assure an open convention, Hoover was encouraging the election of favorite sons and unpledged delegates. Hanford MacNider, Iowa's favorite son, was, in reality, a stalking horse for Hoover. The former President disappointed his onetime aide, Robert A. Taft, who had hoped for Hoover's endorsement. Within the Hoover circles, there were suggestions of Hoover-Dewey and Hoover-Bricker tickets. But there was little enthusiasm among GOP leaders for the man whom the nation had so overwhelmingly rejected in 1932. Almost nobody gave Hoover any kind of a chance to capture his third Republican nomination.[6]

The most remote possibility of all, political observers were in general agreement, was the erstwhile liberal Democrat Wendell L. Willkie. Dewey and Taft were far out in front of the Republican pack, with the New Yorker in a comfortable lead.

CHAPTER NINE

THE FIRES OF SPRING

By February 1940, Russell W. Davenport sensed that Willkie was running out of time. It would be just four months until the Republican National Convention, and his candidate had not yet shown up in the polls or captured a single delegate. "If you are going to do anything, you had better do it pretty quick," he wrote Willkie in a blunt-edged February 18 memorandum. "The time has come for you to make preparations for hitting the country with a bang, when and if the strategic moment comes.

"The way you are going along now," Davenport concluded, "the whole thing will be a fizzle. By fizzle, I don't mean that you won't get nominated. You probably won't get nominated anyway. I mean by fizzle that you will take on too much personally; you'll get tired and worn out and won't be any good to yourself or anybody else; and you'll make mistakes ranging from inaccurate quotations of figures to propositions of major dimensions that you haven't properly thought out. What you are undertaking is a serious thing. You can't just grab your ideas and pronouncements out of the top of your hat, like white rabbits. There's a big difference between being independent, which you must be, and being merely extemporaneous."

Davenport stressed that Willkie, for all his favorable press clippings, still needed to establish his credentials as a genuine presidential contender: "Frankly, I don't think it [Willkie's name] has been before the country as much as you think it has. Newspaper clips are a good indication so far as they go; but when you stop to think how many names the good people of the U.S. are called upon to remember; how many people write for the papers, are quoted in the papers, then it becomes clear that only those names can sink in to which handles have been attached. And I don't think your name has a handle."

There were, he went on, numerous opportunities for Willkie to become better known, including speaking appearances before the right groups and more extensive coverage in national magazines, newspapers, and newsreels. Davenport offered to approach the "March of Time" and make a pitch for a special Willkie documentary. "But I don't think much can be done there," he told Willkie, "until you make more news."

"Of course you can take another tack," Davenport wrote. "You can say that your true aim is 1944. If they take you this year, all right; but you aren't really aiming for this year, but for later on. But if you seriously want to tackle 1940, you'd better PREPARE to get going."[1]

Willkie acknowledged that he should be doing more to advance his candidacy and agreed to step up his public activity.[2] First, though, he was putting the finishing touches on an article for the April issue of *Fortune* that Davenport wanted to serve as his political platform. He had provided Willkie with a research assistant and, in addition, commissioned a critique of the New Deal by a panel of lawyers, investment bankers, and corporate executives. Willkie's first draft had been choppy and without a central theme. Davenport wrote Willkie in another memo that it seemed "rather negative" and that certain segments were "a little half-baked as if the ideas had not been worked out." Another *Fortune* editor, Raymond L. Buell, added, "My general criticism is that it is too much like Tom Dewey—and therefore tends to be commonplace, not for what it says but on account of what it omits. Moreover, it lacks a sense of compassion for the misery affecting at least a third of the nation."

At this point, Willkie collaborated with Davenport and Irita Van Doren on the revision of his article. He particularly liked Davenport's suggestion of a six-paragraph petition to President Roosevelt as a preface to the article. The April *Fortune* was practically a Willkie campaign document. Davenport wrote a two-page editorial all but endorsing him: "The fascinating characteristic of Mr. Willkie's position is that most people will agree with it. He is preaching just plain common sense. . . . The principles he stands for are American principles. They are progressive, liberal, and expansive. One cannot dare to doubt that they will eventually prevail. But whether they will prevail in terms of political candidacy is a question that depends upon the political sophistication of the American people."

In his article called "We the People," Willkie came across as an irate citizen conveying his indignation at the mismanagement of the federal government. With generalities and more than a few clichés, he attacked the New Deal as too doctrinaire but said that it would be a mistake to return to the rigid dogma of Herbert Hoover. Indeed, he made it clear that he accepted liberal reform. "Government, either state or federal, must be responsible not only for the destitute and the unemployed," wrote Willkie, "but for the elementary guarantees of public health." To encourage industrial growth, he urged tax incentives and the elimination of bureaucratic red tape. He favored a balanced budget but said that it would have to wait until government spending had been brought under control. These views were much more progressive than those being articulated by Dewey and Taft. But it was in foreign policy that Willkie differed most sharply with his rivals. "It makes a great deal of difference to us—politically, economically and emotionally—what kind of a world exists beyond our shores," he wrote. He berated isolationists in Congress for blocking the sale of weapons to Finland in the wake of the Russian invasion. "Our foreign policies should be forthright and clear," wrote Willkie. "We are opposed to war. But we do not intend to relinquish our right to sell whatever we want to those defending themselves from aggression."[3]

As Davenport had hoped, Willkie's magazine piece dramatized his political views and established the raison d'être for his candidacy. It was reprinted in *Reader's Digest.* Within two weeks of its publication, Willkie received two thousand invitations to give speeches. He was applauded by leading opinion makers. Gardner Cowles, Jr., publisher of *Look* magazine, who had never met Willkie, wrote him that "We the People" was "the most sensible statement I have seen anywhere of the issues facing America and of the problems which must be solved." Colonel Frank Knox, publisher of the Chicago *Daily News* and a prominent interventionist who had been the 1936 GOP vice-presidential candidate, sent a letter to Willkie pledging his support but cautioned that he shouldn't be too optimistic. "I don't believe the men who compose either convention could be induced to nominate a man for President who cast his first vote for that party in the last previous election," wrote Knox. "I cite this as political fact without the slightest sympathy with it. I would crawl on my hands and knees from here to Washington if, by that act, I could bring about your nomination."[4]

A twenty-eight-year-old Wall Street lawyer was so inspired by the *Fortune* article that he rewrote parts of it into a Willkie for President petition and had eight hundred printed at his own expense. Oren Root, the grandnephew of Elihu Root and a Princeton graduate, shared an office with a young Yale graduate. Using their respective alumni directories, they sent test mailings to the Princeton class of 1924 and the Yale class of 1925. Each petition had space for fifteen signatures. As the return address, Root put his West Fifty-seventh Street apartment. Four days after the petitions went out, Root ordered twenty thousand more.

On April 9, he wrote Willkie that he had not asked permission to launch the petition drive "because I wished to be able to say not only that you had not sponsored it but also that you had not even known of it." Willkie's GOP rivals, he added, "differ from each other only in varying degrees of unfitness. If in this crisis of civilization the Republican party turns to some ponderous isolationist or to some crooning votegetter I say it is morally bankrupt."

"I have no illusions about your being nominated in Philadelphia," he said. "I do know that if nominated you will win. And I am naive enough to believe that even the Republican politicians may see the light if enough work of the right kind is done at once. I propose to contribute to that work with all the vigor and imagination at my command."[5]

In addition to Root's activities, two other events took place on the same day that would significantly contribute to the Willkie boom. Hitler's armies charged into Denmark and Norway, which brought a sudden and chilling end to what Churchill had called the winter of illusion. Denmark fell in just four hours. With the polls showing overwhelming sentiment against U.S. intervention, Willkie had been the only Republican candidate who had advocated military aid for the embattled democracies.

That evening Willkie appeared as a guest on the popular radio quiz show, "Information Please." He had mixed thoughts about going on the program, because some advisers said it would be undignified. Two of the show's regular panelists, New York *Post* columnist Franklin P. Adams and New York *Times* sportswriter John Kieran, finally convinced him to do it. As a result, millions of listeners heard Willkie answer questions with humor and intelligence on topics ranging from *Nicholas Nickleby* to the presidential use of the "pocket veto." Asked for a quotation referring to April, he offered "April showers bring May flowers." Moderator Clifton Fadiman observed approvingly, "That's a simple one." Willkie deadpanned, "That's the only kind I know." *Life* devoted a full page to his performance. After the show, he said, "I never had a better time in my life."

Unhappy about newspaper stories on the Root petition drive, Willkie attempted to snuff it out. His friend Thomas W. Lamont was the senior partner of J. P. Morgan & Co., which happened to be the principal client of Root's law firm. Willkie got Lamont to phone the young lawyer and encourage him to drop his activities. "Willkie expressed a reluctance to telephone me himself," Root said later, "since he feared that I was probably at best an incompetent and at worst an adventurer with the consequent danger in either case that I would use his call for the sake of further publicity." Lamont, however, failed to persuade Root and put Willkie on the phone to confirm his displeasure. When Root still expressed a reluctance to abandon his project, Willkie arranged for him to meet Davenport the following day. Willkie was still apprehensive about a crazy-quilt movement of "Draft Willkie" clubs. "The principal reason," said Root years later, "was that Willkie had his own ideas about how best to obtain the Republican nomination, and my unauthorized publicity was seriously threatening a strategy which had been carefully thought out and had been in process for many months."

Over a long lunch at the Biltmore Hotel, Root managed to convince Davenport that the petition drive should be continued. Davenport set up a breakfast meeting between Willkie and Root at the University Club on Fifth Avenue. Root brought a press release saying that they had met and that Willkie "would not disapprove my action, though he could not approve it." Willkie revised the phrase to read "would not approve nor disapprove" and he added in his scrawled handwriting "and that he [Willkie] would not participate in any organized move to that end."

Within three weeks, Root announced that he had collected two hundred thousand signatures. Bundles of letters, petitions, and campaign contributions soon filled his office at Davis, Polk, Wardwell, Gardiner and Reed. And the firm's switchboard became jammed with calls from Willkie volunteers. He later acknowledged, "The situation there became impossible from both sides." Finally, Root went on leave from his law firm to devote full time to the Willkie clubs. He had carefully preserved all the correspondence and had written personal replies to people indicating an interest in further Willkie activity. He rented a small office at 660 Madison Avenue. With Root's encouragement, Willkie-for-President groups were quickly organized throughout the country. Most of the Willkie amateurs were young, college-educated, and were white-collar professionals who in a later era would have been described as Republican moderates. Marcia Davenport said that Oren Root "was the brains and the core of the volunteer movement."

In the meantime, Davenport and MacVeagh opened a rival headquarters in the Murray Hill Hotel on lower Park Avenue. Their organization was called the Voluntary Mailing Committee for Distributing Willkie's Speeches. Bruce Barton, a highly successful advertising executive then serving as congressman from New York's East Side "Silk Stocking" district, helped recruit public relations men for a publicity build-up. One of them, Fred Smith, later confided to Warren Moscow of the New York *Times* that he had organized nearly two thousand Willkie mailing clubs with the covert assistance of the Edison Electric Institute, trade organization of the public-utility industry. Local power companies furnished the manpower for distribution of Willkie campaign literature in their area. Smith said that the utilities were helping in the Willkie effort because they thought he had done much to bring their industry back into respectability.

Using his *Fortune* letterhead and journalistic contacts, Davenport solicited the support of influential editors and political writers. On April 6, he wrote Raymond Clapper: "The one man in America with the ability and the intellectual and oratorical power to rally these progressive Republican forces is Wendell Willkie. You will, however, go on to point out that Mr. Willkie is not a political reality. Check. But why in the hell don't we make him one?" Davenport added, "It is up to the progressives in the Republican Party, the people, the columnists, and the editors to make Wendell Willkie a political figure."[6]

Clapper, the much respected political analyst for Scripps-Howard newspapers, responded with a series of pro-Willkie columns.

On Sunday, April 23, the Davenports gave a small dinner party at their apartment for Willkie and John and Gardner Cowles, publishers of *Look* magazine, the Minneapolis *Star Journal,* and the Des Moines *Register and Tribune.* The Harvard-educated Cowles brothers were liberal Republicans. "Our views are 90 percent identical on any major subject," John said. Three years earlier, they had started *Look,* the hugely successful biweekly magazine, which gave them an opportunity to shape public opinion on a national scale. Gardner Cowles personally approved every political article that appeared in *Look* and had been looking for a presidential candidate to support. The Cowles brothers talked with Willkie until nearly three o'clock Monday morning. "They thought my philosophy was right and that I had the power to advocate it," Willkie said afterward, "but, they didn't know how much discount to give me as a resident of New York City, a public-utility man and a former Democrat."[7]

The Cowleses told Willkie that he was going about his campaign all wrong. If he wanted the nomination, they argued, he would have to fight for it. Willkie replied that Dewey and Taft were headed for a convention deadlock and that if this happened, he had a chance. "My brother and I said to Willkie that he was nuts," Gardner Cowles recalled in a 1978 interview. "We told him that there was no way the convention would turn to him as a compromise candidate if none of the delegates knew him. I told him that he didn't have any past relationship with the party and that as a prominent former Democrat and Wall Street utility tycoon the delegates would be afraid to turn to him."

Offering to set up several meetings in the Republican heartland, the Cowles brothers suggested that Willkie begin a whirlwind courtship of his adopted party's convention delegates. As a test run, Willkie agreed to go on the road. Opening night was scheduled for May 11 in St. Paul, Minnesota. John Cowles purchased a half hour on the CBS radio network for Willkie's speech and arranged for Minnesota's governor, Harold E. Stassen, already chosen as the GOP keynote speaker, to introduce Willkie. Only thirty-three years old, Stassen was known as the boy wonder of American politics and widely regarded as a future presidential contender. Until FDR, Minnesota had been such a Republican stronghold that a Democratic presidential candidate had never carried it. Vandenberg and Dewey had both chosen Minnesota as the kickoff site for their presidential bids, and GOP leaders considered it the bellwether of the Great Plains states.

On a hot, muggy night, more than five hundred of the Minnesota faithful were packed into the Hotel Lowry's nonair-conditioned ballroom for Willkie's political debut. It began poorly. Without passion, he stumbled through the text, attacking the New Deal's spending and, at the same time, calling for increased aid to European democracies. "It was no good," Gardner Cowles said later. "Wendell never did learn to read a speech. You just had to turn him loose. Wendell knew it had been a flop. The applause was so light you could hear the radio announcer say, 'We now return you to our regular program.' Wendell then took his speech and fluttered the pages over the crowd."

Taking off his coat and glasses, Willkie stepped back from the podium and shouted: "Now that I'm off the air and I don't have to use so damn much fine language. What I've been trying to say is, we've sure got to get rid of that bunch and I'll tell you how to do it." Raising his voice, he snorted, "Every time Mr. Roosevelt damns Hitler and says we ought to help the democracies in every way we can short of war, we ought to say: 'Mr. Roosevelt, we double-damn Hitler and we are all for helping the Allies, but what about the $60 billion you've spent and the 10 million persons that are still unemployed?" The crowd burst into applause. Willkie said that he admired Stassen, then added, "But I say to him, in all seriousness, that if he as keynoter for the Republican Convention attempts to put the Republican party on record as saying what is going on in Europe is none of our business, then we might as well fold up."

For ten minutes, the crowd roared its approval. Willkie later told Janet Flanner of the *New Yorker* that the response of this Minnesota audience made him decide to become an active candidate. Later that night, John Cowles gave a reception for Willkie at his brick-faced home. Stassen, who had earlier made a commitment to Dewey, pulled Cowles aside and whispered that he was now leaning to Willkie. Four delegates announced flatly that they would support Willkie in Philadelphia.

Five days later, Willkie delivered a rip-roaring speech before thirty-five hundred Iowa Republicans at the KRNT Theater in Des

Moines. Gardner Cowles had instructed him not to read from notes or a text. Moving back and forth across the stage, Willkie ignored the microphone and spoke in a gravelly voice that brought the audience to its feet. "After these two occasions, Wendell got almost fanatical about it," Gardner Cowles said years later. "He wanted to meet every state delegation he could. For the next month, my brother or I were with him all the time. Wendell almost killed me. We flew in small planes all over the country."

Hitting his stride as a campaigner, Willkie seemed confident and upbeat. "I'm the cockiest fellow you ever saw," he told a Kansas crowd. "If you want to vote for me, fine. If you don't, go jump in the lake and I'm still for you." He welcomed questions about his liabilities. "If any of you have any doubts about my availability because I'm in business," he told a group in Lincoln, Nebraska, "go ahead and vote against me. I'm in business and proud of it. Nobody can make me soft-pedal any fact in my business career. After all, business is our way of life, our achievement, our glory."

As for the turncoat issue, Willkie said, "Some reference has been made to the fact that I was a Democrat in 1932 but I want to say that the New Deal wasn't on the ticket, and the New Deal has no reference or relationship to democracy." Oddly enough, none of his opponents bothered to point out that he was backdating his conversion to the GOP by seven years. Even if they had, it probably wouldn't have mattered. Events in Europe suddenly became the campaign's dominant issue.

On May 10, 1940, the Nazi blitzkrieg struck France and the Low Countries. Belgium and Luxembourg were quickly overpowered. And, following Hitler's brutal air raids on Rotterdam, Holland was crushed in five days. With ruthless efficiency, the German war machine smashed through the Maginot Line. On May 21, the Nazis reached the English Channel, cutting off nearly 350,000 British and French soldiers on the beaches of Dunkirk. Churchill, who succeeded Neville Chamberlain as Britain's Prime Minister on May 10, wrote FDR that he expected the Germans to attack his country next and pleaded for U.S. military assistance. Walter Lippmann wrote, "If the offensive which Hitler has now launched succeeds, we shall know no peace in our lifetime." Charles Lindbergh, the aviator hero who had become a leading isolationist, declared, "We have to face the fact that before we could take effective action the German armies may have brought all Europe under their control. In that case Europe will be dominated by the strongest military nation the world has ever known, controlling a population far larger than our own."

For months, Willkie had been warning about the specter of a Hitler-controlled Europe and calling for American aid to the democracies. Dewey continued to rule out U.S. intervention of any kind. Taft accused President Roosevelt of injecting war hysteria into the election and stated that the New Deal posed a greater threat to American democracy than Nazi Germany. Hitler might well defeat England, Taft declared in St. Louis, but a German victory would be preferable to Americans getting into another war. Several weeks earlier, former President Hoover had brushed aside a question about the Nazi threat to France and England with the comment that it was too unrealistic a scenario to deserve an answer. Vandenberg called for the "insulation" of the United States from all foreign conflicts.

Willkie said that he "trembled for the safety of the country" whenever he thought one of his isolationist opponents might be the next President of the United States. He ridiculed Taft as "a blind, foolish and silly man" for suggesting that it did not matter which side won the European war. From the beginning of his campaign, Willkie linked the events in Europe to the security of the United States. "If Germany and Russia get away with what they are doing now," he told reporters in Minnesota, "someday we'll probably have to meet them in a contest of arms." Willkie contended that it would be much more dangerous for the United States to retreat into isolation than it would be to send weaponry to the embattled allies. "The lights of liberty are going out in Europe today one by one," he said in Kansas. "The only thing this fellow Hitler respects is strength."

"As soon as the Allied defenses fall," Willkie told an Indiana audience on May 15, "our security will be at an end." Two weeks later, speaking before his old American Legion post in Akron, he called France and England "our first line of defense against Hitler" and urged sending them military aid "in every way we can, short of declaring war." In St. Louis, Willkie asserted, "The curse of democracy today, in America as in Europe, is that everybody has been trying to please the public. Almost nobody ever gets up and says what he thinks." He berated the other Republican contenders for their stubborn isolationism and said that FDR had seen "more clearly than most men, the real threat of Hitler." Willkie also chided Roosevelt for inadequate military spending and urged a massive buildup of the nation's defenses.

Willkie's forthright position on the European war earned him the full-fledged support of Henry R. Luce, the interventionist publisher of *Time, Life,* and *Fortune.* Luce had been favorably impressed with Willkie when they had met at Davenport's country home in August 1939, but he had been less interested in American politics than the unfolding drama in Europe. During the spring, Luce went to France and witnessed the crumbling of Western Europe's democracies. His old friend Joseph P. Kennedy, U.S. ambassador to England, told him in London that the British would be defeated. Luce insisted that Britain would survive. In a cable to *Time* editors, he confided his disillusionment with the Republican hopefuls. "Unless the others move awfully fast," he wired, "it looks like Davenport's man is the only Republican who can get this homecoming vote."[8]

Luce's publications, which had already been friendly to Willkie, abandoned any pretense of objective coverage of the Republican contest and portrayed "Davenport's man" as the defender of U.S. democracy. *Life* published eleven pages of Willkie puffery in its May 13 issue. "In the opinion of most of the nation's political pundits," it began, "Wendell Lewis Willkie is by far the ablest man the Republicans could nominate for President at Philadelphia next month." A campaign report in the June 10 *Time* said, "While Tom Dewey, with bravado, was fumbling with the topic of foreign affairs, while Taft appeared to be running toward the wrong goal posts, Willkie seized the ball." *Time* went on to say that Willkie's defiant words were "what many a U.S. citizen believed."

In May, Davenport resigned as managing editor of *Fortune* to become Willkie's full-time campaign manager. Willkie advised Davenport not to make such a financial sacrifice, but he replied that he was over twenty-one and capable of making his own decisions. For much of the spring, Davenport had been working behind the scenes in an effort to get the endorsement of a prominent Indiana Republican, which would call attention to Willkie's Hoosier background and help to offset the allegation that his campaign was being run from Wall Street.

Congressman Charles A. Halleck, only thirty-nine years old, was already recognized as one of the Republican party's most astute strategists. Dwight D. Eisenhower would later describe him as a political genius. In 1940 Halleck turned down offers from Vandenberg and New Hampshire Senator Styles Bridges to manage their presidential campaigns. Halleck was an Indiana University graduate and had been a member of Willkie's fraternity. He had met Willkie at a Beta alumni party and had been "tremendously impressed." Republican National Chairman John D. M. Hamilton, a close friend of Halleck's, had privately settled on Willkie as his candidate. Hamilton joined Davenport in urging Halleck to endorse Willkie and place his name in nomination at Philadelphia. "I indicated a possibility that I might be willing to go along with that because it looked to me like we had to do something pretty drastic," Halleck said years later.[9]

Shortly before he addressed the National Press Club on June 12, Willkie drank a cocktail with Halleck in a small reception room. The congressman told Willkie that the Indianapolis *News* was set to publish a report that he was coming through with the endorsement. "If you're ready to go, I am," said Halleck. Willkie took the podium a few minutes later and said, "Gentlemen, this is on the record. I'm going to be a candidate for President of the United States. And my good friend Charlie Halleck from Indiana is going to place my name in nomination." Many reporters who had just sat down to lunch scrambled for the telephones to file for their afternoon editions.

Two weeks later, Willkie confidently told Massachusetts Republicans in Boston that he would be their most formidable candidate in the general election. He ruled out a suggestion that he might consider the vice-presidency. Although Bay State delegates were committed to Joseph Martin as a favorite son, Willkie managed to get more than a few pledges of support once the House Minority Leader released his delegation. Among these were Republican National Committeeman Sinclair Weeks and Christian A. Herter, who would later become Eisenhower's second Secretary of State. Weeks and Samuel Pryor of Connecticut flew down to Washington and had dinner with Martin. The New England GOP leaders gently suggested that Martin release his delegates. Despite their long friendship, Weeks said that Martin's candidacy was going nowhere and the times "demanded a man of Willkie's type." Martin, still hopeful that he might become a contender in the event of a deadlock, told Weeks and Pryor that Willkie wasn't a serious candidate.[10]

In early June, Willkie and Taft attended a dinner honoring Lord Lothian, the British ambassador, at the home of New York *Herald*

Tribune publisher Ogden Reid. Among the other guests were avowed Willkie supporters Thomas Lamont, Dorothy Thompson, and Lewis Douglas, FDR's former budget director who would later serve as U.S. ambassador to the Court of St. James's. After Lord Lothian talked about the British war effort, Taft was noncommittal on sending American aid. Willkie called for all-out military assistance and said that he would support President Roosevelt over an isolationist Republican. The normally unflappable Taft lost his temper and got into a shouting match with Miss Thompson. The *Herald Tribune* columnist said a few days later that Taft "fails to comprehend the kind of world in which we are living."

Soon afterward several accounts of the Reid dinner appeared in print that portrayed Taft in unflattering terms. The Ohio senator, wrote Walter Lippmann, "made Neville Chamberlain look like a far-sighted and strong statesman." Although Taftites would later cite the dinner as proof of an Eastern Establishment conspiracy to put over Willkie's nomination, the *Herald Tribune*'s active support of Willkie was so well known at the time that the only surprise of the incident was that Taft accepted Reid's invitation.

Willkie assessed his Republican opponents with characteristic saltiness. In an interview with the Philadelphia *Evening Bulletin,* he said that Taft was impractical and "too school-teacherish." He added, "Tom Dewey is on the wrong track, thinking he can win with his 'everything's wrong with the New Deal preachments.'" He also jumped on the GOP's two most recent presidential nominees: "If the Republicans repeat the stupid tactics of the Hoover and Landon campaigns, they are licked before they start."[11]

Public opinion polls showed Willkie steadily gaining ground. In March the Gallup poll reported that he had been the first choice of less than 1 per cent of Republican voters. On May 8, Dewey had 67 per cent, Vandenberg 14, Taft 12, and Willkie 3. By the end of the month, Willkie had climbed to 10 per cent. By the middle of June, Dewey had slipped 15 points, and Willkie had overtaken Taft for second place with 17 per cent. That same week, German soldiers overran Paris.

Dewey's strategists were even more troubled by their own private polls, which showed that Willkie was picking up strength at their expense. Gerard Lambert showed Dewey his findings and said that it looked as if Willkie would overtake him in the polls during the convention and quite possibly win the nomination.[12]

Herbert Hoover privately appraised the Willkie boom as "a sort of reaction from disappointment as to candidates." In a letter to Walter H. Newton, the former President added that he could not "conceive that it [Willkie] will get anywhere in the convention, although it is very popular in business circles. Many of the people who have been backing Dewey financially have now switched over."[13]

Exhilarated over his dramatic leap in the polls, Willkie said, "I would like to think it means I'm a hell of a fellow. But I think it means I represent a trend or am ahead of a trend."[14]

CHAPTER TEN

"WE WANT WILLKIE"

Philadelphia, the first capital of the United States, has always been a special city. As William Penn's City of Brotherly Love, it became the leading metropolis of the New World. A century later it was the place where the founding fathers drafted the Declaration of Independence and the Constitution. Few cities in the world are more conscious of their past than America's founding city. In the spring of 1940, Philadelphia was the third largest city in the nation, yet it remained in many ways an old-fashioned provincial town with its cobblestone streets, double-deck buses, and city "squares" instead of blocks.

Arriving from the north by train, Republican delegates passed through Fairmount Park, the magnificent wooded preserve that extends for more than ten miles along the banks of the Schuylkill River and Wissahickon Creek. Moving south, it was more than likely they would catch a glimpse of sculling races in front of the Victorian boathouses of the rowing clubs. And then, rising above the park, was the Philadelphia Museum of Art, a splendid Greek temple that houses some of the world's greatest art treasures. Moments later, the train reached Philadelphia's Thirtieth Street Station, a massive neoclassic building that seemed oversized for the setting and was less impressive than the great Chicago and New York railroad palaces.

Philadelphia's skyline was dominated, then as now, by Alexander Milne Calder's statue of William Penn atop City Hall. Since 1894, there had been an unwritten ordinance that no other building could be taller than Penn's hat. Even so, Philadelphia had some of the most remarkable high-rise architecture in America, including George Howe and William Lescaze's sparkling, glass-encased Philadelphia Savings Fund Society Building on Market Street. Along the same street could be found several of the country's biggest department stores–Daniel Burnham's grandly scaled John Wanamaker's, Strawbridge and Clothier, Gimbels, and, with its nineteenth-century cast-iron façade, Lit Brothers. There were rows and rows of antique shops and bookstores, one of which, Leary's, had served as the model for Christopher Morley's popular novel, *The Haunted Bookshop.* A few blocks to the west were the Georgian doorways and elegant townhouses of Delancey Place and the stately apartment buildings overlooking Rittenhouse Square, the city's most fashionable address.

For years, Philadelphia had been overshadowed by New York, its glamorous neighbor to the north. The once-proud Athletics and Phillies were the two worst teams in Major League baseball. To much of the country, the Philadelphia of 1940 seemed remote and isolated. The development of a large portion of Center City had been prevented by the so-called Chinese Wall, a large brick causeway, one block wide, which held sixteen parallel railroad tracks and went from West Philadelphia to City Hall. The city was considered so dreary that W. C. Fields, one of its best-known sons, quipped that he wanted his tombstone to say, "On the whole, I'd rather be in Philadelphia."

There were a few hints, though, that Philadelphia might be on the verge of a comeback. In 1939 Philip Barry's play, *The Philadelphia Story,* had been a smash on Broadway and would soon become a popular film with Bryn Mawr's Katharine Hepburn as Tracy Lord, the Main Line golden girl, Cary Grant as Dexter Haven, her playboy ex-husband, and Jimmy Stewart as Macaulay Connor. Another story about a Main Line girl, Christopher Morley's *Kitty Foyle,* had been a runaway best-seller, and in 1940 Ginger Rogers was playing the title role in the motion picture.

To help revive the national image of America's birthplace, Philadelphia's civic and political leaders aggressively sought the 1940 Republican Convention. Among other things, they offered the GOP National Committee the free use of Convention Hall and a cash gift of $200,000, which proved enough to outbid Chicago, Philadelphia's leading competitor. Another factor in the committee's decision was that Philadelphia's politics were dominated by an entrenched, corrupt Republican machine while Chicago was a Democratic stronghold. In the 1930s, local GOP officials had turned down $60 million in federal funds from FDR's Public Works Administration, which seemed to confirm all the jokes about Philadelphia.

Some of the most dramatic moments in American political history had already taken place in Philadelphia. Except for Chicago, Philadelphia had hosted more national conventions than any other city. In 1848 Henry Clay's last bid for the presidency fell short during the Whig convention in Philadelphia's Museum Building.

On June 17, 1856, the first Republican National Convention was called to order at Musical Fund Hall on Locust Street. On the first ballot, John C. Frémont, the dashing explorer of the American West, was chosen as the new party's presidential nominee. In addition, a former Illinois congressman, Abraham Lincoln, drew his first national attention by making a strong though unsuccessful bid for the vice-presidential nomination.

Eighty-eight years later, Lincoln's party was about to convene in an atmosphere made tense by world events. Four days before the convention opened, President Roosevelt jolted GOP leaders by naming two prominent Republicans to his Cabinet–Henry L. Stimson as Secretary of War and Frank Knox as Secretary of the Navy. Stimson, seventy-three, had held the same post in the Taft administration, later served as Hoover's Secretary of State, and ranked with the former President as his party's elder statesman. Knox, sixty-six, had been the Republican vice-presidential nominee in 1936, a Rough Rider with Teddy Roosevelt at the battle of San Juan Hill, and, as publisher of the Chicago *Daily News,* an early Willkie supporter. Alf M. Landon had turned down FDR's invitation to join the cabinet when the President left open the possibility of seeking a third term. In Philadelphia Landon was so shaken by the news about his old friend and running mate, Knox, that he could not finish eating his meal.[1] Republican National Chairman John D. M. Hamilton angrily read Stimson and Knox out of the party, snorting, "These men can no longer be qualified to speak as Republicans."

One week before the Republicans opened their convention, Hitler conquered France. Humiliating French leaders, the Nazi führer presented his harsh terms in the railroad car at Compiègne, where Germany had surrendered in 1918. A jubilant Hitler called it "the most glorious victory of all times" and ordered flags to be displayed throughout the Third Reich for ten days. Under Hitler's armistice, Germany occupied more than half of France and, in the remaining territory, a puppet government headed by the senile Marshal Pétain collaborated with the Nazis. Great Britain repudiated Pétain's regime and officially recognized Charles de Gaulle's Free French movement. The fall of France was going to have a dramatic effect on American politics, and it cast a shadow over the GOP convention.

In his final preconvention appearance, Willkie noted that England now was "standing in imminent fear of being crushed" and called for Americans to rally to its defense with all aid short of war. "America, instead of being afraid," he declared, "should grow stronger and measure up to its true destiny."

Nazi agents were using subterfuge in an attempt to influence the events in Philadelphia. Their conspiracy would not be made public until 1956 when the State Department declassified secret documents of the German Foreign Ministry that had been captured during World War II by Allied forces. The Hitler government had been working for some months in an effort to help bring about the defeat of FDR and the election of an isolationist President. These efforts were directed by Dr. Hans Thomsen, Germany's chargé d'affaires, in Washington. Like many other political observers, the Germans expected the GOP to nominate an isolationist for President. In addition, they wanted to make certain that Republicans adopted an isolationist platform. Thomsen, in his cable to Berlin, referred to the Philadelphia scheme as "a well-camouflaged blitz propaganda campaign."[2]

The plan had been developed by George Sylvester Viereck, the most enterprising and treacherous German spy in America. His cover job was as Washington correspondent for a Munich newspaper, but he was, in fact, chief of intelligence at the German embassy. Viereck established working relationships with many isolationist senators and congressmen and even managed to get paid German spies on some of their payrolls. Thomsen submitted Viereck's two-part proposal to the Foreign Ministry:

> 1. A well-known Republican congressman who works in close collaboration with the special official for press affairs (Heribert von Strempel, German press and political attaché), will invite fifty iso-

lationist Republican congressmen on a three-day visit to the party convention, so that they may work on the delegates of the Republican Party in favor of an isolationist foreign policy. Three thousand dollars are required.

2. In addition the Republican in question is prepared to form a small ad hoc Republican Committee, which . . . during the Party convention would publish in all the leading American newspapers a full-page advertisement with the impressive appeal "Keep America Out of the War."

New York Congressman Hamilton Fish, the grandson and namesake of Ulysses S. Grant's Secretary of State, invited fifty of his isolationist colleagues to Philadelphia and paid their expenses so they could testify before the platform committee. And, on Tuesday, June 25, Fish signed full-page advertisements in a half-dozen leading newspapers, including the New York *Times,* which urged Republican delegates to "Stop the March to War! Stop the Interventionists and Warmongers!" One of the vice-chairmen was Harold Knutson, a Minnesota congressman actively opposed to Willkie's candidacy.

Landon was chairman of the platform committee's foreign affairs subcommittee and, as a moderate, worked to achieve a pro-Allies plank. In the wake of the Stimson and Knox appointments, Landon found it difficult to overcome the committee's hard-line isolationists, headed by Senator Henry Cabot Lodge, Jr., of Massachusetts and Illinois senate nominee C. Wayland "Curly" Brooks. The plank, as shaped by Landon's committee, declared: "The Republican Party is firmly opposed to involving this Nation in foreign war. . . . The Republican Party stands for Americanism, preparedness and peace. We accordingly fasten upon the New Deal full responsibility for our unpreparedness and for the consequent danger of involvement in war." Landon was able to insert an amendment that read: "We favor the extension to all peoples fighting for liberty, or whose liberty is threatened, of such aid as shall not be in violation of international law or inconsistent with the requirements of our own national defense."

Britain could take little encouragement from the GOP's foreign policy plank. Indeed, Thomsen told the German Foreign Ministry that the platform had been "taken almost verbatim from the conspicuous full-page advertisements in the American press published upon our instigation." H. L. Mencken wrote that the platform "is so written that it will fit both the triumph of democracy and the collapse of democracy, and approve both sending arms to England or sending only flowers." Walter Lippmann added that it was "rather less intelligible and decidedly more illiterate" than Warren G. Harding's 1920 Republican platform.

Fueled by the build-up in the Luce and Cowles magazines, Willkie's popularity surged. In the final preconvention Gallup poll, published on Friday, June 21, Willkie had 29 per cent to Dewey's 47. Taft and Vandenberg were tied for third with 8 per cent and Hoover had 6 per cent. Gallup described Willkie's rise as the most astonishing phenomenon in the brief history of polling. One of the reasons for the Willkie boom was the European war and the fact that he, alone among the Republican contenders, was an advocate of aid to Britain. But another factor in his sudden momentum were the efforts of the nation's most influential publishers. More than anything, it was Willkie's massive and highly favorable exposure in the public prints that made him a national political force. David Halberstam reported in *The Powers That Be* that, in addition to his political views, Willkie's rugged good looks made him a favorite with Luce and the Cowles brothers. Willkie, Halberstam wrote, "had a wonderful face for the era of modern photojournalism. He was a Republican who did not look like a Republican, the rarest of things in those days, a Republican with sex appeal."

Willkie's face was splashed across a half dozen of America's most popular magazines during convention week. "Reprints of pro-Willkie editorials, news stories and magazine articles, all appearing as though by magic within the last few days, are being scattered around the Republican National Convention hotels," Paul Hodges wrote in the June 21 Cleveland *News*. "Early arrivals among the delegates are talking of little else."

Time's June 24 issue offered a convention preview including "The Story of Wendell Willkie," a three-page feature written in adoring prose: "Win or lose, the spectacular campaign of Wendell Willkie belonged with the great U.S. political stories." David Lawrence's *U.S. News* published a cover photograph of Willkie in his World War I uniform and a strong endorsement. The *Saturday Evening Post,* published on Philadelphia's Independence Square, gave Willkie most of its June 22 issue, including an article by General Hugh Johnson which said that he would be a great President, an article by Willkie titled "Five Minutes to Midnight," and an editorial which said that the world crisis required bold new leadership.[3] On June 19, the Scripps-Howard newspaper chain endorsed him, saying, "With all due respect to other Republicans who seem to have a chance, Willkie stands out among them like an oak in a thicket." *Look* published Willkie's article, "Roosevelt Should Run in '40." Willkie had told the Cowles brothers in Minnesota, "I want to see us beat the champ, I don't want to see us beat Tony Galento." Two-Ton Tony Galento was a rotund, beer-guzzling New Jersey heavyweight who had recently been knocked out by the champion, Joe Louis. In *Look,* Willkie made the argument that only with FDR as a candidate would there be a full discussion of the New Deal as a major campaign issue. "With Mr. Roosevelt in the fight, defending this philosophy, we can obtain a clean-out verdict," Willkie wrote. A *Look* sidebar characterized Willkie as "the leading compromise candidate," "the dark horse to watch in the convention," and "the ablest of any Republican."

In an era when national magazines shaped public opinion, Willkie became an instant celebrity, a star. Having the support of *Life, Look,* and the *Saturday Evening Post* were roughly the equivalent of CBS, NBC, and ABC getting together on a candidate in the age of television.

The GOP gathering at Philadelphia was the first convention ever televised. It was a brand-new medium that had made its debut in 1939 at the New York World's Fair. Four NBC cameras were installed in Convention Hall, linked to New York by 108 miles of special coaxial cable. According to NBC, the convention was watched by about fifty thousand people, mostly in the Northeast but some as far away as Tulsa, Oklahoma. Close-ups of the speakers were clear, but crowd scenes tended to be fuzzy and lack detail. Street noises, especially the honking of automobiles, sometimes drowned out the speakers. It would be twelve years before TV introduced gavel-to-gavel coverage of the conventions and changed forever the balance of American politics. Chalmers Roberts, a young reporter for the Washington *Daily News,* seemed to sense, if he did not know, the potential influence of television. "Lucky for some of the speakers the public doesn't have television this campaign," wrote Roberts. "Some speakers are terrific face twitchers and it's a wow on the air."

It had been Davenport's strategy to cast Willkie as a real-life version of *Mr. Smith Goes to Washington,* the earnest and irate citizen fighting the corrupt politicians of both parties. So, while Taft established his headquarters in one hundred and two rooms at the Bejamin Franklin, Dewey in seventy-eight at the Walton, and Vandenberg forty-eight at the Adelphia, it was Davenport's idea for Willkie to have just two rooms on the sixteenth floor of the Benjamin Franklin. As a result, some of Willkie's top strategists were without hotel space. Harry Shackelford, Willkie's college roommate and advertising manager of the Johns-Manville Corporation, was appalled to find Congressman Halleck, Willkie's point man, in a matchbox room at the Walton. Shackelford gave Halleck $200 for expenses and arranged for him to stay in the Bellevue Stratford's sample apartment on the mezzanine level. Halleck's room at the Bellevue was so crowded with visitors that he held private conferences in a tiny bathroom with a pull-chain toilet. On Saturday, Halleck met in the bathroom with Governor Raymond Baldwin of Connecticut, who confided that he was prepared to deliver his state's sixteen delegates on the first ballot. Another key New England Republican, Governor Leverett Saltonstall of Massachusetts, made a commitment to Halleck that the Bay State would switch to Willkie after fulfilling its obligation to favorite son, House Minority Leader Martin, in the early roll calls.

Wearing a straw boater and a rumpled pinstripe suit, Wendell L. Willkie arrived at Philadelphia's Thirtieth Street Station on Saturday afternoon. His train fare, it turned out, had been paid by several newspaper reporters. He had left his money at home. "Willkie was a most disorganized person," recalled Turner Catledge of the New York *Times*. "If you visited his hotel room, you'd likely see his clothes scattered everywhere—shirt under the bed, socks on the chandelier."[4]

With a bundle of newspapers under his arm, Willkie conducted an impromptu press conference on the terminal's underground platform. "Ask me any damn thing in the world," he began, "and I'll answer it. Nothing is off the record, so shoot, ask anything you want." Willkie said that he did not have a campaign manager or a campaign fund. His headquarters, he added, were under his hat, and he was having the time of his life. He flatly predicted his nomination and dismissed speculation about a Dewey-Taft "Stop Willkie" coalition as "a lot of bunk."

"I haven't the faintest idea of how many delegates will be for me on the first ballot," he said, "and I don't think it matters. This is a wide-open convention, and anyone who says he can deliver a certain number of delegates to a certain candidate at a certain time is wrong."

Willkie then got into a limousine with Davenport and Halleck and went to Broad and Chestnut streets, just south of Philadelphia's City Hall, where he marched down the sidewalk followed by a large crowd. As he walked on, more and more people fell in behind him. Willkie grinned, shook hands, and bantered with the throng. "Mr. Willkie's progress was noisy, undignified and at times tumultuous," Emmet Crozier wrote in the New York *Herald Tribune*. Willkie stopped at a storefront "Willkie Club" office at Broad and Locust streets and then walked across the street and into the lobby of the Bellevue Stratford, the gray-stone Victorian hotel that was the convention's official headquarters and nerve center.

A roar went up as Willkie made his way through the crowd. Walter Tooze, chairman of the Oregon delegation and a McNary delegate, confronted Willkie about his views on reciprocal trade agreements. Willkie said that he favored them "in principle" and thought they would work to America's benefit after the war. Tooze walked away, growling that he had been given a "run around." Willkie placed his hand on the Oregon Republican's shoulder and said that he would answer anything. When Tooze started expounding his own views, Willkie said, "If you will stop talking, I will try and answer you. Yes, I am for the principle of the reciprocal tariff. As a matter of fact, I believe the reciprocal tariff was initiated by President McKinley and carried on by President Taft.

"That's my position," declared Willkie. "You can vote for me if you want to, or not."

"I didn't get the answer I wanted," Tooze responded, "but I've got to hand it to you–you're not afraid to talk up and say what you think."

With the procession still following him, Willkie walked into the Bellevue's dimly lit Hunt Room bar and ordered a scotch and soda. "Lots of us followed him into the bar to get a close peek at him," wrote Broadway columnist Damon Runyon. "Everybody that could get near him had something. He was so big and tough that he never budged an inch from his place at the bar when everybody was scrimming and scrouging trying to have something and somebody said it was a good thing he was not one of the fellows we figured on picking our ticket from or they would have got lost in the shuffle or knocked down and crippled.

"Then he said let's have another and he began shaking hands around and every time he shook hands he ruined somebody's dukes. He left the Bellevue and went all over town shaking hands and he left hundreds of guys so they couldn't pick up a knife or a fork for a week."[5]

Not everyone found Willkie so engaging. In the lobby of the Benjamin Franklin Hotel, he approached a group from Indiana that included former U.S. Senate Majority Leader James E. Watson. An old-line conservative, Watson was supporting Dewey and bluntly told Willkie that he was not "my type of Republican." Willkie acknowledged that he was a former Democrat.

"Well, Wendell," said Watson, "you know that back home in Indiana it's all right if the town whore joins the church, but they don't let her lead the choir the first night."

Everyone–including Willkie–laughed, but the presidential hopeful recognized that, in spite of his dramatic gains in the polls, his Democratic past still made him unacceptable to a great many Republican leaders. David S. Ingalls, Taft's cousin and campaign manager, attacked Willkie without mentioning his name, asserting that "the next president should be a Republican" who was "deeply experienced in the science of government." Philadelphia oil millionaire Joseph Newton Pew, the porcine little man who controlled Pennsylvania's seventy-two delegates, denounced him as a reformed New Dealer. Willkie retorted, "I don't like Joe Pew's brand of politics." In an interview in the Philadelphia *Evening Bulletin,* Willkie said, "I don't know Joe Pew personally and would not allow myself to become part of his policy of returning to the uncontrolled days of Harding and Coolidge."

Willkie and his wife were getting into a taxi in front of the Benjamin Franklin at around midnight Saturday when New York *Times* Washington correspondents Arthur Krock and Turner Catledge arrived at the hotel. Krock, the fifty-three-year-old chief of the *Times* Washington bureau, had been the first major political columnist to suggest that Willkie was presidential timber. Catledge had covered Willkie's battle with the TVA. Willkie greeted them warmly, explaining that he and Edith were going across town to stay in an apartment at the Warwick Hotel instead of spending the night in the Ben Franklin headquarters suite. He invited the newsmen to come along for a drink, and they readily accepted.

Krock, a courtly, imposing figure, was arguably the most powerful journalist in Washington as national affairs columnist and bureau chief of the nation's pre-eminent newspaper. Like Willkie, he was a Woodrow Wilson liberal. Krock had, in fact, accompanied Wilson to the Paris Peace Conference and won a citation from the French government for his coverage. He had already won two of his three Pulitzer Prizes, the second for a 1938 interview with President Roosevelt. Krock enjoyed his role as the confidant of the select and mighty and was himself a formidable political power broker. Since his February 1939 column about Willkie's presidential prospects, Krock had written frequently about his favorite dark horse.

Willkie told Krock and Catledge that he was growing increasingly optimistic about his chances of winning the nomination. The three men talked in the living room while Edith slept in an adjoining bedroom. Willkie called room service and ordered a bottle of scotch. Krock blandly asked whether Willkie had settled on a floor manager. The *Times* reporters were stunned when Willkie said he did not know what Krock was talking about and asked whether it was necessary to designate someone for the job. Krock and Catledge explained that the floor manager was critical at any convention.

In his memoirs, Krock wrote, "We explained that since it was secondary support Willkie was seeking, and his task was to get more votes on each ballot–taken from his reserve strength after Dewey and Taft had had their 'runs'–he must have a group that would manage the accessions, the rate of these accessions, etc. We described how it was necessary for him to have well-known politicians, being known (unlike himself) to the state leaders, to roam the floor, to say to this delegation that the other was about to 'plump for Willkie,' and regulate the pace of his bid when the time came to make it."

Willkie was responsive and asked for the names of some possible floor managers. He respected Halleck and had been impressed with the Indiana congressman's early efforts. Both Krock and Catledge said that Halleck's work on the resolutions committee was not yet finished and it would be too much to expect him to handle Willkie's floor responsibilities and the nominating speech. Krock recommended Baldwin, whom Willkie indicated had been friendly. Willkie then asked about Stassen. Krock said that as keynoter the Minnesota governor would have to be neutral and could not take such a visible role. Catledge, however, noted that Stassen might make such a move after delivering his Monday night keynote speech.[6]

Going into the convention, Dewey was the front-runner, claiming that he was within a hundred votes of the nomination. The New York district attorney had swept the primaries and, though his ratings had recently sagged, had led the Gallup poll for more than a year. Dewey's strategy was to go for an early knockout, but there was growing talk among the delegates that he was turning out to be like all those fighters who came from Philly and sparkled in the preliminaries but faded once they got into the main event. Pollster Gerard Lambert urged Dewey's other advisers to hold fifty delegates in reserve on the first ballot, so that they would be assured of gaining strength on the second. "The men met this suggestion with the most annoying, patronizing air I have encountered in my entire life," Lambert said years later. "They explained that I didn't know anything about politics. They must keep up the morale of the delegates. They must start high." Lambert warned that shooting the works would be a major error, but he was overruled.

After the fall of France, a popular joke in political circles was that Dewey had become the first American casualty of the Second World War. It was not so much his isolationism as his youth and seeming uncertainty in foreign affairs that raised grave questions about his capacity for leadership. "There's no way that the Republicans are going to nominate a thirty-seven-year-old kid for President," Dewey's New York ally, Edwin F. Jaeckle, had told a GOP meeting in May.[7] "As a presidential possibility," wrote columnist Westbrook Pegler, "Dewey is preposterous, and his election would be a calamity which, happily, does not seem imminent." A week before the convention, CBS radio canceled "Gangbusters," the thriller for which Dewey had been the prototype.

On Saturday, Dewey drove from New York to Princeton and picked up Lambert; then the two men motored to Philadelphia. That afternoon Dewey opened his headquarters in the Hotel Walton, which had been William McKinley's command post during the 1900

Republican Convention. "The battle has just begun," he told more than a thousand supporters in the Crystal Room. At daily press briefings, Dewey was cool and controlled in attempting to put the best possible face on his declining fortunes. On Sunday, however, he became distracted and momentarily lost his composure when some onlookers began talking in the back of the room.

Dewey, looking fresh and dapper in a blue suit, had already mastered the politician's art of saying as little as possible in dealing with the press. He deflected questions about the Willkie boom by saying that his strategists had seen little evidence of movement to the Commonwealth and Southern president. He resisted an opportunity to challenge Willkie's Republican credentials. Would he take the vice-presidential nomination? "I hope that question is totally academic," he replied. His youth, Dewey acknowledged, had become a handicap, and he noted wryly that good health was "the only political advantage that I have discovered in being young."

Senator Robert A. Taft, who commanded impressive support from the GOP's organizational and congressional heavyweights, still trailed Dewey in committed delegates but was increasingly viewed as the favorite for the nomination. President Roosevelt and Democratic National Chairman James A. Farley both picked Taft on an early ballot. "Ninety out of every one hundred experienced reporters here," wrote Richard L. Strout in the *Christian Science Monitor,* "believe that Taft has the edge." The Ohio senator predicted that he would win the nomination on the fourth roll call.

On the eve of the convention, Taft claimed two hundred votes on the first ballot, with most of his strength concentrated in Ohio, Texas, and the Deep South. In order to capture the nomination, Taft's forces needed to wrest control of Illinois from Dewey and pick up Pennsylvania's seventy-two votes when Pew dropped favorite-son candidate, Governor Arthur James. Taft also hoped that former President Hoover might come through with an endorsement or, at the very least, quietly bring California's forty-four votes into his column. During World War I, Taft had been among Hoover's youthful aides. And, later, Taft had backed his former chief for the presidency on three occasions. While Hoover appreciated Taft's past loyalty, the GOP's elder statesman was still playing for a deadlock in the hope that the convention would turn to him.

Taft and his wife Martha left Washington by car early Saturday morning and arrived in Philadelphia in midafternoon. At his headquarters in the Benjamin Franklin Hotel, Taft was not amused when his staffers rented a pigmy elephant named Blossom. "Get that damned Blossom out of my bedroom!" he snapped.[8] During a news conference, Taft dismissed the possibility of a deadlock, stated that he expected to be the nominee, and ruled out taking the vice-presidency if he failed to get the top spot.

Unlike Dewey, Taft conceded that Willkie was proving to be a genuine contender and had won over some of his delegates. "Willkie has not cut into my first-choice strength at all," he told reporters, "but he has made some inroads into my second-choice strength." It rankled Taft that a political amateur could move in and threaten the front-runners. Privately, he denounced Willkie as a "demagogue" and a "Wall Street and public-utility candidate."

Senate Minority Leader Charles L. McNary, too, viewed the Willkie phenomenon with considerable distaste. As a tough old party professional, he resented a lifelong Democrat getting any consideration for the nomination. McNary also had long been skeptical of Wall Street and holding companies. Checking into the Bellevue Stratford on Sunday, McNary ripped into Willkie. "The West, which the Republican party must carry, will go against us if Mr. Willkie heads the ticket," he said. The Oregon senator alleged that Willkie was nothing more than "a tool of Wall Street" and would get no more than fifty votes. Ralph Cake, Oregon's GOP National Committeeman, worried that McNary's blast was counterproductive, making Willkie seem stronger than he actually was.[9]

Although McNary had once hoped to capitalize on a Taft-Dewey stalemate and emerge as the presidential candidate, he was enough of a realist to know that his time had past. "This game is only for millionaires or those that have their support," McNary wrote his sister Ella in a longhand note. "Tree growers better stay at home."

On the eve of the convention, McNary had certain votes from Oregon, California, Minnesota, and Delaware. There was widespread speculation that Dewey hoped to clinch the nomination by tapping McNary for the vice-presidency. The Philadelphia *Inquirer* reported that Oregon and Colorado were ready to support Dewey on the condition that McNary would go on the ticket. There was only one problem. McNary did not want to be Vice-President and he preferred Taft or Vandenberg over Dewey. "While at Philadelphia I told a number of delegations not to waste any votes on me as I was not at all interested," McNary wrote his wife. "I shall be glad when it is settled. When I left yesterday, I thought the drift was toward Mr. Taft. He would make an excellent President."[10]

Arthur H. Vandenberg, the erstwhile front-runner, was met by a cheering, banner-waving delegation from Michigan when he arrived at Thirtieth Street Station on Sunday afternoon. With his wife and his son, Arthur, Jr., at his side, Vandenberg waved his straw hat at the crowd, climbed into the back seat of a black convertible, and went to his headquarters at the Adelphia Hotel.

Standing on a wobbly chair in the Adelphia ballroom, the Michigan senator declared his candidacy and predicted his nomination on the sixth ballot. In what he termed "a completely free and open convention," Vandenberg saw himself as the least objectionable alternative. "Everybody's mad at everybody else around here except me," he asserted. Referring to FDR's expected domination of the upcoming Democratic convention, the senator deadpanned, "The only smoke-filled room this year will be in Chicago, and the smoke will come from one long cigarette holder."

On the preceding Tuesday, Vandenberg and Willkie had met for breakfast at Washington's Carlton Hotel. A number of Vandenberg's early supporters, including Baldwin and Colorado Governor Ralph Carr, were moving to Willkie in the wake of Vandenberg's crushing defeats in the primaries. During the breakfast, Willkie sought the senator's endorsement. "He said that all he needed to put him over was the support of some outstanding, recognized Republican leader like me," Senator Vandenberg wrote in his diary. "I thanked him and told him that I thought the final showdown would come between the two of us. We parted good friends—but nothing doing."[11]

Dewey, too, approached Vandenberg, and the New Yorker offered the vice-presidential nomination in return for his support. Vandenberg, however, had rejected a chance to become Landon's running mate in 1936, and his attitude had not changed in the intervening four years.

Vandenberg sent Dewey a counteroffer. If the district attorney would take the second spot on the ticket, Vandenberg pledged to step down after one term and support Dewey in 1944. The senator then suggested "a sporting proposition" that they meet "and flip a coin to see which end of the ticket we each take." Dewey did not bother to answer Vandenberg's proposals.

While Dewey still had a large plurality over the GOP field, his lead appeared to be softening. It was not just that many delegates considered him too inexperienced for national leadership at a time of world crisis, but that Dewey had alienated one of his most powerful supporters and faced an internal war over control of the New York delegation. Dewey had chosen an unfortunate time to do battle with Kenneth Simpson, the tweedy, pipe-smoking Republican National Committeeman from New York and chairman of the New York City GOP.

Simpson, forty-five years old, was the shrewdest Republican leader in New York since Thomas Collier Platt. It had been Simpson's efforts that made Dewey the city's first Republican district attorney in memory and brought Fiorello La Guardia a second term as mayor in an uphill fight. And it had been Simpson who managed Dewey's remarkable 1938 campaign for governor in which he came within a percentage point of upsetting the popular incumbent, Herbert Lehman.

During the thirties, it had been Simpson who challenged and brought down Tammany Hall, the most celebrated political machine in America. Although he liked to drink with the pols, Simpson was not a product of the Bourbon-and-branch-water atmosphere of clubhouse politics. He had been a classmate and friend of Edmund Wilson at the Hill School in Pottstown, Pennsylvania, then later attended Yale and Harvard Law School. An army officer in World War I, he served on the Western Front. During the 1920s, he worked as an assistant federal prosecutor before going into private practice and Republican politics. He was a man with uncommon interests, an art collector and Manhattan socialite whose circle of friends included Gertrude Stein and Alexander Kerensky, former premier of Russia. Simpson was an outspoken liberal. He muted Dewey's criticism of the New Deal in the gubernatorial campaign. Simpson also made a public attack on former President Hoover that drew cross fire from the Republican right.

Simpson and Dewey got along well enough until the district attorney commented that he would have been elected without Simpson's organization. A conflict between the two strong-willed, ambitious New York Republicans became inevitable. By the spring of 1940, the feud had become a full-scale war. Simpson hinted that he might back Willkie for the nomination. And Dewey, with the aid of upstate conservatives, narrowly ousted Simpson as national committeeman on June 12.

In the tradition of New York political bosses, Simpson did not get mad. He got even. On that day he served notice that he would take revenge in Philadelphia. One of Simpson's closest allies, Manhattan Congressman Bruce Barton, endorsed Willkie later the same day and said that he would deliver a seconding speech at the convention. Simpson planned to sandbag Dewey's presidential hopes by splitting the New York delegation and breaking up other blocs of pro-Dewey delegates. On the eve of the convention, Simpson's friend, Mayor Rolland B. Marvin of Syracuse, announced that he was switching from Dewey to Willkie.

Almost as soon as he arrived in Philadelphia, Willkie began receiving delegates in his small, sixteenth-floor suite at the Benjamin Franklin. "I don't want to be president enough to be intellectually dishonest with you," he told a group of California delegates. "I'm not a cagey politician–I don't know the arts of that trade. I'm glad I don't. I have the satisfaction of knowing that the man who is looking for a job is my chief supporter. The big boys may still be hostile, but the man who works with his hands or wants to have a chance to get a job is rooting for me." Defending his utilities background, he told Indiana delegates, "If you can find any successful accusation against me, I want you to be against me." To another group, he said, "I haven't any trades to make. Take me or leave me."

For most of the week, the hallway outside Willkie's suite would be packed with delegates, political amateurs, clubwomen, and reporters waiting to see him. In his cramped room, Willkie got so wet with perspiration that he paid a messenger to go buy him some fresh shirts. On Monday he hosted a dozen state delegations. By midnight Tuesday, he had met with delegates and alternates from thirty-four states. As he explained his views and took questions, Willkie often made chopping gestures with his right hand as if he were a football coach giving a halftime pep talk to his players.

On Sunday night, Willkie delivered a rousing speech before more than four thousand cheering fans in the Academy of Music, the handsome old opera house that had been the scene of Ulysses S. Grant's renomination in 1872. Introduced as "President Willkie," he declared that building a strong national defense would be the overriding issue of the campaign and said that his program would create jobs for millions of unemployed workers and, in the process, restore the nation's economy. "Three months ago no man had less notion than I that I might occupy public office," he said. "No one was more amazed than I at the way the talk about my availability for the presidency grew." Willkie said that he had spent less than $4,000 in traveling expenses and telephone bills and "paid it all myself." If he won the nomination, Willkie added, "I will be under obligation to nobody except the people."

Later that night, Krock arranged for Willkie to see former Kansas Governor Alf M. Landon, the 1936 GOP standard-bearer and still a major influence in national politics. Until the New York *Times* columnist interceded, Landon had declined to meet with Willkie. "If he had ever held a public office, and was not a utility man, he would be a real contender because of his robust personality and ability to express himself," Landon had written Senator Arthur Capper on June 5.[12] But since coming to Philadelphia, Landon had been troubled by allegations linking Willkie's campaign to Wall Street big-money interests and reports that some of their methods were unethical if not illegal. Willkie convinced Landon that he was personally honest and had nothing to do with the questionable and unauthorized activities of some supporters. Willkie had, in fact, persuaded several Philadelphia newspapers to withdraw full-page advertisements that had been placed without his approval. Though impressed with Willkie, Landon opted to back Dewey.

By the time the convention opened on Monday, Halleck, Simpson, Baldwin, Saltonstall, and Wyoming Congressman Frank Horton were among the Republican luminaries actively working for Willkie's nomination. Halleck presided over daily strategy meetings. "Really, I was way over my head," the Indiana Republican would recall years later. "The only way I knew was to try to swim out."[13]

Halleck's raids on the delegations of other candidates had been successful. So had Willkie's own efforts, and a large bloc of isolationist congressmen decided that everything possible should be done to block the Democratic renegade's nomination. On Monday morning, forty GOP representatives and five senators signed a manifesto urging the convention to choose "a leader with a past record consistently supporting Republican policies and principles and whose recognized position and recent pronouncements are a guarantee to the American people that he will not lead the nation into a foreign war." Many of the signers had been recruited by the German embassy and brought to Philadelphia. Years later, one of them, Karl Mundt of South Dakota, denied any knowledge of the German connection and said that the group opposed Willkie because he was an interventionist.

"That's a lot of spinach," Willkie shot back on learning that the group of Republican congressmen had repudiated his candidacy. Taft's forces were hopeful that Willkie had been dealt a major blow. "The Willkie boom has struck a snag," campaign manager Ingalls said, "and has been losing momentum since yesterday noon." Senator McNary, while not signing the anti-Willkie petition, said that it represented the views of a majority of western Republicans. "We can win," McNary said, "if this convention selects as its candidates the men who stand for the advanced and traditional Republican ideals and if the nominees are selected in an unbossed convention."

Despite the "Stop Willkie" movement, the tousle-haired maverick continued to make gains. Governor William H. Vanderbilt of Rhode Island, who had been for Dewey, announced that he was switching to Willkie. It was reported that half of New Jersey's thirty-two member delegation was ready to break in Willkie's favor. Colorado's Governor Carr, one of Vandenberg's longtime allies, abandoned the Michigan senator and said that he would second Willkie's nomination. Governor Charles A. Sprague of Oregon, McNary's close friend and campaign chairman, acknowledged that the Senate Minority Leader's prospects had all but vanished. In a telegram to his executive assistant Sigfrid Unander, a McNary delegate, Sprague instructed Oregon delegates to stick with McNary on the early ballots, but he said they should consider an alternative. "That would be Wendell Willkie," Sprague wired. "Prime issues now are neither control of utilities, reciprocal tariffs or past party labels but developing sound foreign policy, organizing America for defense and restoring financial and industrial security."[14]

On Monday morning, Republican National Chairman John D. M. Hamilton opened the 1940 GOP Convention and Philadelphia Mayor Robert E. Lamberton made a brief welcoming speech. After forty-five minutes, Hamilton ended the morning session. Over the weekend, Hamilton had participated in Willkie's strategy sessions and pledged his behind-the-scenes assistance. Years later, Hamilton said that he had "toyed with the thought of seconding Mr. Willkie's nomination," but felt that he could be more effective by remaining publicly neutral.

Philadelphia's Convention Hall, a huge two-level indoor arena with a capacity of fifteen thousand people, had been designed as a place for national political conventions. Four years earlier, FDR had chosen it as the setting for his second nomination. A thousand-pound bronze eagle was attached to the podium, and the stage was decorated with red, white, and blue bunting. The forty-eight state coats of arms were hung from the balconies, and between them were bronze eagles. Each state standard held a silhouette of the Republican elephant with a small American flag in its trunk. Maine and Vermont, the only states that went for Landon in 1936, were seated in the front row next to the large Michigan and Indiana delegations.

On Monday night, the delegates returned for Governor Stassen's keynote speech. Among the celebrities in the audience were former heavyweight champion Gene Tunney, singer Rudy Vallee, radio personalities Lowell Thomas and H. V. Kaltenborn, and Grantland Rice, dean of American sportswriters. Two wives of former presidents were there–Helen Herron Taft, who would see her son's name placed in nomination for the presidency, and Mary Scott Lord Dimmick Harrison, widow of President Benjamin Harrison. Wearing a black gown, Mrs. Harrison declined any comment on the presidential race, but her son-in-law confided that he was for Willkie.

The Oyster Bay branch of the Roosevelt family was well represented in Convention Hall. Colonel Theodore Roosevelt, Jr., worked the floor for Dewey and had been among his top strategists. His brother, Archie, was actively supporting Willkie. And their sister, Alice Roosevelt Longworth, backed her good friend Bob Taft. When Joseph Alsop suggested to Mrs. Longworth that Willkie's support seemed to come from the grass roots, she replied, "From the grass roots of ten thousand country clubs."

On Monday night, a group in one of the balconies shouted "We Want Willkie" during delays in the program. The chant brought scattered applause, but the delegates seemed indifferent. The Philadelphia Orchestra opened the night session with a stirring rendition of Earl Robinson and John LaTouche's "Ballad for Americans." Denis Cardinal Dougherty, Archbishop of Philadelphia, referred in his invocation to "so many parts of the world lying in ruins" and asked for divine guidance for the convention's delegates as they reached their decision.

Governor Stassen, though drawing big applause with his plea to "keep burning the light of liberty," rambled on for nearly an hour and left the audience bored. An underwhelmed H. L. Mencken wrote in the Baltimore *Sun* that Stassen's age appeared to be somewhere between seventeen and thirty-three.

His keynote speech may have been less than a triumph, but Stassen still commanded influence as Minnesota's governor and the party's freshest face. Willkie felt that an endorsement from Stassen would be a major coup, and the Cowles brothers pressed the governor for a commitment. Soon after completing his speech, Stassen contacted John Cowles and asked for a meeting with Willkie. At 2 A.M., Stassen and the Cowles brothers came to Willkie's suite. Stassen said that he would support Willkie on the condition that he was named floor manager.

At that point, Halleck had been running the convention operation, both plotting strategy and lining up delegates. "Charlie, you've done all the work," Willkie told Halleck. "You've got to be the floor manager." The Indiana congressman replied, "Now look, Wendell, we need help so badly, this thing is so tight; if we can get Stassen and whatever he's got on that basis, I'll step aside." Halleck, always the professional, did just that. Years later Halleck recalled of Stassen: "He hadn't done anything up to that point. He hadn't been to any of these meetings. He wasn't doing anything. Mr. Stassen sat down in front on the floor, and he didn't know a damn bit. He didn't know what was going on."[15]

But Stassen's endorsement, it turned out, did give Willkie a powerful boost on the eve of the balloting. At Stassen's request, the announcement was delayed until Wednesday. "This kills the story that I'm an eastern seaboard candidate," said a beaming Willkie.

Tuesday was Herbert Hoover's day. For weeks there had been speculation that the former President might sway the delegates with his second-night speech. Four years earlier, in Cleveland, his appearance before the GOP National Convention had touched off the week's greatest ovation. This time, with a deadlock in the offing, the last Republican President of the United States held out hope that the convention would unite behind him as it had in 1928 and 1932.

"Nine out of ten (delegates) think that because of experience and other qualities, he would make a better president than any of the candidates seeking the nomination," wrote Mark Sullivan. "But many have thought that while Mr. Hoover would be a better president, he would not be as good a nominee." In short, there was a feeling that Hoover was a sure loser in a return match with FDR.

As befitted a former President, Hoover was the last of the 1940 contenders to arrive in the convention city. When he stepped out of a long black limousine in front of the Bellevue, a tanned and smiling Hoover found himself surrounded by several hundred well-wishers. Hoover's long-shot candidacy received a lift when John L. Lewis, president of the Congress of Industrial Organizations and a dominant figure in the American labor movement, came to Philadelphia and asserted that Hoover deserved credit for the policies that had the nation on the way to recovery from the Great Depression. Instead of a symbol of failure, Hoover should be revered as an American hero, said Lewis. It was only the "self-seeking politicians" that blamed Hoover for the nation's economic ills, Lewis added.

To the strains of "California, Here I Come," the former President strode down the center aisle of Convention Hall that night with his son, Allan, and Pennsylvania Governor James at his side. A great roar erupted and, for seven minutes, the crowd of fifteen thousand stood and cheered. In a burst of enthusiasm, delegates from seven states pulled out their standards and began parading through the hall. Hoover, looking much the same as he did during the White House years, wore a double-breasted suit and the high, starched collar that had become his trademark. The nation's only living ex-President stood at the rostrum and waved somewhat awkwardly until, finally, House Minority Leader Joseph W. Martin, the convention's permanent chairman, banged his gavel and restored order.

It was Herbert Hoover's home-run shot. If there was to be a third presidential nomination, he knew this was the time to make it happen. He had been working on the speech for many weeks, and those who read the text thought it was the best-crafted effort of his long career. "We are here faced with the task of saving America for free men," Hoover solemnly declared. He asserted that his administration had begun to turn the nation's sagging economy around and that the New Deal had prolonged the Depression. He compared the Roosevelt administration to the failed governments of Western Europe.

Hoover condemned Nazi Germany's aggression but added, "The first policy of calm realism is not to exaggerate our immediate dangers. Every whale that spouts is not a submarine. The three thousand miles of ocean is still a protection."

By the time he had finished, it was evident that Hoover had struck out. His delivery had been so poor that many delegates were chanting "Louder! Louder!" Newsmen sitting in the section behind the podium had been unable to hear him. So it was not surprising that the crowd's enthusiasm quickly diminished. There were later rumors that Hoover had been suffering from a sore throat, which was not the case. The former President's remarks had been perfectly audible to the national radio audience. Hoover himself suspected that he had been the victim of a political dirty trick—perhaps the installation of a defective microphone prior to his speech. "It was deliberately rigged," charged Hoover associate James P. Selvage. Hoover asked a friendly newspaper columnist, George Sokolsky, for some photographs of Stassen giving his speech. "I have good reason to want to see what sort of a microphone set-up he had," Hoover explained. Seven years later, Hoover obtained an affidavit with a firsthand report that an electrician had been given written orders to switch microphones by Samuel Pryor, a Willkie strategist who was in charge of GOP convention arrangements. After Hoover's speech and the hall was empty, the original microphone was reportedly put back into place so the next day's speakers would be heard.[16]

On Wednesday morning, Hoover once again had difficulty making himself heard when a drum corps marched through the Bellevue-Stratford's lobby during his press conference. Still clinging to the remote possibility that it might turn to him, Hoover said, "This should be an open convention." He declined to say anything positive about the other contenders and did not rule out jumping into the race after the balloting began.

With typical audacity, Willkie challenged his rivals on their home turf. On Tuesday, he crashed the Pennsylvania delegation's breakfast for Governor James and upstaged their favorite son by getting the greater applause. On Wednesday, he had breakfast with Taft's Ohio delegates and made a pitch for their support if the senator's candidacy should fade. Later in the day he went before the New York delegation and, while taking pains not to offend Dewey's backers, said he would like to be their second choice. In an attempt to soften his opposition and blunt the former President's participation in the "Stop Willkie" movement, he paid a courtesy call on Hoover.

For most of the week, Senator Taft had been in seclusion seeking the counsel of assorted Republican kingmakers. "We'll get the delegates first, then think about the voters," Taft said. Taft's camp exuded confidence. Their convention strategy called for Dewey to collapse on the third ballot with the bulk of his support going to Taft. On Sunday night, Taft dined with Pew at the Union League, and political insiders spread word that the Pennsylvania boss pledged to throw his seventy-two delegates to the Ohio Republican on the third ballot. On Tuesday, Taft held conferences with delegates and his own strategists from 9 A.M. to midnight. On the basis of these discussions, Taft and Ingalls believed that they had the best strategic position going into the final stretch.

On Tuesday night, Dewey operatives J. Russell Sprague and Ruth Hanna McCormick Simms came to Taft's suite at the Benjamin Franklin and suggested pooling their strength to gain firm control over the convention. Dewey's managers made the argument for a Dewey-Taft ticket with the New Yorker getting top billing since he was the closest to the magic number required for nomination.

Taft's long-held premise was that he had more staying power than Dewey in a deadlocked convention. So Ingalls proposed the same combination in reverse order. But the negotiations were cut short when neither candidate would agree to take the second spot. "We are in either to win top place or nothing," declared Charles P. Taft, the senator's brother and aide.

Shortly before the Wednesday night session, Martin and Hamilton had reason to be concerned about matters other than politics. Philadelphia detectives and the Pennsylvania State Police informed them that they had uncovered a terrorist plot to disrupt the GOP gathering. To avoid throwing the convention into panic, the authorities asked the party officials not to say anything to the delegates. The conspiracy had been infiltrated by an undercover policeman who had been designated by the terrorists to place a bomb near Convention Hall. At the last minute, the policeman feigned illness and alerted police headquarters.

Several homemade bombs filled with nuts and bolts that would explode into shrapnel were to have been hidden in Convention Hall and other key Republican meeting places. Two of the bombs had been recovered Wednesday night, and the alleged conspirators, Adolph Heller and Bernard Rush, were arrested. The Philadelphia *Inquirer* reported later that the terrorist group had conspired to assassinate a number of the GOP's top leaders. Heller and Rush were convicted by a Philadelphia jury in 1941 of possession of a bomb, but it was overturned by the presiding judge and in 1942 the state dropped the case.

On Wednesday night, Convention Hall was noisy and crowded as the nominations began. John Lord O'Brian of New York nominated Dewey first, pledging that the district attorney would keep the nation out of war if elected President. In a slam at Willkie, O'Brian took note of the fact that Dewey had been "a lifelong Republican." For twenty minutes, Dewey's delegates paraded through the hall waving cardboard posters, state standards, and a six-foot-high oil painting of the diminutive racket-buster. While it was a long demonstration, Dewey's forces appeared to be somewhat lacking in passion.

Upstate New York newspaper publisher Frank Gannett's name was the second placed in nomination. His candidacy was a rich man's vanity. Westbrook Pegler described the Gannett campaign as "a total rebuttal of all his criticism of the New Deal for wasteful spending on useless things." To finance his campaign, Gannett had plunked down $500,000 of his own money, much more than any other GOP candidate. Although he sanctimoniously refused to publish liquor advertisements in his newspapers, Gannett was the only candidate who maintained an open and well-stocked bar for delegates in his convention headquarters. He obtained an elephant troupe from Pierre Bernard, the metaphysician known as "Oom the Omnipotent" and the pachyderms marched outside Convention Hall wearing Gannett placards. His campaign manager, Nelson Sparks, gave Philadelphia cab drivers $500 to induce them to plug Gannett, yet it was reported that they were promoting Willkie instead. Gannett suffered from such lack of identity that his nominator, New York Congressman James Wadsworth, mispronounced his name before the convention. For Gannett's demonstration, he hired several busloads of ragged and unshaven derelicts from Philadelphia's Vine Street flophouses, paying each of the men a dollar. A red-haired man wearing a torn jacket and no shirt held a Gannett banner and asked Meyer Berger of the New York *Times,* "Who is this guy, Gannon? What's his racket?"

Senator Robert Alphonso Taft was then nominated by Grove Patterson, editor of the Toledo *Blade*. Patterson claimed that the senator had "never dodged an issue," and he drew cheers from Taftites by shouting, "And always he has been a Republican." The Taft demonstration was louder and more spirited than Dewey's had been. Photographs of a tight-lipped Taft sprung up throughout the hall, and bright balloons dropped from the rafters. Taft delegates blew horns and noisemakers. They carried banners that said, "Statesmanship Not Showmanship," "Trust in Taft," "Taft for Balance," and "A Top Scholar: Bob Taft." A half-dozen Taftites started up the chant "We Want Taft!" and soon it seemed that half the delegates had joined in. They ignored Martin's call for quiet and kept shouting until Taft's floor manager, R. B. Creager of Texas, asked them to stop.

Without the knowledge of his adversaries, the galleries had been packed for Willkie. In mid-May, Oregon's Taft-leaning GOP National Committeeman, Ralph E. Williams, chairman of the convention's committee on arrangements, suffered a stroke at the Bellevue-Stratford and died. Samuel F. Pryor of Connecticut, a Willkie insider, replaced Williams as chairman and took charge of credentials. As Richard Reeves has written, credentials are the coin of a national convention, and it was Pryor's decision how they would be spent. The engraved tickets were guarded around-the-clock by Pinkerton detectives and Philadelphia police in a room at the Bellevue-Stratford to which Pryor held the key.

Pryor cut by half the ticket allocations for the Dewey and Taft delegations of the Far West, Deep South, and border states. Pro-Willkie delegations, such as Connecticut, got their full share. Simpson rather than Dewey was given control over New York's tickets. Pryor eliminated the blocks of tickets for wealthy GOP contributors and sharply reduced the allotment given to party officials. As a result, local Willkie activists held more spectator tickets than Governor Arthur James. Finally, Pryor issued standing room tickets to Willkie partisans admitting the holders to Convention Hall's gate 23. "Those tickets went to the average people on the street who, I knew, were ardent supporters of Wendell Willkie," Pryor admitted years later.[17] Neither Taft nor Dewey were informed about these gallery passes. And nobody knew that the men and women in the galleries would have a great deal to say about the convention's verdict.

It was with some trepidation that Congressman Charles A. Halleck stepped from the stage to the podium. Since coming out for Willkie, the thirty-nine-year-old Halleck had received so much hate mail from isolationists and his party's right-wing fringe that he was having his letters screened by aides. Halleck anticipated that the Taft and Dewey forces would vent their emotion at him during the speech. With that in mind, he pulled out a pint of bottled spirits and drank "two or three good slugs."[18] Then Halleck took center court.

The Indiana congressman began by breaking political tradition. Always before, it had been the custom for the nominating speaker to withhold the identity of his candidate until the very end of the address. But Halleck and Davenport decided to meet their opposition "head-on." In a deep voice, Halleck said, "I nominate Wendell Willkie because, better than any man I know, he can build this country back to prosperity."

Halleck's next sentence was drowned out by boos, hoots, and catcalls. "It was really rough," he said years later. "It just stunned me." Then, suddenly, the galleries exploded in a chorus of "We Want Willkie! We Want Willkie! We Want Willkie!" Outnumbering the Taft and Dewey delegates on the floor by more than ten to one, the pro-Willkie galleries overwhelmed the hecklers. Creager, learning of the standing room tickets, angrily threatened to bring the matter before the full convention, and Martin, trying to avert a bitter floor fight, promised to investigate. But on Wednesday night, the cries and shouts for Willkie filled the hall with excitement and provided the convention's most dramatic moment.

From then on, Halleck was in control of his audience. It was a defiant speech that struck hard at the weaknesses of Willkie's adversaries and suggested that the GOP was courting disaster if it did not nominate the former Democrat. "Is the Republican party a closed corporation?" Halleck asked. "Do you have to be born in it?" The galleries shouted, "No! No!"

As Halleck finished, the crowd of fifteen thousand was on its feet. Halleck and Davenport had not planned a demonstration. The galleries resumed their deafening chant, and the New Jersey, Indiana, and Connecticut standards were lifted from their sockets and carried by Willkie delegates. A fistfight broke out in the New York delegation when Mayor Rolland Marvin of Syracuse grabbed the state standard and was challenged by Frank Bruschi of the Bronx, a Dewey man. The powerfully built Marvin, who looked like a football tackle, quickly won possession and led the Willkie parade. A few minutes later Bronx district leader Peter Wynne went after Marvin, and they wrestled until Philadelphia police intervened. Judge William F. Bleakley of Westchester, chairman of the New York delegation, told the police to let Marvin have the standard, and the demonstration went on. Police also broke up a scuffle within the Virginia delegation, and a Willkie delegate grabbed the standard. In the Pennsylvania delegation, three delegates stood guard over their state's standard. Though disorganized and chaotic, the Willkie demonstration was described by veteran political analysts as the most spirited since the days of Teddy Roosevelt.

Even more remarkable, though, was the public outpouring of support for Willkie. Nothing quite like it had ever happened before in presidential politics. During convention week, more than a million letters, telegrams, and postcards urging Willkie's nomination were delivered to the thousand delegates. On Thursday, Western Union reported that it had carried forty thousand telegrams into Convention Hall. It became part of the convention's lore that the mother of a rival candidate wired, "Son, stop your foolishness and get behind Willkie, he's fascinating." A Minnesota delegate received a telegram from the doctor who had just performed surgery on his daughter: "Operation successful, daughter doing well, drop Taft and vote for Willkie." The New Jersey delegation alone received 100,000 pro-Willkie messages.

Much of this paper blizzard had been generated by Root's Willkie Clubs. It was later alleged that thousands of the letters and telegrams were canned and fraudulent. Landon personally answered several thousand and, on his return to Kansas, found eighteen bags of replies that were stamped "Address Unknown." *Editorial Research Reports,* however, conducted a survey in five eastern states and reported that "no person questioned denied having sent a message which bore his signature. It was found also that telegrams sent from New York by supporters of Thomas E. Dewey urging delegates to switch to Willkie also were no less genuine."[19] In Philadelphia few of the delegates could dispute that thousands of the pro-Willkie messages were authentic and represented the views of a growing number of American voters.

On Thursday morning, Joseph Alsop and Robert Kintner disclosed in their political column that Wendell L. Willkie had surged past Dewey in the Gallup poll and was now the favorite of the GOP's rank and file. George H. Gallup, an honorable and much respected pollster, had decided not to release the poll until after the convention to avoid any suggestion that he was trying to influence the outcome. In the poll, taken during the convention, Willkie had 44 per cent, Dewey 29 per cent, and Taft 13 per cent. Although Gallup did not publish the results until July 7, the Alsop and Kintner column provided delegates with dramatic evidence of the Willkie boom.

The New York *Herald Tribune,* the nation's most influential Republican newspaper, carried a front-page editorial urging the convention to choose Willkie. Irita Van Doren, Dorothy Thompson, and Helen Rogers Reid had been among the *Herald Tribune* powers working for Willkie's nomination in Philadelphia, and the newspaper's pro-Willkie bias had been known for weeks. But, for maximum impact, the *Herald Tribune* waited for the day of the balloting to publish the first front-page editorial in its history. "Extraordinary times call for extraordinary abilities," the editorial said. "By great good fortune Mr. Willkie comes before the convention uniquely suited for the hour and for the responsibility." It called him "heaven's gift to the nation in its time of crisis."[20]

Throughout the week, the European war made front-page news. On Thursday morning, Philadelphia newspapers reported that Japan was seeking to cut a deal with Nazi Germany over the Far Eastern colonies of France and the Netherlands. Churchill had spent the previous night inspecting antiaircraft weaponry on Britain's east coast. And it was reported that the French fleet was in the North African harbor of Casablanca, where they had refused to surrender to the Germans. H. E. Homan, cartoonist for the Brooklyn *Citizen,* pictured the menacing figure of Hitler standing smack in the middle of Convention Hall above the caption, "The uninvited guest."

The balloting started at 4:35 P.M. For the first time since 1924, there was genuine suspense over the outcome of a national convention. From coast to coast, millions of radio listeners tuned in to find out whether Willkie was for real or just an overnight phenomenon. The conventional wisdom had Taft as the favorite but with the outcome in some doubt. Taft's forces believed that the votes of Illinois, Michigan, and Pennsylvania would probably be decisive. Halleck, who planned Willkie's convention strategy, did what Dewey refused to do, holding some votes in reserve so that Willkie would be certain of making gains on subsequent ballots. "If we ever lost strength," said Halleck, "we were dead."

Willkie was listening to the convention on the radio in his suite at the Benjamin Franklin with such political associates as the Cowles brothers and a roomful of reporters. His mood was upbeat. Predicting that he would get one hundred votes on the first ballot, Willkie said that the nomination would be his "on the fourth or fifth ballot." If he lost the prize, Willkie said, "it won't be worth anything anyhow." When asked about reports that the galleries had been packed, he grinned and pulled five tickets from his coat pocket. "I had only ten tickets myself," he said, "and I had these five left over."

Convention Hall's galleries were once again filled with Willkie's youthful, well-scrubbed supporters. Undaunted by the Taft manager's threat of a floor fight over credentials, Pryor had distributed the standing room passes for the second time in as many days. Each time a Willkie vote was announced, the five thousand Willkie fans shouted, "We Want Willkie! We Want Willkie! We Want Willkie!" Their chant was so overpowering that some delegates complained of not hearing the roll call. One of the reasons that the Taft and Dewey forces were caught by surprise was that there had been few instances in convention history where the galleries had stampeded the delegates. In 1860, supporters of front-runner William H. Seward had been locked out of the Republican convention in Chicago, and the galleries were packed for the local favorite, Abraham Lincoln. When Seward failed to get nominated on the first ballot, the cheers for Lincoln swayed enough delegates for the rail-splitter to score a stunning upset on the third ballot. On this night, however, the galleries were not supposed to have that kind of influence.

As expected, Dewey led on the first ballot. His 360 votes, however, were considerably under the 400 that the district attorney had claimed. Taft's 189 votes were also a disappointment to the Ohio senator's strategists, who had estimated they would get more than 200. Willkie received 105 votes, Vandenberg 76, James 74, Martin 44, MacNider 34, Gannett 33, and Hoover 17, with the rest scattered among favorite sons. In his suite at the Walton, Dewey heard the vote with his close associates Ruth Hanna McCormick Simms, John Foster Dulles, and Paul Lockwood. "The results are great," Dewey said, "and I am greatly pleased. I expect a gain on the second ballot."

Dewey dropped on the next roll call, an indication that his candidacy was doomed. No presidential candidate has ever gone on to win a major party's nomination after losing strength on any ballot. With that in mind, Halleck had held back five votes in Maryland and seven in Missouri, which he released on the second ballot. Simpson broke loose an additional five votes from New York. And, in a major break, Willkie picked up nine votes from Maine. Throughout the roll call, the galleries roared, "We Want Willkie! We Want Willkie!" At the end of the ballot, it was Dewey 338, Taft 203, and Willkie 171. Chairman Martin adjourned the session for dinner at 6:50 P.M.

During the next hundred minutes, the competing Republican forces worked to regroup. It was a time for secret meetings, backroom deals, and promises that would soon be forgotten. Both Willkie and Taft were now struggling for an additional three hundred votes, many of them committed to favorite-son candidates. Stassen called Willkie and asked for permission to talk with Pennsylvania's Joseph Pew, who controlled seventy-two delegates. "You are gambling with the biggest thing you've ever gambled with," said Stassen. But Willkie turned him down, saying that he could not deal with Pew as a matter of conscience. Later in the evening, Willkie snorted "Pew be damned" when another adviser broached the subject. The Taft camp thought it had an agreement with the Sun Oil millionaire, and they hoped to get Pennsylvania's votes on the critical third ballot. Unhappily enough, when a Taft strategist placed a call to Pew's suburban mansion, a servant informed him that the Republican boss was taking a bath and had left strict orders that he was not to be disturbed.

Willkie's handlers were hopeful of getting the eighteen votes of the Kansas delegation that had just been released from its favorite son, Senator Arthur Capper. William Allen White of the Emporia *Gazette,* the founder and national chairman of the Committee to Defend America by Aiding the Allies, was pressing his fellow Kansas delegates on Willkie's behalf. A round-faced, gray-haired little man, White was America's favorite small-town editor and had long been active in the GOP's progressive wing. White's political ally, Alf M. Landon, however, controlled the delegation and he was still for Dewey.

Shortly after 8 P.M., Stassen met for twelve minutes in a freight elevator with Landon, the party's titular head. The Minnesota governor asked him to swing Kansas behind Willkie. Landon indicated that the majority of the delegation would be switching to Dewey for the next several ballots. In a 1976 interview, Landon said that he felt that Stassen had double-crossed Dewey by reneging on an earlier commitment to the New Yorker and that he was wary of making any agreement with the youthful Minnesotan.[21] Landon told Stassen that he was neither for nor against Willkie.

The convention resumed at 8:30 P.M. Dewey now found himself under pressure from his own advisers to make a graceful withdrawal and release his delegates. But the district attorney was adamant about going on for at least another ballot, when he hoped to inherit the delegates of several midwestern favorite sons. While Dewey did gain eleven votes from Kansas, his lines were cracking elsewhere. Walter Mack, president of the Pepsi Cola Company and a Willkie delegate from Manhattan, told Halleck that he was going to demand a poll of the New York delegation, because Willkie was being undercut by Judge Bleakley, the pro-Dewey chairman. Halleck told Mack that it would be too time-consuming and was not worth the risk of a confrontation. Much to Halleck's surprise, Mack went ahead and asked Chairman Martin to poll the ninety-two Empire State delegates. The galleries booed. As a result of Mack's poll, though, Willkie received twenty-seven New York votes instead of the previously announced seventeen. "It turned out he [Mack] was smarter than I was," Halleck said later.[22]

The galleries were stomping, crying, shouting "We Want Willkie!" As Dewey's numbers slipped, Taft's froze. Hoover, who had expressed opposition to Willkie and preference for Taft, stubbornly refused to give up his thirty-two delegates. In his eleventh-floor suite at the Bellevue Stratford, the former President still thought he might be the convention's compromise choice. Taft's forces were also frustrated by the reluctance of the favorite sons to release their delegates. On the convention floor, it was Willkie who garnered the majority of the delegates breaking away from favorite sons. Massachusetts switched to Willkie from Joseph W. Martin—Governor Saltonstall delivering on his bathroom conference with Halleck. Half of New Hampshire's delegates abandoned Senator Styles Bridges for Willkie. And, led by former U.S. Senator George Wharton Pepper, fifteen Pennsylvania delegates dropped Governor James and threw in with Willkie. While the clerks totaled the votes cast on the third roll call, spectators in the balcony thundered, "We Want Willkie! We Want

Willkie!" Willkie, gaining 88 delegates, moved into second place with 259 votes. Taft, adding just 9 votes, fell to third with 212. Dewey, still leading, dropped to 315 votes.

Only the bell could preserve Thomas E. Dewey's shaky lead, and he moved quickly in an attempt to get the convention adjourned. The district attorney telephoned Vandenberg and, according to the Michigan senator, "begged" for help. Vandenberg instructed his floor managers to work something out with Dewey's aides at Convention Hall. In his diary, the senator wrote that these efforts collapsed because Taft's managers "insisted they could win by battling straight through without a further recess." Hoover, nursing ambitions of his own, urged Taft to press for immediate adjournment after the third ballot. "I did not have any luck convincing the Taft forces they were in danger," a Hoover floor manager wrote several weeks later.[23] Meanwhile, Taft sent his brother-in-law, Thomas Bowers, to Dewey's headquarters in another attempt to form an alliance against Willkie.

"Yes, Dewey is definitely out," Willkie commented after the third ballot. "It's a race between the senator and myself." As the balloting went on, Willkie chain-smoked cigarettes and settled down in an overstuffed chair. When he realized that he had gone without lunch, Willkie ordered a room-service dinner and ate steak, baked potato, and a bowl of fresh raspberries. On a doubtful state, he would pause from his meal and, if he gained a vote, Willkie waved his fork and smiled. He kept in touch with his floor managers by a direct telephone line that Pryor had installed. Willkie would step into the next room to take the calls from Convention Hall and then would tell reporters what to expect on the next roll call. After a delegation came up a vote short of what his tally had indicated, he cracked, "There's one liar in that state."

Following his third-ballot surge, Willkie was glowing with confidence. "Boys, I think I am in," he said. As he heard the "We Want Willkie" chant drowning out the radio commentators, he joked, "There goes that paid-for gallery again. There ought to be an investigation." At 9:55 P.M., he declared that his vote would be more than three hundred on the fourth ballot. As it turned out, Willkie had underestimated his strength by seven votes. "See," he said, "I wouldn't kid you."

On the fourth roll call, the shouts from the balconies grew even louder as Willkie climbed into first place and Dewey fell to third. For a moment, the carnival atmosphere became even more confused when a cable from one of the radio networks became connected to the public address system and the voice of a newscaster blared out through the amplifiers. Once order was restored, it soon became apparent that it was a Willkie-Taft contest. Dewey, losing 65 more delegates, slipped to 250. Willkie added 47 and moved ahead with 306. Taft, however, was finally making his move. The Ohio senator gained 20 delegates in Illinois, 42 overall, and squeezed past Dewey with 254. There were reports in Convention Hall that Pennsylvania was now ready to give Taft its 72 votes. Taft was also reported to have reserve strength in Iowa, Wisconsin, California, and Oregon. Rumors swept through the hall that Vandenberg was going to release Michigan's delegates to Taft.

Between the fourth and fifth ballots, Willkie took a series of calls from Convention Hall in the bedroom of his Benjamin Franklin suite. Willkie confided to John Cowles, who was the only other person in the room, that he had turned down two blocs of Taft votes, one in exchange for a cabinet post and the other in return for the vice-presidential nomination. Cowles said that Willkie "flatly and unequivocally rejected the idea of making any deal of any kind."

"After hanging up the telephone," Cowles recalled several years later, "Willkie turned to me and said, 'Apparently Taft is going to be nominated on the next ballot and we have lost. But it has been a grand fight and I would rather lose the nomination than win it by making any deal. Let's slip out of here and get away from the crowds before Taft is nominated.'"[24]

Although his mood was grim, Willkie could not leave without talking with the group of friends and reporters who had spent the evening and much of the week with him. As he moved into the next room, Willkie tried to put a good face on what he felt was almost certain defeat. "Well, I scared them," he said. "They didn't think I could do it. At least we can say we stirred 'em."

Meanwhile, Dewey, failing to get the adjournment, reluctantly admitted he was beaten and released his delegates. Embittered over Willkie's sabotage of his fragile coalition, he maneuvered to block the Hoosier's nomination. Drew Pearson and Robert S. Allen reported that the district attorney had decided to address the convention and personally urge his followers to get behind Taft. Dewey put his hat on and was heading for the elevator when he learned that the fifth ballot had begun and it was too late to get across town. In a 1969 letter, Dewey recalled, "Before the sixth ballot, it appeared to me that I could not be nominated and I released my supporters, asking them to vote for Senator Taft."[25] The New Yorker then telephoned Hoover and urged him to drop his undeclared candidacy and help Taft. The former President, however, refused to give up his small bloc of California delegates and suggested that Dewey "stand fast and not release any delegates."

On the fifth ballot, Taft got off to a fast start, increasing his strength in Arkansas and picking up most of Hanford MacNider's Iowa delegates. As Alf M. Landon rose to announce the Kansas vote, a hushed silence came over the hall. In his brassy voice, Landon announced that his state's eighteen votes were all for Willkie. The galleries rocked Convention Hall with their screaming and clapping. In his hotel suite, Willkie recognized that he had scored a major breakthrough. "Well, it looks as if it might be either one of us," he said. Kentucky's chairman drew hooting from the balconies when he referred to "that lifelong Republican, Senator Taft." And, when a Washington state delegate announced sixteen votes for a "real Republican, Senator Robert Taft," Chairman Martin responded, "This is a Republican Convention and all of the candidates before this body are Republicans."

"They've used that argument too often," observed Willkie. "It's working against Mr. Taft now."

The galleries exploded when Willkie gained 40 delegates in New York. But Taft had increased his strength in the South, Midwest, and Far West. As the fifth ballot ended, Willkie and Taft had each gained 123 delegates. The vote stood Willkie 429, Taft 377, Dewey 57. Had Pew swung his 51 James delegates to the Ohio senator, Taft would have been just one vote behind Willkie. Taft was still counting on Pennsylvania for the next ballot. The roll call confirmed Taft's scenario that it would come down to Pennsylvania and Michigan. Ohio Governor John W. Bricker rushed to the podium and asked Martin for an adjournment. "I can't do that," Martin said. "In announcing the vote at the end of the last ballot, I asked the convention to prepare for the sixth ballot. A motion to adjourn would be out of order." If Willkie and Taft were still locked in a close race, Martin told Bricker that he would ask for a recess following the sixth ballot.[26]

Willkie, staying in close touch with his floor managers, told the group in his sitting room that he had vetoed any move to adjourn the session. It was after midnight, and Willkie made no effort to conceal his emotions. He loosened his necktie and brushed his face and hands with a handkerchief. His voice was strong and calm. On hearing that the Ohio senator had gained in one state, he said, "Taft can still win." Then, when a break went his way, Willkie said, "I don't see how they can afford to pass me up."

John D. M. Hamilton had been working the Pennsylvania and Michigan delegations. He advised Governor James that Willkie was probably going to win and suggested that he release his delegates. Margery Scranton, Pennsylvania's GOP National Committeewoman, said to the governor, "Arthur, please release me so I can vote for Willkie." Governor James told Hamilton, "You may think I am selfish, but I still have a chance to be nominated."

With Senator Vandenberg out of the running, Michigan was set to break for Willkie or Taft. Vandenberg's own preference was Taft, and his wife sent a note to the delegation urging them to back the Ohio senator. Hamilton, however, had performed an important favor in 1936 for Frank D. McKay, Michigan's Republican boss. "Young man, remember you have a balance in my bank and you can draw on it any time you want to," McKay told Hamilton in a meeting at the Bellevue Stratford. At the beginning of the fifth ballot, Hamilton asked McKay to deliver his delegation for Willkie. McKay expressed concern that Willkie might turn over patronage appointments to the Willkie Clubs instead of the regular organization, saying that he wanted to be assured control over federal judgeships in Michigan. Hamilton took McKay over to Sam Pryor, who called Willkie and relayed the request. "To hell with the judges," said Willkie. "Tell McKay he can have them if we get the votes." Pryor scribbled out a note that said, "Wendell said 'okay as to the judges'" and handed it to McKay.[27]

At 12:20 A.M., nearly eight hours after the balloting started, the sixth roll call got underway. In the early going, the lead changed hands several times. Taft outgained Willkie in California and Colorado, but the Hoosier picked up strength in Florida and Illinois. The galleries were chanting "We Want Willkie! We Want Willkie!" Martin, trying to maintain order, said, "Well, if you'll be quiet long enough, maybe you'll get him."

In a moment of high drama, Howard Lawrence, Vandenberg's campaign manager, went to the podium and announced that the Michigan senator had released his delegates. Convention Hall fell silent as Lawrence reported Michigan's vote. "The chairman of the delegation has asked me to announce the result as follows: For Hoover, one; Taft, two; Willkie, thirty-five."

Pandemonium broke loose in the galleries. Convention programs, souvenir fans, and hats were thrown into the air. "We Want Willkie! We Want Willkie!" the spectators roared, realizing for the first time that their long shot was about to win. Senator McNary released his delegates, and Oregon, too, went for Willkie. There were boos when Pennsylvania passed. Willkie's vote stood at 499, two short of the magic number, when, near the end of the roll call, former Senator David Reed grabbed the microphone and announced, "Pennsylvania casts 72 votes for Wendell Willkie."

The miracle had happened. "I am thoroughly convinced that the nomination of Willkie was managed by the Holy Ghost in person," H. L. Mencken wrote New York *Daily News* reporter Doris Fleeson a few days later. "At the moment the sixth ballot was being counted I saw an angel in the gallery. It wore a Palm Beach suit and was smoking a five-cent cigar, but nevertheless it was palpably an angel."[28]

Willkie's eyes misted as he heard the news, and his voice cracked. "I'm very, very appreciative, very humble," he said, "and very proud." Within a few minutes, he had taken congratulatory phone calls from his fallen rivals–Dewey, Taft, and Hoover. Then Willkie shook hands with his friends and the press entourage before taking the elevator to the Benjamin Franklin's crowded lobby. More than three thousand people cheered as he waved and, with the assistance of a police escort, found his way to a limousine.

He looked weary when he returned to his pine-paneled suite on the twelfth floor of the Warwick. The wife of the hotel manager poured him a scotch and soda. "You need a drink, you look pretty haggard to me, Mr. Willkie," she said. Willkie sipped the drink and celebrated with his wife and several friends. The Republican presidential nominee celebrated until 4:40 A.M. when Mrs. George Lamaze, whose apartment they were occupying, suggested that his guests let him get some sleep.

Less than thirty minutes after Willkie went to bed, he was awakened by a telephone call from Ralph Cake, Oregon's GOP national committeeman, who asked to see him. Although groggy, Willkie invited Cake up for a brief visit. Wearing a blue silk bathrobe, Willkie answered the door when the Oregonian arrived. "I wouldn't blame you if you kicked me out," said Cake. "I came here to talk about Senator McNary."

Willkie assumed that Cake was there to talk about the vice-presidency. The prospect of a Willkie-McNary ticket had already been suggested by publishers Helen Reid, Gardner Cowles, and Roy Howard. They noted that the Far West had been Willkie's weakest region at the convention and McNary, Oregon's four-term senator, was its most popular political figure. Willkie told Cake that he had already made a commitment to Connecticut's Governor Baldwin, but his advisers thought that such a ticket would lack the required geographical balance. As for the selection process, Willkie told Cake that his advisers would be coming to his Warwick suite at 10 A.M. to discuss several possibilities and make their recommendation. "I suggest you shower, shave, and come over," said Willkie. "If they are willing to select Senator McNary, I'll take him."[29]

From the wee hours of Friday morning, Senator McNary had been receiving telephone calls from Oregon politicians urging him to give consideration to the second spot. "I have been awake most of the night answering telephone calls from Philadelphia and stating over and over that I did not want to be nominated for Vice President," he wrote in a letter to his sister. "I have given it out to the news boys to be published in the press and I hope that settles it."[30]

But when Willkie's group convened to discuss the vice-presidency, they did not accept the Senate Minority Leader's rejection as final. For more than two hours, Davenport, Halleck, Simpson, Stassen, the Cowles brothers, John S. Knight, Luce, Roy Howard, Helen Reid, Martin, Pryor, and Cake rated the strengths and weaknesses of prospective running mates. Taft and Dewey were immediately eliminated because of their repeated disavowals of candidacy. According to Cake, the finalists soon became McNary, Vandenberg, and Governors Bricker and Carr.

House Minority Leader Joseph Martin, McNary's junior partner in the Republican congressional leadership, made a strong pitch for the Oregon senator. "McNary would balance the ticket," he told Willkie. "You are known as a utilities man. McNary has sided with the public power boys. You're supposed to represent big business interests. McNary was the sponsor of the McNary-Haugen farm bill. You aren't supposed to know much about the legislative process. McNary is a master of it. I think you'd make a perfect team."[31] For many of the same reasons, John D. M. Hamilton advised Willkie to go with McNary, stressing that he would enhance GOP chances in the farm belt and Far West.

Willkie summoned Governor Baldwin to his private suite and ruefully explained that "the oldsters" among his advisers felt that it was important for him to balance the ticket with a running mate from the Far West. Baldwin took the news gracefully and released Willkie from his commitment.

With the group approaching a consensus, Willkie suggested that Martin telephone McNary and offer him the nomination. The Oregon senator's acceptance was still highly questionable. McNary had made some bitter attacks on Willkie during the convention and had been less than overwhelmed by his nomination. He believed that his influence as Senate Republican Leader was much greater than it would ever be in an office which he characterized as "a damn totem pole." Shortly before Martin placed the call, McNary had discussed the vice-presidency with Ebert Burlew, FDR's Assistant Secretary of the Interior. "That is one thing they cannot hand me," said McNary. "Philadelphia was such a mess. The man who was nominated for president was not supposed to be nominated."[32]

"Hell, no, I wouldn't run with Willkie," McNary growled when Martin extended the invitation. Ralph Cake then took the telephone and made the argument that his acceptance would be a singular honor for Oregon, which had not had a place on a national ticket since before the Civil War. After a long pause, McNary suddenly seemed less adamant about saying no. Martin followed up with an appeal to the senator's sense of party loyalty. "You have got to consider the Republican party," said Martin. "You are in a position to do the party a great service. Your presence on the ticket would give it great strength. We'd have a better chance to win."

McNary, listening to his political associates, reluctantly accepted. "I was innocent of the job until yesterday morning; then, pressure was turned on, and I finally yielded because of the implorations of the Oregon delegation who loyally supported me and who wanted the old state recognized," he confided in a letter to his wife. He later told a crush of reporters that he did not want the vice-presidency. "I recognize, though, that there are some things you have to do for the sake of party," said the Oregon senator. "If the demand is in the nature of a draft, I will be a good soldier and do my part." A few hours later, on learning that McNary was Willkie's choice, the convention unanimously drafted the Oregon senator.

The Willkie-McNary ticket was the dominant topic of discussion at FDR's cabinet meeting on the final day of the Philadelphia convention. "It was the general opinion that the Republicans had nominated their strongest possible ticket," Interior Secretary Harold Ickes wrote in his diary. "The President spoke particularly of McNary. He said that McNary had deserved the nomination and he was glad that it had gone to him, adding that he had always liked McNary, which is the fact." Democratic National Chairman James A. Farley told Roosevelt that Willkie was a formidable candidate and McNary added to his strength.[33] Supreme Court Justice William O. Douglas advised FDR that Willkie would be a tough campaigner. And Ickes, the old curmudgeon, told the President that he, FDR, was the only Democrat who could defeat Willkie. "Nothing so extraordinary has ever happened in American politics," Ickes commented.

Despite their promises to campaign for Willkie, the fallen Republican contenders found it difficult to contain their bitterness. In an off-the-record meeting with New York reporters, Dewey alleged that Wall Street financial interests had been responsible for Willkie's triumph. Senator Robert A. Taft said that Dewey himself was to blame for not getting out of the race one ballot earlier. Taft also felt that Joseph Pew had let him down. And he complained privately about the newspaper and magazine coverage given Willkie. Herbert Hoover speculated that the defective microphone had stalled his own drive and blamed Sam Pryor for manipulating Willkie's nomination. "The stalemate did not appear," wrote Senator McNary, "as the outfield with plenty of financing back of him ran away with the ball [*sic*]." Senator Vandenberg, the most graceful loser, wrote in his diary: "The Willkie blitzkrieg hit me just as it hit everybody else."[34]

Willkie's nomination sent ripples overseas. Lord Lothian advised London that Willkie's nomination assured them of having a friend in the White House no matter which party won the November election. The Republican's views on the European war, Lothian reported, were virtually the same as President Roosevelt's. In a private conversation, Willkie told the British Ambassador that he favored doing "everything possible" to help Great Britain because of its importance to U.S. security. The Yorkshire *Post* called Willkie's victory "one of those minor miracles of which the Allied cause stands in need." A high-ranking British official added, "The nomination of a candidate so friendly to the cause of democracy as Mr. Willkie has shown himself to be must, frankly, be a source of great pleasure to this beleaguered island."

In Nazi Germany, Willkie's victory was perceived as a major blow. "From the standpoint of foreign policy, Willkie's nomination is unfortunate for us. He is not an isolationist," Thomsen wrote the German Foreign Office, "and his attitude in the past permits no doubt that he belongs to those Republicans who see America's best defense in supporting England by all means 'short of war.'" Thomsen noted, "Neither his membership in the American Legion nor his pure German descent have so far had any influence in diverting him from his pro-Allied stand."[35]

The European war had, more than anything, set Willkie apart from his Republican rivals. Years later, Gardner Cowles said, "It wasn't the packing of galleries or the flood of telegrams that nominated Willkie. Adolf Hitler nominated Willkie. With the fall of France and the Low Countries, American public opinion shifted overnight—and that was responsible for Willkie's nomination."[36] On the same theme, Henry Luce wrote, "Except for one thing, Dewey would probably have been nominated—or perhaps Taft. That one thing was Adolf Hitler. [The convention gathered at] one of the most stupefying moments in the history of Western Civilization. . . . In this situation the delegates and guests in Philadelphia, and all the letter-sending station-wagoners, came to feel, as if by a sort of prairie fire osmosis, that the man to nominate was Willkie. Why? Essentially because Willkie looked like the biggest and strongest man around."[37]

A survey of delegates from five states taken by *Editorial Research Reports* indicated, though, that Willkie himself had a great deal to do with his convention triumph. According to this poll, 50 per cent of the delegates had been influenced by meetings with Willkie, 30 per cent by the deluge of telegrams, and 20 per cent by talks with other delegates. While none of those sampled would acknowledge that the galleries had been a factor in their switch to Willkie, the shouting and cheering had certainly added to the outsider's momentum.[38]

On Friday afternoon, Willkie shattered another political tradition and went to Convention Hall. It was the first time that a Republican presidential nominee had gone before the delegates who had chosen him. This was the kind of dramatic gesture that Willkie loved to make. When it was announced that Willkie was on his way, the delegates and guests stood on the floor and on seats and benches for more than ten minutes in hushed anticipation. As Wendell L. Willkie made his entrance, a deafening roar went up. "It was a Niagara, a frightening torrent that poured down from the balconies and up from the delegation's floor," wrote one observer. Enjoying his moment, Willkie grinned and waved both arms at the crowd. Thousands of balloons and a shower of confetti dropped from the steel rafters and the band struck up his campaign song, "Heigh-ho, Heigh-ho, It's Back to Work We Go," from the recent Walt Disney motion picture, *Snow White and the Seven Dwarfs*.

Willkie brushed some confetti out of his hair and looked across the great indoor stadium with wonderment. In a voice husky with emotion, he declared, "I stand before you without a single pledge, promise, or understanding of any kind except for the advancement of your cause and the preservation of American democracy. It is a moving and appealing and almost overwhelming thing to be the nominee of a great free convention of this kind. I doubt if any man who has not experienced it could imagine and understand the full import of the emotion it brings to one when such obligations come to him."

Addressing the faithful of his adopted party as "you Republicans," Willkie pledged to conduct an "aggressive, fighting campaign." He touched on the European war. "Democracy and our way of life is facing the most crucial test it has ever faced in all its long history; and we here are not Republicans, alone, but Americans, to dedicate ourselves to the democratic way of life in the United States because here stands the last firm, untouched foothold of freedom in all the world."

As Willkie finished speaking, the organist played "God Bless America," and many in the audience began singing Irving Berlin's patriotic ballad. Wendell L. Willkie then returned to the front of the podium and shouted, "And now, I'm going to sleep for a week."

CHAPTER ELEVEN

LIMELIGHT

Following the "Miracle at Philadelphia," Wendell L. Willkie was America's candidate, the bold amateur who had defeated the political bosses on their home court. On his return to New York, he went to the movies at Radio City Music Hall and the crowd of six thousand stood and cheered. A few days later, attending the Broadway comedy *Life with Father,* he stopped the show. "There is no doubt," Alf M. Landon wrote, "that you have caught the imagination of the American people."

In the White House, Franklin Delano Roosevelt privately commented that Willkie's nomination had been "a Godsend to the country" because it removed the war issue from the campaign. Robert E. Sherwood, FDR's aide, later wrote, "It guaranteed to the rest of the world–and particularly to the warring nations–a continuity of American foreign policy regardless of the outcome of the election." At the same time, FDR acknowledged that Willkie was his most formidable opponent in thirty years of politics. "He's grass-roots stuff," the President told Walter Winchell. "The people like him very much. His sincerity comes through with terrific impact. The people believe every word he says. We are going to have a heck of a fight on our hands with him."

One of Willkie's first visitors in New York was Turner Catledge, to whom he confided that he expected to have trouble with Old Guard Republicans. With a giggle, Willkie joshed that the first thing he had to do after the convention was switch his registration from Democrat to Republican.[1]

Willkie had a great deal to learn about running a national campaign. Despite the fact that John D. M. Hamilton had played a key behind-the-scenes role in his nomination, Willkie decided to oust him as Republican National Chairman. In the spring, Hamilton aided Willkie's cause by designating Stassen as the keynote speaker and putting Pryor in charge of credentials. He also encouraged Halleck to give Willkie's nominating speech and had considered stepping down as chairman to second the nomination. At a breakfast meeting, Willkie put his arm around Hamilton's shoulder and said that he wanted him to continue as chairman. The other leading contenders gave Hamilton the same assurances. Most political observers rated him as the GOP's most effective chairman since Mark Hanna. Following the debacle of 1936, Hamilton paid off the party's debt and began rebuilding. After going to England and studying their durable political parties, Hamilton established the first permanent Republican National Headquarters. In recognition of the importance of local organizations, he personally visited more than three thousand county chairmen. To many of them, Hamilton was the embodiment of the Republican party. Halleck and Pryor implored Willkie to retain Hamilton.

During the convention, Halleck was troubled by reports that Willkie was set to dump the chairman. Confronted by the Indiana congressman, Willkie reiterated his support of Hamilton: "He'll be chairman, don't you worry." Yet the speculation intensified. Approaching Willkie a second time, Halleck found that the reports were true. "Goddamn it, Charlie, don't bother me with that anymore," said Willkie. "I've got to finesse it. That's all there is to it."

On the night of his nomination, Willkie received advice to get rid of Hamilton from *Herald Tribune* publishers Ogden and Helen Reid, who thought the chairman was too isolationist and conservative in his views. What made him unacceptable, they argued, was Hamilton's strident message reading Stimson and Knox out of the party. For the same reason, William Allen White urged Hamilton's ouster. Willkie's amateurs, Davenport and Root, thought it symbolically important for him to select a fresh face, a new personality.

Meeting with party leaders in his Pine Street office, Willkie disclosed his plan to name a new chairman. Halleck, who had been regarded as a likely choice, said, "I'll tell you one thing, it ain't going to be me."

"Why in the hell not?" asked Willkie. "Who are you loyal to?"

"I'm loyal to you–and John Hamilton, too," replied Halleck. "And before we're through, you're going to find out."[2]

One option that he was considering was eliminating the chairmanship and placing control of the Republican party in a committee of five. Willkie proposed Charles Evans Hughes, Jr., a New York lawyer and son of the Chief Justice, as the "moderator." The other members he had settled on were Davenport as his personal representative and Hamilton as liaison with political organizations. Outlining the plan to Raymond Moley, Willkie talked with enthusiasm about how such a change would symbolize the new direction of the GOP. Moley said bluntly that Willkie's scheme would never work and pleaded that he seek the advice of Will Hays, former Republican National Chairman and movie censorship czar.

"There are a million little people running the Republican party," Hays told Willkie. "Upon them depends your success. They work on the doubtful, keep the party fires going, get out the vote. They must, when they look up through the ranges of party machinery, see way up at the top a chairman they can understand. One who speaks their language, knows their needs–one who will not forget them."[3]

Although Willkie had been reluctant to seek the advice of the conservative Hays, the former chairman convinced him to drop the committee plan and keep the traditional party apparatus. That still left the problem of the chairmanship. With Halleck out of the running, Willkie quickly narrowed the field to House Minority Leader Martin and Minnesota Governor Harold E. Stassen. He settled on the Massachusetts congressman, but Martin politely turned him down. Willkie had anticipated a negative response and turned on the pressure. Landon, Mrs. Reid, and Colonel Robert McCormick telephoned Martin and urged him to reconsider. Then Willkie himself applied the treatment. His acceptance, Willkie argued, would forge a stronger link between the presidential and congressional wings of the party and unify all factions going into the general election. Years later, Martin recalled, "I have never known a man so hard to say no to."[4]

When Martin took the chairmanship, Willkie said, "I feel like a member of the Northwest Mounted Police. I got my man."

To ease the blow to Hamilton, Willkie gave him a four-year appointment as executive director of the Republican National Committee at the same $25,000 annual salary he had been receiving as chairman. Hamilton was also put in charge of the Willkie campaign in the West and Midwest with headquarters in Chicago's La Salle Street financial district. Hamilton was not happy about the arrangement, but he took the job at the urging of Republican allies. "Willkie carved the heart out of John Hamilton," said Joseph Pew, the chairman's longtime confidant.

As a consolation prize, Governor Stassen became chairman of the campaign advisory committee. Russell Davenport, Willkie's personal representative, was the committee's dominant influence. Sam Pryor was given responsibility for the eastern campaign. And Oren Root continued as national chairman of the Willkie Club movement.

For many of the same reasons he had removed Hamilton from the chairmanship, Willkie was set to fire Pittsburgh steel mogul Ernest T. Weir as Republican finance chairman. "Some leading Republicans advised Willkie that he was an inappropriate symbol for the party and should be replaced," recalled Martin. "When he came to me about it, however, I persuaded him to abandon any idea of dismissing Weir. It struck me as an unnecessarily harsh thing to do. It would have caused all sorts of dissension."[5]

On July 8, Willkie announced his resignation as president of Commonwealth and Southern. That morning his son, Philip, had dropped by the office and suggested that Willkie reconsider his decision. "You see, Dad, you may not win," he explained. "You are giving up a good job, a sure thing. If you lose the campaign, perhaps you couldn't find another position of $75,000 a year." Willkie assured him that he would have numerous options if he lost the election and that whatever happened the family would be financially secure.

Later that morning, he conferred with Thomas E. Dewey. Although Willkie frequently interrupted their discussion to take phone calls, Dewey managed to make his points about the general election campaign. The district attorney pledged to campaign anywhere his efforts might be considered useful. In addition, he offered the assistance of his most talented aides–pollster Gerard Lambert, Press Secretary Lamoyne Jones, and economic adviser Elliott Bell, which Willkie promptly accepted. Willkie cut him short, however, when Dewey started telling him how and where he should campaign. "Tom," snapped Willkie, "since when did the party make you the nominee?"[6]

In the afternoon, Willkie took a plane to Washington for his first meeting with Senator McNary. When the Oregon Republican came to his suite at the Willard Hotel, Willkie was taking a bath. Without embarrassment, Willkie invited McNary into the tiled bathroom. McNary later commented that his running mate had "a very human side to him that was charming."

By all accounts, Willkie and McNary hit it off, a remarkable feat considering the Oregon Republican's comments in Philadelphia. The Senate Minority Leader made it clear to Willkie that his role in the campaign would be a subordinate one. The presidential nominee said that he was eager to have McNary make some appearances in the corn belt. *Life* reported that small-town movie audiences watched FDR and Willkie without emotion but broke into applause when the newsreels showed McNary. McNary said that he would do whatever was asked of him and agreed he would be most effective before farm and rural gatherings. The Oregon senator advised Willkie to cut down on the one-liners, because many voters did not like their politicians to be comedians. "Don't forget, young fellow," said the old incorruptible, "in politics you'll never get in trouble by not saying too much."

Following their conference, Willkie and McNary spent several hours with Republican congressmen and other officials. That night, Martin and Halleck hosted a unity dinner for the GOP ticket, and among the guests were Taft and Vandenberg. "I was pictured until I was almost paralyzed," McNary wrote his wife. "A banquet followed with some more pictures and when I got to bed I was quite unnerved." The vice-presidential nominee added, "I like Mr. Willkie very much. He is open and forthright and able. There are some traits he has that I would modify."[7]

On July 9, Wendell and Billie left the nation's capital by United Airlines charter for a five-week vacation in Colorado Springs. The Willkies stayed at the luxurious Broadmoor Hotel, a sprawling concoction of Mediterranean architecture whose pale pink buildings with red tiled roofs were set on the rim of a large artificial lake. The Italian Renaissance resort fit snugly into the rugged Pike's Peak landscape. Willkie went for hikes in the mountains, swam in the hotel's Olympic-size pool, and stretched out on the well-manicured lawns and terraces. For vacation reading, he had brought along a biography of literary critic Margaret Fuller recommended by Irita Van Doren;

The Dissenting Opinions of Mr. Justice Holmes; and *The Heart Is a Lonely Hunter,* a new novel by Carson McCullers.

When the Willkies arrived at the Broadmoor, they were accompanied by only one male secretary. San Francisco *Chronicle* editor Paul C. Smith, summoned by the presidential nominee to Colorado Springs, said later, "It was obvious that he had not the faintest realization of the impact it would have upon his private life, which from that time on was nonexistent." Smith recalled, "I found the secretary sitting in a small bedroom, staring as if hypnotized at a high mound of mailbags, while Edith and Wendell Willkie were running madly from room to room of their three-room suite in a slapstick effort to answer three telephones that had been ringing constantly and simultaneously ever since they had arrived. Both were near collapse from their naive effort to get away from it all." Smith promptly hired three stenographers and organized a makeshift Willkie staff. A special switchboard with sixty lines and around-the-clock operators was installed to handle the GOP candidate's phone calls.

"He had learned suddenly," said Smith, who would later join the Willkie campaign, "that there was no escape and that no waking moment would be free of the burdens now heaped upon him, until election night. Curiously, the dimensions involved were totally new to him, even though he had long been in so-called big business."[8]

With an entourage of a dozen reporters, Willkie spent his second week at the Broadmoor in a lounge chair listening to the Democratic National Convention on a portable radio. Although the outcome was never in much doubt, FDR was being challenged on the third-term issue by a pair of ranking members of his administration, Vice-President John Nance Garner and Postmaster General James A. Farley. Skillfully dodging all questions about his availability, the President chose Chicago as the setting for the 1940 convention with confidence that Mayor Edward J. Kelly would deliver. When Farley was nominated by Senator Carter Glass, Kelly's ward heelers drowned him out with jeering and booing. Visibly tense and chain-smoking cigarettes, Willkie told his companions that he was "afraid" FDR might withdraw, which would take the excitement out of the fall campaign.

Willkie's mood changed as he heard a gravelly voice shouting over the Chicago Stadium loudspeakers, "We Want Roosevelt! We Want Roosevelt!" The voice, it turned out, was Chicago's superintendent of sewers, Tom Garry, who was yelling into the public-address system from a tiny basement room. As the delegates and galleries picked up the chant, Kelly's men led a demonstration on the floor. "Boys," said Willkie, "I think my worries are over."

Breezing to a third presidential nomination, Roosevelt jolted party regulars by choosing Agriculture Secretary Henry A. Wallace as his running mate. The bosses resented Wallace as a former Republican and a political mystic. Facing open rebellion in Chicago Stadium, FDR sent word that he was prepared to reject the nomination unless Wallace was approved. Even so, Wallace barely squeaked through. And there was such bitterness over his selection that FDR's aides persuaded Wallace not to address the convention. In a radio address from the White House, Roosevelt said that he had looked forward to retirement but could not decline "to serve my country in my personal capacity if I am called upon to do so by the people of my country."

Willkie said that he was "deeply gratified" to "meet the champ" and predicted "a great campaign." A few days later, he taunted FDR for suggesting that he sought a third term because of "noble motives." Said Willkie: "I am not going to tell you of my unselfish sacrifices in seeking to be president. I frankly sought the opportunity because I have some deep-seated convictions I want to present."

With the New Deal coalition showing signs of wear, Willkie pegged his general election strategy to splitting the Democratic vote. Encouraged by Democratic bitterness over the Wallace selection and the third-term issue, he predicted that some of the party's heavy hitters would actively support his candidacy. "I do not know of any reason why any Democrat who subscribed to and believed in the 1932 Democratic platform or believes in the historic principles of the Democratic Party or who was a Woodrow Wilson Democrat," said Willkie, "should not vote for me in preference to the President."

For the next month, he made hundreds of telephone calls to disgruntled Democrats, seeking their endorsements. From the Broadmoor, Willkie announced the formation of "Democrats for Willkie," headed by former New Dealers John W. Hanes and Lewis W. Douglas. This group, said Willkie, gave independents and traditional Democrats "a nucleus around which they can coalesce." FDR, bothered by the defection of Hanes and Douglas, said at a press conference that they had always been more interested in dollars than humanity. When former New York Governor Alfred E. Smith came out for him, Willkie shot back, "I hope that nobody suggests that the warmhearted Alfred E. Smith is one of those persons who is actuated by love of money rather than love of humanity."[9]

Some southern Democrats proposed the nomination of Willkie on a Constitutional Democratic ticket. FDR had made powerful enemies of such southern senators as Carter Glass and Harry Byrd of Virginia, Walter George of Georgia, Pat Harrison of Mississippi, and E. D. "Cotton Ed" Smith of South Carolina. While they expressed sympathy for Willkie, only Smith came through with an endorsement. As much as the southern conservatives opposed FDR, they could not ignore polls which showed him with almost 90 per cent support in the Deep South. Glass and Byrd endorsed the President.

None of this bothered Willkie. The Cowles brothers thought Willkie should concentrate on northern industrial states and the midwestern heartland. Lambert's polls indicated that it would be "a waste of time" for Willkie to make appearances in the South. Displaying his charts and data in the candidate's living room at the Broadmoor, Lambert similarly advised Willkie. "He literally yawned in my face and said he had heard that he was doing slightly better down there now," said Lambert, "and that he was going." Ruth Hanna McCormick Simms, who also came to Colorado Springs, reported to Dewey: "Mr. Willkie is fundamentally indifferent to party labels and he believes that more Democrats will ultimately support his candidacy than I think likely."[10]

Most "Democrats-for-Willkie" were political has-beens. Senator Edward R. Burke of Nebraska had just been defeated for renomination by a Roosevelt loyalist. Among the others supporting Willkie were two victims of the 1938 FDR purges, former New York Congressman John J. O'Connor and former Oregon Governor Charles H. Martin. Others included New York Judge Samuel Seabury, former Michigan Governor William Comstock, and former Oklahoma Governor William H. "Alfalfa Bill" Murray. These endorsements were of dubious value. As Philadelphia Democratic boss Peter J. Camiel later observed, "There is nothing as useless as a former mayor, a former officeholder, a former candidate. There is just nothing they can do for you."

It rankled Herbert Hoover that Willkie seemed to be paying so much attention to the Democrats and ignoring the only living former President. "There are many people among his friends who have the same feeling that Landon had in 1936," which was to shun him, Hoover wrote a friend. "Having had one experience I shall not be put to the same humiliation." Gardner Cowles, however, arranged to have Willkie invite Hoover to the Broadmoor. The former President came and agreed to make speeches in the fall campaign and encourage his supporters to unite behind Willkie.

During Hoover's visit, Willkie learned that Elliott Roosevelt, FDR's son, was also staying at the hotel. Impulsively and much to Hoover's discomfort, Willkie invited young Roosevelt to join them in his sixth-floor suite for cocktails. "Wouldn't you like to stay for a bite?" asked Willkie as the President's son settled in a chair. "We had a delightful time," Roosevelt recalled in a 1982 interview. "Among other things, we discussed the ardors of campaigning. Willkie was already worried about his voice. I told him that I commiserated. Willkie said that while he had a great deal of respect for Father, it was time for the country to take a new direction. With the threat of another world war, Willkie argued that he could do a better job in preparing the country."

"More power to you," replied Roosevelt. "But Father feels strongly that he's the only one who can handle the crisis. In spite of the fact that you are antagonists in the campaign, I want you to know that my father has much respect for you."[11]

Hoover, still embittered over his 1932 loss of the presidency to FDR, had been offended by Willkie's friendly gesture to his son. "He was obviously quite upset," recalled Roosevelt. "Even though he was polite and cordial, it was clear that my presence in the room inhibited him. He was there to give advice and felt that I was intruding on his time." The former President later told Cowles that he should have stayed home. "My original hunch that I should not class myself with the politicians, publicity hunters and the smear guard of the press who were flocking to Colorado Springs proved itself correct," wrote Hoover.[12]

Not everyone who called on Willkie was seeking publicity. Nelson A. Rockefeller, then only thirty-two years old, flew west under the name "Mr. Franklin" for a meeting with his party's presidential nominee. Despite the fact that Rockefeller was supporting Willkie and his family had contributed a huge sum to the campaign, the handsome young millionaire had been invited to join the Roosevelt administration as coordinator for the office of Inter-American

Affairs. As Rockefeller described the dilemma of a Willkie Republican going to work for FDR, Willkie interjected, "If I were president in a time of international crisis and if I asked someone to come to Washington to help me in foreign affairs, and if that man turned me down—well, I don't need to tell you what I would think of him." Rockefeller took the job.[13]

Several days later Willkie omitted Hoover and Landon from a list, which he made public, of the political leaders whose advice he valued. Senator McNary and Chairman Martin were the only prominent Republicans mentioned. In an off-the-record conversation with reporters, Willkie showed contempt for the former President, dismissing his importance with a circular wave of his right hand.[14]

On Willkie's invitation, Martin came to Colorado Springs. The Massachusetts congressman told him he was talking too much. "These legislative issues are Roosevelt's responsibility, not yours," said Martin. "You're still on the outside. You don't have to comment on every bill. Don't voluntarily assume positions unless you have to. Wait and see how the questions come up in the campaign. There will then be some issues on which you will want to comment, but let's avoid these unnecessary conflicts as much as possible." No sooner had Martin left than Willkie resumed his policy of answering every Democratic criticism, each question from the press.

Appalled by the chaos at the Broadmoor, Oregon Republican leader and editor E. Palmer Hoyt implored Willkie to bring more professionals into the campaign. "The amateurs won the nomination," said Willkie, "and they can win the election." On a one-day side trip into Iowa, he addressed Willkie Club members as "fellow amateurs."[15]

It was supposed to be a restful vacation, but Willkie could not restrain himself from making campaign appearances. When it was announced that he would attend a fish fry on the western slope of the Rockies, nearly ten thousand people showed up. More than 100,000 cheered him in Salt Lake City's Covered Wagon Days parade. Attending the opera in an old gold mining town, he waved his arms and smiled when the audience chanted "We Want Willkie."

At the Broadmoor, he found it difficult to get any privacy, and the strain had begun to show. One night more than three hundred persons started shouting "We Want Willkie" in the dining room, and it took a personal appearance by the visibly tired candidate to restore order. "All the screwballs in the United States visited him while he was out there," Sam Pryor told Herbert Parmet. "He was mentally fagged out before the campaign started and didn't recover from it until the day he died."

Willkie's advisers felt that his retreat in the mountains had stalled his candidacy. Gardner Cowles told him that he had wasted five weeks. Walter Lippmann wrote Willkie: "The momentum behind you has slowed down since you were nominated because you have not shown the road you intend to take, and your well-wishers have been moving in several directions at once." Years later, Lem Jones acknowledged, "We spent too much time in Colorado. We let what was the hottest thing in the world get cold."[16]

Ending his thirty-seven-day Colorado vacation on August 16, Willkie flew to Indiana aboard the United Airlines "Willkie Special." As he stepped from the silver aircraft, Willkie doffed his straw boater and raised his arms in a gesture of victory. A band struck up "Back Home in Indiana" and several thousand Hoosiers crashed through police barriers. With the gusto of a seasoned campaigner, he worked his way through the crowd to his black convertible. In a scene that would soon become a ritual, Willkie stood in the back seat, arms outstretched, and was splashed with confetti and ticker tape as the motorcade moved through the streets of downtown Indianapolis.

Leaving town, Willkie's motorcade tore recklessly over fifty-five miles of narrow, winding road. What had begun as a small caravan of 24 automobiles soon grew to 150. Red flares had been placed along some of the highway and the motorcade raced through small towns with horns blaring. "It was the wildest ride I have ever experienced," Richard L. Strout wrote his bureau chief. "The only police escort was right at the front and the whole outward traffic movement from Indianapolis joined our procession, three abreast, dashing forward in irregular line at 50 and 60 miles an hour. Our driver was pretty poor, and always slammed on the brakes at the last moment."[17]

At each intersection, crowds had gathered in the hope of catching a glimpse of Willkie. In Greenfield a huge "We Want Willkie" banner was stretched across the road in front of Hoosier poet James Whitcomb Riley's home. By the time Willkie arrived in Rushville, it was nearly midnight, yet all six thousand inhabitants were on hand to greet him. "You can understand that being here again unlooses wells of emotions," he told them. "There comes to me here an overwhelming sense of humility when I think that I am called to a position of leadership in one of the most critical moments in the world's history to preserve the kind of life you people live here."

His mother-in-law, Cora Wilk, wore an American-flag Willkie badge and, in her window, had placed a poster of her son-in-law captioned "The Pride of Rushville." That night she prepared Willkie's favorite meal, fried chicken and hot cherry pie. After dinner, Wendell and Billie spent the night at the home of their longtime friend Mary Sleeth.

In the morning, the Willkies took a special train to Elwood for the Republican National Committee's notification ceremony. For nearly two months, Willkie's hometown had anxiously awaited this political folk festival. Homer E. Capehart of Indianapolis, a wealthy phonograph manufacturer who would later become a U.S. senator, took charge of the arrangements. With preliminary estimates indicating that 250,000 people might attend, Capehart rejected Willkie's old high school as the site for the ceremonies and chose Callaway Park on the outskirts of town.

To handle the traffic flow, Capehart persuaded Elwood's city council to pass special regulations converting the town's four roads into one-way streets. And, for parking forty thousand automobiles, he rented 240 acres of farmland on which fences were removed and wheat and corn were cleared. Thirty-five thousand seats were unfolded and set up at the park and a huge wooden platform was constructed for the main event. Capehart was especially proud of the latrines. "Each one is a 32-holer!" he told H. L. Mencken. Elwood's twelve-man police force was expanded to more than eight hundred with assistance from law enforcement agencies as far away as St. Louis and Chicago.

In this carnival atmosphere, Elwood merchants anticipated their biggest boom in a half century. The town fathers lifted curfew restrictions. Slot machines in the local Elks Club never cooled down. Restaurants and coffee shops jacked up prices 20 per cent. Every shop in town was selling Willkie mementos. "Do Your Part," said one sign, "Buy Willkie Stamps." There were Willkie hats, neckties, playing cards, license plates, tie clips, pillow cases, and glass tumblers with a fuzzy image of Willkie frosted on the outside. Frank McCarthy, a tomato canner, charged a 20-cent admission to the two-story frame house at 1900 South A Street where the presidential candidate was born. A few blocks away an Anderson Street doctor put up the notice, "This isn't the Willkie home, but you are welcome anyway." At Callaway Park, Shipwreck Kelly stood on a flagpole to advertise Kroger's coffee, and a pitchman offered live foxes "on the hoof" for fur neck pieces.

It was unbearably hot. For much of the summer, central Indiana had been stricken by drought. And on Willkie's day, it was 103 degrees in the shade. The crowd began gathering at Callaway Park shortly before dawn. By 10 A.M., seven hours before Willkie was scheduled to speak, the throng had grown to 60,000. Despite the heat, Willkie managed to draw about 150,000 people to this quiet Indiana town of 10,000 for what would become the largest political rally in American history. They came in 60,000 automobiles, 63 special trains, 300 Pullmans, and 1,200 buses. Richard L. Strout wrote in the *Christian Science Monitor* that Elwood had assumed an "unreal" atmosphere "that was a blend of World's Fair, Army encampment and old-fashioned revival meeting."

Early in the afternoon, Willkie arrived from Rushville. The Indiana University band led the parade down Anderson Street, Elwood's Main Street and 249 other bands marched in the procession. Willkie stood informally in an open car and was swarmed by thousands of shirt-sleeved well wishers. The surging crowd stopped Willkie's car several times and he shook every hand he could reach. *Life* magazine later described the John D. Collins photograph of Willkie riding through Elwood, flags waving, people cheering, as the greatest campaign picture ever made. Willkie insisted on making a brief stop at his old school, but his driver forgot Capehart's instructions to pull away from the police escort and turn into the school grounds. Instead, he came to an abrupt stop in front of the school steps, and Willkie was mobbed.

Once inside the building, Willkie nearly passed out. He was exhausted, hot, and more than a bit tense. Within a few minutes, he recovered and joked with the crowd from an upstairs window. Lighting a cigarette, he shouted, "They didn't use to let me do this in this building."

Always disorganized, Willkie forgot to bring the text of his acceptance speech. Just before getting on the train in Rushville, Willkie borrowed a friend's car, threw in his luggage, and took Joe Martin on a quick tour of the town. When they returned to the train, Willkie left behind the suitcase that contained his marked-up copy of the speech. Before reaching Elwood, he realized his mistake, and staffers arranged to have the speech brought to him by special police motorcade.

At Callaway Park, the Indiana University band struck up "Back Home in Indiana" as Willkie stepped out on the great wooden platform and the crowd's roar shook the trees. For ten minutes, the crowd cheered Willkie before he could begin his speech. Just before he started, Willkie threw away a wad of chewing gum, and people sitting in the front rows laughed and cheered. Chairman Martin officially notified Willkie that he had been nominated and said, "I hope it will not come as too much of a surprise."

In urgent tones, Willkie asserted that his campaign was nothing less than a crusade to preserve American democracy. "Party lines are down," he said in a thick Hoosier twang. "Nothing could make that clearer than the nomination by the Republicans of a liberal Democrat who changed his party affiliation because he found democracy in the Republican Party."

With the sun beating down on his face and sweat misting his glasses, Willkie appeared to be wilting in the heat. On this afternoon, he was one of the few people at Callaway Park wearing a coat and tie, and he looked uncomfortable. While the speech was well crafted, his delivery was awkward and ineffective. "He's dying on his feet," Lyle Wilson of United Press commented in the press area. "Willkie's poor delivery was a surprise to everyone," Strout wrote his bureau chief. "I had underscored lines and said to myself, 'Here's where he'll bring the crowd up cheering!' But he read over such passages without even a change of emphasis in many cases." Strout attributed Willkie's lackluster performance partly to the heat and the possibility that "he had exerted himself too strenuously in the preliminary sessions with the crowd."[18]

Referring to his Indiana boyhood, Willkie spoke of himself in the third person. "As I look back upon him," he said, "I realize that he had plenty of faults. But he also had three steadfast convictions. He was devoted to the ideal of individual liberty. He hated all special privileges and forms of oppression. And he knew without any doubt that the greatest country on earth was the United States of America."

In the last part of his speech, he sipped Coca-Cola from a paper cup and his tempo picked up notably. Before an audience that was overwhelmingly isolationist, he pledged "to outdistance Hitler in any contest he chooses." Vowing to revitalize America's industrial might, he said, "Only the strong can be free. And only the productive can be strong." In closing, Willkie challenged FDR to a series of debates on public platforms across the country. The President later replied he was too busy.

Willkie's performance had been flat and he knew it. Indeed, he told Martin that it would be the last time he attempted to compete with Roosevelt on radio. "The whole thing was hell," Marcia Davenport recalled. In Halleck's judgment, "The speech didn't go worth a damn." Such Willkie insiders as Martin, Hanes, Root, and Pryor were disappointed. Norman Thomas called it "a synthesis of Guffey's First Readers, the Genealogy of Indiana, the collected speeches of Tom Girdler, and the *New Republic*. He agreed with Mr. Roosevelt's entire program of social reform and said it was leading to disaster." Democratic National Chairman Edward J. Flynn felt that the speech exposed Willkie's vulnerability. "When Willkie made his long acceptance speech," he said later, "we knew we could beat him."[19]

Partly because of the heat, Elwood's merchants had not fared much better than Willkie. Restaurants and stores that stockpiled food were left with an unwanted surplus. In the white dusty heat, beer and soda pop were selling at scalper's prices, but few people had appetites for anything heavier. A vendor who had bought 24,000 boxes of candied popcorn was left with 23,980. Another sold just 1,200 of 20,000 Eskimo Pies. The next day tradesmen cut their losses, offering 120 hot dog rolls for a quarter, three watermelons for a penny, and Willkie souvenir bats for a dime.

After his speech, Willkie took the train back to Rushville. For the next month, Wendell and Billie stayed in a three-story brick house on North Harrison Street loaned to them by a longtime friend, Mrs. Charles Mauzy. The central Indiana farm town demonstrated an almost naive enthusiasm for Willkie. Along Main Street, each store window displayed his photograph above the caption "Rushville's Renowned Son-in-Law." Another placard boasted, "The only real estate he owns in the world is located here."

He owned five farms which formed a semicircle around the town and enjoyed giving visitors a running commentary on his Hereford cattle and assorted varieties of hogs. Once he pointed to a large hog and told a guest that its name was Waterman. Asked whether it was really the hog's name, Willkie quipped, "No, just his pen name." Mary Sleeth, who managed the farms, observed wryly, "It's getting so every time a cameraman shows up, the hogs run right over and strike a pose."

On his farms, Willkie refused to pose in overalls and wore a dark business suit. When Republican publicists depicted him as a dirt farmer, he was genuinely embarrassed. "There is one error I want to correct at once," he said, "this talk of being a Rush County farmer. I am purely a conversational farmer. I have never done a stroke of work on a Rush County farm in my life, and I hope I never have to."

Disdainful of sham, he scoffed when the same image makers portrayed him as a devout churchgoer. "I usually sleep on Sundays," he noted.

His main reason in staying in Rushville was an effort to become more identified with his native Indiana and less with Wall Street. While it struck some of his critics as synthetic and unconvincing, he felt very much at home in the sleepy little farm town. Willkie confided to reporters that he hoped someday to retire in Rushville and write books. One morning he showed newsmen a forty-acre forest tract and told them he wanted to acquire it. "I'd give anything to have this," he said. "It's the finest hardwood. Isn't this great? This is the way this country was when the Indians had it, and it had to be cleared."

During his month in Rushville, Willkie held daily press conferences on his borrowed front lawn. He often dropped in on reporters who were staying at the Lollis Hotel. With disarming candor, he told them that he planned to buy a country newspaper for his son Philip. Once, when his house was crowded with political guests, he stepped aside to play historical trivia games with a reporter. In ten minutes, he jotted down the names of British Prime Ministers and their terms in office since the reign of George I.

One newspaperman characterized Willkie as "a master of timing releases, issuing denials before edition time, adding punch to a prepared speech, or making one on the spur of the moment letter-perfect enough to have been memorized, treating editors, publishers, and reporters with the skill needed to suggest that they were the sole beneficiaries of his gratitude and confidence." Damon Runyon called him "the frankest talker in American politics."

"He is a fast thinker and makes a story in everything he says, and a picture in everything he does," Richard L. Strout wrote his bureau chief. "I needn't tell you that Willkie loves the press and seems to prefer them to politicians. He's master of any situation and can meet anyone on an equality."[20]

"Our principal problem," recalled Bill Lawrence, then a youthful United Press correspondent, "was Wendell Willkie himself. He was simply too accessible, too willing to be quoted on any subject, entirely too available for interviews, exclusive or otherwise. If one reporter saw him alone and got a good story, another reporter would go to Willkie to complain about being left out of the first interview. Willkie would appease the second reporter by giving him a better story than he had given the first one. And a third might top the first two."[21]

"Finally," said Lawrence, "in a treaty of self-preservation, most of us agreed informally to write nothing about Willkie that we did not all get at the same time."

In the midst of a world war, some Willkie backers thought his Indiana activity seemed frivolous. Henry R. Luce told Davenport he hoped Willkie dropped "this cracker-barrel dawdling" and got on with the campaign. "Running for President may be fun for Mr. Willkie," Luce said, "but it's a Goddamn serious thing for 130 million Americans and maybe for the world." Luce used his magazines to prod Willkie into political combat. "Mr. Willkie's ambition seemed to be to become a political columnist, to make the front pages daily with a new wisecrack," wrote a *Time* correspondent. "But many thought Ray Clapper and Westbrook Pegler were still doing a better job."

Although far removed from Washington, Willkie had become deeply involved in the politics of war. On the two major issues of national defense policy, he gave FDR important support. The peacetime draft was an unpopular idea, yet Willkie declared in Indiana that he would rather lose the election than make it a partisan issue.

The Selective Service bill was introduced in early August of 1940 by Senator Edward Burke, a conservative Nebraska Democrat, and Representative James Wadsworth, a moderate New York Republican. It was opposed by liberals, conservatives, isolationists, students, the Communist party, and clergymen. The Reverend Harry Emerson Fosdick called the bill immoral. Labor leader John L. Lewis said that enactment of the legislation would mean "dictatorship and fascism." Senator Burton K. Wheeler of Montana declared, "If you pass this bill, you slit the throat of the last democracy still living." The Burke-Wadsworth bill was not designed to build an overnight Army but, rather, to create a reserve of 16 million men so that the United States would be prepared for war. In September of 1939, there were only 500,000 men in the nation's armed forces, and the United States had 400 antiquated tanks with deficient firepower. After the fall of France, Americans recognized their vulnerability to the Nazi threat. According to the Gallup poll, the American public had been split fifty-fifty on the peacetime draft in June, but had shifted to 65 per cent in favor by August. Even so, Willkie's advisers urged him to hold back. "People don't want their sons in uniform," Joe Martin told Willkie. "Go slow on this thing. It is not necessary for you to take the initiative."

But Willkie thought otherwise. Largely because of his influence, Senator McNary and House Minority Leader Martin voted for the Selective Service bill, and Republican isolationist Senator Hiram Johnson wrote privately that Willkie "broke the back" of the opposition to the peacetime draft. When it passed both houses of Congress in mid-September, FDR called the nation's first peacetime draft "America's answer to Hitlerism." In October, 900,000 men were drafted. The President later acknowledged that the Selective Service Act would not have been possible without Willkie's assistance.

Willkie also gave FDR his tacit approval for the destroyers-for-bases pact with Britain. Following Dunkirk, Churchill begged Roosevelt to send fifty of America's World War I destroyers. Though anxious to help Britain turn back the Nazi threat, Roosevelt had been warned by his advisers that he could lose the election if he granted the request. So FDR actively sought Willkie's endorsement of the deal. Archibald MacLeish, Librarian of Congress and a friend of Russell Davenport, made the Administration's initial contact with Willkie. Joseph Alsop approached Davenport and strongly recommended that Willkie support transfer of the destroyers. The President's main intermediary with Willkie, though, was William Allen White, chairman of the Committee to Defend America by Aiding the Allies.[22]

The Kansas editor called on Willkie in Colorado Springs and told him of the impending deal with Britain. Willkie indicated that he favored sending the warships to Britain but was not inclined to give the President a public endorsement. "It's not as bad as it seems," White informed FDR. "I have talked with both of you on this subject during the last ten days. I know there is not two bits difference between you on the issue pending. But I can't guarantee either of you to the other, which is funny for I admire and respect you both. I realize you in your position don't want statements but congressional votes. Which by all the rules of the game you should have. But I've not quit and as I said it's not as bad as it looks."[23]

On learning of the secret negotiations, Thomas E. Dewey contacted Willkie in Colorado and offered to make a public declaration supporting the destroyer deal if it would make it easier for the presidential nominee to take such a position. Willkie abruptly informed Dewey that the situation was under control and he did not need outside help.[24]

Oddly enough, Willkie did not consult with Senator McNary about the destroyers. And in a major breakthrough, Roosevelt got McNary's tacit support. The Senate Republican leader, an isolationist, passed word to the White House that he could not vote for the deal but would not make trouble if grounds could be established for bypassing the Senate. On September 3, Roosevelt issued an executive order transferring the warships in exchange for long-term U.S. leases on military bases in the West Indies.

Once the deal was announced, Willkie came under tremendous pressure from GOP leaders to denounce it. He had ignored their advice to oppose the peacetime draft, but this time he was more receptive. Issuing a statement that supported the transfer of destroyers for naval and air bases, Willkie criticized FDR's method in executing the deal. "This trade is the most dictatorial action ever taken by any president," he asserted. "It does us no good to solve the problems of democracy if we solve them with the methods of dictators or wave aside the processes of democracy." Months later, Willkie told Ben Cohen he regretted those words more than anything else he said in the campaign.[25]

In an effort to smooth differences between the party organization and independent Willkie Clubs, he summoned eighty midwestern and eastern Republican officials to Rushville. They conferred in the Masonic Lodge over the Princess Theater. Local matrons of the Eastern Star charged 75 cents for a fried chicken lunch. Willkie said what they wanted to hear. If elected, he promised to distribute patronage through regular party channels. He made a recording of this pledge for GOP officials to play at their district headquarters. "Just as the leader expects loyalty and cooperation from every member of his party, and cannot succeed without such cooperation," said Willkie, "so is the rank and file of the party entitled to the support and loyalty of the candidate."

By the end of the meeting, Willkie had thoroughly charmed the Old Guardsmen. On the front lawn of his temporary home, he stood with a group of politicians and called out, "Is there any doubt that Willkie and McNary are going to be elected? If there was a discordant note in the conference, I did not detect it."

Privately, though, there had been complaints from party leaders that Willkie had waited too long for the campaign. His stock had dropped sharply in the polls since Philadelphia, and the momentum had clearly shifted to the President. And for the rest of the fall, he would be playing catch-up against the consummate professional.

CHAPTER TWELVE

THE CAMPAIGN OF 1940

In the fall of 1940, American movie audiences lined up to see *Gone With the Wind* and *Knute Rockne: All American.* In the latter film, a boyish Ronald Reagan gave a winning performance as Notre Dame's legendary George Gipp. Ernest Hemingway published *For Whom the Bell Tolls,* his classic novel of the Spanish Civil War. Grandma Moses won critical acclaim at her first major art exhibition. Glenn Miller's big-band sound dominated the hit parade. Bob Wills and his Texas Playboys recorded "San Antonio Rose," launching a new movement in country music. Tony Zale, boxing's "man of steel," captured the middleweight title for the first time. And Michigan halfback Tommy Harmon, setting a Big Ten scoring record, was awarded the Heisman Trophy.

With Hitler controlling Europe, there was a growing sense that the United States was approaching its most critical election since the Civil War. Since August, Nazi planes had been raining destruction on British cities. Each night, Edward R. Murrow of CBS radio brought the war into America's living rooms from London. Even popular music was influenced by the war. Among the season's biggest hits were "The Last Time I Saw Paris" and "A Nightingale Sang in Berkeley Square." A young Harvard graduate, John F. Kennedy, chose the war as the topic of his first book, *Why England Slept,* in which *Time* publisher Henry R. Luce wrote the foreword as a thinly disguised argument for Willkie's candidacy. In late September, the Gallup poll reported that a majority of Americans favored assisting England at the risk of war.

"I felt that the country was on the verge of a profound change," wrote Marquis W. Childs, who followed Willkie's campaign for the St. Louis *Post-Dispatch*. "I think the people sensed it, too, that fall. Much in America we had known was to go. A greater, stronger America might come out of the ordeal ahead of us. Or we might forfeit our birthright, the wonderful heritage of spirit, of earth, of people. But nothing would be quite the same again. The high wind of change was in the air."[1]

In mid-September, two and a half months after his nomination, the dark green, twelve-car *Willkie Special* pulled out of Rushville. "I will not talk in quibbling language," he vowed. "I will talk in simple, direct Indiana speech." Over the next seven weeks, he would wage the most aggressive and vigorous campaign since the 1896 crusade of William Jennings Bryan. Moving along rusty freight spurs that had never carried a passenger train, the 1940 GOP nominee and his entourage of thirty staffers and forty-six reporters traveled 18,789 miles through thirty-one states. Willkie spent five nights in hotel rooms and forty-two in the *Pioneer,* his mahogany-paneled private car, which had often been used by FDR.

Willkie's rear Pullman contained a posh, heavily carpeted living room; glassed-in observation lounge; private dining room and kitchen; compartments for maids, secretaries, two bodyguards; and bedrooms for the candidate, his wife Edith, and his brother Edward, the six-foot-six former Navy football star who had taken a leave from his Chicago firm to serve as confidant, companion, and one-man security force.

One result of the campaign was that Willkie was forced to make adjustments in his private life. He saw Van Doren less frequently than he would have liked. Since the Philadelphia convention, Willkie appeared at public functions with his wife at his side. Though hurt and resentful over her husband's involvement with Van Doren, Edith dutifully supported his political efforts. In *State of the Union,* the fictional motion picture treatment of Willkie's campaign, Katharine Hepburn played the estranged wife who rejoins her industrialist husband, Spencer Tracy, when he runs for President. "Campaigning in America is done with wives," Theodore H. White has written. "Wives are on public display. The code calls for their participation however unrealistic that code may be."

In Philadelphia Mrs. Willkie offered to accompany her husband on his national whistle-stop tour "if I'm not excess baggage." Assured by reporters that she would be an invaluable asset, Edith poignantly replied, "Oh, I hope people tell him that. It would be a good excuse for me to go and I love to travel." Something she did not enjoy, though, was the glare of the spotlight. When an NBC reporter plunked a microphone in front of her at Convention Hall and attempted to get an interview, she looked stricken. Frantically, she telephoned Willkie and asked whether she could get out of doing it. "Don't," her husband responded, "if you don't want to." The interview never took place.[2]

During their Colorado vacation, Mrs. Willkie resented the intrusion of photographers and reporters. Finally, she lost all patience and refused to show up at a scheduled photo session in the Broadmoor's garden. When there were some complaints, Willkie overruled his wife and told her to get ready for the photographers. She went into the bathroom, filled the sink with water, and dipped her head. Edith, her hair sopping, then opened the door, making it clear to Willkie and his press aides that there would be no pictures. Later, she explained, "I just don't like to have my picture taken."[3]

Appearing with her husband on the back platform of the *Willkie Special,* she smiled, accepted flowers from local dignitaries, and waved to the cheering throng. A band often played "Let Me Call You Sweetheart." In city motorcades, she sat at Willkie's left in the back seat of their open car and was warmly received by sidewalk crowds. She made it through the campaign without delivering a speech. Despite the constant strain, she maintained her poise and a sense of humor. At one point, looking at her husband, she quipped, "Politics makes strange bedfellows."[4]

By mutual consent, Van Doren stayed in the background, but Willkie kept in contact. At least once a day, he telephoned or wired her. One of Willkie's trusted aides was designated to place the calls. Raymond Clapper was advised that Democrats had intercepted some of Willkie's correspondence with Van Doren, which they gleefully referred to as "dolly letters." In his memoirs, Supreme Court Justice William O. Douglas claimed that Democratic officials were using the letters as insurance against Willkie's men making public some embarrassing letters from Henry A. Wallace to a religious mystic, whom he addressed as "Guru."

When FDR found out that the Republican National Committee

had obtained letters from Wallace to Nicholas Roerich, a White Russian mystic, he told political aide Lowell Mellett that Willkie's relationship with Van Doren could be publicized to counter their disclosure. "We can't have any of our principal speakers refer to it," said Roosevelt in a taped conversation made public by *American Heritage* in 1982, "but the people down the line can get it out. I mean the Congress speakers, and state speakers, and so forth. They can use the raw material. Now, now, if they want to play dirty politics in the end, we've got our own people. Now, you'd be amazed at how this story about the gal is spreading around the country."

"It's out," Mellett replied.

"Awful nice gal," FDR said of Van Doren, "writes for the magazine and so forth and so on, a book reviewer. But nevertheless, there is the fact. And one very good way of bringing it out is by calling attention to the parallel" between Willkie and former New York Mayor Jimmy Walker. The President recalled that Mayor Walker had an attractive girl friend with whom he lived, but when he went on trial on charges of corruption, he paid his estranged wife $10,000 to attend Mass with him.

"Now, Mrs. Willkie may not have been hired," said Roosevelt, "but in effect she's been hired to return to Wendell and smile and make this campaign with him. Now, whether there was a money price behind it, I don't know, but it's the same idea."

The Wallace letters were not leaked that fall. FDR's adviser Samuel Rosenman said that Willkie kept them private in a statesmanlike decision to emphasize issues rather than personalities in the campaign. Whatever the reason, the Democrats did not raise the question of the GOP nominee's private life as an issue.[5]

From the beginning of the campaign, Willkie drew huge crowds. Opening his western tour in Chicago, he did not make a promising start. In the stench of the Union Stockyards, Willkie was received with indifference if not hostility by men in bloodied aprons. The roaring of elevated trains within a few hundred feet of the platform drowned out his words. Later, appearing in Cicero, he blundered. Willkie started attacking Chicago's Kelly-Nash Democratic machine, when someone in the audience reminded him he was in Cicero. "Well, then," shot back Willkie, "to hell with Chicago." His comment made front-page headlines in the Chicago *Times*, Marshall Field's strongly pro-Roosevelt tabloid, and it clearly did not enhance his prospects in Illinois. That same afternoon Willkie received a tumultuous welcome in Chicago's downtown shopping and financial districts as a ticker tape blizzard sprinkled confetti in his hair and showered his thirty-car motorcade. "I need to clean out the mess of the last seven and a half years," he shouted. "It will take several shovels just to clean out Chicago."

In his last appearance of the day, Willkie promised eight thousand blacks in the American Giants Baseball Park that his administration would eliminate racial discrimination, abolish Jim Crow laws, and press for an antilynching statute. His voice was getting hoarse.

With the fervor of an old-fashioned evangelist, Willkie moved into downstate Illinois. If even a handful of bystanders had gathered by the tracks, he would impulsively pull the bell cord and have the conductor back up the train so he could step on the back platform and say a few words. Such sudden stops were physically taxing and put him off schedule, but he insisted on meeting every group that turned out.

Willkie had looked forward to doing battle with FDR but grew bitter and frustrated when the President ignored him. In Joliet, attacking Roosevelt's foreign policy, he got careless, blaming him for the Munich Pact. FDR, he charged, had telephoned Hitler and Mussolini "and urged them to sell Czechoslovakia down the river." While the allegation made good campaign rhetoric, it was untrue. Lem Jones, Willkie's press secretary, quickly acknowledged that the Republican nominee had "misspoken" and had meant only to say that the President had recommended a peace settlement at Munich. Secretary of State Cordell Hull, responding for the Administration, said Willkie's comment demonstrated that he was "grossly ignorant" in world affairs.

Though politically damaging, Willkie's foreign policy gaffe was of less immediate concern to his advisers than his used-up voice. While the candidate was in Indiana, a friend, radio comedian Walter O'Keefe had suggested lessons in voice placement, which would make it easier for Willkie to give frequent speeches and improve his delivery. The American people were tired of soporific radio voices, Willkie snorted. Voice lessons, he added, were for sissies. He didn't want to sound like an announcer.

In the first two days in Illinois, Willkie stubbornly refused to use a microphone and shouted at his audiences. When he asked Halleck how he was doing, the Indiana congressman urged him to make the speeches "half as loud and half as long." His voice cracked in Chicago. "He was too free and easy," recalled Henry Cabot Lodge, who was on the same train. "You can't make that many speeches and not pay a heavy price." Willkie's voice grew more rasping at each downstate stop. By the time he reached Galesburg, it was reduced to a croak. Dr. Francis Lederer, a Chicago throat specialist, was hastily summoned, but it took a major effort by Willkie's men to get the candidate to sit still for an examination. The doctor ordered him not to give any more speeches until he had time to recuperate. Willkie had been so abrupt with him that Lederer snapped indignantly that what he needed wasn't a doctor but a policeman. Willkie, however, followed the advice and had Halleck give the speeches while he stood in silence and waved to the train station crowds. In Rock Island, he whispered into a microphone, "The spirit is completely willing, but the flesh is weak."

With the rest of his tour threatened, Willkie's advisers desperately sought the help of leading throat specialists. The movie actor Robert Montgomery arranged for Dr. Harold Gray Barnard, a Hollywood physician and throat specialist, to become a full-time member of the campaign staff. "Lean back and open your mouth," Barnard told Willkie at their first meeting. "Go to hell and take your tools with you," said the presidential nominee.[6]

"Personally, I don't give a damn," said Barnard. "But that throat of yours right now is the only way some twenty million Americans can express themselves. Lean back!"

Willkie grinned and opened his mouth. Dr. Barnard told him to talk less and get several days of rest. A difficult patient, Willkie stopped campaigning for just a day and kept on talking. When Barnard, in his pleading, lost his voice, Willkie chortled.

Willkie kept going. In scratchy voice, he alleged at a rally in Coffeyville, Kansas, that FDR had been negligent about America's defenses. The Administration, he claimed, was misrepresenting the strength of the U.S. military. While this was true enough, one of the problems with the argument was that congressional Republicans had obstructed FDR's efforts to rebuild the nation's defenses.

Willkie got carried away with his rhetoric in cattle country by falsely charging that the Administration was giving preference to Argentine beef. He would revive the nation's economy, Willkie stated, by having "the American Navy eat American beef instead of Argentine beef." Willkie was attempting to rekindle the controversy of 1939 when the Navy bought $7,500 of tinned beef from Argentina. He was unaware that Congress had since passed legislation forbidding the Navy to buy foreign beef. Leading political analysts were quick to point out Willkie's error.

It also was Willkie's misfortune to get caught in the middle of perhaps the year's most bitterly fought primary fight. Because of the intense Senate contest between incumbent Lynn Frazier and Governor William Langer, Hamilton had urged Willkie to bypass North Dakota "to avoid any disagreeable circumstances." Oblivious to local political concerns, Willkie campaigned in North Dakota and, as Hamilton predicted, Frazier, Langer, and other hopefuls boarded the train. "At each whistle-stop," recalled Hamilton, "there was a fight between them as to who would make a speech along with Mr. Willkie, several of which resulted in fisticuffs. It was rather an undignified thing to see three or four men on the rear platform of the train struggling with each other to get hold of the microphone."

Since the Philadelphia convention, Willkie's campaign had been notorious for its disorganization. Republican leaders, already cool to his candidacy, complained about unanswered phone calls, letters, and telegrams. He nearly lost his position on the Wyoming ballot by failing to respond to GOP counsel Henry Fletcher's letter with the official registration form. Willkie made it known that he would have nothing to do with Pennsylvania Republican boss Joseph N. Pew or Ohio Governor John W. Bricker. On weekends, Willkie would have his train parked in freight yards outside of town so that he might avoid local politicians, who were derisively nicknamed "boll weevils" by his circle.

In New England, a frustrated Republican official, J. W. Farley, stormed into the Willkie staff car and complained about last-minute schedule changes which had ruined weeks of planning. Unable to get an audience with Willkie, Farley approached Pierce Butler, a senior aide, and demanded to know who was running the tour. "Have you ever been in a whorehouse on a Saturday night when the Madam was away and the girls were running it to suit themselves?" deadpanned Butler. "That's how this campaign train is run."

Willkie was responsible for the disarray. Even though it had been three months since his nomination, he had not settled on *the* campaign manager to whom matters of strategy and administration could be delegated. Martin, Davenport, Hamilton, and Pryor had each been given a title suggesting they were in charge, yet none commanded the authority of FDR's Edward J. Flynn. To a large extent, Willkie served as his own campaign manager and press secretary. It was impossible to keep his speeches under wraps, because he would leak key details to reporters well before they were delivered. The candidate radiated such self-confidence that some political associates decided it was futile to offer further counsel. "Giving advice to Willkie," said one Republican politician, "is as effective as giving castor oil to the sphinx." Willkie declared, "Free advice is worth what it costs."

"I feel that the campaign has demonstrated one thing so far," Senator Taft wrote Dewey on September 17, "that is that no convention should nominate a candidate who has never been engaged in a political campaign before. I am sure that Mr. Willkie has made a good many minor mistakes which we would not have made. I don't have much confidence in my judgment as to public opinion, and it may be that wisecracking which keeps the nominee on the front page every day really gets results, but I rather doubt it."

Other experienced political observers—and not just his defeated rival for the nomination—were beginning to question Willkie's capability. "By two tests," Raymond Clapper wrote in his column on September 20, "the Willkie campaign falls so short that grave doubts are raised, at least with me, about the kind of job he would do as President. One test is Willkie's skill as an organizer. The other test is to be found in the policies upon which he offers himself for the job. By neither test does Willkie seem to live up to earlier expectations of at least this one of his friends.

"Seldom has there been more chaos in a presidential campaign," Clapper concluded. "If the Willkie Administration in the White House functioned with no more unity, co-ordination and effectiveness than the Willkie Administration in the campaign, then the government would be almost paralyzed."[7]

At the beginning of September, Willkie had been in a virtual dead heat with Roosevelt in the Gallup poll and held a slight edge in projected electoral votes. On the same day that Clapper's unfavorable column appeared, Willkie received even more distressing news. The Gallup poll reported that FDR had moved in front by ten points in the popular vote and was running ahead in thirty-eight states with 453 electoral votes. In the September 20 survey, Roosevelt had 55 per cent to Willkie's 45 per cent. "Franklin Roosevelt is not running against Wendell Willkie," said Republican Congressman Dewey Short. "He's running against Adolf Hitler." Another GOP official added, "With Willkie a poor third."

In an off-the-record conversation with reporters on his campaign train, Willkie acknowledged that he would probably lose the election if the war was still on. A leading public opinion survey showed Willkie winning by 5.5 per cent if the war ended, but losing by 18 percentage points if there was a possibility the United States might enter the world war. Most of the forty-six members of the Willkie press corps thought his chances were fading fast. At the same time, they liked Willkie. Bill Lawrence recalled that the GOP candidate frequently dropped into the press room "drink in hand, on the prowl for companionship."[8] He would often leak strategic decisions and major policy statements, sometimes inadvertently, in bull sessions with reporters. His staff chafed, but he seldom got burned. Willkie permitted a pool reporter to stand with him on the back platform of the train. Once, the *Willkie Special* pulled off, leaving a group of reporters, who started running down the tracks. Without his glasses, Willkie didn't recognize them and, thinking they were Republican fans, stood on the platform and waved as the train moved out of town.

Willkie's staff was perpetually on the verge of mutiny. Within a few days, the amateurs and professionals were barely speaking. There were complaints that Willkie's youthful activists had exacerbated tensions between the campaign and party organization. It rankled staffers that Edward Willkie and Davenport were the only aides with regular access to the candidate. Halleck, who was the senior professional, recalled, "I was in the back end of the train all the time, but I never was invited by Wendell Willkie to come in there and have lunch or anything of that sort. I had to fight my way up through."

It did not help staff morale that working conditions were crowded and dirty in what newspapermen termed "The Squirrel Cage," and Marcia Davenport called "a traveling equivalent of Andersonville." In the cramped staff car, the plumbing rarely worked and compartments doubled as offices and bedrooms. "Everything related to physical order and cleanliness, including laundry, was a nightmare," said Mrs. Davenport, who joined the campaign as a speech writer. "Some of the wildest tales of the Willkie train are stories of lost laundry which never caught up with the men who had left their shirts in a town which seemed to have slunk off the map when anybody tried to connect with it again."

Willkie's entourage included the Davenports; Halleck; Senator Henry Cabot Lodge of Massachusetts; John B. Hollister, Ohio GOP leader and Senator Taft's law partner; tour director William J. Gallagher; press secretary Lem Jones; foreign policy adviser Raymond Leslie Buell, on loan from Luce's *Fortune;* economics adviser Elliott V. Bell, former New York *Times* financial writer; Pierce Butler, Minneapolis lawyer and son of a Supreme Court justice; Bartley Crum, San Francisco civil liberties lawyer; and Paul Smith, editor of the San Francisco *Chronicle*. "Those on the train had very little in common," said Willkie's friend Joseph Barnes, "except the desire to see Roosevelt defeated."

Most of the grievances were directed against the dark, intense Davenport, who was indecisive, disorganized, and insisted on rewriting the speeches of his subordinates. Since Philadelphia, the former managing editor of *Fortune* had been a target of Republican conservatives, who held him responsible for putting over Willkie's nomination. Davenport was less than tactful in his relations with Old Guard Republicans. While in California, he turned down Hamilton's request that Willkie meet with a prominent fund raiser and party official because the candidate was "too busy getting his speeches ready to see a lot of God-damned politicians."[9] Lambert concluded that Davenport was "a great handicap to Willkie." Following a visit to Willkie headquarters, political columnist George Sokolsky wrote Herbert Hoover, "There seems to be conflict, jealousy and differences. I think it would be best straightened out by the instant elimination of Davenport who, able as he may be as an editor, has no particular place in this picture."

"Obviously Willkie is not having the advantages which would come if he had some seasoned and trained advisors on the train who know the best liars and sound thinkers in the various states and would steer the candidate away from trouble spots," A. L. "Dutch" Shultz of the Topeka *State Journal* wrote Hamilton on September 15. "There is lots of energy and steam on the train, but am afraid a good deal of it doesn't mean much. Apparently nobody on the personnel staff ever saw a presidential campaign train before and I am not optimistic as to what will happen."

A few days later Shultz sent Hamilton an updated report: "The organization work, if there is much organization work, appears to be in the hands of the Boy Scouts. Unless there is a groundswell against Roosevelt, I don't believe these boys will get the job done."

For all his critics, Davenport still had the confidence of the man whose vote counted. Willkie, who affectionately nicknamed him The Zealot, defended the former editor against his vociferous attackers. "The real basis of the anarchy," said Mrs. Davenport, "was not so much Russell's disorganized methods as the bitter warfare between the Republican professionals and Willkie's wild-eyed amateurs." Had it not been for Davenport, Willkie knew that he would never have been seriously considered for the presidency. Willkie would be willing to fire other members of his senior staff, but he made it clear that Davenport was not expendable.

One of the reasons that Mrs. Davenport joined the train on the West Coast was to help restore order to her husband's speech-writing operation. Lodge, Bartley Crum, and former New Deal brain truster Raymond Moley also assisted in drafting Willkie's speeches, but Davenport, still the editor, rewrote them all, sometimes in a style too formal and stilted for the candidate's breezy personality. As a result, Willkie would often not receive the finished version of his speech until minutes before it was delivered, which usually showed in his performance on the platform. On learning this, Luce diplomatically attempted to persuade Davenport to delegate more responsibilities, writing that he had "no choice but to risk upsetting you because so many people say that they won't or can't tell you 'the truth.'" Davenport, though, refused to consider Luce's proposal.[10]

Of Willkie's advisers among the publishers, Luce was the most intimately involved in the fall campaign, and it was he who wrote the first draft for Willkie's foreign policy speech in San Francisco. On a daily basis, he sent suggestions and comments to the *Willkie Special.* Several of his top executives took active roles in the campaign. *Time* general manager Charles L. Stillman prepared background materials for Willkie on industrial mobilization, and the newsmagazine's managing editor, John Martin, used his month's vacation to work in Willkie's New York headquarters. Buell, director of the *Fortune*

Round Table, became Willkie's principal foreign policy adviser. Luce became irritated when *Time* kept reporting Willkie's blunders and embarrassed when the New York *Post* reported that his magazine had soured on the GOP nominee. "*Time* thinks just as highly of Wendell Willkie today as it ever did," Luce wrote in a letter to the *Post,* "which is, admittedly, pretty high."

Meanwhile, Willkie struggled to find a central theme for his campaign. Republican leaders urged an all-out offensive on FDR and the New Deal, which Willkie dismissed as too negative. At a chance meeting in the barber shop of the Waldorf-Astoria in New York, James A. Farley pressed him to emphasize the third term as his major issue. Beyond quoting the founding fathers a few times, Willkie chose not to argue the question of a third term. Foreign policy, counseled Walter Lippmann, was the fundamental issue. "Your opportunity arises out of the fact that people feel insecure and want the assurance of a strong, competent man," he wrote Willkie. "Roosevelt is not a strong, competent man and that is where you can beat him if you take 'the hard line' and summon the people rather than vaguely trying to please them all." In the early phase of the campaign, Willkie took Lippmann's advice and attacked FDR as too soft, an appeaser. Luce, the son of Presbyterian missionaries, pushed an evangelical theme: "The campaign must be a Crusade for Free Men in a Free Land." Willkie picked up Luce's slogan. In Long Beach, he asserted, "This is not a campaign, it's a crusade. I call upon each and all of you to join it. I ask each of you to be a soldier in the fight to keep our liberties."

Willkie's main differences with FDR were in domestic affairs. He still held the views that had carried him into the battle with the TVA—namely, that government should not be in competition with private enterprise. Influenced by the writings of Carl Snyder, a friend and New York Federal Reserve Bank economist, Willkie called for a rollback of federal regulations to provide incentives for industry, help create more jobs, and stimulate the economy. "Roughly, Willkie believes that private capitalism can carry the ball alone," wrote Clapper. "New Dealers believe private capitalism alone is inadequate and that public spending must supplement it."[11]

It was hardly surprising that Willkie took issue with FDR on corporate capitalism. By tradition, the GOP was the party of business and the candidate himself was a Wall Street industrialist. Of greater significance was the fact that Willkie promised to keep intact many of the New Deal's social welfare programs. He vowed to expand Social Security, continue relief for the unemployed, farm credit, crop insurance, and rural electrification; and maintain the Wagner Labor Relations Act and the Wage and Hour Act. Thirty-five years before the Humphrey-Hawkins Bill, he advocated full employment. At a time when 10 million Americans were unemployed, Willkie promised his administration would provide jobs for everyone willing to work. Finally, in a burst of enthusiasm, he said, "I pledge a new world."

On the West Coast, he was in better voice, for Willkie grudgingly was learning microphone technique. During Willkie's speeches, Barnard stood in the audience and would signal brother Edward to cut off the candidate when his voice strained. On the train, Willkie listened to recordings of his speeches with commentary from Barnard. He still disregarded much of Barnard's advice. Willkie invariably talked too long, continuing extemporaneously after winding up his text.

In conservative San Diego, Santa Ana, Inglewood, and Long Beach, Willkie's motorcade drew friendly crowds, but his reception in Los Angeles was tumultuous with near crashes at every intersection. Throughout his procession, the crowd roared, and torn paper and ticker tape showered his car. At City Hall, the throng circled him, and he never got to meet Mayor Robert Burns and other local officials.

That night, Willkie's entrance into the Los Angeles Coliseum had the pageantry of a Cecil B. De Mille production. With golden spotlights cutting through the clear evening sky and hundreds of American flags waving in a soft breeze, seventy thousand people chanted "We Want Willkie!" and the band struck up "God Bless America." Within a few minutes, Willkie dimmed the crowd's enthusiasm with a dull, rambling speech about taxation.

At Fresno, in John Steinbeck's San Joaquin Valley, he was booed and heckled by young men when he spoke at a park in the center of town. A large percentage of those in the crowd were children let out of school to see their first presidential candidate. This appearance marked one of the few times that reporters on the Willkie train noticed poverty-stricken people in an audience. "Here and there men were lying on the grass, itinerant workers in ragged overalls, lying in a state of such indifference or exhaustion that they gave no sign they

knew the crowd was there or the voice was speaking," wrote Childs. "It was as though they had been barred from the normal, prosperous world that Willkie addressed."[12]

Willkie's foreign policy address in San Francisco was forcefully delivered and well received. He ripped the Roosevelt administration's inconsistency, ridiculed the idea that FDR was an indispensable leader, called for U.S. air bases in the Pacific to protect American interests against Japan, and reiterated his call for aid to Britain short of military intervention. "We must rid ourselves of the fallacy that democracy can be defended with words, with poses, with political paraphernalia designed to impress the American people and no one else. We must send, and we must keep sending, aid to Britain, our first line of defense and our only remaining friend."

Heading north into Oregon, Willkie confronted his most vulnerable issue, public power, and gave assurances that if elected he would complete FDR's huge Columbia River dam projects of which Senator McNary had been the principal sponsor. "Wendell Willkie will presumably go out here with a spade and dig up Bonneville and Grand Coulee," he said wryly. "The United States government has $270 million invested in Bonneville and Grand Coulee and I have more conception of the value that that investment represents than all the New Deal crew put together and piled up double." The power generated from government dams, said Willkie, should be sold for the people's benefit, and it should be their decision whether the distribution lines are owned by the government or private industry. "Don't let any bunk artist come along and tell you Wendell Willkie's views are different from that," he snorted. "And I may say I know how to operate such things for the benefit of those for whom I work and I shall be working for the people of the United States."

Senator McNary did not accompany Willkie on his swing through Oregon, although the presidential candidate had expressed hope that he might visit his running mate at his farm, Fir Cone, just north of Salem. As it turned out, McNary had already been scheduled to open his campaign in the Midwest when Willkie was in Oregon and, oddly, the presidential candidate's handlers did not make a serious attempt to persuade McNary to change his plans.

As the train moved back across the country, there were rumors Willkie planned a major shake-up. He had privately accused Hamilton of "sulking in his tent" and had threatened his removal as executive director. Aware of the threats, Hamilton was "incensed by Willkie's attitude, not only toward me but toward the organization." Coming aboard the *Willkie Special* in Milwaukee, Hamilton was informed by Shultz that the presidential candidate had soured on Joe Martin. A few minutes later, Edward Willkie told Hamilton his brother was waiting for him.

In the privacy of the *Pioneer,* Willkie conferred with Hamilton. The presidential candidate took off his shoes, loosened his tie, opened his collar, and flopped on the bed. "I am getting rid of Joe Martin," he said, "because he is double-crossing me, and I want you to take over the chairmanship." Years later, Hamilton said, "I think I have never been more dumbfounded during the forty years I spent in public life. To me, the whole proposition was politically preposterous."

What set Willkie off were reports that Martin had said the presidential ticket would probably lose the election but Republicans had a fair chance of winning the House of Representatives. Willkie himself had expressed private doubts about his chances, yet he did not think it was proper for his national chairman to say the same thing. Hamilton, still resentful over being fired as national chairman in July, had warned Willkie that the House Minority Leader would give congressional races priority over the presidential election. According to Hamilton, he told Willkie that Martin was symbolically important, had served him loyally, and that it would be a political mistake to dismiss him.

"I directed his attention to the fact that if he were elected President of the United States," recalled Hamilton, "he would undoubtedly carry the House with him and Joe would be its Speaker." Hamilton said that Willkie could not afford to begin his administration with a House Speaker "who was personally antagonistic."

Hamilton, who had been Landon's campaign manager in 1936, gave a personal reason for declining Willkie's offer. Even though the outcome of the election was uncertain, he said, most voters had probably made their decision "for better or for worse, and that if Willkie won, Joe was entitled to the credit and if he lost, I did not want the discredit of losing another national election."

Willkie's response was not recorded, but he kept Martin in place at the GOP National Committee. While less than effective as chairman, Martin proved to be a durable congressional leader, who would later serve two terms as House Speaker. Following the election, Willkie urged Martin to continue in the chairmanship.[13]

Three weeks of aggressive campaigning failed to check Willkie's slippage in the polls. On October 6, the Gallup poll reported his projected electoral vote had dropped from seventy-eight to thirty-two. Extending his popular vote margin to twelve points, FDR was now leading in forty-two states. For Willkie, it was the low point of his campaign, although the main factors in his decline were beyond his control. Roosevelt, who still considered Willkie a dangerous opponent, told House Democratic leaders Sam Rayburn and John W. McCormack that the numbers were misleading. "I said in–about the first of August–I said you watch these polls, you watch the Republican timing of this campaign. I think the polls couldn't possibly make it Willkie. They're going to show Willkie in pretty good shape the first part of August. Then they're going to put him through a bad slump, bad slump, so that I'll be well ahead on the first of October. And my judgment is that they are going to start Willkie–pickin' up! pickin' up! pickin' up!–from the first of October on. And you know what a horse race is–it's like–what they're going to do is to have their horse three lengths behind, coming around into the stretch. And then, in the stretch, in the first hundred yards, he gains a length, and the next hundred yards, he gains another length, and gives people the idea that this fella still can win–he's got time to win. He can nose out the other horse. Now, I don't know whether that's their game, but I'm inclined to think it is. I'm wrong on my dates. They didn't start the first of October. Next Sunday, in the Gallup poll, we'll have a great many–too many–votes handed to us, 500. A great many too many."

The President was skillfully exploiting his role as commander-in-chief. Instead of campaigning in the traditional sense, he was making "inspection tours" of defense plants. The destroyer-bases deal and enactment of the first peacetime draft underscored FDR's symbolic prominence as commander-in-chief. These actions also produced a patriotic surge in Roosevelt's political stock.

Willkie was forced to re-evaluate his strategy. Running well behind in the polls, he sought an issue that would undercut FDR's popularity. The Republican candidate's personality and style were enormously appealing, but his platitudes about a "crusade for liberty and the democratic way of life" were no different than the utterances of many politicians. His attacks on New Deal regulations were well received in corporate boardrooms but had not caught on with the masses. "The trouble with Willkie," Roosevelt told Rayburn and McCormack, "is that he will say anything to please the individual or the audience that he happens to talk to." The President showed anxiety over Willkie's frequently repeated promise to find jobs for the nine million unemployed workers in America. "After he's said it thirty or forty times, he's made a real issue of it [until the voter says] 'Willkie's the fella who's goin' to put nine million men to work, I'll vote for him.' It's the iteration—'promise, promise, promise' every single morning, noon, and night. After a while, people get to believe it." Willkie had scored points with his charge that Roosevelt had failed to lift the nation out of the Depression and had been negligent in rebuilding America's defenses, but neither issue seemed likely to turn the election in his favor.[14]

For the majority of Americans, only one issue really mattered—the world war. Until this point, Willkie had been a more ardent interventionist than FDR. Prior to his nomination, he declared it was possible the United States might have to enter the fighting. Had he been defeated in Philadelphia, Willkie stated his preference for Roosevelt over an isolationist Republican. In the summer, he said he would rather lose the presidency than make political capital of the peacetime draft. Early in the fall, Willkie struck the theme that Roosevelt had not been tough enough in meeting the Nazi threat, attacking him as an appeaser. For the most part, though, Roosevelt and Willkie were in agreement on foreign policy. So much so, in fact, that the Republican hinted he would retain Cordell Hull as Secretary of State.

In later years, Willkie was eulogized as the political rarity who would rather be right than President of the United States, yet when confronted with a test of principle in the fall of 1940, he buckled to expediency. Since the convention, Republican leaders persistently urged him to denounce Roosevelt as a warmonger, but he continued to give the Administration important bipartisan support. As he slipped in public esteem, Willkie suddenly became less unbending in his principles and more receptive to compromise. Paul Smith prepared a foreign policy speech in which Willkie would have "gone all the way" in support of the Allies. Chicago *Tribune* publisher Colonel Robert McCormick and Scripps-Howard publisher Roy Howard talked him out of making the speech and urged him to pledge that no

American soldiers would be sent abroad. Smith got Willkie's assurance that he would not make any such commitment. But several days later, Willkie was echoing the isolationist line.[15]

Instead of the principled maverick, he was acting like a normal politician. At Shibe Park, in Philadelphia, Willkie charged that FDR had caused "a drift toward war. We must stop that drift toward war. We must stop that incompetence. Fellow Americans, I want to lead the fight for peace."

In a nationally broadcast speech, he alleged that Roosevelt had made secret agreements which would commit the nation to war. "We are being edged toward war by an administration that is careless in speech and action," he said. "We can have peace but we must know how to preserve it. To begin with, we shall not undertake to fight anybody else's war. Our boys shall stay out of Europe."

Throughout the isolationist Midwest, Willkie kept repeating that if FDR's promise to keep American boys out of foreign wars was no better than his 1932 promise to balance the budget, then "they're already almost on the transports." In St. Louis, he shouted, "We do not want to send our boys over there again. If you elect me President, they will not be sent. And, by the same token, if you re-elect the third-term candidate, I believe they will be sent."

Willkie's foreign policy flip-flop brought him into a temporary alliance with people for whom he had contempt, including such isolationist stalwarts as Hamilton Fish, Charles A. Lindbergh, and Colonel Robert McCormick. He actively sought and succeeded in getting the endorsement of California's crusty isolationist senator, Hiram Johnson, and paid tribute to the recently deceased Idaho isolationist, William E. Borah, as one of his political heroes.

The Republican candidate's flirtation with isolationism disappointed a great many of his backers. *Herald Tribune* columnists Walter Lippmann and Dorothy Thompson, perhaps his best-known journalistic sponsors, abandoned his cause. Ending his service as an informal adviser, Lippmann took a neutral stance in the election. "As for Willkie," he wrote privately, "I feel very badly indeed. I hoped and believed he would be the man this country needs, but I think he set his campaign on a fundamentally wrong line." Following a luncheon with Willkie in which she explained her decision, Miss Thompson endorsed FDR. Her change of heart was professionally costly. It was the major reason she was fired by the *Herald Tribune* in March 1941. Luce was appalled at Willkie's handling of the war issue, arguing that he should have "told the truth and gone down, with greater honor, in a far greater defeat." In a letter to a relative, Senator Taft wrote that the GOP nominee was "a very able man," but "he is of the salesman type, anxious to make a good impression on those who are immediately in front of him. Whether he will really stand up against pressure I have some doubt."[16]

Political analyst Richard H. Rovere noted, "By the time the campaign was over, Willkie was as much in opposition to the man he had been a few months earlier as he was to his opponent." In a 1981 interview, Oren Root acknowledged that Willkie's sudden conversion on the war issue was nothing more than a cynical appeal for votes. Despite his rhetoric, Root noted that Willkie had not shed his long-held convictions.[17]

Willkie's tactics revived his candidacy and alarmed Democratic strategists. Within two weeks, the Gallup poll reported he had trimmed the President's popular vote margin by half. Willkie had moved ahead in five midwestern states and was surging in the industrial Northeast. The New York *Daily News* poll indicated the Empire State was a toss-up. On Wall Street, the betting odds against Willkie dropped from twelve-to-five to seven-to-five.

From the beginning of the campaign, Roosevelt expected a close election, maintaining privately that Willkie was the most dangerous rival of his political career. Democratic National Chairman Edward J. Flynn and First Lady Eleanor Roosevelt suggested he drop the "inspection tours" and launch an old-fashioned campaign. Interior Secretary Harold Ickes told FDR bluntly that he would not bet a nickel on his chances unless he fought for re-election. "I am fighting mad," the President replied, confiding that he would soon respond to Willkie's allegations. Samuel I. Rosenman, Roosevelt's longtime political aide, said FDR was forced into action as a result of Willkie's dramatic gains.[18]

In the Oval Office, Roosevelt made the claim that he was too preoccupied with affairs of state to follow Willkie's speeches, yet he carefully studied them all. Willkie struck a presidential nerve in quoting Winston Churchill's long-forgotten criticism of the New Deal's economic policies. In 1937 the British statesman had alleged that the Roosevelt administration was waging "so ruthless a war on private enterprise that the United States is actually at the present moment leading the world back into the trough of the Depression." Roosevelt demanded that Churchill repudiate Willkie's use of the Prime Minister's words against his re-election.

Grateful for the President's strongly pro-British policies, Churchill sent word to the White House that while he had "criticized certain aspects of the New Deal," he nonetheless had "always entertained lively admiration" for FDR. With Willkie coming on strong, the British were hedging their bets. Lord Lothian cabled London that a change in administrations would not be harmful to the Anglo-American alliance. Francis Biddle, Roosevelt's solicitor general, advised the British embassy that Churchill's quotations were hurting the re-election bid and suggested the Prime Minister blunt their effect by speaking out in the House of Commons. Nevile Butler, British minister in Washington, cautioned the Foreign Office that any comment would be construed as intervention in the American election. When Churchill asked for transcripts of Willkie's quotations, Butler sent the material with the warning that the Republican candidate "is now considered to have quite a good chance" and British action "would be too late to do any good but so timed as to be extremely conspicuous" and risk "queering the pitch with whom we may have to be working after November 5th." After examining Willkie's quotations, Churchill verified their accuracy and told his private secretary, "It was all too true. Less said soonest mended. Do nothing."[19]

Willkie was stung by Democratic allegations that Nazi Germany favored his election. Henry A. Wallace, FDR's running mate, charged in his acceptance speech that European dictators were pulling for Willkie. "They'd do anything in the world to have me licked," FDR said privately. At a White House press conference, Roosevelt smiled when asked if Germany and Italy were working for his defeat. The President quoted from an article by New York *Times* foreign correspondent Herbert L. Matthews which said, "The Axis is out to defeat President Roosevelt." New York Governor Herbert Lehman, keynoting his state's Democratic convention, declared, "Nothing that could happen in the United States could give Hitler, Mussolini, Stalin, and the government of Japan more satisfaction than the defeat of the man who typifies the kind of free, humane government which dictators despise–Franklin D. Roosevelt."

Campaigning in Michigan, Willkie expressed shock "that a man of Governor Lehman's character and responsibility should stoop to a kind of politics that can only jeopardize the safety and welfare of the American people in a critical hour." Willkie said he had given bipartisan commitment to FDR's foreign policy, but that Lehman's words "tend to destroy the unity." Oswald Garrison Villard, editor of the *Nation,* told the governor that his declaration "touches the low-water mark of unfair, unjust and intolerable partisanship" and accused him of "playing upon passions and prejudices which you ought to be the last man in the State of New York to do." The New York *Times,* which had endorsed Willkie, said: "We are under no illusion that Hitler and Mussolini like Mr. Roosevelt. We are under no illusion that they will like Mr. Willkie any better, in case he is elected, for Mr. Willkie is just as vigorously pro-America, and just as bitterly anti-Axis, as Mr. Roosevelt, and it is entirely possible that, by preventing economic disintegration in the United States and assuring a more rapid production of airplanes and other war supplies, he would give the Axis even more to worry about."

In the fall of 1940, it was true that the Axis desired Roosevelt's defeat, for its leaders feared that his re-election would bring the United States into the war. Under the circumstances, they preferred Willkie, an unknown quantity, to the proven hostility of FDR. Two years later, Hitler's Minister of Propaganda, Joseph Goebbels, was to write in his diary: "Willkie as President would possibly be even more dangerous to us than Roosevelt, for he is an opportunist, a politician without character and firm convictions, with whom nothing can be done. He would certainly be the man to intensify the United States war effort."[20]

There were slurs and whispering campaigns about Willkie's German ancestry. Unsigned pamphlets linked him with Hitler's theory of the master race and stated that his sister was the wife of a Nazi naval officer when, in fact, she was married to the U.S. naval attaché in Berlin. Democratic Senator Joseph Guffey of Pennsylvania disclosed that after sending photographers to take pictures of the Willkie family plot in Indiana, he had found that the grave markers bore the Germanic spelling of "Willcke."

Outraged, overcome by emotion, Willkie stood in the auditorium of a Brooklyn high school and fired back, "I understand that a whispering campaign is going on about me because one of my parents was born abroad. I say any man who questions my patriotism is a coward and a cur and I care not what position he occupies, public or private. I only want the votes of intelligent, free-thinking Americans."

His voice breaking, Willkie recalled how his father had attempted to enlist against Germany in World War I at the age of sixty and noted that he and his older brother had gone to war and their sister had worked for the government as a translator. His eloquent and moving address more than offset the whispering campaign of his faceless accusers, but another low blow jolted the Republican candidate. In October the Democratic National Committee's minorities division released a statement that Willkie's hometown in Indiana had signs saying, "Nigger, don't let the sun go down on you." It also quoted Willkie as frequently wisecracking, "You can't do this to me, I'm a white man." Willkie described it as "the most scurrilous and indecent" political document of the campaign. Democratic National Chairman Edward Flynn disowned the leaflet and fired Julian D. Rainey as chairman of the committee's minorities division.

Willkie was making a strong bid for the black vote, which had been Republican since the Civil War and had not broken for FDR until 1936. He gained the endorsements of such leading black newspapers as the New York *Age,* Pittsburgh *Courier,* and the *Afro-American.* Willkie also had the support of heavyweight boxing champion Joe Louis, the most popular black figure in America. Republicans quickly manufactured campaign buttons with the legendary Brown Bomber's picture and the slogan, "Joe Louis for Willkie." In his memoirs, Louis said he had supported FDR in 1936 only to be disappointed by his performance on civil rights. "When I listened to Willkie," said Louis, "I fell in love with him. I thought Willkie would have been one hell of a President. He made me feel that things would have been better for blacks."[21]

His commitment to civil rights was unflinching. He repudiated the endorsement of radio priest Father Charles Coughlin's anti-Semitic newspaper, *Social Justice.* "Not only am I not interested in that kind of support, but I don't want it," said Willkie. "There is no place in my philosophy for such beliefs. I don't have to be President of the United States, but I do have to keep my beliefs clear in order to live with myself."

Emotions were running high, and the ugliest phenomenon of the campaign was that Willkie found himself the target of more violence than any presidential candidate in a generation. A man was apprehended in Madison Square Garden as he pulled a loaded revolver from his coat just a short distance from Willkie. Two New York City detectives, Stephen Buckley and Rudolph McLaughlin, accompanied Willkie throughout his travels and dodged more flying objects than a pair of hockey goalies. Willkie laughed when reporter Bill Lawrence, standing with him on the train's rear platform, was struck by an egg and the broken yolk dripped and stained his coat.[22] One of the most enduring images of the campaign was a wire-service photograph which showed the GOP candidate as he was struck in the left temple by a frozen egg in Chicago's LaSalle Street Station. In Pontiac, Michigan, he hardly noticed when an egg splashed on the platform, and returned to his Buick convertible. Then, suddenly, an egg swished within inches of Mrs. Willkie's head, hitting the back of the driver's seat and splattering her dress and stockings. Willkie's face tightened, he reddened with anger and moved toward her assailant, then held back.

Entering Detroit's Cadillac Square, Willkie ducked a cantaloupe thrown from a hotel window, but a wastebasket aimed at him split open a young woman's head. Riding through Boston, Willkie was hit by a potato. Several rocks broke the window of the train's dining car and showered glass on Philadelphia *Inquirer* reporter William Murphy. Willkie's press corps kept a daily running count of the missiles thrown at the candidate, which included telephone directories, chairs, ashtrays, stones, oranges, eggs, and tomatoes. "He had more assorted sizes and kinds of vegetables thrown at him," said *Time,* "than anyone since the old Mississippi showboat days." Washington *Post* correspondent Robert C. Albright told his colleagues on the train that working conditions would no longer be hazardous, because it was the last week of the tomato season.

President Roosevelt, calling the attacks on Willkie "reprehensible," urged the swift prosecution of his attackers. National Chairman Flynn denounced the hecklers as "hoodlums." Willkie cracked that New Deal supporters made so few hits that they must be declining as baseball players. In a display of sportsmanship, he wired Pontiac school officials and asked them to lift the suspension of a young man who had thrown the egg on the grounds that he had probably been influenced by older persons. Later, it developed that some Chicago schoolchildren had been paid to throw missiles at the Republican candidate.

Edith Willkie committed a political gaffe in suggesting to the Philadelphia *Record* that the eggs had been thrown "by some poor boy whose family probably is on relief." For the most part, though, Mrs. Willkie was showing grace under pressure. Kathleen McLaughlin wrote in the New York *Times:* "During the campaign, Mrs. Willkie's poise has dominated her self-consciousness. Nothing ruffles her. She moves serenely amid minor and major crises." Like her husband, she earned high marks for her candor with reporters. Early in October, she admitted that she had not yet registered to vote in the fall election. On her return to New York, she managed to do so just under the deadline. Asked about her husband's chances, Edith replied, "You can never really be sure of anything." Entering the final weeks, Mrs. Willkie confided to a reporter, "I'm a little tired of all this campaigning. It makes you nervous seeing so many people." Though plainly uncomfortable with a public life, Edith said, "I believe a woman's job is to adjust herself to her husband's way of living and help him do what he wants."

The Republican candidate was going for broke. On the morning of his nomination, he had pledged strict adherence to the Hatch Act, which placed a $5,000 ceiling on individual campaign contributions. In Colorado Springs, he reprimanded GOP counsel Henry Fletcher for having the effrontery to suggest loopholes in the newly passed law. Now, however, he was more than willing to listen. As the race tightened, Willkie's advisers persuaded him of the necessity of changing his views on campaign money. Only weeks after denouncing Philadelphia millionaire Joseph N. Pew, the party's biggest contributor, Willkie invited him aboard the train. "Sooner or later in every political campaign," wrote Scripps-Howard columnist Thomas L. Stokes, "no matter how illuminated with idealism it is at the outset, there comes the time of compromise with the practical powers." The Pew family contributed $108,525 to Willkie's campaign war chest. The Du Ponts of Delaware gave $186,760, and the Rockefellers gave $59,000. Following the election, the GOP National Committee reported expenditures of $14,941,143, compared to the Democratic expenditures of $6,095,357. Oren Root's Willkie Clubs of America, in addition, reported expenditures of $1,309,925.

On the *Willkie Special,* the candidate showed new optimism. He asked Turner Catledge of the New York *Times* for a candid assessment of his chances. The newspaperman replied that it appeared

Roosevelt would probably win. For the moment, Willkie conceded that his friend was right but noted public opinion was rapidly moving his way. Willkie seemed upbeat and supremely confident of his ability to overtake FDR in the stretch.

His running mate had a much different outlook. "I am not setting any eggs on the results this fall," Senator McNary wrote his sister. "It seems inconceivable that the Republicans can beat the war in Europe and the $15 million now being expended in all matter of enterprises, including reliefers, farm bonuses and war activities."

Willkie's failure to build a working relationship with his partner on the ticket deprived him of the advice of perhaps the shrewdest legislator in Washington. During the fall campaign, they met only once, when McNary introduced him at Forbes Field in Pittsburgh. "Saw Willkie only at speaking stand," McNary wrote his wife. "You would not have had much fun. Willkie tried to rest, eat alone." Halleck said years later that McNary nearly quit the ticket on more than one occasion. "I don't know if I should be the vice-presidential candidate," he told his cousin Carlton Savage. "I'm not enough of a partisan."

The Oregon senator's relaxed campaign style contrasted with Willkie's revivalist fervor. McNary worked harder for the ticket than had been expected, though turning down Martin's request for more campaign appearances in the Northeast with the argument he would be most effective in the farm belt and Pacific Coast regions. On a trip to Minnesota, he took the train with his Democratic opponent Henry A. Wallace, and the two men sat together for hours. They had been friends since the 1920s when Wallace, as a young farm editor, was a leading advocate of the McNary-Haugen farm bill. A few weeks later, the vice-presidential nominees once again found themselves on the same train and had breakfast together.

A reluctant candidate, McNary regarded the campaign as an ordeal. "I shall feel as happy as a pardoned prisoner when it is all over," he wrote his wife. In a letter to another relative, he confided, "I should be happy if I were heading homeward. The home-minded man has no business chasing around the country, but sometimes events are thrust upon us in such a fashion that we cannot follow our own course."[23]

Franklin Delano Roosevelt had no such problems. Few American presidents have campaigned with such zest and enthusiasm. On October 23, his ten-car *Presidential Special* took him to Philadelphia, and he opened his bid for a third term with a vintage performance. "I will not pretend that I find this an unpleasant duty," he stated in golden voice. "I am an old campaigner and I love a good fight."

Without mentioning his opponent by name, FDR called Willkie a liar and heatedly denied signing secret agreements committing the nation to war. Although the President privately believed it would be necessary for the United States to soon join the world war, he was not above using the rhetoric of peace in challenging Willkie for the isolationist vote. "We will not participate in any foreign wars," he said in Philadelphia, "and we will not send our army, naval, or air forces to fight in foreign lands outside of the Americas except in the case of attack."

One week later, FDR gave his controversial Boston Garden speech in which he solemnly pledged to keep the nation out of war. "I have said this before," he began, "but I shall say it again and again and again. Your boys are not going to be sent into any foreign wars."

Willkie, listening to the Boston speech on the radio, turned to his brother and snapped, "That hypocritical son of a bitch! This is going to beat me." Within FDR's camp, there had been considerable debate over the Boston speech. Rosenman argued that he should have added the words "in case of attack." Robert E. Sherwood, a strong interventionist, urged him to make the pledge without qualification. Mrs. Roosevelt thought he should not go so far. But Roosevelt, too, was playing for keeps.[24]

In Madison Square Garden, the President responded to Willkie's charge that his administration had neglected American defense with a biting attack on the Republican congressional leaders who had voted against defense appropriations–including McNary, Taft, and Vandenberg. Accusing the GOP of "playing politics with the national security of America," FDR made a sarcastic reference to isolationist congressmen "Martin, Barton, and Fish," which became legendary buzz words. Ticking off other defense measures, he asked his audience who had opposed them, and it roared back, "Martin, Barton, and Fish." Willkie said later, "When I heard the President hang the isolationist votes of Martin, Barton, and Fish on me, and get away with it, I knew I was licked."[25]

Herbert Hoover passionately hated FDR and, though ignored by

Willkie, was anxious to help bring about the defeat of the man who had ousted him from the White House. The former President was looking for a knockout blow. On October 17, he wrote Chief Justice Charles Evans Hughes, whom he had appointed a full decade earlier, and urged him to resign "with a declaration to the country of the complete necessity for a change in administration." Hoover added, "I would not do it if I did not believe that the whole future of the American people hangs upon the decision of this election."[26] Twenty-four years earlier, Hughes had stepped down from the Supreme Court and reluctantly accepted the Republican presidential nomination. This time, however, he refused to consider leaving the bench. At the age of sixty-eight, Hughes had long since moved beyond partisan politics. The Chief Justice told Hoover's aide, Lawrence Richey, that quitting the court would be pointless, because FDR would promptly name a replacement and his influence would fade overnight.

The competition for last-minute endorsements was fierce. Willkie thought he had a secret weapon in the anticipated support of Joseph P. Kennedy, FDR's ambassador to the Court of St. James's. Kennedy, who had been Roosevelt's severest foreign policy critic within the Administration, indicated to Clare Boothe Luce in London that he would endorse Willkie on his return to the United States. The ambassador made the private boast he would "put 25 million Catholic votes behind Wendell Willkie to throw Roosevelt out." To be sure, Kennedy had an inflated opinion of his political clout, but it was certain his defection would be an important breakthrough for Willkie in his pursuit of the isolationist and Catholic vote. Arrangements were made for Henry Luce to meet Kennedy at the airport shortly before the dramatic announcement on national radio.

Fully informed of Kennedy's plans, the President denied him permission to return home. The ambassador's response was that he would publicly indict FDR's policies unless the decision was reversed. Crossing the Atlantic, Kennedy received a message from Roosevelt which asked him "not to make any statement to the press on your way over, nor when you arrive in New York, until you and I have had a chance to agree upon what should be said. Come straight to Washington as I want to talk to you as soon as you get here." When Kennedy arrived in New York on October 27, he was met by presidential aides and summoned to the White House. Lyndon B. Johnson, then a young Texas congressman, said he was with FDR when he took Kennedy's phone call. After hanging up, the President drew his forefinger across his throat razor-style, Johnson recalled.

Roosevelt and Kennedy had dinner at the White House that evening. No written record of the meeting was kept, and there have been conflicting versions of what transpired. Sir William Stephenson, British intelligence agent, the man called Intrepid, said the President got Kennedy's support by threatening to make public transcripts of indiscreet conversations in London. Kennedy told Clare Boothe Luce he traded his support in exchange for FDR's promise to support Joseph P. Kennedy, Jr., his eldest son, for the Massachusetts governorship. James Roosevelt said his father warned the ambassador that bolting the party for Willkie would mark him as a turncoat and ruin his dream of political careers for his handsome sons. John F. Kennedy said later that FDR hinted he might support the Kennedy patriarch for the presidency in 1944 if he came through with a timely endorsement of the third term. Whatever the reasons, Ambassador Kennedy purchased time on CBS radio and endorsed the President just two nights later.[27]

"Unfortunately, during this political campaign, there has arisen the charge that the President of the United States is trying to involve this country in the world war," said isolationist Kennedy. "Such a charge is false."

Crestfallen, Willkie said ruefully that FDR had deluded Ambassador Kennedy on the probability of war. Oren Root felt Kennedy's speech had been a turning point of the campaign. For Willkie, it was a profound disappointment. The President triumphantly introduced Kennedy as "my ambassador" at Boston Garden. Their shotgun marriage was brief. Soon after the election, FDR fired Kennedy for insubordination when the Boston *Globe* published an interview in which the ambassador criticized the President.

Willkie was more successful in the wooing of John L. Lewis, bushy-browed president of the CIO and the United Mine Workers, and the most influential labor leader in America. Four years earlier, Lewis had contributed $500,000 to FDR's re-election, and he had been regarded as a key leader of the New Deal coalition. Since then, however, relations between the two strong-willed men had deteriorated. Lewis became embittered when the President opposed his handpicked choices in a special congressional election and for the

Pennsylvania governorship. The old coal miner was outspoken in blaming FDR for mass unemployment and failing to cure the nation's economic ills. He berated the Administration for awarding defense contracts to antiunion companies. Most of all, he opposed FDR's foreign policy, which, Lewis charged, would inevitably lead to war. In an effort at reconciliation, FDR met with Lewis upstairs at the White House, but the union leader stormed out when Roosevelt was unresponsive to his accusation that the FBI had him under surveillance.

At a secret meeting on September 28, Willkie assured Lewis that labor would have a major voice in his administration and some of its leaders appointed to high positions, including Labor Secretary. The CIO president, skeptical of Willkie's foreign policy, thought the Republican candidate would be less prone to go to war than FDR. Lewis offered his endorsement if Willkie went public with his pledge to appoint a Labor Secretary from the ranks of organized labor. Five nights later Willkie kept his part of the bargain but got into trouble in departing from the script. Speaking to a labor rally at Forbes Field, he received a thunderous ovation with his announcement that the Secretary of Labor would be chosen from their brethren. Then, he blurted out, "And it will not be a woman either." The President, who was listening on the radio, told Labor Secretary Frances Perkins, "That was a boner Willkie pulled. He was right. He was going good when he said his appointment of a Secretary of Labor would come from labor's ranks. That was legitimate political talk, but why didn't he have sense enough to leave well enough alone? Why did he have to insult every woman in the United States? It will make them mad, it will lose him votes." It was one of the campaign's ironies that Willkie was the first presidential candidate to run on a platform supporting an Equal Rights Amendment "providing for equal rights for men and women."

As a further condition of his support, Lewis wanted his speech broadcast on all three major radio networks. Chairman Martin asked Hamilton to quickly raise between $75,000 and $80,000 to fund the broadcast. Hamilton, who viewed Lewis as a rabble-rouser, said he was dubious about the value of the endorsement and suggested it might undermine Willkie's GOP organizational support. Finally, Hamilton agreed to raise the money if given an opportunity to try and talk Willkie out of accepting the CIO president's backing.

Willkie told Hamilton the Lewis endorsement was "a ten-strike." In an emotional meeting in Willkie's private car, Hamilton urged him to keep his distance from the labor leader. "I know of no instance where I came nearer to begging on my knees than I did on the occasion of this conference," he said later, "but I was not persuasive and Mr. Willkie overruled me on every score." He said Martin had asked him to raise funds for the Lewis broadcast, but Hamilton wanted a "specific request" from Willkie, which the candidate promptly made. The tenacious Hamilton then enlisted the help of Ohio Governor John W. Bricker. "He told me that John L. Lewis was personally obnoxious to him, that Lewis had insulted him and had made speeches against his candidacy in the past," recalled Hamilton, "and he told me in so many words that if Willkie accepted the Lewis support, he did not see how he could continue the active support of Mr. Willkie." Hamilton triumphantly brought the Ohio governor into the *Pioneer* and reiterated his case against Lewis. Angered that Hamilton had invited Bricker into the dispute, Willkie insisted Lewis would give his candidacy a terrific boost.

The next morning Martin told Hamilton they did not require his services in raising the funds because a wealthy contributor had underwritten the broadcast. At the time, it was announced that the program had been paid for by Democrats-for-Willkie. After the election, it was learned that William Rhodes Davis, an oil millionaire with Nazi connections, had been the real sponsor. Willkie told Marquis Childs that he had never heard of Davis until Pryor told him about the oilman's interest in putting up the money and thought it was nothing more than a fortunate windfall. "My feeling," said Childs, "was that a candidate whose managers were about to accept so substantial a gift under the circumstances should have known more about the giver," but that Willkie "did not want to ask questions."

Had he known about the oilman's shady background, Willkie said he would have turned down the offer. If the Democrats had found out before the election, the Davis connection would have been politically devastating.

The Lewis broadcast more than lived up to Willkie's expectations. In his deep Shakespearean voice, the CIO president delivered a stem-winder, denouncing FDR for turning his back on the working class, failing to come up with an effective response to the Depression, and leading the nation into world war. Willkie, argued

Lewis, had a better understanding of labor's problems and said that to reject him for FDR "would be a national evil of the first magnitude." With a dramatic flourish, he concluded by saying he would resign the CIO presidency if Roosevelt won the election. His ultimatum was a political bombshell, and it caught FDR by surprise. Democratic strategists were fearful that Lewis was undercutting the party's blue-collar foundation with his attempt to turn the election into a referendum on his leadership of the labor movement. Sidney Hillman, Roosevelt's most prominent labor ally, found the President uncharacteristically depressed by Lewis's threat. Hamilton was so impressed, he told friends that he had been wrong in his efforts to prevent the speech. Pollster George Gallup, whose survey was continuing to show a strong Willkie trend, thought Lewis might be the decisive factor in a handful of key industrial states which were within the margin of error.[28]

Mocking the Lewis claim that Willkie was a friend of low-income workers, the President quoted a socially prominent Philadelphia lawyer's snobbish remark that "only paupers" were supporting his re-election. "There speaks the true sentiment of the Republican leadership," thundered FDR. "Those paupers are only the millions who have helped build this country."

In the final hours of the campaign, Willkie's speeches took on a new urgency. The candidate immodestly called his presidential bid "the greatest cause that ever was." Buoyed by his comeback in the polls and the size and enthusiasm of his crowds, Willkie appeared more poised and confident. When reporters asked him how he could possibly get along with congressional isolationists if he won the election, he replied impatiently that with the power of the presidency behind him, they would have to be cooperative.

On election eve, he brought his crusade to an end with a tremendous rally in Madison Square Garden. For twelve minutes, a throng of twenty-two thousand people roared, "We Want Willkie!" shaking the rafters of the old boxing arena. In his speech, Willkie referred to the United States as "the last untouched land of freedom in the world" and said FDR's re-election could bring the "destruction of our democratic way of life." He shouted, "Help me, help me, help me save it!" For the last time, he said, "I want to unite all people in America."

Drained of energy, Willkie managed to project an image of youthful vigor even though he had campaigned harder than anyone in memory. On closer examination, he showed signs of wear. An old friend, Wall Street lawyer John W. Davis, thought he seemed punch-drunk, physically and mentally. "He was tired at the end," said Henry Cabot Lodge. "He couldn't take on quite as much as he wanted."

The candidate flung himself on the bed in Martin's suite at the Commodore Hotel and asked the national chairman point-blank, "How are we coming out?"

Cautiously, Martin responded, "We've got a chance to win. It's a very close race. There are twelve or fourteen important states—like Wisconsin, Illinois, New York, Indiana, Ohio, and Iowa—that hang in the balance right now. They are going to be decided by a small margin. If we get what they call that last week's pay-up, we can win. If we don't, we won't."

Willkie was noncommittal.

"The difficulty that we're really under," said Martin, "is that we've got to take all of them."

Not wanting to upset Willkie, Lambert assured him that it looked as if he were going to win the election. In fact, the pollster had already sent out several telegrams predicting a narrow victory for the President, and he was far from alone in holding that view. "Our party is making inroads," Senator McNary wrote his wife. "We have a fair chance. But the odds are so great. We must fight a war and billions of dollars in benefit payments."[29]

Most political observers were predicting the closest national election since Woodrow Wilson narrowly won a second term in 1916. In the final Gallup poll, Roosevelt had 52 per cent of the popular vote and Willkie 48, but the poll reported a "strong trend" for the Republican challenger which put him "within easy striking distance of victory." According to Gallup, Willkie had pulled into the lead in the battleground states of New York, Pennsylvania, Ohio, Illinois, Indiana, and Missouri and was nearly even in Massachusetts, Minnesota, and New Jersey. Nineteen states with 274 electoral votes, Gallup said, were very much in doubt. A *Newsweek* survey of fifty leading political writers found them almost evenly divided. Four years earlier, only one member of the panel had failed to predict the FDR landslide. This time, twenty-seven picked Roosevelt, twenty-two predicted Willkie, and one called it a toss-up. Raymond Clapper wrote privately that he liked FDR in a close finish. H. L. Mencken wrote a friend, "Willkie is making a magnificent fight but can't win."

On election eve, Willkie told Root, "I think we have a real chance. I believe there will be a big silent vote." Root thought Willkie no longer seemed confident of his chances to overtake FDR, and he himself was increasingly doubtful.[30]

For a brief time on election night, it appeared that Willkie might have a chance of pulling a second political miracle. At Hyde Park, a visibly concerned FDR closed the doors of his study and gave his bodyguard strict orders that no one, including family members, should be permitted to see him.

Meanwhile, Willkie chain-smoked Camels and lounged in an overstuffed chair in a green-carpeted suite on the fourteenth floor of the Commodore. The early returns were encouraging. "They generally pile up big majorities early in the evening, don't they, Wen?" asked Edward Willkie.

"Almost always," the candidate hoarsely replied. "The eastern city vote is always the first in, and it's Democratic." A young aide entered the room and handed Edward a sheet of paper. Edward took a quick glance and passed it to his brother. "Looks good, Ed," said Willkie. "They'd have to carry New York City a lot bigger than it looks like they're going to."

Willkie's mood turned somber when John B. Hollister brought a report from Ohio. On the basis of returns from swing precincts, Hollister told Willkie that FDR would carry the state by 100,000 votes. No Republican had ever won the presidency without carrying the Buckeye State. "I recommend an early concession," said Hollister.

Stubborn-faced, Willkie insisted, "I still have a statistical chance. The rural vote." Hollister pointed out that his strength in rural areas had been well below their expectations. The state was definitely in Roosevelt's column.

"I can still win," said Willkie.

He was trailing in early returns from Indiana. "That's probably Gary," he said. It was. Willkie eventually carried his native state. Late into the evening, he clung to the hope that returns from rural areas and small towns would reverse the FDR tide. Willkie's brother, Edward, restlessly switched the radio dial, comparing the returns from the three major networks.

At eleven o'clock, Elmer Davis, the most authoritative of radio commentators, declared that the President had won his third term. By narrow margins, Roosevelt appeared to have captured New York, Pennsylvania, Ohio, New Jersey, Massachusetts, and Illinois, all of which Willkie had hopes of carrying. In his upstate home, the President was finally able to relax and had the doors of his study opened for friends and family. Shortly afterward, Willkie blinked but was silent as the radio announcer disclosed that his running mate, Senator McNary, had just conceded the election. From his Oregon farm, McNary congratulated Roosevelt and Wallace, saying, "We are a unified country. The two-party system is secure. We shall try to afford Mr. Roosevelt and his associates a worthy and vigilant opposition."

Willkie was quiet and subdued as aides told him that his own concession would be a gracious and conciliatory gesture. "I've no hope now," Edith said in an adjoining room. "I wish Wendell would get ready to go home."[31]

By the time Willkie marched into the Commodore's Grand Ballroom at twenty minutes after midnight, fewer than a thousand volunteers and staffers remained. They took up the chant, "We Want Willkie!" Another cry went up, "We'll elect you in '44." The candidate raised his right hand and waved to his faithful fans. "I first want to say to you that I never felt better in my life," he said. He promised that whatever the election's outcome, their ideals would ultimately prevail. "Don't be afraid and never quit," he concluded without admitting that he had just lost an election.

Late Wednesday morning he finally sent the President his concession message: "Congratulations on your re-election as President of the United States. I know that we are both gratified that so many American citizens participated in the election. I wish you all personal health and happiness."

Willkie then went to lunch with editors of the *Herald Tribune*. "He was frank, cheerful, fair and appreciative," recalled Nicholas Roosevelt, then an editorial writer. "He showed no bitterness toward FDR, nor did he seem to blame anyone in his entourage for his defeat. He admitted mistakes of political judgment. He had warm praise for all who worked for him. His was the reaction of a big man in adversity."

In a handwritten letter Secretary of War Stimson commended

Willkie for "the courage, independence and force with which you have carried on your campaign." Stimson added, "I think I have been in a position to peculiarly appreciate the courage and vision which it took for you to come out as clearly as you did in favor of helping the British and adopting the Selective Service act and I think you rendered a great service to your country in doing so. The good effect of that service may be felt for a long time yet in the future. I am glad that you are going to continue your interest and efforts in the guidance of the country on national and international questions and I believe you will have ample opportunity for fine service."[32]

In a record turnout, FDR had received 27.3 million votes and Willkie 22.3 million. Though losing the election, Willkie had received the largest popular vote in his party's long history, a record that would not be surpassed until Dwight D. Eisenhower's election in 1952. He had slashed Roosevelt's 1936 winning plurality by half, polled five million more votes than Alf M. Landon, increased the GOP's share of the major party vote by 8 per cent, and more than doubled the number of counties carried by the national ticket. With Willkie heading the ticket, Republicans picked up five Senate seats and made a net gain of two new governorships. Roosevelt, carrying thirty-eight states, received 449 electoral votes to Willkie's 82, but the President's margin had been uncomfortably close in the battleground industrial states. Warren Moscow, who followed the campaign for the New York *Times,* pointed out that a shift of 600,000 Roosevelt votes in ten states would have produced a Willkie victory. The Republican candidate's edge was slight in the ten states he carried. Moscow noted that 225,000 votes taken from the Willkie column and scattered in those states would have given FDR an electoral college shutout.

Willkie's strongest showing was in the Great Plains region, where he carried Iowa, Kansas, Nebraska, and both of the Dakotas. In North Dakota, his percentage of the vote was 25 per cent higher than Landon's in 1936. McNary's presence on the ticket was an undeniable asset in the farm belt. By narrow margins, Willkie carried his native Indiana and Michigan. He won Maine and Vermont, which had been Landon's only states four years earlier. In the Rocky Mountain region, his percentage of the vote was 11.5 points higher than the party had received in 1936, but Colorado was the only state in which he edged FDR. In New York Willkie received more votes on the Republican line than FDR on the Democratic, but the President managed to overcome this deficit with the American Labor party vote. On the Pacific Coast, where FDR never lost a state in his four presidential races, Willkie increased the Republican vote by 10 per cent.

Postelection surveys indicated that FDR had consolidated his New Deal coalition. Half of his national winning plurality had come from the traditionally Democratic South. And, though the defection of John L. Lewis probably helped Willkie carry Michigan, it was quickly apparent that FDR had captured the overwhelming majority of the blue-collar vote. Willkie made gains in the suburbs, small-towns, farm belt, and rural areas, but FDR had swept the nation's largest cities, lower-income groups, and minorities. "It was a class-conscious vote for the first time in American history," wrote political analyst Samuel Lubell. "The New Deal appears to have accomplished what the Socialists, the I.W.W. and the Communists never could approach. It has drawn a class line across the face of American politics."

On separate occasions, Willkie and McNary told Ralph H. Cake that the world war had been the most important factor in Roosevelt's re-election. A postelection survey reported that 11 per cent of the President's vote had been cast as a direct result of the war. By contrast, only 2 per cent of Willkie's supporters listed it as a compelling factor in their vote. "The collapse of the Allies made Roosevelt's election a certainty no matter what Willkie did," said Joe Martin. "The fall of France and the imminent danger of Britain filled the American people with a fear of switching administrations. 'Don't change horses in the middle of the stream' was never a more potent argument in American history than it was then."

Even so, some political professionals blamed Willkie for losing the election. Sam Pryor told him that retaining Hamilton as GOP National Chairman and making more of an effort to cooperate with party regulars would have made the difference. Democratic National Chairman Edward J. Flynn wrote, "One of the main reasons for Willkie's defeat was the lack of support given him by the regular Republican organizations. The organizations certainly did not want him to be nominated. He overwhelmed them in Philadelphia. Unquestionably they left the convention with no kindly spirit toward their candidate. This feeling got worse, aggravated by the fact that Willkie took every opportunity he could to insult directly or indirectly the politicians in the Republican party. This course of action never wins an election, and it can certainly help to lose one."[33]

Ten days after the election, Herbert Hoover lunched with Willkie in the former President's Waldorf Towers suite and tactlessly pointed out that the GOP nominee had run behind the ticket in many states. The war, Willkie replied, had been a decisive factor in the defection of interventionist Republicans to FDR. Unpersuaded, Hoover virtually ghosted a column for his longtime friend Mark Sullivan, which made the argument that Willkie had blown the election by not running a traditional Republican campaign.

Beginning in the middle of November, Willkie and his wife went on a six-week vacation at Sam Pryor's winter cottage on Jupiter Island in Hobe Sound, Florida. When Sullivan's column appeared, Willkie was irritated enough to respond in two private and confidential letters. On November 24, he wrote Sullivan: "In my judgment, the reason we did not prevail was due to two reasons—one, defense money and the inevitable consequent prosperity. This was most evident in Connecticut, although it was well localized in key states. Second, Republican congressional record on conscription, international affairs, and defense. This was most evident in New England and New York."

One day later Willkie sent the columnist a follow-up in which he defensively noted that he had carried Michigan and Indiana while incumbent Republican governors were defeated; that he had run nearly 120,000 votes ahead of the Republican governor of Kansas; and in New York he had received 150,000 more votes than the U.S. Senate candidate (it turned out to be 300,000).

"I write you because I am quite anxious to be of assistance in the next few years in bringing the Republican Party to a viewpoint more representative of the times," wrote Willkie. "I do not believe that such objective can be accomplished if certain of the congressional leaders are misled into believing that the policies they had adopted would have won the election. I think any dispassionate analysis of the results will show that such is not the case. I appreciate that there is a very aggressive propaganda being carried on by certain leaders in the Republican Party to create the impression that the congressional record, if followed, would have won the election. With this I completely disagree and I think if you will apply your own analytical judgment to it, you will come to the same conclusion.

"I am sorry to bother you so much about this," Willkie concluded, "but I really am quite anxious about this not because I have any future political ambitions but because I think it would be almost tragic if the Republican Party falls back into old-guard reactionaries in the belief that it could have won if that had been its program in 1940."[34]

Visiting Willkie in Florida, Gerard Lambert confessed to the defeated candidate that he had "deliberately lied" about the outcome of the election, for he had known that FDR would win the election but had not wanted to upset Willkie before his final speeches. "He smiled," Lambert wrote later, "and said that if I would remember, he in turn had told me he thought he would win, but he was lying too, because he knew he wouldn't."[35]

In late November, he took a one-day break from his vacation and addressed the National Interfraternity Conference in New York. Showing good humor, he talked about his recent political defeat. "I recently received a letter from a friend of mine down in Mississippi," Willkie began, straight-faced, "and he was complaining about the outcome of the election. He said that if every county in the United States had shown the same percentage of increase for the Republican candidate his county did, 'you would have been overwhelmingly elected. In 1936, the Republican candidate in this county received two votes. In 1940,' he said, 'you received three.' "

On a more somber note, Willkie expressed regret that politicians "on both sides" had "abandoned dispassionate discussion" in the 1940 campaign "and some of them engaged in pure vilification and personal abuse." Willkie said democracy could function "satisfactorily and effectively," only if the channels of public discussion were kept "completely open" and free from ad hominem attacks. During the weeks ahead, he promised to devote his efforts to the elevation of public discussion in America.

He sounded very much like the forthright man of the previous spring. "We must continue to help the fighting men of Britain to preserve that rim of freedom which is gradually shrinking and which, if we permit it to continue to shrink, will shrink to the edge of our own shores."

In closing, he stressed the importance of national unity. Then, holding his wineglass high in the air in a sweeping gesture, Wendell

L. Willkie brought his audience of thirty-six hundred people roaring and applauding to their feet as he proposed a toast "to the health and happiness of the President of the United States."

Some took up the chant, "We still want Willkie!" In the White House, FDR told his son Jimmy, "I'm happy I've won, but I'm sorry Wendell lost."[36]

First Lieutenant Willkie, 1918.

Russell Davenport quit as *Fortune*'s managing editor and launched Willkie's bid for the 1940 Republican nomination. Colorado Springs, Colorado, July 1940.

Irita Van Doren.

Willkie supporters in the gallery learn that New York has switched from Dewey. The "We Want Willkie" chant was deafening in Convention Hall, Philadelphia, June 1940. REPUBLICAN NATIONAL COMMITTEE

In a display of GOP unity, Willkie and 1936 presidential nominee Alf M. Landon shake hands on the Philadelphia podium. REPUBLICAN NATIONAL COMMITTEE

Willkie impressed FDR in selecting Senator Charles L. McNary as his running mate, for the Democratic President had talked privately about inviting McNary to join him on a wartime fusion ticket. REPUBLICAN NATIONAL COMMITTEE

Showered with confetti, Willkie and his wife make a triumphant appearance at Philadelphia's Convention Hall. U.P.I.

Senators Robert A. Taft (left) and Arthur H. Vandenberg congratulated Willkie after he defeated them for the 1940 presidential nomination. REPUBLICAN NATIONAL COMMITTEE

Willkie's western vacation in 1940 provided a colorful backdrop, but his advisors thought it cost him momentum. Here he is at Cheyenne, Wyoming. U.P.I.

Rushville, Indiana, cheers its renowned son-in-law, August 1940. U.P.I.

Willkie banters with the press. REPUBLICAN NATIONAL COMMITTEE

Senators Robert A. Taft (left) and Arthur H. Vandenberg congratulated Willkie after he defeated them for the 1940 presidential nomination. REPUBLICAN NATIONAL COMMITTEE

Willkie's western vacation in 1940 provided a colorful backdrop, but his advisors thought it cost him momentum. Here he is at Cheyenne, Wyoming. U.P.I.

Rushville, Indiana, cheers its renowned son-in-law, August 1940. U.P.I.

Willkie banters with the press. REPUBLICAN NATIONAL COMMITTEE

Willkie and King George VI of England at Buckingham Palace, 1941.
BRITISH INFORMATION SERVICE

On his return from England, Willkie testified in favor of lend-lease before the Senate Foreign Relations Committee. WIDE WORLD PHOTOS

In Iran, Willkie lunched with the youthful Shah, Muhammad Riza Pahlavi. INDIANA UNIVERSITY

Much to the discomfort of his traveling companions, Willkie was captivated by Madame Chiang Kai-shek and proposed bringing her back to the United States on their return flight. Chungking, 1942. WIDE WORLD PHOTOS

Ending his 1944 comeback in Omaha in April, after a crushing defeat in the Wisconsin primary, Willkie insisted he had no regrets about his effort. WIDE WORLD PHOTOS

CHAPTER THIRTEEN

THE POLITICS OF WAR

Wendell L. Willkie had just lost the presidency, yet he remained a youthful and vital national figure. At the age of forty-eight, his future could not have looked more promising. More than anything in his life, his lost presidential campaign would shape and strengthen his character and contribute to his growth as a public man. Henry Cabot Lodge recalled, "Willkie was in a state of evolution–intellectually and in other ways." Gardner Cowles said Willkie had regretted bowing to expediency and became iron-willed in his determination to be absolutely forthright about every major political issue. Years later, John Morton Blum observed, "He had come close enough to the presidency to feel its great burdens."[1]

On Armistice Day, he delivered a national radio address from his political headquarters at the Commodore. He spoke not only to the 22 million people who had supported his candidacy but to the entire country. "In the campaign preceding this election," he said, "serious issues were at stake. People became bitter. Many things were said, which, in calmer moments, might have been left unsaid or might have been worded more thoughtfully. But we Americans know that the bitterness is a distortion, not a true reflection of what is in our hearts. I can truthfully say that there is no bitterness in mine. I hope there is none in yours. I was the target of most of the shafts and if I can forget, surely you can.

"We have elected Franklin Roosevelt, President," he went on. "He is your President. He is my President. We all of us owe him the respect due to his high office. We give him that respect. We will support him with the best efforts for our country. And we pray that God may guide his hand during the next four years in the supreme task of administering the affairs of the people."

This did not mean, however, that Willkie was making himself available for a position in a coalition government. Since the election, there had been feelers from the Roosevelt administration, and some political commentators had urged his appointment to a high federal position as a symbol of wartime unity. "An American president could fill his whole cabinet with leaders of the opposition party," he said, "and still our administration would not be a two-party administration. It would be an administration of a majority President giving orders to minority representatives of his own choosing. These representatives must concur in the President's convictions. If they do not, they have no alternative except to resign. . . . We, who stand ready to serve our country behind our Commander-in-Chief, nevertheless retain the right, and I will say the duty to debate the course of our government. Ours is a two-party system. Should we ever permit one party to dominate our lives entirely, democracy would collapse and we would have dictatorship.

"Ours is a very powerful opposition," he said, "let us not, therefore, fall into the partisan error of opposing things just for the sake of opposition. Ours must not be an opposition against–it must be an opposition for–an opposition for a strong America." He asked the Willkie Clubs to continue their political activity but under other names. "I do not want this great cause to be weakened," he said, "by even a semblance of any personal advantage to any individual. I feel too deeply about it for that. Nineteen forty-four will take care of itself."

In closing, Willkie said, "I want to see all of us dedicate ourselves to the principles for which we fought. My fight for those principles has just begun. I shall advocate them in the future as ardently and as confidently as I have in the past. As Woodrow Wilson once said, 'I would rather lose in a cause that I know some day will triumph than to triumph in a cause that I know some day will fail.' "

No other defeated presidential candidate had ever received such an avalanche of mail. In 1936 Landon received around 6,000 letters. One month after the election, Willkie had drawn 100,000. A majority of the letters came from women, pledged continued support for the defeated candidate, and were idealistic in tone. An Iowa newspaper publisher wrote, "This crusade must continue. You must be the leader." A precinct worker from Pasadena added, "There are thousands and thousands of people in every city and rural community who still think of themselves as Willkie crusaders." A Peoria barber wrote, "God be with you and give you strength to lead this army of millions who look to you as head of the Republican Party."

"A strong opposition party is needed here more than ever," wrote a tire dealer from Racine, Wisconsin, "and you must remain its leader. Twenty-two million think you're okay. Hold them fast. Four years is not so far away." A young San Mateo, California, mother said: "I would like to see you reorganize the Republican party and rid it of the old mossbacks and crooked politicians. Under a leadership such as yours, I think this could be done. If not, I would like to see a new party organized." A Springfield, Massachusetts secretary added: "Make the people of the country understand that Wendell Willkie is not stepping out of the picture. For myself, it will not matter who is in the White House . . . I love my country and I believe in you with all my heart."

Overwhelmed by the public's response, Willkie said his main regret was that it would be impossible to respond personally to each letter, but his secretarial pool was kept busy for weeks in the preparation of form letters. Most of the letters, Willkie said, were remarkably free of political dogma. "It might be that these people are striving for the simple things they learned in early school days," he said, "things, for example, like thrift, and work, and production and growth. The writing indicates something in the nature of spiritual revival."

U.S. News editor David Lawrence and former GOP National Chairman Hubert Work strongly urged him to become Republican National Chairman. If he took the chairmanship, Willkie would, Lawrence wrote, "become the most constructive minority voice the country has ever known." Willkie, however, thought the position would be too confining and helped persuade Martin to remain in the chairmanship.[2]

Willkie had less success in trying to keep Hamilton as executive director. Two days after the election, he told Hamilton in New York that he should have a vacation before returning to Washington and setting up permanent headquarters. "I told Wendell I was getting out of politics," said Hamilton, "and had come solely to express my regrets at the outcome of the election and to do him the courtesy of letting him know of my decision before writing Joe my formal letter of resignation." At the time of Hamilton's appointment, Willkie had assured him that it was for a four-year term at an annual salary of $25,000. Willkie asked if Hamilton was dissatisfied with the money or position. The former chairman replied that he was anxious to resume his law practice, but the real reason, which he tactfully did not mention, had been Willkie's removal of him from the chairmanship. "Willkie's refusal to accept me was ample evidence in my mind that the party would not accept the English theory of permanency of personnel in organizational activities," Hamilton wrote in his private memoir. "Had there been any evidence of a stable future in politics, I would have gladly remained in the organization."[3]

Raymond Clapper suggested in his column that Willkie ought to consider a new career as a college president, and he was plainly intrigued by this possibility. There was a good deal of alumni support for his appointment as president of Stanford University although a friend wrote that the trustees were concerned about whether he might use the office as a political springboard. "You may say to anyone, with full authority," he replied in December, "that I do not intend to devote my time to any form of organizational politics." Unconvinced, Stanford's trustees passed him over, for nearly everyone expected him to attempt a political comeback by 1944.

Even so, Willkie was flooded with offers from Wall Street law firms, blue-chip corporations, newspaper syndicates, and national magazines. He would eventually sift through more than two hundred offers of employment. Financially independent and still winding down from the campaign, he was in no hurry to make a career move, and it would be weeks before he reached a decision.

Already he was becoming conscious of the dangers of overexposure. "One thing I do not want to do," he wrote David Sarnoff, "is keep talking every few days. The people of the United States rapidly get weary of a man expressing his opinion on all kinds of subjects, particularly when he holds no official position."[4] Few presidential also-rans were confronted with such problems. Landon and John W. Davis had been quickly forgotten. Not since William Jennings Bryan's near-miss in 1896 had a defeated presidential candidate managed to hold the public's attention. Yet it was clear that Willkie would not fade from the national political scene.

A major factor in Willkie's durability was his favorable treatment by the press. Luce, Krock, the Cowles brothers, and the Reids were close personal friends, but it was not just management that had a special affection for Willkie. His popularity extended beyond the corner suites and into the newsrooms. He was always accessible to reporters and paid careful attention to their needs, taking many of them into his confidence with inside political gossip and information. He became a regular source to influential columnists Drew Pearson, Raymond Clapper, Marquis Childs, and Roscoe Drummond. Other prominent Republicans were clumsy in their dealings with the press, but Willkie had a magic touch. While his cultivation of the press worked to his political benefit, it was not contrived. He genuinely liked reporters and they liked him.

Early in 1941, Childs organized a dinner for Willkie in Washington with the correspondents who had followed his campaign. "On such an occasion, Willkie is at his best," Childs said. "His talk is frank and uninhibited, salted with his convictions and prejudices freely and bluntly expressed. He loves it, talking with men in a room through a long and convivial evening." William L. Shirer, then a CBS war correspondent, had been among a group of journalistic luminaries invited to separate *Herald Tribune* lunches with Dewey and Willkie. Dewey struck them as cold and insensitive, and the roomful of reporters sat in silence as he droned on. When Willkie came a few days later, he sat down and asked questions through the lunch hour and into the evening. "Before we knew it," said Shirer, "it was midnight. Willkie was a guy who had what so many politicians lack—intellectual curiosity."

Indeed, Bill Lawrence once observed that "a really great reporter" was lost when Willkie went into law rather than journalism.[5] So many of his friends were newspapermen that Willkie himself would have liked nothing more than to have joined their fraternity and came close to doing just that. In the meantime, he served as a talent scout for his publisher friends. Following the 1940 campaign, he recommended Lawrence, then a twenty-four-year-old United Press reporter, to the Cowles brothers as well as Krock and Arthur Hays Sulzberger of the New York *Times*. Both of the news organizations were responsive to Willkie's suggestion and came through with offers. Lawrence chose the *Times,* where he became one of the most respected political reporters of his generation. "We got to know Willkie intimately," Lawrence recalled. "In my case, he became a friend for life, and a kind of public relations man for me."

In his dealings with the press, he performed countless favors and services. When United Press correspondent Joe Alex Morris sought to return home from London, Willkie contacted Secretary of State Hull about getting him on a special charter. He represented Turner Catledge in his negotiations to become managing editor of the Chicago *Sun*. A longtime friend, Associated Press foreign correspondent Eddy Gilmore, asked for his help when Soviet officials were set to exile his Russian girl friend to Siberia. Appealing directly to Stalin, Willkie blocked the proceedings. "I never thought of myself as a cupid before," he said, "but, on reflection, I don't see why I am not qualified."

Following the election, Willkie resumed his relationship with Van Doren. "I am very much pleased and relieved that you did not think my recent political activities void me from the list," Willkie wrote from Hobe Sound. "Maybe you will even let me review another book for you." Willkie and Van Doren gave a dinner for members of his campaign staff at her West Side apartment, which FDR thought was politically risky because his defeated rival was still in the limelight. Willkie, however, had no such inhibitions and invited numerous journalists to Van Doren's, including Robert Kintner, Joseph Alsop, and Shirer. He teased Van Doren about Dorothy Thompson's switch to Roosevelt. "I am still chuckling over Dorothy. I recall how you jumped on me when I told you some time ago that Dorothy's motivation was a desire to ride the winner. Someday you will have faith in me."[6] Because of Van Doren, he remained Thompson's friend. At a *Herald Tribune* forum, the Republican audience was booing Miss Thompson when Willkie, the featured speaker, walked across the hall and warmly embraced her. Soon after the election, Van Doren invited Thompson for dinner with Willkie.

During his six weeks in Florida, Willkie made the determination that military aid to Britain should become his next political cause. It would be the most fateful decision of his public career. The President introduced the Lend-Lease Act, a military aid program designed to circumvent neutrality legislation and provide weaponry "to the government of any country whose defense the President deems vital to the defense of the United States." A number of Willkie's prominent backers in the 1940 campaign were pressing him to continue attacking FDR as a warmonger. Nearly the entire leadership of his party was aligned in opposition to lend-lease.

Publisher Roy Howard, with whom Willkie had worked closely in the campaign, telephoned and told him lend-lease gave him an opportunity to expose FDR "as a dictator." Willkie said he needed time to carefully study the legislation. A few minutes later, the Scripps-Howard executive called back and offered to help with the preparation of Willkie's "blast." There wasn't going to be any blast from him, he replied. Even though Willkie thought lend-lease granted wider presidential authority than he felt was necessary, he supported its overall objectives. Following this conversation, Howard telephoned a third time and boasted that Landon and Hoover had joined him in opposition and he was drafting their statements. Willkie said he would have something to say in a few days.[7]

The President compared his program to lending a garden hose to a neighbor whose house was on fire. Senator Taft countered, "Lending war equipment is a good deal like lending chewing gum. You don't want it back." The Chicago *Tribune* labeled it "the war dictatorship bill." Senator McNary came out against lend-lease because it gave "extraordinary and total power to one person." Senator Burton K. Wheeler claimed it "will plow under every fourth American boy." Senator Vandenberg asserted that it gave FDR authority "to make undeclared war on any country he pleases at any time he pleases." Lend-lease, said Dewey, "would bring an end to free government in the U.S."

In a letter to Robert S. Allen, Willkie wrote, "I remained silent after the campaign for a couple of months, making only off the record talks about my views, but when Messrs Hoover, Landon, Dewey, Taft and Vandenberg all came out in a frontal assault on the Lend-Lease Bill, I thought I owed a duty to speak for it."[8]

On January 13, 1941, he announced his support of lend-lease. "Under such dire circumstances," Willkie said, "extraordinary powers must be granted to the elected executive. Democracy cannot hope to defend itself in any other way." He favored some minor revisions, Willkie said, including an amendment that underscored congressional authority to declare war. "The United States is not a belligerent, and we hope shall not be. Our problem, however, is not alone to keep America out of war, but to keep war out of America." He berated critics of FDR's program. "Appeasers, isolationists, or lip-service friends of Britain will seek to sabotage the program of aid to Britain and her allies behind the screen of opposition to this bill."

That was not all. Willkie disclosed that he would soon be going to England for a firsthand look at the war. He had telephoned Secretary of State Hull and received permission for a passport, and FDR had invited him to the White House before his departure. Even before Willkie approached Hull, the President had been hoping to send him to England. In a meeting with British intelligence agent William Stephenson, Roosevelt had asked if he could make some gesture to hearten the English. "What could be better," Stephenson replied, "than sending Mr. Wendell Willkie, your opponent in the recent bitter elections." The President immediately liked the idea. "Roosevelt felt," said Frances Perkins, "that the leader of the opposition party would carry more reassurance than a political friend of the President's." At a New Year's party, FDR's confidant, Justice Felix Frankfurter and publisher Harold Guinzburg made the suggestion to Van Doren. "We broached the idea to Irita," wrote Frankfurter, "that Willkie could profitably make a trip to England as a means of putting himself in a position to reply, on the basis of firsthand knowledge, to the Republican isolationists who are ganging up on him."[9] Van Doren passed on Frankfurter's proposal and Willkie was receptive.

Willkie said later that he decided to make the trip while working on a speech about aid to Britain. "In the course of my writing," he wrote Robert Allen, "I became conscious that there were certain points which I was making which were perhaps beyond my knowledge. The thought then flashed through my mind, why don't I go to England and find out?"[10] Helen Reid and Geoffrey Parsons, of the *Herald Tribune,* and John Cowles were consulted, and all recommended that he make the trans-Atlantic journey. He invited Cowles to accompany him, and the Minnesota editor promptly accepted.

Over breakfast, Willkie informed his wife of his planned journey. "I'm going to England," he told her, "because thousands of people keep asking me personally and by letter what I think of the whole situation abroad. I want to see for myself, so I can have an honest answer that's my own. A lot of persons probably will shout that it's a grandstand play and blame me for a theatrical gesture. But I can't help that. I'm going to see for myself."

Joe Martin opposed the trip because it would be politically exploited by Willkie's enemies in the GOP. "I wouldn't take it," he told Willkie. "What are you going to get out of it? You can't do anything over there."

"I can see the debris from the bombing and conditions of the war," said Willkie.

"Well, sure you can see *that,*" he agreed.

"Anyhow," Willkie said, "I'm going."

"I wouldn't do it," Martin argued. "You stand in pretty well now as the head of the loyal opposition. All I can say is that Roosevelt is just trying to win you over. This won't be well received by the Republicans."[11]

From the moment he endorsed lend-lease and announced his trip, Willkie's leadership in the Republican party was strongly disputed. Senator Warren Austin, Massachusetts Governor Leverett Saltonstall, and Oregon Governor Charles A. Sprague were among the few prominent GOP officials who sided with him. Senator Taft declared that he no longer spoke for the party. "There is no essential difference between Mr. Willkie's position and Mr. Roosevelt's position," stated Landon, "which is to go to war if necessary to help England win. If Mr. Willkie had revealed it before the Republican National Convention, he would not have been nominated." The Chicago *Daily News,* published by Navy Secretary Frank Knox, Landon's former running mate, claimed that it was "precisely because Willkie's views were known and coincided with the views of a majority of Republicans, that he won the nomination over his faint-minded rivals." Colonel McCormick's Chicago *Tribune* assailed him as a turncoat and read him out of the party. Senator Arthur Capper wrote Landon, "Willkie does not speak for me and I don't believe he voices the wishes of the Republicans of the Middle West."[12]

"Willkie's statement and his subsequent trip to England," John D. M. Hamilton wrote to a GOP leader, "resulted in a breach between himself and the Republican members of Congress, which, in my opinion, is irreparable. . . . Out of the 190-odd Republican members of the House and Senate, Willkie couldn't dig up ten friends if his life depended upon it."[13]

On the night of his lend-lease announcement, Willkie accepted Roy Howard's dinner invitation. The diminutive Howard and Bruce Barton spent much of the evening attempting to talk Willkie into not making his trip. "All the time and effort I have spent on helping you has been wasted," the publisher told him. By supporting lend-lease, he went on, Willkie had missed "the biggest chance in his life." Barton told Willkie he was an ingrate. When Willkie insisted he was going through with his plans, Howard snapped that his newspapers would "tear your reputation to shreds" and "break" him. "If Howard wasn't such a little pipsqueak," Willkie later told Frankfurter, "I'd have felt like knocking him down."

The vain, petty Howard declared open season on Willkie in his chain's news columns. General Hugh Johnson, Howard's hatchet man, denounced him as a "Hoosier hick." When leading advertisers complained about the assault on Willkie, Howard sought a reconciliation with his onetime friend. "I know you wouldn't want to injure me," the publisher told Willkie and offered to see him off at La Guardia Airport in full view of newsreel cameras. Willkie declined.

On January 15, Willkie discussed his upcoming trip during dinner at Van Doren's apartment with Justice Frankfurter, Guinzburg, and Dorothy Thompson. "I hadn't seen Willkie since before the campaign," Frankfurter wrote in his diary. "He still strikes me as an unusually honest, attractive fellow, on the right side in general, not at all an intellectual, sometimes a bit naive, but thoroughly admirable and likeable."

Willkie confided that a wealthy isolationist, Jeremiah Milbank, had offered to put up $2 million for him to use for radio and personal expenses if he would lead the campaign against aid to Britain. He also disclosed that he had been approached in Florida by Verne Marshall, the Cedar Rapids, Iowa editor, and William Rhodes Davis, the Nazi-tinged oil mogul, who urged him to consider supporting a negotiated peace with Hitler. It was with these men in mind that Willkie made the link between isolationists and appeasers in his lend-lease statement.

He said that business and political associates were suggesting that he also go to Germany to see whether he "couldn't fix things up," or possibly make a tour of France "to report on the need for food." Frankfurter told Willkie that he "would come under great suspicion if he were to try to visit Germany, and that there wasn't any use in visiting France, which is not an international factor in its own right at the present time." Willkie said that he had never seriously considered going anywhere except England.[14]

In a parting shot at his critics, Willkie told the National Women's Republican Club: "Let me say to you, that if the Republican Party in this year of 1941 makes a blind opposition to this bill and allows itself to be presented to the American people as the isolationist party, it will never again gain control of the American government. I beg of you, I plead with you, you people who believe as I do in our great system of government, please do not in blind opposition, do not because of hate of an individual—and of all persons in the United States I have least cause to hold a brief for him—forget the critical world situation which confronts us."

On the night before FDR's third inaugural, he received Willkie at the White House. For the first time, they were meeting as allies rather than adversaries and FDR proposed their wartime cooperation. Roosevelt joked that he wished "Wendell" would be taking the oath in the cold instead of himself. "When I'm over there where the excitement is, you'll wish you were me, too," Willkie replied. "At regular intervals," Jimmy Roosevelt said, "great bursts of laughter could be heard coming through the closed doors." FDR's secretary Grace Tully recalled, "It was clear to me that the two men enjoyed being together." "The President," Willkie said later, "was obviously trying to make me feel that we were buddies." Perkins wrote, "The interesting thing is that he took an immediate liking to Willkie and he hadn't expected to."[15]

Discussing Willkie's trip, FDR helpfully suggested that he might confer with Averell Harriman, who had just been assigned to London to help coordinate American military aid shipments. "You'll like Averell," said the President. "He contributed to our campaign, you know." Embarrassed, Roosevelt said he had not meant to boast about his political contributors, but he had been appreciative of Harriman's help.

"Oh, that's all right," Willkie grinned. "Harriman did contribute to *our* campaign. Harriman gave me money for my pre-convention campaign before I got the nomination, but then he contributed to your election campaign."[16]

Roosevelt indicated he was naming former New Hampshire Governor John G. Winant, a New Deal Republican, as ambassador to England partly because he anticipated a "social revolution" over there after the war. Some British Tories were alarmed when prominent New Dealer Benjamin V. Cohen was appointed as Winant's legal adviser.

The President asked that Willkie get together in London with

Harry Hopkins, his closest aide, who was supervising the implementation of lend-lease. Willkie promised to meet Hopkins but asked FDR why he had retained the frail adviser in view of his unpopularity with so many politicians. "Some day you may well be sitting here where I am now as President of the United States," he said. "And when you are, you'll be looking at that door over there and knowing that practically everybody who walks through it wants something out of you. You'll realize what a lonely job that is, and you'll discover the need for somebody like Harry Hopkins who asks for nothing except to serve you."[17]

Roosevelt handed Willkie a letter for Churchill addressed to "a former naval person," a reference to the Prime Minister's World War I service as First Lord of the Admiralty. "Wendell Willkie will give you this," FDR wrote, "he is truly helping to keep politics out over here." The President added, in his own handwriting, Longfellow's verse, which, he said, "applies to you as it does to us."

Sail on, O Ship of State!
Sail on, O Union strong and great!
Humanity with all its fears,
With all the hopes of future years,
Is hanging breathless on thy fate!

Soon afterward, the President told Secretary Perkins that he felt Willkie could make a major contribution to wartime unity. "You know, he is a very good fellow," said FDR. "He has lots of talent. I want to use him somehow." Perkins said Roosevelt thought Willkie's mission would be invaluable in the development of a bipartisan foreign policy. "For a long time," she said, "it had been clear in Roosevelt's mind that our foreign policy, with the possibility that we might have to enter the war, must not be the province of one party or a President, but the conviction of both parties and their leaders. Roosevelt knew that Willkie's trip would help toward unity."[18]

The President later told Ickes that while liking Willkie, he wondered about his judgment. "In this connection he mentioned the name of Mrs. Van Doren, who everybody says was Willkie's mistress until he became an active candidate. The President said, incredible as it might seem, Willkie, after the election gave a dinner to some of the most important people in his campaign and that this dinner was given in Mrs. Van Doren's home. There might be some interesting complications if Mrs. Van Doren insisted on returning to her present status as mistress, if, at the same time, Mrs. Willkie should refuse to be pushed into the background."[19]

If Roosevelt had attempted to give Willkie advice about his personal life, it would have had little impact. After the year apart during the campaign, Willkie had eagerly resumed his relationship with Van Doren. But, so long as he was politically active, it was unthinkable to change his marital status.

His Washington visit, though brief, stirred considerable excitement. In the lobby of the Carlton, several hundred people mobbed him as he came downstairs to greet Secretary of State Hull. Even at the White House, he was the focus of attention. Eleanor Roosevelt said, "The household was so anxious to get a glimpse of him while he sat waiting in Franklin's study on the second floor that suddenly many people had errands that took them down the hall. I would have gone myself, but I didn't hear of his visit until Franklin told me of it later."[20]

On January 22, he loped down the pontoon walkway at La Guardia Airport, stepped aboard Pan American's *Yankee Clipper* and was off for England. "His journey captured the imagination of people on both sides of the Atlantic," wrote Childs. "It was the most brilliant stroke he had made since Philadelphia."[21] What made Willkie's trip so extraordinary was its wartime backdrop and the fact that leading political figures did not engage in shuttle diplomacy in this bygone era. Senator McNary, who had much influence in foreign affairs as the GOP leader, had never traveled abroad. Nor, for that matter, had the late William E. Borah, who built a reputation as the Senate's most knowledgeable authority on world affairs. Not since Woodrow Wilson had an American President crossed the Atlantic while in office. FDR had not been in a plane since his 1932 flight to Chicago when he accepted the Democratic presidential nomination, and it would be two years before he flew into a war zone.

"I want to find out all I can about everything I can," Willkie wrote Robert Allen a few days before his departure. "An overall notion of my objective is to see what I can learn in England to help me in advocating the cause of increasing American aid to Britain." Willkie said he was especially interested in meeting with Ernest Bevin and other representatives of labor. "I have a feeling that the social developments in England will at least to a certain extent, set the pattern of American social conditions following the war."[22]

After brief stops in the Azores and Portugal, Willkie arrived in London four days after leaving New York. "I am here as Wendell Willkie," he announced. "I am representing no one. I am very glad to be here in England, for whose cause I have the utmost sympathy. I want to do all I can to get the United States to give England the utmost aid possible in her struggle for free men all over the world."

Willkie soon heard the hail of German bombs. For more than five months, the Nazi Luftwaffe had rained destruction on London. During the first four months of the Blitz, more than thirty thousand people were killed or severely wounded. One thousand German bombers and fighters pounded the city's docks, rail terminals, factories, gas works, and neighborhoods. For fifty-seven consecutive nights, the Nazis bombed London, and they also struck in the daytime. On the night of December 29, 1940, it appeared that the entire city was engulfed by flames. Churchill would admit years later that he feared that London "except for its strong modern buildings, would gradually and soon be reduced to a rubble heap." Other cities were even more devastated than London. In the middle of November, Germans wiped out seventy thousand homes in Coventry and destroyed historic Coventry Cathedral.

Throughout the Blitz, more than a third of London's people were forced to live in shelters and underground stations. The shriek of falling bombs, warning sirens, breaking glass, and the screams of the dying were all part of wartime London. "The individual's reaction to the sound of falling bombs cannot be described," said Edward R. Murrow. "The moan of stark terror and suspense cannot be encompassed by words, no more than can the sense of relief when you realize that you were not where that one fell."

On Willkie's first night in London, his voice cracked with emotion in visiting five underground shelters amidst the blast of explosions and falling incendiary bombs. "I have been through four or five shelters," he told a packed air-raid shelter audience. "I've seen probably several thousand people. I haven't seen one that was afraid." Later, he said, "I never saw such spirit. It was a great emotional experience. I exchanged greetings with hundreds of people and they all seemed so brave and calm I had to turn my head away once or twice." In another shelter, he rasped, "I'm a tough old egg, I think. But this moves me very deeply. I am almost spilling over."

When Churchill heard that his American visitor had been walking through London without a steel hat during a Nazi air attack, he immediately sent Willkie six white helmets and three gas masks. At each stop, Willkie was instantly recognized as he descended into the shelters. "He's the fellow in the white hat," some Englishmen shouted as he made an appearance at the Ministry of Home Security.

As Willkie made his way into another shelter, an old man with a harmonica played "The Star-Spangled Banner" and the Londoners began singing America's national anthem. One seventy-year-old man told Willkie he was prepared to sleep underground forever "if it would help win the war." Slapping the big American on his back, a woman told him, "Go home, and tell them we can take it." At Mickey's Shelter, in the borough of Stepney, which had been built for five thousand people, he saw nearly twice that many crowded into the large room. It was said at the time that there were no civilians in London, and he had seen more than enough evidence to support that claim.

Willkie was a person who responded to such visceral experiences. Foreign Secretary Anthony Eden later told Frankfurter, "I saw a great deal of him when he first came to London. We had a pleasant time but he was full of doubts and worries and criticisms. Then he went off by himself to see the English men and women, and it is that experience that stirred in him the feelings that he afterward expressed about the people in England."[23]

With bombs crashing outside, Willkie listened to a Labor member of Parliament denouncing the Churchill government in the House of Commons for its suppression of the *Daily Worker*. "It was the most dramatic example of democracy at work anyone could wish to see," he said later. "Here Britain is fighting a war for her life. Yet a free House meets and the people can get up and denounce the administration." At St. Paul's Cathedral, a church official presented him with a fragment of an incendiary bomb that had landed on Christopher Wren's dome and burned itself out. He was appalled by the destruction in London's book row, where three million volumes burned from Nazi flames.

Soon after his arrival in London, Willkie was grief-stricken to learn of Kenneth F. Simpson's death. Earlier in the month, Willkie and his political ally had conferred on lend-lease, and the congressman had introduced an amendment which incorporated the suggested revisions on legislative authority and a time limit for the presidential emergency powers. The New York GOP organization offered Willkie the nomination for Simpson's seat in Congress. "Not interested," he cabled Thomas J. Curran, New York Republican chairman.[24] Though he would have been an overwhelming favorite in the special election, Willkie felt that he had much greater influence as national party spokesman than would be the case if he were a freshman minority member in the House of Representatives. Without holding public office, he had managed to capture the presidential nomination and was considered a strong contender for another. It had been sixty years since a congressman had been elected to the presidency, and that was the only political office Willkie really wanted.

In his conversations with Churchill, Willkie was told that what England wanted from the United States was not troops but technicians and tools. The Prime Minister expressed confidence that the island would survive the Blitz. England's greatest danger, he told Willkie, was that Nazi submarines and dive bombers had the capacity to cut its supply lines. On his return, Willkie said he would urge that fifty more destroyers be sent. Churchill gave Willkie an official luncheon at 10 Downing Street and later had him as an overnight guest at Checquers, his country estate. In his memoirs, Churchill recalled "a long talk with this most able and forceful man."

When Churchill mentioned that his staff had been unable to find out the author of the poem FDR had sent him, Willkie informed him that it was Longfellow. In a dramatic wartime speech, the Prime Minister gave this public reply: "What is the answer that I shall give, in your name, to this great man, the thrice-chosen head of a nation of 130 million? Here is the answer which I will give to President Roosevelt. Put your confidence in us. Give us your faith and your blessing and under Providence all will be well. We shall not fail or falter. We shall not weaken or tire. Neither the sudden shock of battle nor the long-drawn trials or vigilance and exertion will wear us down. Give us the tools and we will finish the job."

Willkie had been greatly impressed by Churchill's intellect and force of personality. Addressing a trade union group, he paid tribute to the Prime Minister's "dauntless courage" and "inspirational leadership." Privately, he suggested that Churchill was too rigidly conservative to provide effective leadership once the war was over. At a party given at the Dorchester Hotel by Rebecca West, Willkie spoke candidly about Churchill. "Mr. Willkie went on to say how greatly he had been impressed by the Prime Minister, and what a grand leader he was for a country to have in times like these," wrote a Foreign Office official. "He was not so sure, however, that Mr. Churchill would be so valuable a leader when it came to the postwar period and economic adjustments and reconstruction were necessary." The official noted with disapproval that Willkie's comments were applauded and called it "a dreadful lack of stage management" for the visitor to be exposed to "argumentative intelligentsia."[25]

In Willkie's view, the dinner with leading English writers had been a highlight of his trip. "Most people liked him very much," Rebecca West wrote in 1981. "I also remember he complained that somebody else's dinner party was too frivolous." Willkie and Miss West sent Van Doren a series of cablegrams. "Everybody in England is amazed at my youthful appearance," the forty-eight-year-old Willkie cabled on January 29. The next day he added, "Impressions of youth persist despite every effort to play down." Following the dinner, he cabled, "Miss Rebecca West authorizes me to say to you that her deliberate judgment of my age is 42 as ever."[26]

Churchill wrote in his memoirs that "every arrangement was made by us, with the assistance of the enemy, to let him see all he desired of London at bay."[27] He visited with Lord Beaverbrook, Minister of Aircraft Production; Ernest Bevin, Minister of Labor; Clement R. Attlee, Lord Privy Seal; and Sir Kingsley Wood, Chancellor of the Exchequer. With A. V. Alexander, First Lord of the Admiralty, he looked through the British Admiralty's secret map room. He inspected airplane factories, chemical works, hospitals, and fire stations. On the heavily bombed South Side, he was mobbed by Cockneys and drank tea with the crowd. A policeman noted, "He autographed everything from a package of tea to a ukulele." Willkie hopped on a bicycle and pedaled down the street with the crowd following. When a police unit attempted to break up the crowd, Willkie waved them aside. "We don't need the cops," he said. "Everything's dandy." He nearly got ejected from a double-decker bus when he paused by the fare box to look for the correct change, not knowing that London passengers give their fare to the conductor after taking their seat. "Get on or off," conductor Theresa Bowers said, and Willkie good-naturedly rushed to a seat.

At the Old Chesterfield Arms, a pub in Shepherd's Market, he ordered a pint of beer and bought a round of drinks for a party of soldiers. He was challenged to a game of darts by Albert Phillips, a demolition squad worker, scoring a double with his first shot but losing the match. "He was a nice fellow," said Willkie, "but he was too hot for me—and he knew the rules." Word of the American visitor's presence spread quickly and the pub was soon crowded. The bartender showed Willkie how to work the handles which drew beer up from the cellar, and he stepped behind the bar and helped serve drinks to Chesterfield regulars. The pub's owner brought out a bottle of champagne which he had been saving for the armistice and said Willkie's visit was reason enough to celebrate. "He stood as a Republican," said an Irish soldier, "but he's the best Democrat I ever met."

Splashing through the mud along the English Channel, he viewed the coastal defenses and watched antiaircraft guns open fire on Luftwaffe planes. He talked with troops and joked with Americans serving in the British forces. In Liverpool he stood on the docks with a large crowd as a fifteen-ship convoy arrived from the United States. "Good old Willkie," shouted dockworkers and he moved into the crowd to visit with them.

In Manchester, several thousand people gathered outside his hotel and cheered until he made an appearance on his balcony. Later, he walked through the ruins of homes and the mud of demolition sites in areas of the city hit hardest by the Germans. At each stop, he talked with residents, demolition workers, and young people. When a woman rushed up to him with a bottle of beer, he drank it. Hundreds of people shook his hand although police attempted to keep the crowds back a short distance. "He frequently stopped men, women and children whom he casually encountered while seeing some sections of the city which had been most seriously damaged by the German air raids," reported American Consul George Tait. "He expressed surprise when he saw the extent of the indiscriminate damage and destruction wrought."

"I am certain now," Willkie said, "that this country is united in an unbelievable way. No other nation in the world could have been so united in a cause as you are. I do not divide people into classes. You do. But it has been the same wherever I have gone—you are united. I have asked individuals in your different groups, and you are all the same now."

A message was handed to him that German radio had advised the people of Manchester to demonstrate against his visit. "That's amusing, isn't it," said Willkie. "If they have demonstrated, they have not been successful in the way Germany would want."

For Willkie, the motorcades and boisterous crowds were reminiscent of his campaign tour. "He received a most enthusiastic and cordial welcome from the entire city," Tait reported from Manchester. "Large crowds turned out and frequently waited for considerable periods of time along the route which it was anticipated and hoped he would follow."[28] In Conventry hundreds of men and women waited for more than an hour to catch a glimpse of Willkie in front of City Hall. Walking through the ruins of the great cathedral, he said that the damage inflicted by the Nazis had exceeded his expectations. "Your sacrifice was worthwhile," he said, "because of the confidence it gave our people in you. Any totalitarian attack, either in America or Britain will fail against the brotherhood of this country and the United States."

In a private airplane, he flew to Dublin and talked for ninety minutes with Irish Prime Minister Eamon De Valera. The State Department and Churchill had been apprehensive about Willkie's meeting with the old revolutionary.[29] Willkie, noting America's close bond with the Irish people, urged De Valera to consider modifying his policy of neutrality and opening the coastline for lend-lease bases. In the event of a German invasion, De Valera acknowledged he would probably seek British help, but until then he would not permit Churchill to use Irish ports and bases against the Nazi counterblockade. Even though Willkie's efforts were fruitless, he was of the opinion that it had been a constructive meeting. The American embassy shared this view. "Whatever may have been Mr. Willkie's motives in coming to Ireland," an official wrote Hull, "I feel that it has turned out well for us. I am in fact unable to explain Mr. De Valera's cordiality and apparent desire to receive Mr. Willkie, unless it is his cryptic way of signaling the inauguration of a more pro-Ally line of policy."[30]

Willkie later confided to Robert Kintner that he had been "brutally frank" in telling De Valera that Ireland's special relationship with the United States would be jeopardized unless the Dublin government cooperated with London against the Germans. De Valera referred to the seven-hundred-year-old struggle between Ireland and England, and Willkie interrupted that neither of them could do anything about that situation under present conditions. And when De Valera lamented that England had isolated Irish Catholics in the northern counties from southern Ireland, Willkie said that problem would have to be deferred in view of the war. Willkie told De Valera that it was "foolish" to think that Ireland could remain out of the war by remaining neutral, saying that Hitler might strike its coastline at any time. De Valera complained that England had not supplied the weapons that Ireland had hoped for. "Of course not," said Willkie. Nor, he added, should any help be expected unless De Valera made a conciliatory gesture.

On Willkie's return from Ireland, he was met at the London airport by the King's secretary and driven by limousine to Buckingham Palace. There, he chatted with King George VI and Queen Elizabeth. He joked with the Queen about the isolationist politics of former Ambassador Kennedy and told her that she was "doing a better job on me than on another person." Elizabeth retorted, "Well, Mr. Willkie, it wasn't because I didn't try on him."[31] During the meeting, one of the King's uniformed footmen grabbed John Cowles's sleeve and timidly asked if he could get Willkie's autograph. Cowles said he was certain Willkie would be glad to sign his name for him. But when Willkie came out of the King's apartment, the footman was too shy to approach him and Cowles had to stop Willkie to get the signature.

He addressed the German people over a British Broadcasting Corporation transmitter, noting that his ancestors had fled Germany to escape political repression. "I am proud of my German blood," he said, "but I hate aggression and tyranny. Tell the German people that my convictions are shared to the full by the overwhelming majority of my fellow countrymen of German descent. They, too, believe in freedom and human rights." British planes and the German underground were dropping leaflets of his speech throughout Germany. Although the Nazi press claimed that Willkie could not even speak for his own political party, Propaganda Minister Joseph Goebbels was sufficiently concerned to make the false allegation that Willkie's grandfather had left Germany when a Jewish neighbor cheated him out of his inheritance.

Meeting with Harry Hopkins in London, Willkie pledged to throw his full effort into the lend-lease debate on his return. "Last night I saw Wendell Willkie," Hopkins cabled FDR. "He told me that he believes the opposition to Lend-Lease is going to be vehemently expressed and it should not be underrated under any circumstances. It is his belief that the main campaign against the bill will be directed from Chicago and heavily financed. As perhaps he told you it's his opinion that Herbert Hoover is the real brains behind this opposition. Willkie said he hoped that you would make a radio speech, preferably from Chicago, and thereby take your case right to the people. He said that he himself might make some speeches after he returns home in about two weeks. He said that he approved the bill with some amendments but did not specify what they were. He is receiving all the attentions which the British know so well how to provide for distinguished guests."[32]

With the outcome of the lend-lease vote far from certain, the Roosevelt administration took up Willkie on his offer. Secretary of State Hull cabled him in Dublin and requested that he cut short his journey in order to testify before the Senate Foreign Relations Committee's hearings on lend-lease.[33] Anticipating Willkie's response, the State Department had made special arrangements with Pan American for his return flight. He promptly agreed to come home. When it was announced that he was returning to testify in Washington, Willkie received a telegram from a leader of the isolationist America First threatening that his reputation "would be the subject of debasement in every town in America."

On February 5, Willkie and his party left England. His trip had been acclaimed a personal triumph. Admiring Londoners nicknamed him the "Indiana Dynamo." *The Times* of London, pronouncing him the most interesting American public figure in thirty years, with the exception of FDR, said, "Everywhere and with everyone he has left the impression of sincerity, friendship, boundless energy and radiant high spirits which has been most heartening." Mark Sullivan wrote that Willkie's diplomatic mission had been "more stirring to national interest than any journey ever taken by any other American in public life." In the White House, Roosevelt gave Willkie high marks for his effort. "Many people thought Roosevelt would be jealous of the attention Willkie got," said Frances Perkins. "I watched him closely, and I am sure he wasn't. He was pleased with the effect Willkie had in England, and it was a considerable effect."[34]

His return trip took five days. From London, he flew to Lisbon and boarded Pan American's *Dixie Clipper*. The flight from Portugal to New York was over an experimental route of 7,459 miles, twice the distance of the direct route via the Azores and Bermuda, but avoiding the winter head winds. Willkie's first stop was on the island of Bolama, which was 360 miles south of Dakar and off the coast of West Africa. The plane's crew took Willkie hunting for big game, but they only managed to shoot a few wild ducks. The American's friendly manner got him into an embarrassing predicament. On the edge of the jungle, he met the chief of the Bijagós tribe and asked how he could support his twenty-seven wives. The chief replied that each time he married he got a new field hand. Willkie said he had seen the tribal chieftain's wives and daughter bathing in the river. Other members of the party knew that he had committed a faux pas, because it was a tribal custom that men did not mention another man's daughter except in proposing marriage.

The Bijagós chieftain accepted what he took as the American's offer to marry his daughter. Willkie, unaware of what had transpired, returned to the plane. The next morning a canoe approached the aircraft shortly before takeoff, and crew members met the native bride, her mother, and several retainers. Explaining that there would not be enough room for the bride on this trip, the crew assured her mother that the money would be paid at once. The crew took up a collection and paid the mother twelve silver dollars. Not until the plane was airborne did Willkie learn that he had almost taken a second wife.[35]

On Sunday, February 9, 1941 the *Dixie Clipper* touched the water at the Marine Terminal of La Guardia Airport, and more than one hundred people had gathered for Willkie's arrival. "The most stimulating experience in my life," he said of the historic trip. "What the British desire from us is not men, but materials and equipment." John Cowles told Raymond Clapper that Willkie came back with stronger convictions that the United States should do everything possible to keep England fighting its battle against the Nazis. Willkie said he still supported lend-lease but would make no further comment until his Senate testimony.[36]

The lend-lease debate was approaching its climactic showdown. Secretary of State Hull, Dorothy Thompson, and New York Mayor Fiorello La Guardia had testified on behalf of FDR's program, while General Hugh Johnson, Colonel Charles A. Lindbergh, and Alf M.

Landon had spoken against it. Landon had come to Washington when Taft told him he was "the only Republican leader whose testimony will combat the idea that Willkie speaks for the party."

Willkie had already been repudiated by the most influential Republicans on the Senate Foreign Relations Committee–Hiram Johnson, Arthur Capper, Arthur Vandenberg, and Gerald P. Nye–and he expected to face hostile questions from them and Democratic Senator Bennett Champ Clark of Missouri. On New York *Times* letterhead, Krock advised Willkie on his testimony: "Avoid every aspect of cockiness on the stand. Disclaim any thought of posing as a military expert. Some very smart people will be laying for you. Take one or two fundamental tacks and decline to be diverted to others by questions that will be asked.

"Say that you are simply giving your impressions of a brief visit among a people under attack; that you know nothing of military or aviation affairs from the expert viewpoint; that guidance to these should come from experts, and everyone–including the President–should accept the same guidance.

"If another administration had been chosen last November, you believe it would be proceeding toward all-out British aid in a simpler and more specific way, without ambiguities, with preliminary consultation with leaders of all parties in Congress. That administration would already be moving to relinquish certain powers, such as those over the dollar which were acquired to deal with a wholly different economic situation.

"But the people re-elected this administration, and it is determined to have the British-aid bill in the form introduced into Congress as HR 1776. Therefore, all who believe as you do that this assistance must and should be given to Britain and certain other countries if the United States is not to be left to defend democracy utterly alone, are obliged to support the general form of HR 1776 with modifications designed to protect our constitutional system and fully reserve to Congress the powers of the purse and of the sword."[37]

Even before sunrise, the crowd began gathering outside the Senate Office Building, although Willkie was not due to testify until midafternoon. By the time he appeared, nearly twelve hundred people were squeezed into the Caucus Room, more than double its supposed capacity. Mrs. Henry A. Wallace, wife of the Vice-President, found standing room just behind the committee table. Joseph Alsop and

Robert Kintner described "the vivandières of isolationism, Mrs. Nicholas Longworth, Mrs. Bennett Champ Clark, and Mrs. Robert A. Taft, who sat like sirens disappointed of Ulysses, in a special row of chairs, joking among themselves." On taking his seat, Willkie opened his briefcase and discovered he had left his prepared testimony in his hotel room. For forty-five minutes, he talked informally with the senators about his trip until a messenger brought the document. Mimeographed copies were passed out to committee members, and the room turned quiet.

Leaning forward into a large microphone, Willkie asserted, "Britain needs more destroyers. She needs them desperately. The powers asked for are extraordinary. But in my judgment, this is an extraordinary situation." He had not had time to rest since his return, and there were signs of fatigue in his eyes, but his delivery was forceful and confident. Willkie made the argument that lend-lease offered the "best clear chance" for the United States to avoid war. "If Britain can stand through the summer," he said, "then at last the effects of our long-term assistance will begin to be felt."

Senator Vandenberg, who had attacked him as the "*Clipper* ambassador," asked whether he favored going to war if necessary to save Britain from defeat.

"In my judgment, there is only one body with power to declare war," he replied. "If I were a member of Congress, I'd never vote for war until the American people wanted it."

"That's an excellent statement," said the Michigan Republican.

"I think I answered your question," he said.

"I'm sorry," Vandenberg replied, "but I don't."

He could not be more precise, Willkie explained, because it was difficult to predict what might happen in the future.

Senator Robert R. Reynolds of North Carolina asked if it was possible the United States might have to intervene in the war.

"Yes," said Willkie. "Two madmen are at large and we cannot say where they will strike. If Britain collapsed tomorrow, we'd be in the war one month later."

Willkie was indignant when Senator Guy Gillette of Iowa suggested he had shifted his views on aid to Britain.

"Not in the slightest," he said. "As a matter of fact, in April, prior to my nomination, I made a speech in Akron, Ohio, in which I called upon the Secretary of State of the United States to ask Britain what we could do to help her."

Gillette said Willkie's speeches evidently did not have much impact.

"They brought about my nomination," he snapped. "I was not elected. But I got the nomination."

Senator Bennett Champ Clark of Missouri was the most strident in his cross-examination, suggesting that the Nazis could capture weapons sent to Britain.

"If by sending bombers we were to help weaken Germany," countered Willkie, "we might still be in a stronger position than if we kept bombers."

Senator Clark persisted. "Suppose the Germans got our bombers and used them against us?"

"If all the hazards of war go against us," said Willkie, "we will get whipped."

"You have flown halfway around the world to advise this committee," Clark replied sarcastically.

Willkie interjected, "I did not fly halfway around the world to advise this committee or anybody else. Let us be fair in this."

At one point, Senator Clark addressed him as "Mr. President." Laughing, Willkie said, "Senator, you merely speak of what should have been."

Senator Clark brought up Willkie's campaign charges that FDR would lead the nation into war if re-elected. "I made a great many statements about him," said Willkie. "He was my opponent, you know."

"You would not have said anything about your opponent you did not think was true, would you?" asked the Missouri isolationist.

"Oh no," said Willkie, "but occasionally in moments of oratory in campaigns we all expand a bit."

When Senator Clark kept pressing the issue, Willkie responded that he saw no constructive purpose in discussing his old campaign speeches. "I struggled as hard as I could to beat Franklin Roosevelt and I tried to keep from pulling my punches," he said. "He was elected President. He is my President now. I expect to disagree with him whenever I please." His remarks drew so much applause that Senator George, the committee's chairman, warned spectators that he would clear the room unless they were quiet.

Senator Nye asked Willkie about a campaign speech in which he had predicted that FDR would have the nation at war by April of 1941. The North Dakota isolationist asked if Willkie still believed "that might be the case."

"It might be," he answered. Then, with a smile, he wisecracked, "It was a bit of campaign oratory."[38]

Although some members of the committee and the majority of the audience laughed with Willkie, the flip comment touched off a political controversy. For the rest of his life, it would be used against him by conservative and isolationist critics. The Chicago *Tribune* said it discredited everything he had ever stood for. The Roman Catholic bishop of Seattle declared in a sermon that Willkie owed his party and the nation an apology. William Allen White praised Willkie for his candor. "I think one of the most courageous things any man ever said in public life was Willkie's campaign oratory statement," said White. "It was not discreet, but it was deeply honest. The pretension that a candidate's utterances are omniscient when everyone knows he is talking damned nonsense is one of the large reasons why the American people lose faith in democracy."[39]

Senator Hiram Johnson, ranking Republican member of the Foreign Relations Committee, denounced Willkie's performance as "a one-man circus intended to influence the citizens." It did. According to the Gallup poll, his testimony had helped swing public opinion behind lend-lease, including a plurality of rank-and-file Republicans. Gallup also reported that 60 per cent of the American public thought Willkie would have made a good President had he won the 1940 election. "Whatever influence he has lost among professional Republican politicians," wrote Ernest K. Lindley, "has been more than offset by his increased prestige among those who voted against him."[40]

The day after Willkie testified, the Foreign Relations Committee recommended passage of lend-lease by a vote of fifteen to eight, with all but one of the committee's Republicans against him. On March 8, the full Senate approved the bill by nearly two to one. The President gave Willkie much of the credit for his legislative triumph. "There's no question that Willkie was the real hero," said Carlton Savage, Hull's top aide.

Barely three months after the 1940 election, Willkie was disowned by a large segment of his party. Senator Taft saw "no justification in precedent or principle for the view that a defeated candidate for president is the titular head of the party." Senator Nye called Willkie's support of lend-lease "a betrayal" and a step toward the destruction of the two-party system. Hamilton Fish charged that Willkie "is now beating the war drums more furiously than the interventionists and war makers of the Democratic party." In Indiana's State Senate, the Republican majority defeated a resolution commending Willkie for his trip to England. Raymond Clapper said Willkie had become "the hated target of most of the influential politicians in the Republican Party." The columnist wrote, "They hate him more than they hate Mr. Roosevelt."[41]

On Capitol Hill, there was even discussion of formally reading Willkie out of the Republican party. "I fought these efforts to a standstill," recalled Joe Martin years later. "The party would have been finished if it had expelled Willkie." While in Washington, Willkie persuaded Martin to defer his planned resignation as Republican National Chairman until after the midterm elections.[42]

In an off-the-record meeting with reporters, Willkie was asked by Detroit *News* correspondent Jay Hayden if the GOP would revert to its old-time isolationism after the war.

"Look," Willkie replied, raising his index finger in an assertive gesture, "if we go back, it will be so far back that neither you nor I nor anyone in this room can be a party to it. It will be way back. We can never let that happen."[43]

At the White House, Secretary Ickes predicted to FDR that Willkie was finished as a political force in the Republican party. "My guess," Ickes wrote in his diary, "was that Willkie had lost whatever chance he might have to be nominated on the Republican ticket in 1944." *Newsweek* reported, "Another alternative which is being discussed, not altogether facetiously, over Washington highballs, is that the Hoosier might make a good Democratic nominee for '44." Roosevelt and Ickes both agreed that seemed a definite possibility. The President said Willkie would probably continue to make the front pages for another year and gradually fade from the scene. In the meantime, he expressed gratitude for the efforts of his defeated rival and indicated to Frances Perkins that he would welcome Willkie back into the Democratic fold.[44]

When Secretary of the Navy Frank Knox came out against Willkie's proposal to supply England with from five to ten destroyers a month, the President summoned him to the White House and had the secretary soften his comments. Stephen Early, FDR's press secretary, said, "No controversy exists among the President, Knox, and Willkie." In his meeting with FDR, Willkie had been led to believe that the Administration would furnish the additional warships.

Finally, in frustration, Willkie sent Churchill a cablegram expressing concern at the conflicting signals between London and Washington. He suggested that the Prime Minister find a method to keep American friends informed "as to changes of needs." The Prime Minister drafted a reply that said Britain was in urgent need of destroyers, long-range bombers, and convoys. "I have never said that the British Empire cannot make its way out of this war without American belligerence," Churchill wrote, "but no peace that is of any use to you or which will liberate Europe can be obtained without American belligerence towards which convoy is a decisive step. Every day's delay adds to the length of the war and the difficulties to be encountered."[45]

Before sending this message to Willkie, the Prime Minister gave a copy to Ambassador Winant, who cabled it to FDR. Furious, the President told Winant: "I wish you would explain very confidentially and entirely off the record to Former Naval Person that I am frankly placed in a most embarrassing situation in regard to Willkie's telegram and the suggested answer.

"Quite aside from the Logan Act," FDR went on, "and solely on the formation and maintenance of public opinion here, it would be very serious if it became known publicly that Mr. Willkie, who is giving splendid cooperation to all of us, were communicating directly with the Prime Minister and receiving direct replies, especially in view of the fact that communications go through the Consul General in New York.

"Such communications are almost sure to leak out and the revulsion of feeling in the Congress and the Administration would be very bad. I can only suggest that the Prime Minister send a friendly reply thanking Willkie for his telegram, going into no details, agreeing that obviously the joint policy must be flexible and constantly changing, and suggesting that Mr. Willkie keep in touch with regard to details with the British ambassador and me.

"I think the Prime Minister should maintain the friendliest of relations with Mr. Willkie but direct communication is a two-edged sword."[46]

Not wishing to offend FDR, the Prime Minister followed his instructions. Churchill cabled Willkie: "Most grateful for your telegram and all you are doing. Please have a talk with Lord Halifax who knows the situation." For the next three years, Willkie and Halifax were in frequent contact.[47]

In the winter of 1941, Willkie briefly considered making a trip to China and Australia for another look at the war but held back. Through Luce, he became a director of United China Relief. "We should help China," he declared, "because she is standing up against an aggressor who is tied in with the European aggressors who are attacking freedom. We must help the Chinese preserve their freedom."

Speaking at a United China Relief rally, he defined his view of the world as a marketplace for the American producer and said isolationists had failed to grasp the importance of global economic interests. "The isolationist believes that while international trade may be desirable, it is not necessary. He believes that we can build a wall around America and that democracy can live behind that wall. He believes that America can be made self-sufficient and still retain the free way of life. But the internationalist denies this. The internationalist declares that, to remain free, men must trade with one another—must trade freely in goods, in ideas, in customs and traditions and values of all sorts."

One result of his trip to Britain was that he had become a symbol of wartime unity among the English-speaking peoples. In March he went to Canada and received a hero's welcome in opening the national war drive fund. The Toronto *Star* reported that he had been more warmly received than any previous American visitor and with an enthusiasm comparable only to that accorded to the King and Queen in 1939. As he stepped from the train at Toronto's Union Station, Willkie shook hands with a few dignitaries, then walked across the tracks and grasped the hands of overall-clad railroad workers. Almost reluctantly, Willkie was led from the workingmen and joined the official party in his motorcade. With red-coated Mounties leading the procession, he rode through the city in an open car and, waving his felt hat, drew resounding cheers and was showered with confetti and streaming ticker tape. More than 100,000 Canadians turned out to welcome him. At City Hall, the mayor welcomed him as "one who has performed a great service to humanity." A local newspaper headline said, "Wendell Willkie Is Worth More Than Spitfires."

"With our help and your help, they're going to win," Willkie shouted at City Hall. "We are going to beat Hitler. It may be tough, but we are going to beat him." Later, he addressed the Ontario legislature and had dinner with Canadian Prime Minister W. L. Mackenzie King at the York Club. That night the Prime Minister introduced the American at a great rally in Maple Leaf Gardens and hailed his efforts on behalf of lend-lease. Willkie presented Mackenzie King with a check from American contributors to purchase a Spitfire airplane for England, which he called "a symbol of the interest which the people of the United States have in the successful outcome of the war." In a stirring speech, Willkie received his biggest cheers when he departed from his prepared remarks and called on the United States and Canada to send England more destroyers. "Give ships until it hurts," he shouted.

"Mr. and Mrs. Willkie's reception by Torontonians was unexpectedly enthusiastic," American Consul General Herbert C. Hengstler reported to the State Department. "There is no doubt that Mr. Willkie's visit has further strengthened friendly relations between Canada and the United States."[48]

Willkie inspected Canadian war plants and talked of his experiences in England. "Every time we accomplish something in the United States or Canada," he said, "every struggling man in Britain takes a new cheer and every Nazi leader gets a chill."

Even though it was raining, more than twenty thousand people showed up at the Windsor Street Station in Montreal for his final appearance of the Canadian tour. After the war, Willkie said he hoped the United States and the British Commonwealth might establish a world peace organization. In a special appeal to French Canadians, he praised the Resistance movement and called on Quebec's French-speaking people to help drive the Nazis from Europe. The crowd chanted "We Want Willkie" and frequently interrupted his remarks with applause.

On his return to New York, Willkie announced that he was going back into law practice as senior partner in the Wall Street firm of Miller, Owen, Otis, and Bailly. He had given serious thought to other options but concluded that only a law partnership afforded him the flexibility for political activities that he now required. In April the firm was renamed Willkie, Owen, Otis, and Bailly, and he moved into a twenty-seventh-floor corner office with a commanding view of New York Harbor and the Statue of Liberty. He would concentrate on trial work and select his own cases. He also took part in the firm's conferences and helped shape its policies. His return to law practice inspired a verse by Melville Cane that began:

Let the so-called welkin tingle,
Ring the bells both near and far,
Wendell Willkie's hung his shingle
Wendell Willkie's back at the bar.

More and more, Willkie was becoming involved in the politics of war. By this time, he was considered the leading interventionist spokesman in America. Charles A. Lindbergh, the renowned aviator, had emerged as the most prominent isolationist. In the spring of 1941, Willkie and Lindbergh debated the war in the pages of *Collier's* magazine. Lindbergh, who had visited Nazi Germany, claimed that Hitler's military might was greater than the combined forces of Russia, England, and the United States. He attacked the Roosevelt administration for creating a record deficit and leaving the nation unprepared for war.

"If we don't leave it to them [the Administration]," answered Willkie, "to whom are we to leave it under our constitutional system? Without revolution we cannot have a different administration for four years. I certainly did all I could to remove it from power last November. But the democratic process spoke. I believe in the democratic process. I accept its verdicts."[49]

Until Pearl Harbor, Willkie and Lindbergh would continue debating the dominant issue of American politics. In Philadelphia, Colonel Lindbergh charged FDR was more of an aggressor than Hitler "when he says that it is our business to control the wars of Europe and Asia." The isolationist, noting the convergence of foreign policy views between Roosevelt and Willkie, charged that the American people had been denied a free choice in 1940 and urged "new leadership" that would "place America first."

At a mass rally in Chicago, Willkie said Lindbergh's comments had been "reckless and misguided." He added, "It does no good to say of the President of the United States as was said last night that he acts through hypocrisy or subterfuge. No man who was President of the United States at this critical moment could act out of such motives as that."

Roosevelt counterattacked with a vengeance, comparing Lindbergh to the Civil War "Copperheads," which was still a euphemism for traitor in those days. Many interventionists were attacking the famed aviator as a Nazi sympathizer and "fifth columnist." Secretary Ickes scorned him as the "number one Nazi fellow traveler" and the "first American to raise aloft the standard of pro-Naziism."

Willkie thought the Administration had been guilty of overkill in its assault on Lindbergh. "I hope that the Administration will discontinue these constant and bitter attacks on individuals, companies and others who disagree with it," he said. "Democracy should function through orderly and thoughtful discussion and not through adolescent name-calling. Nothing can contribute more to disunity than such attacks. Those of us who are doing our utmost to promote national unity, I believe, are entitled to the help, not the hindrance of the Administration, in our efforts."

At an anti-Fascism rally, Willkie scolded the audience for booing Lindbergh's name. "Let's not boo any American citizen," he said. "We come here tonight, men and women of all faiths and parties, not to slander our fellow citizens. We want all of them. Let's save all our boos for Hitler."

In September Lindbergh overplayed his hand in linking the Roosevelt administration, England, and Jews as the forces behind the interventionist movement. "Instead of agitating for war, the Jewish groups in this country should be opposing it in every possible way, for they will be among the first to feel its consequences," he said. "Their greatest danger to this country lies in their large ownership and influence in our motion pictures, our press, our radio, and our government."

Willkie called it "the most un-American talk made in my time by any person of national reputation." He added, "If the American people permit race prejudice to arise at this crucial moment, they little deserve to preserve democracy." Lindbergh's speech divided the America First movement. The Chicago *Tribune,* which had strongly supported him, disavowed Lindbergh's anti-Semitic remarks. The Lone Eagle was repudiated by other isolationist leaders and, almost overnight, he was no longer in demand as a public speaker for the cause.

That same month, Willkie was back on the front pages as special counsel for the motion picture industry during the Senate Commerce Committee's investigation of alleged war propaganda in Hollywood. His old antagonists, the Senate isolationists, were contending that film moguls had been promoting the Administration's foreign policy on the silver screen. Senator Nye said they were "trying to make America punch drunk with propaganda to push her into war." Willkie felt that anti-Semitism had triggered the hearings in the first place. Throughout the deliberations, Senator Nye condemned the Jewish influence in Hollywood yet insisted he was not anti-Semitic. Willkie, who was not permitted to cross-examine the senators, shot back, "I wish I could ask the senator whether he believes the American public does not recognize the technique he is using."

Another old adversary, Senator Bennett Champ Clark, testified that Hollywood was "turning 17,000 movie theaters into 17,000 nightly mass meetings for war." Darryl F. Zanuck of Twentieth Century-Fox assured the committee that fewer than fifty of the eleven hundred American films produced during the world war could be considered "war" movies.

Willkie chortled when another isolationist senator suggested that a possible solution might be for Hollywood to produce films showing both sides of the war. "This, I presume," said Willkie, "means that since Chaplin made a laughable caricature of Hitler, the industry should be forced to employ Charles Laughton to do the same on Winston Churchill."

In two weeks of hearings, the isolationists failed to produce evidence which supported their charges, and it was apparent that Willkie and the motion picture industry had won the battle for public opinion. Willkie told the committee that the motive behind the investigation had been nothing less than "the sabotage of the country's foreign policy."

Since the passage of the Lend-Lease Act, Germany and the United States had been waging an undeclared naval war in the North Atlantic, and Willkie thought the Neutrality Act of 1939 left the American ships vulnerable to German attack. Throughout the year, he urged the President to seek a repeal of the isolationist-inspired legislation. On October 6, speaking before a GOP gathering at the Waldorf, Willkie called the Neutrality Act "a piece of hypocrisy and deliberate self-deception."

"It is apparent to all thoughtful people," Willkie said, "that this act should be repealed and repealed promptly. The administration is pursuing its usual course at critical moments—consulting the polls, putting up trial balloons, having some of its members make statements that others can deny—the same course that has led to so much of the people's confusion and misunderstanding."

If the party would show leadership in getting the Neutrality Act repealed, Willkie said Republicans would reassume their traditional position as "the American party of world outlook" and force the Administration "to discontinue its feeble and futile policy of trying to follow the people instead of leading them."

Three days later FDR sent a message to Congress in which he sought revision of the Neutrality Act, including the authority to arm merchant ships. Willkie persuaded three Republican senators, Austin of Vermont, Bridges of New Hampshire, and Gurney of South Dakota, to introduce an amendment that would repeal the entire act. More than one hundred prominent Republicans signed Willkie's letter to their party's lawmakers. Among them were Governors Saltonstall, Sprague, and Stassen, California GOP leader William F. Knowland, future Secretary of State Christian A. Herter, and former Pennsylvania Governor Gifford Pinchot.

Early in November, the Senate and House both voted to repeal vital sections of the Neutrality Act. While Willkie had helped force the issue, the vote demonstrated his lack of clout within his own party. In the Senate, Republicans were against repeal by more than three to one. In the House, it was more than six to one. "Willkie is just a stooge for President Roosevelt," grumbled former Pennsylvania Senator David Reed. A Democratic isolationist, Burton K. Wheeler, complained that Willkie seemed to be shaping Administration policy. "He is telling them what to do. He is pushing the President."

On several occasions, FDR paid tribute to Willkie for his contribution to national unity. At a Democratic party dinner, the President declared, "The leader of the Republican party himself—Mr. Wendell Willkie—in word and action is showing what patriotic Americans mean by rising above partisanship and rallying to the common cause."

Such endorsements did not enhance Willkie's stock with congressional Republicans. "I have no patience with those people," he told

Look magazine, "who believe it necessary for America to be aggressive in its attitude toward the totalitarian countries and in its aid to the democracies who yet hold back because they do not trust the President or believe in his domestic policies. I doubt if any Frenchman living in poverty, degradation and enslavement today can find much satisfaction in the thought that he held back because he did not trust Leon Blum.

"After the campaign, having failed to defeat the administration, I decided that I would do all I could to support its foreign policy–in which, in the main–I believed. That policy, unfortunately, has never been sufficiently clear-cut or consistent, but it is on the right track; and only if we unite in its support can I see any hope of destroying totalitarianism."[50]

In July, Willkie lunched with the President at the White House, and FDR said that he had decided to occupy Iceland in order to keep the North Atlantic sea lanes open. Willkie immediately endorsed the military occupation as a necessity for national defense.

Two months later the U.S. destroyer *Greer* was attacked by a Nazi submarine, and FDR issued orders to "shoot on sight" any German warship they encountered. Willkie strongly backed the President. "There are certain things that no nation can concede without losing its strength," he said, "and there are certain things that people cannot yield without losing their souls."

In mid-October, Nazi torpedoes struck the U.S.S. *Kearney,* and Willkie told *Look,* "The United States already is in the war and has been for some time." The American people, he said, should "abandon the hope of peace." In a national radio address, he said, "We can no more negotiate a peace with the warlords of Tokyo than the conquering dictator of Berlin."

Willkie continued to be critical of the insufficiency of the Administration's defense buildup. In an appearance at the Hollywood Bowl, he charged FDR had failed "in the most elementary task of management, the task of delegation, the task of calling in the ablest men in the country and giving them the power to act." It was known that Willkie was more than a little interested in serving as director of mobilization but could not bring himself to ask Roosevelt for such a role.

The President invited Willkie to dedicate the Mount Rushmore National Memorial in South Dakota. "If you can see your way clear," wrote FDR, "you are the man to dedicate it. It seems to me an opportunity to give new and striking emphasis to the vital need for national unity which, I think, should be the theme of the dedication." Roosevelt added, "I would be ingenuous if I did not also mention that, geographically, this region is sadly in need of the kind of speeches you have been making."[51] Because of prior commitments, Willkie was unable to make the trip to South Dakota.

Late in 1941, Willkie was approached about joining the Administration. Presidential assistant David Niles was sent to New York in an effort to recruit him. "I saw Wendell Willkie Friday afternoon at three o'clock in his office," he reported to FDR on October 27. "I first told him that you would like to have him as part of your Administration, and also that you had said this didn't mean that he was to give up any of his partisan ideology. I suggested that he ought not to say 'no' without further consideration and he replied that he would be glad to talk to you about it when you sent for him."[52]

Willkie still had strong reservations about working for Roosevelt. His political advisers and publishing friends were against it. He was open to the idea of another wartime mission, and the Australian Prime Minister asked him to make an official visit. FDR thought he should do it.

"It would give me very great pleasure if you would care to make a short trip to Australia," Roosevelt wrote him on December 5. "I could arrange the official procedure any way you like.

"I leave this matter wholly in your hands as I think you should consult your own convenience–and I think both of us should be extremely careful, if you do go, lest it be said that I am 'sending you out of the country.'

"It would, of course, be of real value to cement our relations with New Zealand and Australia and would be useful not only now but in the future. There is always the Japanese matter to consider. The situation is definitely serious and there might be an armed clash at any moment if the Japanese continue their forward progress against the Philippines, Dutch Indies, or Malaya or Burma. Perhaps the next four or five days will decide the matter.

"In any event, I do wish you would let me know the next time you come to Washington as there are many things for us to talk over."[53]

Then it happened. On Sunday morning, December 7, 1941, Japanese planes struck Pearl Harbor, the U.S. naval base in Hawaii, and wiped out half of the American fleet. More than 2,300 American servicemen were killed. In declaring war against Japan, the President described it as "a date which will live in infamy." Four days later FDR received a unanimous declaration of war against Germany and Italy after the two Axis powers had declared war on the United States. While Japanese leaders gloated over their successful attack, Admiral Isoroku Yamamoto, commander of the Imperial Navy, privately concluded, "I fear all we have done is to awaken a sleeping giant, and fill him with a terrible resolve."

The United States was now fully committed to the war which most Americans had wanted to avoid. Defense bonds were sold out overnight, and recruiting stations were crowded with long lines of young men rushing to enlist. "Our first duty now," Senator McNary wrote his sister, "is to knock down the ears of those little yellow rats of the Orient."[54] Senator Burton K. Wheeler added, "The only thing to do now is to lick the hell out of them."

"We go to war," Willkie told a national radio audience, "because, if we do not, freedom will die with us and with all men."

Irita Van Doren helped him draft his response to the President's letter: "I am unable presently to appraise the potentialities or the wisdom of going to Australia since the Japanese attack. Perhaps it would now constitute a nuisance. I will think about it further.

"I am coming to Washington on Monday, and, if your schedule presents a free moment, would you have one of your secretaries let me know before that date if it would be convenient for me to call on you in accordance with the suggestion in your letter? Please disregard this if you are at all pressed for time.

"In case I do not see you Monday, there is something I would like to say to you. Of late, a few people, friends of yours, have suggested to me various ways in which they thought you might make use of me in our national emergency. Since they have talked to me about this, I am afraid they may also have troubled you. You have incredibly anxious and burdensome days ahead and it should be plain to anyone that you can function with least strain and most effectiveness if you are free to choose your helpers and advisers for whom you must bear the responsibility, without any consideration other than your conception of the public welfare.

"What I am trying to say—honestly, but awkwardly I am afraid, because it is not easy—is this: If any such well-meant suggestions about me are brought to you, I beg you to disregard them. There is on your shoulders the heaviest responsibility any man can carry and I would not add to it in the slightest way. Even to volunteer a willingness to serve seems to me now only an imposition on your attention. Every American is willing to serve."[55]

On December 15, the President hosted Willkie for lunch and discussed the war effort. Leaving the White House, Willkie said he had not been offered an official post. "In times like these," he said, "there is not any American who would not be willing to give everything he had in the service of his country."

CHAPTER FOURTEEN

THE HOME FRONT

With the coming of war, Wendell L. Willkie remained in the political spotlight. The Gallup poll reported that American voters rated him as FDR's most likely successor in the White House. And there were indications that Republican leaders were beginning to listen to their rank-and-file members. In December of 1941, the *Republican* magazine disclosed that a national survey of party leaders showed him as their overwhelming favorite for 1944. Willkie received 42 per cent of the vote, compared with Taft's 19, Dewey's 15, and Hoover's 6 per cent. Some prominent New York Republicans were urging Willkie to seek the governorship in 1942 as a tune-up for a second presidential bid. Walter Lippmann called on FDR to name Willkie as wartime production chief, a position which genuinely interested him.

On January 13, 1942, he met with the President amid rumors that he was being considered for this slot. Just before this conference, Willkie had been offered an appointment by Secretary Perkins as arbitrator for the National War Labor Board. Though it was not the job he had in mind, he promised to consider it. Arriving at the White House, he was irritated to find that Press Secretary Stephen Early had tipped reporters about the labor board offer. He turned it down.

In the Oval Office, Willkie reminded the President that he had called for a single director for the war effort 124 times and was planning another demand that night in his speech before the U.S. Conference of Mayors. Senator Harry S. Truman, chairman of a committee investigating the war effort, had also informed Roosevelt that he was going to issue a public blast.

Late in the afternoon, FDR reached a decision. Although Willkie had powerful supporters for the job, Harry Hopkins had argued persuasively that he might use it as a "political football." The President named Donald M. Nelson, a former Sears Roebuck executive, then serving as director of the government's supplies, priorities, and allocations board. FDR told him to write out his own executive order defining the war production board's powers and he would sign it.[1]

Only a few minutes before he was scheduled to address the mayors, Willkie learned of Nelson's appointment and was forced to make a major rewrite of his speech. While he was disappointed that he had been passed over, Willkie denied that there had been a falling out over this incident. "To say that two men have 'fallen out' implies that there was once some sort of agreement or understanding between them," he said. "I don't have and never have had any personal relationship with President Roosevelt. I saw him perhaps a dozen times in all before I ever thought of becoming a presidential candidate, never on political matters. Those meetings were always pleasant in tone. But in them the President expressed his views frankly and I replied or presented mine equally frankly. Generally, as a matter of fact, we were discussing things in the administration's economic policy with which I didn't agree.

"In the past few years," Willkie added, "when the President's foreign policy has been much along the same lines, I have agreed with him and have frankly said so. When I have not agreed, I have likewise expressed myself and with equal candor. There has never been any understanding between us that I should do or say certain things or that he should do or say certain things."

On this same day, Willkie had a cordial meeting with Churchill at the White House. The Prime Minister later recalled that during his vacation in Palm Beach he had placed a phone call to Willkie–and, through an operator's mistake–found himself talking with FDR. "I presume you do not mind my having wished to speak to Wendell Willkie?" asked Churchill. The President assured him that it was perfectly appropriate and suggested that he invite Willkie to meet him at the White House.

"Churchill asked me," Willkie recalled, "if I were going to be associated with the government. I called his attention to the difference between the American and British constitutional systems. In Great Britain, an opposition leader who joins the cabinet remains a free agent with full right to differ publicly with the head of the government."

Willkie asked the Prime Minister, "Would you have joined the Chamberlain government when you did if you had thereby felt under the obligation to restrain from expressing your views?"[2]

Churchill, who had greatly appreciated Willkie's important role in the lend-lease debate and in rallying public opinion behind England's cause, said that he could understand the difficulty of his position.

In late April, Willkie and Taft clashed over postwar foreign policy at the Republican National Committee meeting in Chicago. "If the Republican party is to remain an effective instrument of party government," said Willkie, "it must not only repudiate completely the doctrine of isolationism but with courage and imagination must recognize that America must take its part hereafter in world affairs and help lead the peoples of the world to peace and democracy." The Chicago *Tribune* denounced him as a political turncoat whose ideas were unworthy of discussion. Chairman Joe Martin, however, still insisted that Willkie was the "head of the party" and pledged his resolution would be given every consideration. Taft submitted his own resolution.

When the smoke cleared, Willkie had won a substantial victory. The GOP National Committee approved a statement that read: "We realize that after this war, the responsibility of the nation will not be circumscribed within the territorial limits of the United States; that our nation has an obligation to assist in bringing about understanding, comity, and cooperation among the nations of the world in order that our liberty may be preserved and that the blighting and destructive processes of war may not again be forced upon us and upon the free and peace-loving peoples of the earth."

James A. Hagerty wrote in the New York *Times,* "Wendell L. Willkie succeeded today in removing the brand of isolationism from the Republican Party." Willkie said the declaration committed the party to a policy of internationalism and world leadership. Senator Vandenberg wrote privately that it was "sheer bunk," because Willkie's resolution was nothing more than "shadow boxing with platitudes."

Interviewed following the national committee's vote, Willkie said, "The next job for Republicans to do is see to it that in the coming primaries candidates are nominated not alone for Congress but for other positions of public influence who have the courage to declare and who believe sincerely these principles and their necessary implications. Thus, the Republican party can win and become a great force for liberal enlightened government."

Willkie had sounded out former Democratic National Chairman James A. Farley about supporting a bipartisan coalition of senators and congressmen who had backed the Roosevelt foreign policy. Farley advised him that it was impractical and refused to have anything to do with such a plan. One of the reasons, no doubt, was Farley's bitter split with FDR on the third term.[3]

The President was more responsive. Willkie approached him about working behind the scenes against the re-election of Hamilton Fish, isolationist Republican congressman from FDR's home district and ranking minority member of the House Foreign Affairs Committee. "It seems to me that the problem of Fish is as much a problem as it was when we talked it over many months ago," FDR wrote Willkie in February. "I have various recommendations for candidates–some are inclined to think that if Warden Lawes could be persuaded to run, he would make the best showing. I think he calls himself an independent Republican."[4] Fish's principal opponent, it developed, was upstate lawyer Augustus W. Bennet, and Willkie campaigned for him.

During the spring of 1942, Willkie considered a race for the New York governorship. The Albany statehouse had little appeal for him, but he recognized that his election would be an important step toward renomination. For more than a year, Joe Martin and Henry Luce advised him to run for governor. Robert Moses, New York's park commissioner and a former gubernatorial nominee, endorsed him and called on Willkie to announce his availability. Ralph Becker, state chairman of Young Republicans, urged his nomination.

Such a bid held considerable political risk. In national polls, Willkie was already the front-runner for 1944 with Dewey trailing. By running for governor, he would be putting his political career on the line in a state election in which his chances were questionable. In a general election, Willkie appeared to be a likely winner. His problem was the nomination. Thomas E. Dewey controlled the state organization and key county chairmen, and the nomination would be determined by convention. Since losing the presidential nomination to Willkie, Dewey had been campaigning full-time for the governorship.

If Willkie entered the contest, he would be starting out far behind in the battle for convention delegates.

The rivalry between Willkie and Dewey had produced mutual enmity and rancor. Always thin-skinned, Willkie had not liked it when Dewey alleged that Wall Street had been responsible for his nomination in 1940. Dewey thought Willkie had been patronizing in rejecting his help on the destroyer-bases deal. Willkie was suspicious of Dewey's conversion to internationalism, especially his last-minute switch on lend-lease. Gardner Cowles said the main reason for the open hostility between Willkie and Dewey was that they both wanted to be President in 1944.[5]

Through intermediaries, Dewey approached his rival and offered to trade the state's 1944 convention delegates for Willkie's support in the gubernatorial race. Rejecting the offer, Willkie was furious when Dewey's men leaked stories that he had suggested the deal. "The facts are these," he wrote Drew Pearson. "Some several months ago, the representatives and associates of Tom Dewey proposed to me that if I would agree to support Tom Dewey for governor, they would assure to me the New York delegation at the Republican National Convention in 1944. I rejected their suggestion, saying to them that the proposal offended both my moral and my common sense."

At a large social gathering, Dewey came up to Willkie and pledged he would serve out the four-year term if elected governor. "I asked him not to say that to me," Willkie told Pearson, "because it suggested the same proposal that had been made to me before."[6]

Willkie made no effort to disguise his feelings for Dewey. Several minutes before the GOP adversaries were to be seated at the head table during the New York Legislative Correspondents dinner in Albany, Willkie asked the group's president, Warren Moscow of the New York *Times,* if he would be required to give a speech. Just a few words, Moscow replied. "Goddamn it," snorted Willkie, "I don't want to speak tonight because I will wind up giving a speech I don't want to make yet—why Tom Dewey shouldn't be nominated."[7]

In an unmistakable reference to Dewey, Willkie suggested his rival's conversion to internationalism was disingenuous. "Frankly," he said, "I'd be more ready to accept as sincere the statements of an out-and-out isolationist, who admitted he had been mistaken and now recognized the responsibility we have in the world of today than to accept the assurances of a 'wobbler' who never had the courage to take a stand one way or another during the trying and critical pre-Pearl Harbor days but who was suddenly converted after war was upon us. If that means I'm dealing in personalities, well, I'm afraid I am."

Everyone in the room, including Dewey, knew what Willkie was talking about, and the prosecutor looked stricken. "The political pot is beginning to boil a little," Dewey wrote his mother, "and our friend Wendell is out to do me dirt. I am not as worried as I ought to be, probably."[8]

Willkie attempted to launch a "Stop Dewey" campaign and sought the endorsement of GOP National Chairman Joe Martin. "Joe, I wish you'd get me a candidate for governor of New York," he said. "If you get me a candidate, a good candidate, I'll stump every street in New York for him."

The Republican chairman explained that it would be counterproductive for an outsider to get involved in New York party matters. "There's only one way to do this," Martin told Willkie, "and that's to run yourself. If you got elected governor, there would be nothing to stop you in '44. It's the path that leads to the White House."

"I don't fancy that job," Willkie replied. "You wouldn't want a man of my stature there."[9] He told John Hamilton that he was under "tremendous pressure" to seek the governorship but did not want to "be put in the position of a perpetual officeseeker."

Except for the presidency, Willkie told *Look* magazine in April that he had little interest in seeking public office. "That is the only political office," he said, "through which fundamental ideas, national and international, can be made effective. I have never been enamored of mere office holding."[10]

On April 4, Willkie released a list of twelve men he considered as viable nominees for governor, including Charles Evans Hughes, Jr., Robert Moses, Congressman James W. Wadsworth, and Wall Street lawyer Allen W. Dulles. Dewey was omitted from the list. "Pick a candidate about whose international views there can be no question," said Willkie, "and I'll campaign for him in every hamlet, town and city in the state if you want me to, or I'll keep still if you think that's best."[11]

In a letter to Drew Pearson, he confided, "I think you know me well enough to know that I am opposing Tom Dewey for the nomination simply because I think he represents, perhaps unconsciously, those forces in the Republican Party and in the country, which may, when this war ends, cause a repetition of the destructive attitude that kept America out of the League of Nations in 1919 and 1920."[12]

Accepting an honorary degree at Union College, in Schenectady, Willkie made another public attack on Dewey, urging his audience to support candidates who stood for something, "not men who examine each shift of sentiment and watch the polls to learn where they stand. I beg of you to vote for straight-out men—not wobblers. This is no time for ambiguity."

Late in the spring, Gardner Cowles sent Willkie an advance copy of a Gallup survey which indicated that Dewey was threatening his lead among Republican voters nationally. "I am tremendously hopeful that somehow you can maneuver the New York situation so that Dewey does not move into the governor's chair," the *Look* publisher wrote Willkie. "If he does, I think we will have a hell of a fight on our hands in the presidential primary of 1944. It seems to me it would be easier somehow to handle Dewey this year in New York state so that he will not be the big problem in 1944."[13]

Willkie could not have agreed more. But stopping the New York prosecutor was easier said than done. Dewey commanded both money and organization, and none of Willkie's prospective challengers were willing to take him on. He urged Congressman Wadsworth to get into the race, but the upstate Republican declined.

The longer Willkie explored the possibility of fielding a surrogate candidate, the more it became obvious that he was the only Republican leader with the stature to threaten Dewey's nomination. Joe Martin claimed to have a poll which showed Willkie comfortably ahead of Dewey among New York Republicans. Willkie indicated to Lord Halifax, the new British ambassador in Washington, that he might change his mind and run against Dewey.[14]

"Wendell Willkie is wrestling with the toughest decision of his political life," Drew Pearson and Robert S. Allen wrote on June 23. "He must choose between taking off the gloves and wading into a powerful Republican officeseeker whose views he detests, or remain silent and permit himself to be elbowed out of party leadership."[15]

When Governor Herbert Lehman announced that he would not seek re-election, many of his liberal Democratic supporters turned to Willkie as an alternative. Lehman's Republican brother-in-law Frank

Altschul, who had been a Willkie organizer in 1940, tried to get him to run. David Dubinsky, president of the International Ladies Garment Workers Union, and other power brokers of New York's American Labor party announced they would support Willkie on any ticket. Sydney Baron, a liberal political activist, suggested that all three New York political parties draft Willkie as a wartime coalition candidate.

Willkie rejected the idea of a fusion candidacy. "Obviously," he said, "this is both impossible of accomplishment and would be unwise if it could be brought about."

After weeks of deliberation, he looked into the possibility of challenging Dewey for the nomination. Frustrated by his inability to find a suitable surrogate candidate and discouraged about his own prospects, he came to a measure of realism and decided against making an active bid that might eliminate him overnight from presidential politics.

For all his tough talk and bravado, Willkie was painfully vulnerable and unwilling to admit shortcomings. At this low point in his public career, his feelings were easily hurt. When Nicholas Roosevelt of the *Herald Tribune,* FDR's Republican kinsman, gently suggested that it was foolish and politically unwise for Willkie to lead the opposition to Dewey before the state convention, he broke off their friendship. With wounded pride, he accused Senator Henry Cabot Lodge of making disparaging remarks about him. Lodge assured him that such reports were untrue. Willkie could not restrain himself from responding in print to a twenty-four-year-old writer's criticism of his economic views. He attacked Forrest Davis, who had worked as an aide in his 1940 campaign and who wrote a Willkie piece for the *Saturday Evening Post,* for taking part in "a plot by the government to destroy me." He scolded Joseph Barnes when it was hinted in print that the foreign correspondent was the real author of *One World,* Willkie's best-selling memoir of his 1942 global mission for FDR. When his former aide, Elliott Bell, went to work for Dewey, Willkie wrote him, "It does make me feel badly when one with whom I was closely associated with says ill things about me." Justice Frankfurter observed, "I think that Willkie, like many people who have made their own way to the heights from pretty humble beginnings, is rather more sensitive to threats and criticism than he should be."[16]

Willkie's brief flirtation with New York politics had left him bitter and disillusioned. The state's GOP leaders had been sharp in their criticism of him and his increasingly liberal policies. On June 18, he stunned his audience at a Louis D. Brandeis Memorial Dinner with the declaration that he was dropping out of politics. "I doubt if I ever will aspire to public office again," he said. "There are some things in which I am so greatly interested that I don't want to see their advocacy tinged with self-interest."

Though Willkie described himself as "old and fat," almost nobody took him at his word that he was retiring from politics. Indeed, his announcement helped fuel a bipartisan "Draft Willkie" movement. Russell Davenport, Herbert Bayard Swope, and Helen P. Simpson, wife of the late New York GOP leader, were among its principal organizers. At a news conference flanked by best-selling authors Rex Stout and John Gunther, book publisher Stanley Rinehart announced that he was heading a statewide "Draft Willkie" committee which would seek the Republican's nomination "by popular acclaim." Another group of writers including Edna Ferber, Carl Van Doren, Clifton Fadiman, Russel Crouse, Howard Lindsay, and newspaper columnists Walter Winchell and Samuel Grafton urged him to run "as a vital contribution to the struggle in which you have already courageously declared yourself on the side of democracy and decency." Freda Kirchwey, writing in the *Nation,* described the Willkie phenomenon as a "product of the war" rather than a "product of politics."

"Men and women are backing Willkie today precisely because they backed Roosevelt in 1940," wrote Kirchwey, "and are pro-Roosevelt still. I suspect the Willkie boom may even have found some measure of encouragement deep in the heart of the administration."

It had. Willkie later told Bartley Crum that President Roosevelt had offered his support as a "private citizen" if he sought the governorship. This would not have been the first time that FDR had endorsed a Republican. Six years earlier the President backed Senator George Norris of Nebraska and had given tacit support to Senator McNary of Oregon. The American Labor party leaders, including Dubinsky, had convinced FDR that he should not have anything to do with New York Attorney General John J. Bennett, the conservative Democratic nominee. Willkie had the American Labor party nomination and FDR's public blessing for the asking—but although both would be powerful assets in the general election, he felt that he would also need the Republican nomination to be successful. "If he had accepted the ALP support alone," recalled Crum, "he probably would have forfeited his position as head of the Republican Party. Besides, Dewey had sewed up the regulars."

Assessing Willkie's chances under the headline, "The People's Choice," *Time* magazine left no doubt that he was still Luce's favorite Republican. While Dewey was conceded to be the front-runner for the nomination, *Time* dismissed him as "a candidate whose mass attraction had long since faded under the hammer blows dealt him in 1940." Dewey's nomination, *Time* said, had been encouraged by "foxy" Democratic boss Jim Farley. "The key figure behind the scenes," the magazine said, "was big, bearlike Wendell Willkie, a much more experienced Willkie but now as ever forthright, plain and clear in speech and purpose, and concerned with the future of the party he is trying to lead toward the light.

"As a matter of party duty," said *Time,* "Willkie cannot refuse the draft. As a matter of modesty, he cannot encourage it. That Willkie would not refuse the nomination was certain, despite a remark he made to the effect that he did not aspire further to high office."[17]

Willkie's camp was hoping for a New York version of the "Miracle at Philadelphia," with Empire State GOP delegates dumping Tom Dewey in a "We Want Willkie" burst of enthusiasm. State Chairman Edwin F. Jaeckle was sufficiently concerned about the possibility of a Willkie stampede to switch the convention site from Buffalo to Saratoga Springs. In Saratoga, Dewey's men would have tighter control of the convention hall and the galleries. Willkie's only chance was to convince New York's county chairmen that Dewey, a loser in his two most recent political campaigns, had used up his credit with the voters. "Leaving out of account all questions of principle," Willkie wrote a Dewey supporter on June 23, "and I have serious differences of views with regard to certain principles from those advocated by Mr. Dewey—I will make you a prediction—if Mr. Dewey is nominated by the Republicans for Governor of New York State, he will be overwhelmingly defeated."[18]

Late in June, Willkie sent representatives to Albany for a meeting of the New York GOP state committee. Rolland B. Marvin of Syracuse and Dorothy G. Hays of Brooklyn were among those promoting Willkie's candidacy. They discovered, however, that Dewey's lead was holding firm despite the Willkie boom. Two months before the Saratoga convention, Dewey had secured the pledges of two thirds of the delegates. "The feeling concerning Mr. Willkie," reported Hays, "ranged from thinly veiled contempt to open hostility and hatred."

Willkie's slashing attacks on Dewey were resented by the conservative party leaders. So, too, was his support of FDR's foreign policy. From Albany, Hays reported to Lem Jones: "He is through in the Republican party, and they as leaders will have nothing further to do with him, will take no dictation from him."[19]

Faced with such long odds, Willkie did not dare get into the GOP contest. On July 2, he asked the various "Draft Willkie" committees to cease their activities. "I long ago declared that I did not intend to become a candidate," he explained, "and I have no intention of becoming one."

Willkie told friends that he had never really aspired to the governorship. "In normal times," he told Lem Jones, "I might run for Governor of New York because of New York's economic importance to the country. But with things as they are, I believe my voice is more needed on the national and international scene than in a state office. And don't tell me that I could get someone else to do the real work of the governorship while I concern myself with other things. When I take on a job, I do it myself."[20]

In the New York primary, Willkie campaigned against Hamilton Fish, whom he berated for obstructing the war effort. The isolationist congressman was renominated by three to one. Senator Taft said Fish's victory demonstrated "the people's conviction that men who opposed our entrance into the war are just as qualified or more so to represent them than those who are trying to smear them."

After Fish's renomination, Willkie promptly endorsed his Democratic opponent and also urged the defeat of another GOP isolationist, Illinois Congressman Stephen Day. Walter S. Hallanan, West Virginia's Republican National Committeeman and an ardent Willkie supporter in 1940, advised Willkie to soften his opposition to his party's reactionaries, because their candidacies were "of relative unimportance." Willkie wired back, "No greater disaster can happen to the Republican party than the election of men like Day and Fish. In repudiating both I think I am making a real contribution to the future success of the Republican party. Likewise their defeat will serve to unify America in this critical time."

Willkie insisted that he had no second thoughts about his decision not to run for governor. At a meeting in his law office with civil rights leader Walter White, Willkie propped his feet on the big mahogany desk and watched a troop ship heading out of New York Harbor. "Look at those kids out there on that ship," he commented. "I believe I can do more in fighting for what they believe and for what they deserve by staying out of public office, even including the presidency. I would gladly say to hell with the presidency and all political offices if I felt I could do more as an individual than as governor or president or anything else."

Even if he was not a candidate, Willkie hoped to exert influence on the direction of New York's Republican party, telling state GOP leaders that he would be available to keynote the Saratoga convention or chair the platform committee. Chairman Jaeckle, the blunt, jowly Buffalo lawyer, responded that Willkie could have a lowly spot on the committee drafting the platform. As Jaeckle had calculated, Willkie was insulted and rejected any such appointment.

As it turned out, Willkie had a better offer. In July he went to Hyde Park and proposed another wartime mission. The President could not have been more delighted. Weeks earlier, Eleanor Roosevelt had expressed concern about the state of the Democratic party, and FDR had replied that the Republicans would be in poorer health when he brought Willkie into the government. In August Willkie announced that he was making a two-month tour of the Middle East, China, and the Soviet Union as FDR's personal representative to find out "about the war and how it can be won."

Some Republican officials fumed that Willkie was running out on his party during the midterm elections. "We have had no trouble from my fat friend for some time," Dewey wrote his mother. "I hear he is going to Russia before the Republican convention, so he will be where he belongs and I hope he stays there until Christmas."[21]

Dewey was nominated by acclamation in Saratoga, and the party's bitterness toward Willkie surfaced when Rolland Marvin introduced a resolution wishing him "Godspeed and success" on his trip. The pro-Dewey delegates, refusing to give Willkie any recognition, voted to send the proposal back to committee. Finally, the party's executive committee passed a resolution that wished Willkie a successful trip but said that the party had many spokesmen in foreign affairs.

CHAPTER FIFTEEN

SPECIAL ENVOY

It was a historic journey which he would remember as the high point of his public career. Over the next seven weeks, Wendell L. Willkie saw the world war on three fronts and met with such important participants as Joseph Stalin, Charles de Gaulle, and Chiang Kai-shek. "I went for three chief purposes," he later wrote. "The first was to demonstrate to our Allies and a good many neutral countries that there is unity in the United States. That was my idea. The second purpose of my trip was to accomplish certain things for the President. The third job I set out to do was to find out as much as I could, both for myself, and for the American people, about the war and how it can be won—won quickly."[1]

Ever since his return from England, Willkie had been anxious to make another trip into a war zone. In July of 1942, three American newspaper correspondents based in Kuibyshev, the Soviet Union's wartime capital, sent Willkie a cablegram urging him to make a goodwill trip to Russia. "Nothing I would like to do so much," he responded to the journalists. Willkie approached Roosevelt about the possibility of an officially sanctioned trip to Russia, China, and the Middle East. FDR was enthusiastic.[2]

"For many reasons," FDR wrote General George Marshall, "Mr. Willkie should take this trip—especially to put some pep into the officials of Egypt, Palestine, Syria, Iraq, Iran, and China."[3]

Within a few days, Willkie was invited to Hyde Park for a meeting with Roosevelt. Both men were in high spirits. Willkie joked that he had been talking too much, telling his friends that he would like to make a trip to Russia and China, and they had taken him seriously. The President replied that he would be glad to help make the arrangements. Roosevelt offered to make him an ambassador-at-large, which would accord him full official status. Willkie, however, turned down that status, because it would have required him to submit any public statements to the State Department and he wanted to be free of any restraint. FDR then suggested that Willkie make the trip as his personal representative, a more loosely defined appointment that would give him official standing without restrictions on his freedom of expression. Willkie was satisfied.[4]

The President directed the State Department to set up Willkie's itinerary in the Middle East, Russia, and China. Because of the delicate political situation in India, it was put off limits to Willkie. Roosevelt got the War Department to furnish Willkie with a Consolidated B-24 transport and crew. He asked the War and Navy departments to assign Willkie a military and a naval aide. Major Grant Mason and Willkie's brother-in-law, Captain Paul Pihl, received these appointments. FDR arranged for Office of War Information chief Elmer Davis to assign two of his deputies, Gardner Cowles and Joseph Barnes, who were friends of Willkie's, as members of the entourage. Roosevelt told another OWI official, Milton Eisenhower, that Barnes was working full-time for Willkie's political comeback.[5]

Edith Willkie was not enthused about her husband's trip and threatened to embark for Puerto Rico where Philip was stationed in the Navy if Wendell went through with his plans. "Not every mama can go to Puerto Rico to see her son," Willkie responded. "It's impossible." When Willkie wired her in Rushville that his trip had been approved by the President, she answered, "Not every mama can go to Puerto Rico, but neither can every papa go to Russia. Love, Billie." In a 1976 interview, Mrs. Willkie said that she would have been interested in going along, but FDR ruled that "no women were allowed." Clare Boothe Luce telephoned her and said, "I want you to get me on that plane going around the world, Edith Willkie. You can do this for me." Somewhat taken aback by Mrs. Luce's audacity, Edith replied, "That would make a good headline, 'Wendell Willkie Accompanied Around the World by Clare Boothe Luce.'" According to Mrs. Willkie, "She never forgave me for that."

On instructions from the President, Secretary of State Hull briefed Willkie on the countries he would be visiting. FDR drafted personal letters to Stalin, Chiang Kai-shek and other political and military leaders asking them to receive his special envoy. He wrote Chiang: "As you know, Mr. Willkie was the candidate against me in the 1940 elections and as such is the titular leader of the opposition. He has given unstinted support to the Government in its foreign policy and in the conduct of the war, and has helped to create the excellent state of unity which exists today. I particularly want him to meet you and your good wife, for I know that much good will come therefrom. I want him to realize your many and great problems and to tell you something of our problems as well."[6]

During the summer of 1942, the Allies had many problems. Germany still controlled Western and Central Europe and North Africa, and threatened to overpower the Soviet Union. Hitler had committed 70 per cent of his armies to the Russian campaign, and they were closing in on the rich oil fields of the Caucasus and had forced the evacuation of the government from Moscow. In North Africa, Germany's legendary "Desert Fox," Erwin Rommel, had dealt the British a series of humiliating defeats. In the Pacific, the Japanese had driven MacArthur from the Philippines and maintained their dominance of Asia with the recent conquests of Burma, Singapore, and the Dutch West Indies. The Americans had rebounded in the Pacific and crippled the Japanese navy at the battle of Midway.

Even so, Roosevelt was somber about Allied prospects during an August 20 lunch with Willkie. "I've got a great regard for you, even though we have differed politically in the past," said FDR. "I think you are private citizen number one. And I want to warn you. I know you've got guts, but remember, you may get to Cairo just as Cairo is falling, and you may get to Russia just at the time of a Russian collapse."[7] The forboding words did not dim Willkie's excitement about his mission.

Among the reasons FDR had encouraged Willkie to make the trip was that it would provide a dramatic demonstration to the world that the Allies were in control of strategic air routes. A German or Japanese plane could not have completed such a wide-ranging journey. In addition, the President did not underestimate the propaganda importance of having his erstwhile rival, the leader of the opposition party, as his special envoy to Stalin, Chiang, and de Gaulle.

On August 26, Willkie took off from New York's Mitchel Field in the four-engined U.S. Army bomber called the *Gulliver*. The plane was operated by a six-member Army crew headed by Major Richard

T. Kight. The flight went to West Palm Beach, then Puerto Rico, where Willkie had a brief visit with his son, who was stationed there in the Navy. The *Gulliver* touched down at Belém and Natal in Brazil, then crossed the South Atlantic to Ascenscion Island, a secret U.S. military base, and, finally, the African Gold Coast port of Accra. The flight was delayed one day in Kano, Nigeria, which Barnes remembered as a "fantastic walled city of mud huts." From there, Willkie went to Khartoum in the Anglo-Egyptian Sudan and spent an evening at the Governor's Palace. Landing in Cairo, Willkie stepped off the plane looking more rumpled than usual in a dark blue suit with a torn pocket.

"I've come for a definite purpose," he declared. "As a member of the party in opposition to the President, I want to say that there is no division in America on the question of both winning the war and establishing a just peace."

He was appalled by the proliferation of rumors and misinformation about the battle for Egypt that was being fought within one hundred miles of the Cairo metropolitan area. While en route, Willkie had heard reports that Rommel was about to capture the city and that Europeans were fleeing. "We heard tales of Nazi parachutists dropped in the Nile Valley to disorganize its last defenses," recalled Willkie. "The British Eighth Army was widely believed to be preparing to evacuate Egypt altogether, retiring to Palestine and southward into the Sudan and Kenya. Naturally, I wanted to check these reports. And Cairo itself was the world's worst place to check anything."[8]

So it was not surprising, then, that Willkie eagerly accepted the invitation of British General Bernard L. Montgomery to inspect the front, at El Alamein. Willkie went to a French department store in Cairo and bought a khaki shirt and trousers "both several sizes too small for me, but the best they had," and borrowed some bedding for the desert. With Cowles and Major General Russell L. Maxwell, commander of U.S. forces in Egypt, Willkie drove an army jeep out of Cairo and into the desert. Montgomery, who had just taken command of the British troops, had improved morale in moving headquarters from a hot, fly-infested desert site to a secluded, much cooler spot on the Mediterranean coast. The wiry, intense Montgomery was on hand to greet his American guest.

Montgomery had reassuring news. He told Willkie that the battle of Alam el Halfa, still in progress but in its last phase, would be a decisive Allied victory over Rommel's Afrika Korps. "Egypt has been saved," the British general said several times. In his makeshift map room, Montgomery reviewed highlights of the battle and explained how his men had blocked Rommel's thrust toward Alexandria. "It is now mathematically certain that I will eventually destroy Rommel," he said. "This battle was the critical test."

A loner who never mixed easily with his peers, Montgomery took pains to cultivate Willkie's favor. That night, he entertained the American with stories of his boyhood in Northern Ireland and his years in the British Army. Montgomery confided that his personal library and family mementos had been destroyed in a German air raid. Willkie later described the general as "scholarly" and "almost fanatical," and passionately addicted to work. Montgomery told Willkie that earlier British setbacks in the desert had been the result of poor coordination of tank, artillery, and air forces. Since his arrival, he noted that the air officer had been brought into his headquarters and they had achieved coordination of attack which had been a major factor in turning back Rommel. His superior, General Sir Harold R. L. G. Alexander, attended the dinner for Willkie in Montgomery's tent. The next morning, Willkie went swimming in the Mediterranean with both of the renowned British generals.

Then Montgomery took Willkie to the battlefields. "All the while we were going over the front," said Willkie, "the British artillery was thundering steadily and British and American aircraft were harassing Rommel's retreating troops. The Germans, in retaliation, were sending squadrons of Stuttgart planes in quick, sharp strafing raids against British artillery positions."

Willkie examined dozens of captured German tanks, most of which had been blown up on Montgomery's orders. In the wrecked tanks, Montgomery pointed out the charred remnants of British supplies. "You see, Willkie, the devils have been living on us," he said. "But they are not going to do it again. At least, they are never going to use these tanks against us again."

General Montgomery asked Willkie to make an unofficial announcement of the Allied victory. Such a statement, he argued, would lift British morale at a crucial time. Asked why, then, he did not make the announcement himself, the general replied that if he commented publicly it might give the Nazis an opportunity to slip away before the climactic battle of El Alamein. Montgomery said that Willkie's words could strengthen Allied prestige without sending the Germans into retreat. With Montgomery's assistance, Willkie prepared a statement and called a press conference in a large assembly tent that the general often used for staff meetings.[9]

"The battle which has just been won is perhaps one of the most decisive in history," proclaimed Willkie. "It is comparable to the Battle of the Nile when Nelson destroyed the French fleet. Egypt is saved. Rommel is stopped and a beginning has been made on the task of throwing the Nazis out of Africa."

Willkie's remarks were censored by British officials, who had been instructed to be ultraconservative in editing reports from the front. "Goddamn it, boys," Willkie growled to reporters, "nobody's got the right to censor anything I say. I'm a responsible person." Churchill later told Willkie that his statement from the battlefield had done the British cause "no end of good."[10]

In his talks with British officials, Willkie was disappointed at their reluctance to talk about dismantling the colonial system at the end of the war. Like FDR, he felt that the colonies held by European powers should be granted independence. The British seemed resentful of any such suggestion. In Alexandria Willkie talked about the colonial system during a dinner at the home of British Admiral Sir Henry Harwood. "What I got," Willkie later wrote, "was Rudyard Kipling, untainted even with the liberalism of Cecil Rhodes. These men, executing the policies made in London, had no idea that the world was changing. The British colonial system was not perfect in their eyes; it seemed to me simply that no one of them had ever thought of it as anything that might possibly be changed or modified in any way."[11]

Willkie attributed the cultural and political stagnation of Egypt to the absence of a middle class. He called on King Farouk at his palace, and the young monarch seemed more concerned about his image in American newspapers than in the welfare of his countrymen. Already known as a gambler and voluptuary, the last of the pharaohs complained to Willkie that he had not received a shipment of American station wagons. Farouk expressed concern over the "bad press" which he was receiving in the United States. The king's secretary noted that he had received a large amount of "fan mail" at the time of his marriage and could not understand why Americans had turned on him.

Farouk's pro-Axis sentiments and his sybaritic life-style were chiefly responsible for his unpopularity in the United States. The British were forced to put military pressure on him before the Egyptian king would honor his country's treaty obligations with the Allies. Even then, Egypt did not enter the war.

Willkie recognized that Farouk was little more than a soft, overindulgent playboy. He was much more favorably impressed with Egypt's pronationalist Prime Minister, the round, genial Mustafa Nahhas. Six years earlier it had been Nahhas who had negotiated the treaty with England which gave Egypt nominal independence in exchange for a mutual defense pact. "I told him if he would come to the United States and run for office," recalled Willkie, "he would undoubtedly make a formidable candidate."[12]

Throughout the Middle East, Willkie sensed a growing discontent with the centuries-old feudal system in which a wealthy elite maintained control over fertile lands and their resources. Everywhere, he was disturbed by the fact that the vast majority of people were impoverished and illiterate and lived in conditions of filth and squalor. Willkie recalled "the most startling example" of bad health was in Teheran, where the city's water supply ran through open gutters along the streets. One result of this practice, he learned, was that four out of every five children were dead before the age of six. On the streets of Cairo, Jerusalem, and Baghdad, Willkie saw little children who had been blinded by trachoma. He made the argument that the developed countries of the West had a responsibility to improve public health services in the region.

From Egypt, Willkie took a Pan-American flight across the Mediterranean and over the Taurus Mountains into Turkey. Because of the government's neutrality in the war, Turkish officials had refused to allow Willkie's army plane into the country and asked that military officers in his entourage wear civilian clothes. At this time, Turkey feared a possible Nazi invasion even though it had signed nonaggression pacts with the Axis and Allied powers. Nazi radio announced that influential Turks were going to shun the American visitor. In fact, Prime Minister Shukru Saracoglu cut short an inspection trip to northeastern provinces in order to confer with Willkie, and a tumultuous crowd showed up to welcome the special envoy at the Ankara airport. The State Department reported that the Turkish press "gave more space to his visit than to any single event in recent Turkish history."[13]

"I had a perfect trip all the way over," he told the throng at the airport. "As a matter of fact, I am feeling in fighting form. Never felt better in my life." He expressed hope that his journey would dispel Axis propaganda "that all of America is not united." Willkie added, "As far as fighting this war and looking for a just peace after it is over are concerned, the United States is 100 percent united."

At a press conference, Willkie was told that Axis broadcasters had protested his presence in Turkey. He deadpanned, "Invite Hitler to send to Turkey, as a representative of Germany, his opposition candidate." Asked about the length of the war, Willkie replied, "I shall not try to predict the day the war is going to be over, but you are going to see the increasing effect of our production and arms very rapidly."

As always, Willkie enjoyed the give and take with newspapermen. "Is there any question anyone would like to ask me?" he said. "If you think it will be embarrassing, you should be sure to ask me."

One reporter asked what plans were being made for the postwar peace. "I think the American people are looking for a peace of no territorial conquest, a peace in which the basic raw materials of the world are made available to all nations, and that the old idea of isolation and a disregard for other countries will pass out. They feel that small nations as well as large must have the right to aspire to democracy."

A second reporter asked about America's chances against Japan in the Pacific. "I don't wish to discuss details of naval strategy," said Willkie, "but there is not the slightest question in the United States that the United Nations allies are going to destroy the Japanese navy piece by piece." The U.S. Navy had just defeated the Japanese in the battle of the Coral Sea and in the key battle of Midway.

Willkie impressed Turkish leaders with his blunt, frank assessment of the North African war, including an admission of Allied mistakes in the desert campaign. Now, however, he reported that the Allies were on the verge of an important victory. Gardner Cowles recalled years later that Willkie persuaded Prime Minister Saracoglu and Foreign Minister Numan Menemencioglu that American industrial production would ultimately doom the Axis powers. The Foreign Minister told Willkie that he hoped and anticipated an Allied victory and asserted that Turkey, though vulnerable, would defend itself against Nazi attack. Willkie gave assurances of FDR's postwar concern for Turkish boundaries and trade agreements.

Near the end of his talk with Willkie, the Prime Minister assured him that Turkey would indeed fight if attacked by Germany and promised not to yield to any Axis demand which violated his country's neutrality. New York *Times* correspondent Raymond Brock said that Willkie's personal diplomacy had been an important factor in winning over Turkish leaders to the Allied cause. "His visit has contributed materially to consolidating our position here and has unquestionably strengthened Turk-American friendship," the U.S. embassy reported to Washington. "What has especially impressed the Turks is the fact that the leader of the opposition party in the United States should have undertaken such a mission with the avowed purpose of supporting the President wholeheartedly."[14]

On the morning of September 10, Willkie flew to Beirut and was met by General Georges Catroux, French military governor of Syria and Lebanon, and Brigadier General Sir Edward L. Spears, head of the British military mission. William M. Gwynn, American consul in Beirut, had arranged for Willkie to be the houseguest of General Charles de Gaulle, leader of the Free French, in the Residence des Pins, an elegant palace. "General de Gaulle had said that he felt that it was his place to receive as his houseguest the personal representative of President Roosevelt," Gwynn wrote Hull, "and I foresaw no objection to that, thinking it would be considered as our modest equivalent to a similar invitation to the White House."

Willkie, though, rebuked Gwynn in front of Catroux and Spears, and told him that he wanted to stay in a hotel. The diplomat, attempting to avoid "a painful scene," asked him to wait until they could discuss it privately. But Willkie was then whisked off in a limousine with General Catroux to the palace. When Gwynn caught up with him, Willkie demanded that he obtain rooms in a hotel. While supporting the Free French, Willkie did not want to offend the Lebanese by staying in the palace.

Instead, Gwynn pulled General Catroux aside and explained his predicament. Willkie's luggage had already arrived and his suite had been prepared, the French official retorted. If the American refused to stay overnight, it would create much embarrassment. "He therefore begged me to attempt to convince Willkie to stay," Gwynn recalled. "We five Americans then went upstairs where breakfast was waiting to talk things over. Witman and I were then asked to leave the Willkie party alone for consultation. Before leaving I requested Willkie in making his decision to give some thought to the position he would put me in if he decided finally to move out of the residence. After quite some time, we were informed, rather grudgingly I felt, that the party would stay and would go through the program roughly as I had outlined it."[15]

Shortly afterward, Willkie conferred with de Gaulle. For more than two years, the tall, strong-willed general had been recognized as the leader of the Free French, the symbol of resistance to Nazi occupation of his native land. In de Gaulle's view, the French had to take a major part in the liberation of France in order to regain a significant role in the world. "Victory must reconcile France with herself and with her friends," de Gaulle wrote FDR in the fall of 1942, "but it will not be possible if she does not participate in it."

De Gaulle complained to Willkie about his treatment by the Allies. While Churchill had given him a base of operations in London, their relations were strained. The British Prime Minister acidly commented that the greatest cross he had to bear was that of Lorraine. FDR considered de Gaulle something of a nuisance and maintained official relations with Vichy, which controlled the French military and had condemned de Gaulle to death as a traitor.

Willkie thought it had been a mistake for the Roosevelt administration to turn its back on de Gaulle. Asked by reporters about U.S. relations with the Vichy regime, he said, "I don't want to discuss that. My views don't correspond with those of the administration." FBI director J. Edgar Hoover had reported to the State Department that Willkie had been in contact in New York with representatives of the Free French movement and was an ardent supporter of their cause.[16]

In his meeting with de Gaulle, Willkie found him vain, brilliant, self-centered, unyielding, and difficult to work with. They conferred in de Gaulle's columned salon, which was decorated with paintings and a statue of Napoleon. The forty-nine-year-old general wore a white dress uniform and Willkie a blue business suit. In their presence, one of de Gaulle's aides compared him to Joan of Arc, and the general accepted the remark without any visible sign of humility while dazzling his American guest with a long monologue about French history and the French people. When Willkie referred to the Free French as a "movement," de Gaulle snapped, "The Fighting French are not a movement. The Fighting French are France itself." De Gaulle asserted that the Free French were entitled to a bigger voice in Allied councils, and he presented the French side in the dispute with Britain over control of Syria and Lebanon. Willkie suggested that de Gaulle renounce the French colonial system. "I cannot sacrifice or compromise my principles," said the general.[17]

Still smoldering over Willkie's bold suggestion, de Gaulle did not come downstairs the next morning for the American's departure ceremonies. "Willkie didn't warm up to de Gaulle," said Gardner Cowles years later. "As Roosevelt would find out later, we thought that de Gaulle had a high opinion of his importance."[18]

On September 11, Willkie arrived in Jerusalem and talked separately with Jewish and Arab leaders about the conflict over Palestine. These meetings were held in the home of Lowell C. Pinkerton, American consul general. The house had a double staircase and, as Willkie would interview representatives of one group, another group left the room by the back staircase and a third group would wait outside the front door. He talked with Moshe Shertok, who called for the immigration of two million more Jews into Palestine, as well as with Zionist hard-liner Arieh Altman, who wanted ten million immigrants to build a Jewish state. Moderate Arab leader Ruhi Abdulhadi told him of the growing discontent with British rule. Arab nationalist Awni Bey Abdul Hadi rejected any Jewish claim to Palestine. Willkie talked for hours with Henrietta Szold, the American Zionist, and they agreed that the British were encouraging Jewish-Arab tensions in order to sustain their political control over the region. In blunt language, Willkie told Sir Harold MacMichael, the British high commissioner, that both the Jews and Arabs should be brought into the government of Palestine. "It is probably unrealistic to believe that such a complex question as the Arab-Jewish one, founded in ancient history and religion," Willkie later wrote, "and involved as it is with high international policy and politics, can be solved by good will and simple honesty."[19]

It was obvious that the British and French did not like to hear his comments about the breakup of their colonial systems. Yet the more he traveled into their empires, the more certain Willkie became of his view of the future. In Lebanon, he did not believe General E. L. Spears's statement that the British had no political ambitions in the region. In oil-rich Iraq, members of the government privately told Willkie that they were suspicious of Britain.

When the *Gulliver* landed in Baghdad on September 12, Willkie was received by a white-uniformed honor guard of Iraqi soldiers and the band struck up "The Star Spangled Banner." Although Willkie stayed in the royal palace, he found time to mingle with the local population in bazaars and coffeehouses. He drank Turkish coffee and watched backgammon being played. "I had an opportunity to see residents of Baghdad who were not government officials, who were not important people, but were just people, which is the finest thing in the world to see anywhere one goes," he said. "I am afraid from what I saw of some of the backgammon games that I had better not start to play backgammon in this community. I'm afraid I would get trimmed."

Willkie drove through the poorest sections of the city, inspected a blanket factory, and laid a wreath on the tombs of Faisal and Ghazi, Iraq's first two kings. Addressing a state dinner at the palace, Willkie said, "After the war is over, the United States intends to use its uttermost efforts for the establishment of a world in which all men—irrespective of whether they are citizens of powerful or small nations—may live free and decent lives of their own choosing." On his departure, Willkie received a spontaneous ovation from thousands of Iraqis as his motorcade headed for the airport.

By the time he reached Baghdad, Willkie had grown tired of the endless receptions and formal state dinners. So when the British governor general had Cowles make arrangements for a banquet, the *Look* publisher booked some entertainment, a group called the "Girls of Baghdad." At the dinner, Cowles was seated next to the horse-faced wife of the governor general, who bored him with trivia about archaeology. The governor general stood and announced, "At the request of Gardner Cowles, we shall now be entertained by the Girls of Baghdad." "The girls" turned out to be the sultry, scantily clad women who ran the brothels. Willkie greatly enjoyed the show and kept shouting to Cowles, but his friend was trapped with his dinner companion and hardly got to look up from the table.[20]

Nuri Pasha, Iraq's Prime Minister, confided to Willkie that he was ready to declare war on the Axis and formally join the Allies. "I even worked with him at his request, on the address which he planned to deliver while I was in Baghdad," Willkie said a year later. "He was particularly anxious to do this during the visit of an American as a demonstration to the world of his country's goodwill to America and her desire to be aligned with America in the struggle against the Axis. He was convinced that the Arab world which looks to Iraq as the only nominally independent nation, would follow his lead." But the British ambassador persuaded the Prime Minister to delay his announcement several months, when it could be most effective for propaganda purposes.[21]

"It is almost impossible to describe the electrifying effect on Iraq," American Chargé d'Affaires William S. Farrell wrote Hull. "Mr. Willkie's visit produced a most happy impression, not only on the government, but also on the Baghdad man-in-the-street, who was gratified by his friendly attitude and democratic manner. Indeed, British comment in Baghdad was that while the visit had strengthened pro-American and pro-Allied feeling, it had nevertheless resulted also in some increase in the anti-British sentiment because of the extreme contrast between Mr. Willkie's democracy and the pukka sahib exclusiveness of the local British community."

Much to his embarrassment, Willkie left behind some confidential papers in his room at the Iraqi palace. The palace staff turned the documents over to the American legation, and they were forwarded to the State Department by diplomatic pouch. Willkie was so disorganized that it was surprising that it had taken this long for him to lose some of his diplomatic portfolio.[22]

From Iraq, Willkie went to Teheran. One year earlier, Soviet and British troops had invaded Iran and overthrown the pro-German Riza Shah. The Allies replaced him with his son, Muhammad Riza Pahlavi. At the time of Willkie's visit, Soviet troops occupied the northern half of the country and British soldiers occupied the south. Willkie lunched with the boyish Shah of Iran in a well-manicured Arabian nights garden on the palace grounds. Willkie slapped the Shah on the back and called him "a great guy." Told that the Shah had never been in a plane, Willkie impulsively took him on a flight over his country. In appreciation, the Shah gave him a handsome Persian rug.

Willkie urged the young Shah to make an open declaration supporting the Allies, but the Iranian ruler said he would have to shape public opinion before he could take such a step. The Prime Minister interjected that the problem stemmed from the unpopular occupation by the Soviets and British, which had created much pro-German sentiment throughout the country. The answer to this question, suggested the Shah, was a strong American military mission which could train Iranian soldiers. He argued that Iran's most pressing need was a strong army to maintain internal security, something that would become an obsession during his thirty-seven-year reign. When the Shah told Willkie that he was interested in a mutual defense pact with Turkey, the American passed word to Secretary of State Hull and it was so arranged with Turkish officials. "Willkie's visit to Teheran was an unqualified success," the U.S. legation reported to Washington. "Willkie's visit has done much to clarify atmosphere here by focusing public attention on real significance of war and by bluntly pointing out to Iranians their own self-interest requires active sincere cooperation."[23]

Edmund Stevens, foreign correspondent of the *Christian Science Monitor,* who followed Willkie's Mideast trip, wrote, "In countries where speech is used to conceal rather than to express thought, Willkie's disarming directness was like a breath of mountain air in a hot, stale room." At one state dinner, Willkie cracked, "If you want to see the United Nations win, don't just sit there in the bleachers and throw pop bottles." The audience responded warmly. "To the semi-colonial nations of the Middle East," Stevens concluded, "desiring emancipation above all other things, Willkie was the Four Freedoms taken out of the realm of the abstract and clothed in a rumpled blue suit."[24]

On Thursday, September 17, Willkie arrived in the Soviet Union. The *Gulliver* sprinted through the skies above the Caspian Sea, across the flats of the Ural River, along the Volga, and landed in Kuibyshev, which had served as the temporary capital until shortly before his visit, when the government returned to Moscow. On his first day in Russia, Willkie met with Soviet Foreign Office diplomats and U.S. ambassador Admiral William H. Standley, former chief of naval operations. Standley had been lukewarm to Willkie's visit on the grounds that it was designed to enhance his political stature. What really bothered the admiral, though, was the fact that FDR bypassed him in sending special envoys such as Willkie, Averell Harriman, and Harry Hopkins to meet with Soviet leaders. Understandably, Standley felt that such luminaries diminished his own standing, and the ambassador turned down Willkie's request to fly directly to Moscow from Teheran. According to Standley, there could be no changes in the itinerary, but Willkie considered it as a resentful act.[25]

On his first full day in the Soviet Union, Willkie spent fifteen hours visiting state farms and factories. At each stop, Soviet workers asked him when the Allies would be launching a second front in Europe to share the fighting against Nazi Germany. Willkie said it was his opinion that a second front would soon be opened. That night he was the honored guest at a dinner given by the Chinese ambassador. Following the dinner, he attended a performance of Tchaikovsky's *Swan Lake* by the Bolshoi Ballet. When Willkie fell behind schedule and arrived fifteen minutes late, he found that the theater had delayed the performance. At the end of the ballet, he leaned over the box rail onto the stage and presented a bouquet to Irina Tikhomirnova, the attractive star ballerina, and kissed her. She threw kisses in his direction when he returned to his box, and the audience roared, "Willkie! Willkie! Willkie!"

On Sunday, September 20, it was cold, gray, and rainy when he arrived in Moscow. The strains of the long trip were beginning to show, and there were pouches under his eyes. At the Foreign Office Guest House, he had a huge lunch that included caviar, smoked salmon, cheese, tomatoes, roast beef, chicken, ham, sausages, grapes, apples, vodka, wine, brandy, and coffee. On Monday, he walked through the streets of the capital accompanied by six Soviet bodyguards. In Red Square, he attempted to see Lenin's tomb but was turned away and told that it was closed for the duration of the war. He rode the subway, visited the Lenin Library, heard a concert, and inspected a munitions factory and the city's antiaircraft defenses.

In a meeting with Soviet Foreign Minister Vyacheslav Molotov, Willkie learned that the Russian situation was much more serious than he had been led to believe. The Red Army was fighting desperately, said Molotov, and the situation in the Caucasus was dangerous. In addition, the Foreign Minister said that the Nazis were seeking to drive a wedge through the center of Stalingrad. Asked for his own opinion on the war, Willkie was optimistic about Allied prospects in North Africa and the Pacific. The American said that Germany would be defeated only by direct intervention and not by bombing, starvation, or internal disaffection. Molotov replied that bombing was, however, of much help.[26]

Stalin's one prime objective was to get the Allies to open a second front against the Nazis, which would relieve the German pressure on the embattled Soviets. In January Allied leaders had assured him they would invade Europe within the year. By the summer, however, the British had vetoed a European front as premature. One month before Willkie's visit, Churchill went to Moscow and broke the news to Stalin.

Churchill informed the Soviet dictator that he and FDR had determined that it would be fruitless to attempt a cross-channel invasion in 1942, but the Western Allies were planning a full-scale invasion of North Africa which would, he argued, be of help to the Soviet Union. Roosevelt had not given Willkie any information about Torch, the invasion of North Africa, and he had got his first intimation that a major operation would soon be underway from General Montgomery in Egypt. Willkie suggested this possibility to Soviet officials and they replied that a Mediterranean operation would not create much of a diversion from the Russian front. "Churchill handled himself very poorly over there," Willkie told Forrest Davis. "He got into foolish arguments with those people."[27]

On Wednesday night, Willkie was summoned to the Kremlin for a meeting with Stalin. In the confusion, he hurriedly looked through his briefcase and luggage in a vain search for the President's handwritten letter to Stalin. When he got back from the Kremlin, Willkie finally discovered FDR's letter crumpled up in a pile of clothes. It was never delivered, Barnes and Cowles later admitted.[28]

The bearlike Willkie towered over Stalin. "Though stockily built, he was shorter than I expected him to be," he recalled. "Actually he would have to stand on his tiptoes to look over my shoulder." Willkie thought it was remarkable that the larger-than-life man of steel portrayed in Soviet war propaganda was a small man. He observed that Stalin's pockmarked white face looked hard and that the Soviet marshal was visibly tired. He wore a gray military shirt, pink whipcord trousers, and black boots.

For nearly three hours, Stalin and Willkie talked about the war. "When he described to me Russia's desperate situation as to fuel, transportation, military equipment, and manpower," said Willkie, "he was genuinely dramatic." The American added, "He asked searching questions, each of them loaded like a revolver, each of them designed to cut through to what he believed to be the heart of the matter that interested him. He pushes aside pleasantries and compliments and is impatient of generalities."

Stalin grumbled that the Allies were not honoring their commitments. Why, he asked, had FDR "allowed Churchill to run the war?" The Soviet leader flared his resentment at the Prime Minister for going back on the promise of a European front. He also accused Churchill of the "theft" of 152 American lend-lease planes from a Soviet-bound convoy in Scotland. "My talk with Stalin," Willkie said later, "was principally about Lend-Lease arrangements with which he wasn't satisfied, and which he wished to have changed. He demanded 10,000 trucks a month, three million bushels of wheat, condensed foods, and so on." On his return, Willkie helped push through more liberal lend-lease terms for the Soviets.

Willkie brought up the Polish question, expressing the hope that Soviets would support a free and independent Poland following the war. Stalin guardedly replied that he would be willing to discuss the matter with Polish officials.

On a lighter note, Willkie told Stalin that he had been much impressed by the quality of Russian schools and libraries and joked, "If you continue to educate the Russian people, Mr. Stalin, the first thing you know, you'll educate yourself right out of a job." Stalin roared with laughter. Willkie went on, "Mr. Stalin, you know I have been in business and at the bar all my mature life. I am rather glad your lot was not cast in America. You would have made tough competition."

"Mr. Willkie," said Stalin, "you know I grew up a Georgian peasant. I am unschooled in pretty talk. All I can say is I like you very much."[29]

Following this meeting, Willkie traveled 130 miles over muddy roads in an American jeep to the Russian front. He was accompanied by Cowles, Barnes, and Major General Follett Bradley of the Army Air Force, chief of a lend-lease mission to Moscow. On his tour, Willkie dropped into dugouts to study maps with Red Army commanders, inspected Soviet defenses, and looked over positions which had been recaptured from the Nazis. He talked with eighteen young Nazi prisoners, who wore loose, floppy uniforms, and saw the damp, decomposing bodies of fallen German soldiers. On a hill overlooking the city of Rzhev, Willkie heard the thunder of German and Russian shells exploding. He asked thirty-eight-year-old Soviet General Dmitri Leliushenko the size of the front the Red Army was defending. The general glared and told the interpreter, "You tell Mr. Willkie, I'm not defending anything, I'm attacking."

Everywhere, he was asked by soldiers, factory workers, peasants, schoolchildren, and government officials about the failure of the Western Allies to establish a second front in Europe. The Soviets had already suffered more than five million casualties and had lost important industrial centers, the most fertile farmlands, and their oil fields. Enormously touched by the courage and strength of the Russian people, Willkie understood their bitterness over the second front. On his own, Willkie decided to speak out on the controversy that had strained the Grand Alliance.

"I have kept asking myself," Willkie declared in Moscow, "what is the most effective way we can help to win our war by helping these heroic allies. Personally, I am now convinced that we can best help by establishing with Britain a real second front in Europe at the earliest possible moment which our military leaders will approve. Perhaps some of them will need some public prodding. Next summer might be too late.

"It is easy to sit in comfort in America and read about Russians dying by the thousands to hold Stalingrad," he went on. "But I found it difficult to explain to one Russian soldier at the front, for example, why America and England were not ready now to fight in Europe in a direct attack on Germany. He was not impressed with the risk our experts had pointed out to me."

Willkie's remarks made front-page news throughout the English-speaking world and reopened the debate over a second front. As FDR's special envoy, it was at first presumed that he was speaking for the President. Roosevelt, however, told reporters at a press conference that he had read the headlines about Willkie's statement but had not thought it worthwhile to read the articles because they were "speculative." The *Army and Navy Journal* denounced Willkie for "complete ignorance of fundamental military principles." Secretary of State Hull told Vice-President Wallace that he blamed Willkie's performance on Joseph Barnes, who he said was "half Communist."[30] Senator Thomas Connally of Texas called it "most unfortunate that Mr. Willkie has been so free with his comment and his newspaper headlines."

Prime Minister Churchill spoke out in the House of Commons on the "undesirability of public statements or speculations as to the time or place of future allied offensive operations." Asked if he was referring to "Mr. Wendell Willkie," Churchill did not answer. Clement R. Attlee, Deputy Prime Minister, asserted that there was "no need for public prodding" and said that Allied war plans "involved the lives of men and women and cannot be affected by demands made by irresponsible people." Lord Croft, parliamentary secretary in the War Office, claimed that the English were already fighting on thirteen fronts. Two leaders of the British Labor party, Emanuel Shinwell and Lord Strabolgi, endorsed Willkie's call for a second front. From Washington, Lord Halifax reported to the Foreign Office that Willkie's comments were "probably increasing his popularity with the man in the street and middle-of-the-road opinion generally."[31]

Willkie was not surprised by the British reaction to his second-front statement, but FDR's flip remark made him furious. At 2 A.M., he was awakened at his guesthouse in Chungking by a newspaper reporter who asked for his response to Roosevelt's statement that his comments were not worth reading. Willkie told reporters later in the day that he had been commissioned by the President to do certain things, and he had performed these duties to the best of his ability. "But when I speak for myself," he said, "I'm Wendell Willkie and I say what I damn please."

On Willkie's last night in Moscow, Stalin gave a dinner for him at the Kremlin, with most of the Politburo and the diplomatic corps as guests. Later, Willkie recalled that he drank fifty-three vodka toasts "bottoms up, glass over the head" during the banquet. Willkie sat at Stalin's right, and when the Soviet leader scolded the interpreters for speaking in dull, flat voices, the American offered a toast to the interpreters as "the only ones who are working here tonight." Stalin raised his glass and took another sip of vodka. Much later in the evening, Major Grant Mason, Willkie's military aide, proposed a toast to the Russian and Allied pilots. When the toast had been drunk, Stalin remained standing and, raising his voice, alleged that the Western Allies had not supplied the Red Army with the planes that had been promised. He charged that Churchill had stolen 152 fighter planes which were being sent to the Soviet Union through lend-lease.

The British ambassador, Sir Archibald Clark Kerr, his face reddened, stood up and said that he had always admired Stalin's candor and wished he would tell the rest of the story. Stalin, however, sat down.

Willkie then rose and made a graceful rebuttal. He looked at Stalin and praised the determination of the Soviets in fighting Nazi aggression. Two years earlier, he noted, the British had stood alone against Hitler. If it had been conquered, Willkie said that Russia's situation would be even more precarious than it was. There were always misunderstandings and tensions in great coalitions, Willkie went on, and if the Grand Alliance held together, he predicted it would win the war. Hitler would like nothing more than to pull it apart. Willkie put his arm on Stalin's shoulder and turned him around so that they were facing each other.

The American lifted his glass and toasted the Allies–Great Britain, Russia, China, and the United States–"united now and who, for the peace and economic security of the world, must remain united after the war." The Soviet dictator drank Willkie's toast. Willkie had upstaged the old master on his own turf. "It was clear to everyone around the table," Barnes later recalled, "that he was rebuking Stalin."

Stalin leaned across the interpreter and told his guest, "You are a plain-speaking man, I see. I like plain-spokenness, but you wouldn't have stolen 152 planes from me."[32]

Ralph Parker, Moscow correspondent for the New York *Times,* reported, "The effect of Mr. Willkie's visit, all are agreed here, was considerable." Parker said that Willkie had obtained a more comprehensive view of the Soviet war effort "than has been afforded any foreigner since the war's outbreak" and added that his personal diplomacy had "important consequences" on Soviet-American relations.[33]

During Willkie's long flight from Moscow to China, he confided his apprehensions about Stalin. He told Cowles that this was the time, when Russia was in a desperate situation, to press Stalin for concessions on the postwar future of Eastern Europe. "He urged that we settle on the terms of the peace when our bargaining power was at its height," Cowles recalled. "He kept worrying about the Russian leaders. When he was talking with Stalin, Molotov, Vishinsky, and other members of the Politburo, he detected in them a rebirth of the brutality and imperialism of the old Czarist governments."

"He kept exploring in his mind during the long flight," Cowles said years later, "how Russia could be bound during the war to participate after the war in a real league of nations strong enough to preserve peace, promote more equality between have and have-not nations and break down trade barriers so all people might have a chance at a rising standard of living."[34]

Willkie also had growing concerns about the war aims of the Western Allies. Prior to his departure, he had discussed the 1941 Atlantic Charter with Secretary of State Hull and brought up the right of colonial peoples to determine their own form of government once the war had ended. "He told me," Willkie said later, "that the Atlantic Charter didn't apply to the Pacific. I was so amazed by this that I couldn't believe my own ears and I went back again, taking along one of my companions on the trip so that he could hear it also and verify my hearing."[35] In early September, Churchill had told the British parliament that he flatly opposed any effort to define postwar goals "when the end of the war is not in sight." In North Africa, the Middle East, and Asia, Willkie had been appalled by the old-fashioned imperialism of British officials. He talked with representatives of nationalist movements in each region and made no secret of the fact that he supported their vision of the future. In China Willkie issued a sweeping attack on Western imperialism and its colonial system. Speaking in Chungking, he reported that the majority of colonial people were supporting the Allied war effort but were increasingly suspicious about the readiness of the Western powers to grant independence to their colonies following the war.

"The colonial days are past," asserted Willkie. "We believe this war must mean an end to the empire of nations over other nations. No foot of Chinese soil, for example, should be or can be ruled from now on, except by the people who live on it. And we must say so now, not after the war.

"We believe it is the world's job to find some system for helping colonial peoples who join the United Nations' cause to become free and independent nations. We must set up firm timetables under which they can work out and train governments of their own choosing, and we must establish iron-clad guarantees, administered by all the United Nations jointly, that they shall not slip back into colonial status.

"Some say these subjects should be hushed until victory is won.

Exactly the reverse is true. Sincere efforts to find progressive solutions now will bring strength to our cause. Remember, opponents of social change always urge delay because of some present crisis. After the war, the changes may be too little and too late."

On the home front, Willkie's blow against imperialism was enormously popular. President Roosevelt told reporters that Willkie was echoing the Atlantic Charter's pledge "to all humanity." FDR strongly favored the independence of colonial peoples after a period of international trusteeship under the kind of timetables suggested by Willkie. Anglophile columnists Joseph Alsop, Dorothy Thompson, and Walter Lippmann criticized Willkie for straining America's ties with Britain in the midst of war.

"By speaking out boldly and clearly at Chungking," said the *New Republic,* "Wendell Willkie has moved from the national to the world arena of leadership. One's hope for a postwar world is renewed by this phenomenon of a man whose innate democracy breaks through his lifetime of capitalist thinking, and on whom the impact of great world events has been to make his mind flexible with what he has learned, rather than rigid with fear."

Willkie's speech created a sensation in England. Churchill was especially touchy about the issue of colonialism. On November 10, the Prime Minister responded to Willkie. "Let me make this clear in case there should be any mistake about it in any quarter," said Churchill. "We mean to hold our own. I have not become the King's first minister in order to preside over the liquidation of the British Empire." One of the reasons Churchill was so upset was that he knew Roosevelt shared Willkie's view on colonialism. From then on, the Prime Minister went out of his way to make disparaging remarks about Willkie. At a White House luncheon, he told FDR that Willkie reminded him of a Newfoundland dog, jumping into the water and coming out, shaking himself, pawing the ladies, and sweeping the dishes off the table as he wagged his tail.[36]

Another reason that Willkie struck a nerve at No. 10 Downing Street was the fact that his defiant words were well received in the British press. *The Times* of London said, "To deprecate the 'liquidation' of the British Empire is surely a false approach. The pride and achievement of the modern British Empire are that it has become in a certain sense a self-liquidating concern, dissolving itself by an orderly process into a commonwealth of peoples united by a common ideal of partnership in freedom." The Manchester *Guardian* commended Willkie for raising the issue and the *Daily Telegraph* described him as "a candid friend."

Lord Samuel, a former high commissioner of Palestine, observed that Willkie had not called for the "liquidation" of the British Empire as much as "the more rapid extension of self-government." Arthur Creech Jones, a British delegate to an international conference in Canada, wrote Harold Macmillan: "The temperature about Britain is pretty low. The references in the Willkie speeches about British colonial policy, colonial status and the rest, are widely held by men everywhere and by practically all the Americans."

Willkie received the biggest, most elaborately staged reception of his forty-nine-day journey in China. Generalissimo and Madame Chiang Kai-shek had been advised that Willkie might well be the next President of the United States, and they spared no effort in seeking his goodwill and friendship. T. V. Soong, the Harvard-educated chairman of the Bank of China and Madame Chiang's brother, had recommended that Willkie be given special attention because it was likely that he would be a participant in the postwar peace conference.[37] "He's to be smothered," American General Joseph Stilwell wrote in his diary. The Chiangs honored Willkie at parades, receptions, banquets, military reviews, and other public celebrations. Their strategy, Stilwell reported, was to keep their guest "well insulated from pollution by Americans. The idea is to get him so exhausted and keep him so torpid with food and drink that his faculties will be dulled and he'll be stuffed with the right doctrines."[38]

"Since President Ulysses S. Grant, who came to China in 1879," said *Ta Kung Pao,* then China's most influential newspaper, "Mr. Willkie is the first leading American statesman to visit China."

In preparation for Willkie's arrival, tight security measures were imposed. The U.S. and Chinese military declined public comment about his itinerary. Japanese scouting planes, looking for Willkie, headed toward Chungking but ran into fog and moved back into occupied territory. One week later, thirty-five Japanese planes bombed a train which they had been told was the one carrying the American envoy on his inspection of the North China war zone. It wasn't. In the front-line trenches along the Yellow River, Willkie and his group abandoned a railway handcar when four Japanese shells exploded nearby, and they walked to a safer vantage point. "There is more danger of my being killed by the kindness of the Chinese than by enemy bullets," said Willkie.

A flag-waving crowd of ten thousand met Willkie at the Chungking airport on October 2. He wore a wrinkled gray business suit and white shirt as he stepped down from the *Gulliver*. "I have fallen so much in love with the Chinese people," said Willkie, "that it is going to be difficult to carry out my fact-finding mission with the correct critical approach."

Though Willkie spoke with warmhearted humor, it turned out that his mature judgment was outweighed by his affection for Chiang Kai-shek and the Soong dynasty. "He fell into every trap," John Morton Blum later wrote, "that caught most of his countrymen who visited wartime Chungking."[39]

The Chiangs put on an extravaganza for Willkie's arrival. One million firecrackers were exploded during his eleven-mile procession from the airport to the capital. The police razed shacks, shut down the shabbiest shops, forced beggars to move outside the city limits, and saw to it that the streets were decorated with banners welcoming the American. U.S. Ambassador Clarence Edward Gauss was annoyed when Willkie chose to stay at an official government house rather than the American embassy. The ambassador stormed out of the airport, telling subordinates that he did not care if he ever saw Willkie again. "By god, I would have voted for Willkie last election," he told an aide. "But in 1944, I'm voting for that Socialist fellow, Elmer Thomas [*sic*]." Davenport had told Willkie that Gauss was "prejudiced, uninformed, disliked" and a stickler for bureaucratic detail. During most of his stay in China, Willkie ignored him.[40]

In his guesthouse, Willkie was furnished with such luxuries as a master chef, silk sheets, a tiled bathroom, and a powerful radio. From his bedroom window, he saw the ridges above Chungking that were crowded with thousands of paupers' shanties. Despite this visible evidence of the widespread poverty of the Chinese, Willkie acclaimed Chiang as a visionary and great wartime leader. "Possibly no other country on our side in this war," he said, "is so dominated by the personality of one man." On meeting the Chinese leader, Willkie later reported that he seemed "even bigger than his legendary reputation."

Theodore H. White, then a young American journalist covering China for *Time,* said that Chiang's influence stemmed from his ability to strike political deals with military chieftains and warlords. Chiang, wrote White, "had no equal in the ancient art of hog-trading." White also noted that Chiang lacked a grasp of fundamental social and economic problems that plagued his land.[41]

Willkie was informed by Chinese and American sources about the corruption of Chiang's regime, yet he felt that the generalissimo himself was honest and incorruptible. He acknowledged, though, that Chiang's loyalty to his family was "sometimes unreasonable."[42] Two of his brothers-in-law had served as China's Premier and another was Finance Minister.

The special envoy was positively entranced by the Wellesley-educated Madame Chiang Kai-shek. At forty-four, she was still beautiful, with huge sparkling eyes, striking features, and soft black hair. She accentuated her supple figure with Chinese dresses that showed more than a trace of *Vogue*. In the fall of 1942, the generalissimo's consort was probably the most powerful woman in the world, an oriental Eleanor of Aquitaine. She was haughty, charming, brilliant, devious, and ruthless, the prototypical Dragon Lady. Veteran China watchers confided that she had married Chiang fifteen years earlier not out of love but because she had selected him as the man most likely to bring her prestige and prominence.

Madame Chiang, the former Meiling Soong, was the best-known member of modern China's most remarkable dynasty. Her father, Charles Jones Soong, a Christian convert, had gone to the United States as a child, then later studied for the ministry at Vanderbilt, and returned to China as a missionary. The elder Soong later made a fortune publishing Bibles and launched a powerful family dynasty. His eldest daughter, Ailing, married H. H. Kung, wealthy banker and later Premier of China. The middle daughter, Chingling, married the legendary Sun Yat-sen, first President of the Chinese republic. Her brother, T. V. Soong, served as China's Finance Minister and later as Premier. In the 1930s, Madame Chiang headed China's Air Force and helped direct air strategy against the Japanese. She served as China's personal liaison with Western leaders and acted as Chiang's interpreter and spokesman with foreign visitors.

From the moment he met Madame Chiang, Willkie was under her spell. Later, he told Cowles and Barnes that it was the first time he had ever really been in love. "There is little doubt," noted American diplomat John Paton Davies, "that Little Sister has accomplished one of her easiest conquests." The China hand reported that Madame Chiang had "wound him around her little finger."[43]

At a tea which she gave for Willkie, Madame Chiang openly flirted with her American guest. "I think Mr. Willkie is a very disturbing personality," she said. "I had a nice speech all ready to read to him and here he comes and shows he is not the sort of person for whom the speech was made. I will have to, therefore, speak from my heart because he is so spontaneous, so warmhearted, so essentially human that anything written down would not express the welcome felt in our hearts for him." She described him as "the embodiment of that warmth, spontaneity, and energy which are also characteristic of the American people."

"If I can contribute anything in my time," Willkie replied, "the one contribution I can make is to howl and howl throughout this world that we shall see to it that all nations and all peoples will be free. . . . Madame and I are going to howl in chorus when this war is over."[44]

When Willkie and Madame Chiang slipped out of a dinner party at the Kung mansion, they were scolded by her brother-in-law when they did not return until the other guests had left. Another time, Chiang and sixty of his blue-shirted secret police came looking for Willkie at the guesthouse when he was elsewhere meeting with Madame Chiang. "I was scared to death," Cowles recalled in a 1978 interview. On Willkie's final day in Chungking, he stopped to see Madame Chiang, and they met privately for more than an hour, much to the discomfort of Barnes and Cowles.

She accompanied Willkie to the airport, and they embraced and kissed as he boarded the plane. Willkie was so infatuated with her that he proposed that she return to the United States on the *Gulliver* and he would see to it that President Roosevelt gave her all the planes and weaponry that China wanted. "Someone from this section with brains and persuasiveness and moral force must help educate us about China and India and their peoples," he told H. H. Kung. "Madame would be the perfect ambassador. Her great ability, her great devotion to China are well known in the United States. She would find herself not only beloved, but immensely effective. We would listen to her as to no one else. With wit and charm, a generous and understanding heart, and gracious and beautiful manner and appearance, and a burning conviction, she is just what we need as a visitor."

Several months later Willkie's predictions came true when Madame Chiang took him up on his suggestion and came to the United States. Speaking before a joint session of Congress, she won a roaring ovation and more wartime aid for China. Willkie introduced her at a United China Relief rally in Madison Square Garden and spent much time with her at the Waldorf-Astoria Hotel. He sent her flowers under his own name and also sent separate bouquets in which he signed cards from Barnes and Cowles. "When I got a note of thanks this morning," he wrote Barnes, "I was fearful that you, with your complete honesty, might write to disclaim having sent the flowers when you receive a letter of thanks. It is hell to have to worry about the transparent honesty of a friend."[45]

Years later Cowles said it had been his impression that Chiang had approved of Madame's relationship with Willkie as part of their effort to strengthen American support for the Kuomintang government. "She saw herself in a position to dominate Asia after the war," said Cowles, "and she thought Willkie could help her."

General Stilwell recorded in his diary that Willkie had been "completely sold" on the generalissimo and Madame Chiang, both of whom were attempting to remove the crusty American as U.S. commander of the China-Burma-India theater. "Willkie is being thoroughly immersed in soft soap, adulation, and flattery," he wrote. The general found Willkie "either worn out or very indifferent to me. Practically nothing to say or ask about. Almost pointed."[46]

With typical irreverence, Stilwell told Willkie that on his visit to the Chinese front near Sian he would see the biggest market in China. On the great bend in the Yellow River, Nationalist soldiers bargained with the Japanese, Stilwell said, for "all the goods they need from each other."

At the front, Willkie looked through artillery telescopes at the muzzles of Japanese guns, but he saw little action. Captain Chiang Wei-kao, the generalissimo's son by a previous marriage, presented him with captured Japanese cavalry swords and bottles of expensive French wines. Willkie watched a military review on a parade ground and was impressed by the white-gloved infantry units, tanks, and cavalry. At the Chengtu Military Academy, he saw maneuvers by several thousand cadets who cut their way through barbed wire, drove across a mine field, and swam a river holding rifles above their heads.[47]

It was a deceptive exhibition of China's military strength. In fact, the Chinese Army had become a national scandal—over half the soldiers were not only underfed but actually starving. The conscription system was notoriously corrupt. The wealthy avoided military service by paying the right officials, and peasants were sent to the front tied with ropes. "In China, just as in Russia," Willkie would later write, "this is truly a people's war. Even the sons of those of high estate enlist as privates in the army." Nothing could have been further from the truth.

Willkie had two lengthy interviews with Chou En-lai, the Chinese Communist leader then serving in Chungking as a member of the People's Political Council. As Mao Tse-tung's representative in the capital, Chou negotiated aid from Chiang's government for the war against Japan. "This excellent, sober and sincere man won my respect as a man of obvious ability," Willkie said. At his urging, H. H. Kung included Chou on the guest list for a dinner party in Willkie's honor. "I was later told," said Willkie, "that it was the first time he had been entertained by the official family of China. It was interesting to see him greeted in a pleasant but somewhat cautious manner by men he had fought against, and with obvious respect by General Stilwell." Chou assured the American that the Chinese Communists were committed to a united front with the Kuomintang Nationalists until Japan had been driven from China. "He left me with the feeling," said Willkie, "that if all Chinese Communists are like himself, their movement is more a national and agrarian uprising than an international or proletarian conspiracy." His judgment was more perceptive than his contemporaries realized, for the Communist revolution that ousted Chiang from power in 1949 was more committed to social reform and internal stability than international revolution.[48]

His Chungking statement attacking imperialism was well received in China. It also helped bring about final negotiations between the United States, England, and China for the relinquishment of extraterritorial rights on the Chinese mainland. These final negotiations, "Willkie had created, literally overnight," Barnes wrote a decade later. "Those who accused Willkie of threatening Allied unity by his attacks on the colonial system were comfortably ignorant of the degree to which this unity was confined to empty eloquence as long as extraterritorial rights in China were maintained."[49]

On October 9, Willkie began his long journey back to the United

States. At Chengtu, he boarded the *Gulliver* shortly after daybreak, flying over the Gobi Desert and Mongolia to Yatsuk, a onetime Russian penal colony. After another landing in Siberia, Willkie's army transport plane crossed over the Bering Strait to Fairbanks, Alaska. From Alaska, he flew over thick Canadian forests to Edmonton, Alberta. "In regard to flippant statements made by certain public officials concerning the expression of my opinion in Russia on the question of a second front," he said in Alberta, "I did not deem it appropriate or in good taste for me to reply to such personalities or flippancies when I was in other countries. I felt it my duty while abroad to uphold the hand of the President and all other United Nations officials, which I continued to do even after such remarks were made."

Willkie was still angry about FDR's press conference flippancy that his comments on the second front weren't worth reading about. Even though the President had later clarified his remark and praised Willkie's performance as special envoy, Willkie had been hurt by the implication of the initial statement. White House Press Secretary Stephen Early sent word to Willkie as he arrived in Minneapolis that the President wanted to meet with him at once.

Arriving in Washington, Willkie was ten pounds lighter than when he had begun his trip, and his tousled hair was even more shaggy than usual, for he had not had a haircut since the summer.

Late in the afternoon, he conferred with FDR at the White House. Their discussion was said to have been heated. "I know that you are President and that you can throw me out," Willkie said that he told Roosevelt, "but until you do I am going to say a few things to you and you are going to listen."[50]

In the notes which he prepared for this meeting, Willkie wrote: "I think I should tell you quite frankly and bluntly that during the entire period of my trip, I uttered no single sentence of criticism of you or your policies, in order to show to foreign peoples this national unity on the war of which I speak. On the other hand, your press references to me were cabled to China the night before I left the country and a few hours before I was to make a statement which I believed, and still believe that I was speaking for a very large number of Americans and in complete consistency with my special mission for you. Unless you have reports to the contrary about what I said or did on the trip, I think you should cooperate in an effort to make the trip a symbol of national unity on the war."

FDR told his special envoy that any reports he had been critical of him were erroneous, and Willkie later told reporters that the President had been friendly and conciliatory. Roosevelt told a different version to Dean Acheson, claiming that he was preparing to name Willkie Secretary of State but changed his mind because they had quarreled during this meeting.

Willkie briefed FDR on each region he had visited. "This is not a pleasant report to make—but the traditions of British rule in the Middle East have created a vacuum as far as the Arab peoples are concerned, a vacuum which we have not filled and which the Germans and Italians are in part filling through our default. It is my personal belief that we must work hard to preserve our military cooperation with the British in this whole area—and this applies especially to Syria and the problems raised by General de Gaulle, but that we must work no less hard to give these people a feeling that they do not have: that we are not committed to an indefinite perpetuation of British imperialism in this area, but rather to the establishment of political freedom and economic liberty."

Willkie passed on Stalin's urgent request for more military assistance. "He gave me no impression that our failure to supply the Red Army with what it needs is likely to lead him to a separate peace as long as his armies can hold out," said Willkie, "but he gave me the very clear feeling that it will most seriously affect our chances of working out any cooperation in the peace."

In China Willkie said "the problem of inflation" was of "equal gravity" with the Japanese invasion. He suggested that the United States establish an independent foreign policy to counter "the deep-rooted suspicion that America has given at least acquiescence to British plans for restoration of its earlier imperial position in Asia."[51]

As he left the White House, Willkie reiterated his call for a second front in Europe. After an overnight stop in New York, he took the train to Rushville and started drafting his radio speech to the American people about the trip.

On Monday, October 26, 1942, Willkie delivered his half-hour "Report to the People" over all four major networks before an audience estimated at more than thirty-six million. "There are no distant points in the world any longer," he said. "The myriad millions of human beings of the Far East are as close to us as Los Angeles is to New York by the fastest railroad trains. I cannot escape the conviction that in the future what concerns them must concern us, almost as much as the problems of the people of California concern the people of New York. Our thinking and planning in the future must be global."

Willkie repeated his call for the breakup of Old World colonial empires. "I can assure you that the rule of people by other peoples is not freedom, and not what we must fight to preserve," he declared. He asserted that America's "reservoir of goodwill" around the world had been threatened "by failing to define clearly our war aims." He condemned "the half-ignorant, half-patronizing way in which we have grown accustomed to treating many of the peoples in Eastern Europe and Asia." Winning a military triumph over the Axis would not be enough, he said. "We must fight our way through not alone to the destruction of our enemies but to a new world idea. We must win the peace," he said. "To win that peace, three things seem to me to be necessary–first, we must plan now for peace on a global basis; second, the world must be free, economically and politically, for nations and for men that peace may exist in it; third, America must play an active, constructive part in freeing it and keeping its peace."[52]

His speech was widely acclaimed. "Last night," said Clare Boothe Luce, "the world heard the message of a global Abraham Lincoln." William Allen White wrote, "For the first time in human history, a major leader of a great republic spoke out specifically, naming names of nations and races, and demanding in terms definite and certain, freedom for all mankind. Mr. Roosevelt and the Atlantic Charter and Mr. Churchill have spoken of freedom but apparently with crossed fingers for Asia and Africa. The Atlantic Charter did not interest 'the yellow and brown and the black,' but Mr. Willkie demanded the end of the colonial system. His demand was a forward step in the battle for freedom."[53] David Lawrence said that Willkie's message "thrilled the peoples overseas even more than it did the people of his own country." The *Christian Science Monitor* added, "Mr. Willkie's trip may turn out to be more important than Phineas Fogg's and Marco Polo's put together."

"Stay in there and pitch," wrote a man from Medford, Oregon. "Thank you for the most honest, thrilling, intelligent speech of the war," wired a group of literary figures from the New York suburbs. From New Orleans, a telegram signed "Two Able Seamen," said, "You got it." A New York City man wired, "It was wonderful." From Corsicana, Texas, a Willkie supporter wrote, "Deep in the heart of Texas, there are a million people who want to vote for you for president."

Willkie's address drew a larger response than any other speech of his public career, and the mail was overwhelmingly favorable.

In his next major public appearance, Willkie was muzzled by the Administration. On November 16, he was set to denounce FDR's policy of cooperation with the Nazi puppet government of France. Willkie had been outraged by the bargain that had been struck between General Dwight D. Eisenhower and Admiral Jean François Darlan, commander in chief of Vichy France's armed forces, as part of the Allied invasion of North Africa. Public opinion on the Darlan deal was sharply divided in Britain and the United States. Edward R. Murrow, the CBS radio commentator, issued a public blast against the alliance with a notorious Vichy leader, suggesting that it could help lose the war rather than win it. Willkie later wrote that he "never accepted without discount stories of the probable losses we would have sustained at the hands of the French if we had gone in directly as Americans without dealing with Darlan."

Less than an hour before Willkie was to give his speech at the *Herald Tribune* forum, he was awakened from his nap by a phone call from Secretary of War Stimson. The old warrior told Willkie that if he went ahead with his criticism of the Darlan deal, it could jeopardize the success of the North African invasion and risk sixty thousand American casualties. Though skeptical about Stimson's claims, he agreed to delete the references to Darlan and FDR's "long appeasement of Vichy."[54] The next day Willkie became angry when the President publicly lamented the "temporary expediency" of the Darlan agreement and suggested that Willkie's criticism had been politically motivated. In an article written for the London *Evening Standard,* he alleged that Administration censorship was being used to suppress free discussion and cover up political mistakes.

Shortly after his nationally broadcast "Report to the People," he started writing a book about his world-encircling journey. The idea had been proposed by Irita Van Doren's son-in-law, Tom Torre Bevans, a top executive with Simon and Schuster, with whom he had long talked about doing a book. Bevans made the suggestion that he publish, in book form, a collection of the speeches he made following his return. Over the years, Willkie had turned down numerous opportunities to write his own political book, but this time he had something he wanted to say. "Willkie's decision to write a book," recalled Barnes, "grew directly out of the reception given to his broadcast speech."

Once he began editing the speeches, Willkie concluded that he could write a much more lively and illuminating book if he took a narrative approach. At his request, Barnes and Cowles prepared extensive memos about incidents and anecdotes from the trip and Major Kight provided technical background about the flight of the *Gulliver*. Though Willkie planned to write no more than thirty thousand words, he produced a manuscript more than twice that length.[55]

For nearly two months, he worked on the project each morning at Van Doren's apartment, talking out his ideas as she recorded them and added her professional touch. Using a heavy black pencil, Willkie reworked the material until he was satisfied it had the right pitch. "I have got so much writing to do in the next few weeks," he confided to Olive Clapper on January 2, 1943, "that every time I think of writing something more, I get nauseated." Even when the manuscript was in galley proofs, he continued making major revisions. He took the galleys with him to Rushville and telephoned New York several times a day with suggested changes in the text. "I write entirely with a purpose," he said. "I pretend no literary skill. I write what I think and then rewrite."[56]

He provided firsthand accounts of his meetings with Stalin, Chiang, de Gaulle, Montgomery, Chou En-lai, and other Allied leaders. In the book, he called for postwar cooperation with the Soviets. "There can be no continued peace until we learn to do so." Condemning Old World imperialism, he urged the developed nations to assist the emerging peoples of the Third World with education, public health, and development of resources. His *One World* philosophy, in short, was to "unify the peoples of the earth in the human quest for freedom and justice." Willkie advocated the establishment of a strong postwar world organization along the lines of the United Nations. "It is inescapable that there can be no peace for any part of the world," he wrote, "unless the foundations of peace are made secure through all parts of the world."

His working title had been *One War, One Peace, One World.* "Why not just *One World?*" asked Bevans. Willkie chose the shorter, more dramatic title. If the book sold 150,000 copies, Willkie said that he would be satisfied. When a Simon and Schuster executive gave him odds of three to one that the book would do even better, Willkie grabbed the bet. As it turned out, he lost the wager but not the money. His friend had the check framed for his office.

One World was published on April 8, 1943. The first printing sold out so quickly that the publisher was forced to run advertisements in fifty newspapers apologizing to the public for failing to keep up with demand. In an effort to fill thousands of orders, five sets of plates were made, and the book was printed in two plants and bound in a third, with crews working in around-the-clock shifts. Within seven weeks, it had sold one million copies. By the end of the year, it reached the two-million mark in trade hardback, paper, and book club editions.

Widely acclaimed, *One World* was a critical triumph on the same scale it was a commercial success. "From every page of it, his exuberant personality bubbles," wrote William L. Shirer. "It is one of the most absorbing books I have read in years, full of humor, shrewd observation, a thousand and one facts you and I never heard of but should have, and fabulous tales of the East told with a skill which a Duranty or a Gunther or a Sheean might well envy." Clifton Fadiman, in the *New Yorker,* said, "He has simply, by an inexplicable miracle, burst all the bonds which might have confined him within the narrow limits of big-business thinking and become one of those 'new men' with 'new ideas' for whom he pleads in his book." Walter Lippmann said *One World* placed Willkie among the "best American observers who have gone abroad. He had the privileges of the insider without the inhibitions. He was able to make a very good use of his privileges because, as this book proves, he has a seeing eye and an understanding heart." *Foreign Affairs* described it as "one of the hardest blows ever struck against the intellectual and moral isolationism of the American people." The *Atlantic* praised Willkie's "courage and candor." "A very remarkable little book," said *Commonweal,* which called it "a moving appeal for self-government among the peoples of the Far and Middle East, for the end of white imperialism everywhere, and for the immediate creation of international machinery that will learn to keep the peace by helping to win the war." Malcolm Cowley said Willkie's political thinking was "exactly 128 years ahead of the State Department." Cowley added, "In this book, Willkie shows us a more appealing side of American democracy: the underlying notion that fixed classes are wrong, that people are pretty much alike in all countries and that they ought to be good neighbors." Reinhold Niebuhr called it "wise" and paid tribute to Willkie's "remarkable grasp of the essential realities."[57]

Harold E. Stassen, reviewing *One World* in the New York *Times,* was among the few dissenting voices. The Minnesota Republican, who was vying with Willkie for the progressive leadership of their party, called it "dogmatic" and "belligerent," criticizing him for "an over-emphasis on the evils of the British colonial system and an understatement of the evils of Communism." Willkie's friend, *Times* publisher Arthur Hays Sulzberger, offered to let him respond to Stassen's barbs, but he declined.

Willkie received thousands of letters about his book, nearly all of them favorable. "You have made an inspiring messenger of confidence and of good will toward men," wrote novelist Ellen Glasgow. "You go far indeed to convince me that the sense of universal fellowship is stronger than instinctive eversion, that it is stronger even than the rule of greed in human affairs." A retired schoolteacher wrote, "My traveling days are over but as long as books that take one around the world in such a way as yours does are published, I shall not mind." An army air force lieutenant wrote, "I believe it was just what we needed at this time to better understand our allies and other friendly nations. It should go a long way in making the isolationists see the true picture of what a great responsibility the United States has after the war." An army private added, "*One World* is by far the best analysis of the situation of the United Nations and their problems, present and future, yet published. I already have a long waiting list from fellow soldiers who also want to read it." "Your book places upon the intellectual doorstep of every American," wrote a Newark, New Jersey, lawyer, "a gift of contemporary world knowledge and world understanding which, if fully availed of, will extend his mental outlook from the limits of his front yard to the ends of the earth."

In the fall of 1943, Willkie said that he had earned $350,000 from his book, including the sale of film rights. Darryl F. Zanuck of Twentieth Century-Fox purchased the motion picture rights and assigned

Lamar Trotti to write the screenplay. Zanuck sought Spencer Tracy to portray Willkie and the actor was interested, but the film was never made. Willkie donated all proceeds from the book to a trust fund which was distributed to war charities, civil rights groups, and other public service organizations.

"The success of *One World* gave Willkie greater personal satisfaction than anything in his life," said Barnes, for it "gave him the feeling that he was being successful in a field he had always revered and in which he had always felt inferior."[58]

CHAPTER SIXTEEN

THE GOOD FIGHT

On November 9, 1942, Willkie appeared before the Supreme Court as the defense lawyer in a landmark civil liberties case. One month after his global trip, he was representing William Schneiderman, secretary of the California Communist party, a Russian-American whose citizenship had been revoked by a federal district court on the grounds that his membership in the party had been concealed thirteen years earlier when he had applied for naturalization. At first, Willkie had refused to take the case. Defending a well-known Communist was certain to be controversial, and his closest advisers warned him of the political consequences. He changed his mind, however, after studying the brief prepared by civil liberties lawyer Carol King, who was representing Schneiderman. "Your original letter came with the brief attached," Willkie later told her. "I put it on the side of my desk as one of the things I wanted to read. It was about a week before I got around to reading the brief. I read it on a Saturday morning. I re-read it. After that, I could not with my beliefs have remained satisfied with myself if I refused the case if two conditions were true—(1) that Schneiderman was a decent fellow personally, and (2) that the record sustained the brief. That was the reason for my making inquiries about Schneiderman and asking you to send me the record."[1]

"I read the record," he recalled, "and decided without further consideration to argue the case. Why? Because I saw myself as the man involved in the case. Here was a radical who had followed his ideal toward his objective. While I did not agree with his views, he was entitled to them and to a fair trial under our system, and to the safeguards of our constitution. He had arrived in this predicament by a series of accidents of life. I had started as he had from pretty much the same point of thinking. My series of personal accidents had taken me down an opposite road. They might well have been different, and if they had I might now be in his predicament and in such event I would have wanted the type of representation and advocacy that satisfied me."[2]

Willkie never wavered in his commitment to civil liberties. "On no single issue throughout both his business and his political career," said Barnes, "was Willkie so consistent or so articulate." In March of 1940, he had written a piece for the *New Republic* in which he slammed the Roosevelt administration for its political prosecutions of Huey Long and Communist party leader Earl Browder: "Justice is not something you hand out at one time because it is convenient and withhold at another for the same reason. Equal treatment under the law means exactly what it says, whether the man before the tribunal is a crook, a Democrat, a Republican, a Communist, or a business man; whether he is rich or poor, white or black, good or bad. You cannot have a democracy on any other basis. You cannot preserve human liberties on any other theory.

"Sometimes," he went on, "hatred obscures this instinct for fair play. It is well to remember that any man who denies justice to someone he hates prepares the way for a denial of justice to someone he loves."[3]

In a letter to Bartley Crum, Willkie said, "I am sure I am right in representing Schneiderman. Of all the times when civil liberties should be defended, it is now."[4]

When Mrs. King brought him a proposed draft of the Supreme Court brief, he rejected it. "Willkie was gentle but firm," she said. "He didn't want to be a 'shirt front.' The brief had to be completely his, a part of his very being, his own expression of the political injustice he had agreed to combat. But he did not regard himself as above criticism or suggestion."

Two days before he argued the case, Willkie checked into Washington's Carlton Hotel and prepared his defense. "Willkie had an informal and not too neat manner of working," said Mrs. King. "Only at our very first conference had he managed to keep his feet on the floor. I would probably never have noticed that his shoes were rarely shined except for the fact that they were always in the immediate foreground. When he was busy, he would go right on talking as he ate a ham sandwich and swallowed coffee out of a container from the corner drugstore. He liked to mark the things on which he was working himself. He would say, 'I can follow my own tracks.' He came to the argument in the Supreme Court with a much tracked-up record, a sheaf of quotations and a page of notes scrawled in pencil. There wasn't much on the sheet either. He obviously talked from the heart and not from his notes."[5]

In his brief, Willkie argued that the decision of the lower court "constitutes a drastic abridgement of freedom of political belief and thought." He noted that Congress had not made membership in the Communist party a bar to naturalized citizenship. Solicitor General Charles Fahy declared before the court that the Naturalization Act required that an alien obtaining citizenship must be "attached to the principles of the Constitution" and be "well disposed to the good order and happiness of the United States." Fahy contended that Schneiderman and the Communist party, at the time of his naturalization in 1927, "believed in, advocated, and taught the overthrow of this government by force and violence."

Willkie, a lock of hair falling over his forehead, countered that the dogma of a political party was not binding to all its members. "Am I to be held responsible for everything Ham Fish says?" he asked. He argued that a Communist had "a right to believe in and advocate changes" in the constitution "by the peaceful process of amendment."[6]

Asked by a justice if Schneiderman believed in "organized government," Willkie said, "Communism is one of the most organized governments that exists. If anything, one of the principal quarrels I would have with it is that it is over-organized."

Quoting Lincoln, "the founder of my party, the Republican Party," Willkie read, "'This country, with its institutions, belongs to the people who inhabit it. Whenever they shall grow weary of the existing government, they can exercise their constitutional right of amending it, or their revolutionary right to dismember or overthrow it.'"

Then, he quoted Jefferson: "God forbid we should ever be twenty years without such a rebellion. . . . The tree of liberty must be refreshed from time to time with the blood of patriots and tyrants."

So, Willkie noted, the founders of America's two great political parties and the Communist party had all advocated the use of violence against oppressive reaction, and "the mildest of the three by far was Karl Marx."

The *Herald Tribune* reported, "Willkie concluded with an argument as forceful as any he ever made on a campaign platform."

For months, the Supreme Court's justices were bitterly divided in their private sessions on Schneiderman's fate. Chief Justice Harlan F. Stone argued that the lower court decision should be upheld. Justice Felix Frankfurter, himself a naturalized citizen, wrote in his diary: "That which to Mr. Willkie seemed so important–to prove that Schneiderman was attached to the Constitution because of his smooth and complete and perfect testimony on the witness stand–looks to me rather in the other direction, for as a judge I do not have to be innocent of that which as a man I know, namely that deception and lies in the interest of their holy cause are well recognized instruments in the tactics of Communist officials."[7] Justice Robert H. Jackson, who had been Attorney General when the Justice Department launched the case against Schneiderman, did not participate in the deliberations.

On June 21, 1943, the high court ruled in Schneiderman's favor by a vote of five to three. Influenced by Willkie's arguments, Justice Frank Murphy wrote the majority opinion: "Under our traditions, beliefs are personal and not a matter of mere association. Men in adhering to a political party or other organization notoriously do not subscribe to all of its platforms or asserted principles."

Those concurring were Hugo L. Black, William O. Douglas, Wiley B. Rutledge, and Stanley F. Reed. Chief Justice Stone wrote a caustic dissent: "A man can be known by the ideas he spreads as well as by the company he keeps." Justices Frankfurter and Owen J. Roberts concurred.

All were in agreement that it was an important decision. "Immediately," wrote Justice Rutledge, "we are concerned with only one man, William Schneiderman. Actually, though indirectly, the decision affects millions." The decision was later used to thwart deportation proceedings against radical labor leader Harry Bridges. "Wendell Willkie was the only man in America," Bridges observed, "who has proved that he would rather be right than be President."

After the court's decision, Willkie sipped champagne out of a paper cup in a celebration at Carol King's law office. "I have always felt confident as to how the Supreme Court would decide a case involving such fundamental American rights," he said. "My bafflement has been as to why the administration started and prosecuted a case in which, if they had prevailed, a thoroughly illiberal precedent would have been established."

Willkie came close to denouncing the Roosevelt administration's internment of Japanese-Americans in wartime concentration camps, which the American Civil Liberties Union termed "the worst breach of civil liberty in American history." At a dinner honoring the late Justice Brandeis, Willkie stopped just short: "I have no trust and faith in any extra-judicial proceedings under which any group will be deprived of their rights, under guise of war emergency."

On March 28, 1942, the *Saturday Evening Post* published an inflammatory article by Milton Mayer entitled "The Case Against the Jew." Willkie denounced what he termed "Mayer's flagellation of the Jews," and the article resulted in a storm of canceled advertising and subscriptions, newsstand boycotts, and the forced resignation of the *Post*'s reactionary editor, Wesley Winans Stout. His successor, Ben Hibbs, responding to the suggestion of many *Post* readers, persuaded Willkie to write a rebuttal.

In "The Case for the Minorities," Willkie wrote with conviction about the dangers of racism and intolerance. His own family had been touched by the wave of anti-German hysteria following America's intervention in World War I. And, as a young lawyer in Ohio, he had fought the Ku Klux Klan. The slurs against his German ancestry had angered him in the 1940 campaign, although his accusers were silenced in the wake of his contributions to the Allied war effort.

"When affairs go wrong the public, by ancient custom, demands a scapegoat," said Willkie, "and the first place to seek one is from the minority. All this would appear ridiculous in our modern age, were it not for the examples of bigotry and persecution we see in countries once presumed to be enlightened; and, even more seriously, were it not for the fact that we are already witnessing a crawling, insidious anti-Semitism in our own country.

"We are living once more in a period that is psychologically susceptible to witch hanging and mob baiting," he wrote. "And each of us, if not alert, may find himself the unconscious carrier of the germ that will destroy our freedom. For each of us has within himself the inheritances of age-long hatreds, of racial and religious differences, and everyone has a tendency to find the cause for his own failures in some conspiracy of evil. It is, therefore, essential that we guard our own thinking and not be among those who cry out against prejudices applicable to themselves, while busy spawning intolerances for others."[8]

Accepting the American Hebrew medal for 1942, Willkie took issue with the official citation which commended him for his efforts to promote racial and religious "tolerance." He declared, "It is not tolerance that one is entitled to in America. It is the right of every citizen in America to be treated by other citizens as an equal. No man has the right in America to treat any other man 'tolerantly,' for 'tolerance' is the assumption of superiority. Our liberties are the equal rights of every citizen."

Unlike many political figures, Willkie observed in his private life what he talked about in public. Following the 1940 election, he took a long vacation in Hobe Sound, Florida. On learning that Jews were excluded from the posh resort, he demanded that the restrictions be dropped or he would move elsewhere. The owners, eager to keep their famous guest, changed their policy.[9]

In the area of civil rights, Willkie became increasingly outspoken in demanding equality for blacks. With the coming of the New Deal, American blacks had dropped their traditional allegiance to the GOP and switched to the Democratic party. Like everyone else, blacks had been helped by the New Deal's relief programs, yet the fact remained that Roosevelt had moved slowly in civil rights. The infamous Jim Crow practices were still in effect, and FDR would not risk his southern white support to challenge them. Under pressure from A. Philip Randolph's 1941 march on Washington, the President established the Fair Employment Practices Commission, but it lacked enforcement powers, and private industry and labor unions still discriminated without penalty. Although Roosevelt integrated federal office buildings, he named few blacks to policymaking positions. In an age when vigilante mobs were lynching blacks, FDR refused to support antilynching legislation, because he did not wish to offend powerful southern congressmen. At times, Roosevelt demonstrated an appalling insensitivity to the plight of American blacks. During the 1940 campaign, he met with three prominent black leaders to discuss the possibility of integrating the armed services. FDR said later that it couldn't be done, but told Secretary of the Navy Frank Knox, "There's no reason we shouldn't have a colored band on some of these ships, because they're darned good at it."[10]

With emotional commitment, Willkie supported black leaders in their effort to integrate the armed forces. "Of all the indignities and injustices Negro men and women have suffered," said Willkie, "the most bitter and ironic is the discrimination and the mistreatment they have received in the armed forces of their country." For the most part, the Army had assigned blacks to noncombatant roles as laborers, servants, and stevedores, while other services were closed to them. Local draft boards inducted whites over blacks. "They should have the right of every citizen to fight for his country," said Willkie, "in any branch of her armed services without discrimination."[11] In the spring of 1942, the Marines, Navy, and Coast Guard were opened to black volunteers. The Merchant Marine and Air Corps soon were admitting blacks. By the end of the war, many barriers had been broken. Not until 1948, though, did President Truman officially desegregate the armed services.

On July 19, 1942, addressing the National Association for the Advancement of Colored People, Willkie identified racism as a national dilemma. "It is becoming apparent to thoughtful Americans," he said, "that we cannot fight the forces of imperialism abroad and maintain a form of imperialism at home." Yet, he said, "We have practiced within our own boundaries something that amounts to race imperialism. The attitude of white citizens toward the Negroes has undeniably had some of the unlovely and tragic characteristics of an alien imperialism—a smug racial superiority, a willingness to exploit an unprotected people.

"Our very proclamations of what we are fighting for have rendered our own inequities self-evident. When we talk of freedom and opportunity for all nations, the increasing paradoxes in our own society become so clear they can no longer be ignored."[12]

On every major civil rights issue, Willkie was unmistakably forthright. Walter White, secretary of the NAACP, became a close friend and political adviser. Under White's leadership, the NAACP had grown more influential than any black organization in history. With A. Philip Randolph, White had organized the 1941 march on Washington that had forced FDR to issue his executive order against job discrimination. In the 1940 campaign, White had spurned efforts by Republicans to get him into Willkie's camp. Following the election, Willkie dropped White a note saying he wanted to meet "the fellow" who had refused to see him. Their attempts to arrange a mutually convenient date were unsuccessful. But one night, at a dinner for a Catholic bishop at the Waldorf, White came up to Willkie and introduced himself. "Before the evening was over," White later recalled, "a friendship developed which grew steadily in warmth and meaning to me to the day of his untimely death."

Willkie went all-out for federal antilynching legislation, a major concern to blacks. Within the span of a few weeks in the fall of 1943, three black men were lynched in Mississippi, yet the Administration would not push for the legislation. Willkie called for repeal of the notorious poll tax, one of the obstacles imposed by southern white officials to keep blacks from voting. A South Carolina registrar was straightforward in saying, "We do that to keep down the niggers." Willkie berated congressional Republicans for not taking the initiative on these issues and reclaiming the legacy of Abraham Lincoln. "The very fact that the Republican party was the instrumentality through which the Negroes were given freedom," he said, "makes them more resentful that it should join in acts which prevent them from obtaining the substance of freedom."

On June 20, 1943, Detroit exploded in the worst race riot in the nation's history. When it was over, thirty-four people were dead, more than seven hundred wounded, and thirteen hundred arrested. Twenty-five of those killed were black, some of them shot by the police. Detroit's mayor blamed the city's blacks for the riots, but an investigation by the U.S. Justice Department indicated that the police had exacerbated racial tensions and contributed to the violence. There were riots in other cities. In Mobile, thousands of white workers in the shipyards attacked black employees when a dozen black welders were promoted. In Beaumont, Texas, two blacks were killed by a mob and fifty were seriously hurt when white vigilantes spread the rumor that a white woman had been raped by a black.

"The situation which flared so tragically in Detroit," Willkie said in an address nationally broadcast by CBS, "has its counterpart, actual or potential, in many American cities. Such instances of mob madness cannot be treated as single cases, because they are profound in their effect in this country and lasting in their impression throughout the world. Two-thirds of the people who are our Allies do not have white skins. And they do have long, hurtful memories of the white man's superior attitude in his dealings with them. Today, the white man is professing friendship and a desire to cooperate and is promising opportunity in the world to come when the war is over. . . . Race riots in Detroit do not reassure them."

In the speech, Willkie called on the American people to join forces against racial discrimination and criticized both political parties for failing to address civil rights questions. "One party cannot go on fooling itself that it has no further obligation to the Negro citizen because Lincoln freed the slave," he said, "and the other is not entitled to power if it sanctions and practices one set of principles in Atlanta and another in Harlem.

"All the forces of Fascism," Willkie concluded, "are not with our enemies. Fascism is an attitude of mind which causes men to seek to rule others by economic, military or political force or through prejudice. Such an attitude within our own borders is as serious a threat to freedom as is the attack without. The desire to deprive some of our citizens of their rights—economic, civic or political—has the same basic motivation as actuates the Fascist mind when it seeks to dominate whole peoples and nations. It is essential that we eliminate it at home as well as abroad."

For many American blacks, Willkie had become a symbol of hope. "It is no exaggeration whatever for me to say that your going out there and making the speech you did," wrote the NAACP's White, "has done more to lift the morale of Negroes than any other thing within the past year. They now see hope where before there was only despair."

Willkie confronted Hollywood moguls for their unfair treatment of blacks in the movies. With the notable exception of the brilliant Paul Robeson, blacks had been stereotyped in films as servants, dancers, and paupers. Every few years, a major studio produced a respectable black film such as *The Green Pastures* or *Stormy Weather,* but these were rarities. Willkie brought White to California for a meeting with leading motion picture executives, pointing out that their films had contributed to racial prejudices. Several years later White recalled that Willkie had told the group that "many of the persons responsible for Hollywood films belonged to a racial and religious group which had been the target of Hitler and that they should be the last to be guilty of doing to another minority what had been done to them." The audience cheered, and many of the producers assured

Willkie that they would take pains to depict blacks more favorably than before. For a short time, it appeared that Willkie and White were making progress. A 1943 western, *The Ox-Bow Incident,* featured a black in a serious role. In *Casablanca,* Dooley Wilson played opposite Humphrey Bogart. And *Cabin in the Sky* was a winning black musical. "A few of the pledges were kept," White wrote in his memoirs. "But Willkie's tragic death damped and almost extinguished the reforms he stimulated. A highly vocal and belligerent minority which insisted that there be no change in film treatment of the Negro soon re-established the goblin of box-office returns in the thinking of Hollywood producers."[13]

In October of 1943, Willkie told *Look* magazine that he considered racial equality the most important issue facing the American people. "We must never forget that, while democratic government rests on majority rule, the essence of freedom is the protection of minorities. The Republican Party has always advocated equal rights for all, irrespective of race, creed or color. Now, above all times, we must make these principles a reality, because the whole world is watching us. Only if we can make individual liberty a reality among Americans, can we hope to gain adherents to our cause among other peoples. We must not protect these rights fitfully, inconsistently and with political purposes, as has the present administration."[14]

Willkie was making strong inroads into Roosevelt's popularity with blacks. "If the candidates are Roosevelt and Dewey," Walter White reported to George Gallup, "75 to 90 percent would vote for Roosevelt. If the candidates are Roosevelt and Willkie, the percentage would be just the opposite." Another leading pollster, Elmo Roper, warned Russell Davenport that Willkie could be playing with political dynamite. "If Mr. Willkie's obvious sense of fairness toward the Negro and his sympathy with his status," said Roper, "somehow got mixed up with the belief that he advocated an aggressive policy which might be regarded as truculent, I think he would most certainly be defeated at the polls."[15]

On this issue, Davenport was confident that Willkie would not be influenced by political considerations. "He took positive joy in the defense of minorities," Davenport observed. Carey McWilliams, the crusading liberal editor, added, "No public figure of the period understood what was happening better than Wendell Willkie."[16]

CHAPTER SEVENTEEN

STARTING OVER

Following his return from the *One World* trip, Willkie began plotting his political comeback. In late October of 1942, he confided his plan to Gardner Cowles and John W. Hanes. "Wendell had been pretty discouraged about his prospects for elective office," recalled Cowles, "but once we got back, he began to get interested and wanted to go after the presidential nomination." The odds against him had never been longer. It had been a Republican tradition that losing presidential candidates were not awarded a second chance. And, although Willkie had grown into a figure of international prestige and prominence, retaining wide popular support in the United States, he had alienated himself from Republican leaders in supporting FDR's foreign policy and in going to distant parts of the globe as a presidential envoy during the most critical weeks of the midterm campaign. Privately, Willkie made the prediction that the GOP would lose twenty seats in Congress and several important governorships.[1] On his return, he gave Dewey a lukewarm endorsement in an effort to ingratiate himself with party regulars, but most of them were still resentful that he had not taken a more active role in the campaign.

The Republicans scored dramatic gains in the November 3, 1942 elections, picking up forty-four congressional seats, nine in the Senate, and four new governorships, including Dewey in New York and Earl Warren in California. Senator McNary, winning his fifth term in Oregon, said the GOP triumph was "only a breeze compared to what will happen in 1944." On the morning after his election, Dewey pledged to serve out his full four-year term in Albany and insisted that he had put aside his presidential ambitions, but almost no one took him at his word. "I think there has been some upturn in Willkie's popularity," John D. M. Hamilton wrote a prominent Minnesota Republican, "but I doubt very much if it goes to the extent of giving him any sizable number of delegates to a convention, were it to be held today." Luce reported that Willkie "had missed a great chance to establish his party leadership by his failure to go on the radio a week or two before election day."[2]

Shortly after the elections, Senators Taft and Vandenberg announced that they would not seek the GOP presidential nomination in 1944. Taft endorsed Ohio's governor, John W. Bricker, as "exceptionally qualified" to be the Republican candidate. What he liked most about Bricker, Taft wrote a friend, was that he was "all against Willkie. There is only one way to beat the New Deal, and that is head on. You can't outdeal them." Vandenberg took himself out of the running with a letter to Detroit *News* political writer Jay G. Hayden. "I am not a candidate and I shall not be a candidate for President," said Vandenberg. "In my opinion, the events of the next eighteen months will dictate our appropriate nominee. In my expectation, he will be found amid the new timber which is richly available for this leadership, and which will become more so as the war progresses."

In December of 1942, Willkie and Taft battled for control of the Republican National Committee in what was widely viewed as a preliminary of the struggle for the presidency. After more than two years as the party's chairman, Joseph W. Martin was stepping down. When the committee met in St. Louis, Taft's candidate for the chairmanship was Werner W. Schroeder, conservative national committeeman from Illinois, and Willkie's surrogate was Frederick E. Baker, thirty-five years old, a Seattle public relations man. "I would find it hard to believe that the National Committee would see fit to select me for any office," Baker wrote privately, but he agreed to run as Willkie's "trial horse."[3] Ralph H. Cake of Oregon, who had become one of Willkie's closest advisers, nominated Baker, and Senator Taft spoke for Schroeder. On the first ballot, Baker and Schroeder were tied with forty votes apiece. On the second roll call, Baker moved slightly ahead but remained well short of a majority. During a recess, Martin persuaded the two candidates to withdraw in favor of Harrison Spangler, an elderly, red-faced Iowa lawyer with close ties to Hoover.[4] Willkie's camp hailed Spangler's selection as a partial victory, yet nothing could have been further from the truth. The new national chairman observed that Willkie's renomination would be most unfortunate for the party.

On February 28, 1943, Everett C. Witkins reported in the Indianapolis *Star* that Willkie would soon launch his second presidential campaign. Witkins said that Willkie's candidacy "may be taken for granted without any formal announcement from him," and he "will fight for the popular vote in every state where delegates are named in primary elections. Mr. Willkie, it may be stated authoritatively, will make a vigorous, whirlwind campaign in primary states."[5]

Willkie was under no illusions about his standing with the party's Old Guard. That same month, Homer E. Capehart wrote him, "The public is with you. The professional politician is against you." John Cowles pleaded with Willkie to mend his relationships with GOP officials. "I am more convinced than ever," he wrote, "that you must personally do a tremendous lot of intensive work both with the Republicans in Congress and with the Republican governors and with the party organization throughout the country. This job is of staggering dimensions but if you will go to it and keep at it week after week, I think you can accomplish it."

He agreed to try, responding to Cowles that he was willing to seek détente with congressional Republicans. "Things are developing," he reported to his friend in March. "One of the things, however, as you have pointed out to me that I have to do is to break down the congressional resistance but I have a difficult time figuring out how to go about that systematically. When I come down to Washington, I find it so difficult to develop a natural way of doing this. Think it over. We have to do something about it."[6]

Since his defeat in 1940, Willkie had frequently blasted congressional Republicans for their isolationism in foreign affairs and conservatism at home. Senator McNary and Joseph Martin had warned him that he was hurting his political stock in the party by becoming so closely identified with the Administration's foreign policy. The view among younger Republican congressmen was that Willkie did not care to hear what they had to say. Raymond Moley wrote, "He essayed to lead a party and also to be independent. He tried to be a free commentator on public affairs, while serving as an actor in those affairs. He tried at once to be Grantland Rice in the press box and Joe McCarthy on the field. A great party leader lectures his followers behind closed doors. Somehow, Willkie conveyed a growing impression that he was, however loyal, the active opposition to his own party."[7]

Willkie's attempts to improve his relations with Republican congressmen were fruitless. He lectured those who politically differed with him, and the result was an even wider breach. In a meeting with freshman congressmen, he thundered, "I know you people are opposed to me. You don't like me. But I am going to be nominated whether you like it or not. Better get right with me. I am going to be your next president." On June 12, 1943, Dewey was the overwhelming favorite in a poll of Republican congressmen on their choice for the presidency, and Willkie finished a distant fourth.

By the springtime, Willkie was devoting his full energies to the campaign. His law offices became the headquarters for his still undeclared candidacy, and several youthful associates were hired as full-time political aides. Cake, Weeks, Hanes, Luce, and the Cowles brothers served as senior advisers and conferred on a regular basis about strategy and tactics. Luce urged him to get out and "meet the folks." With enthusiasm, Willkie replied, "Harry, from being the Republican who knew the fewest party leaders I am going to become the man who knows more of them than anybody else–and I'm going to do this in one year!"

During the first six months of 1943, Willkie campaigned in thirteen states, speaking before large crowds and small gatherings of influential Republicans. He was enjoying the stump more than ever before. Sharing a taxicab with Luce on Park Avenue, Willkie told the Time-Life publisher that he ought to consider getting into politics. There was nothing wrong with journalism, said Willkie, but "this is the sport of kings."

Willkie's opponents were plainly troubled by his fast start and the phenomenal success of *One World,* which had outsold any political book in the history of publishing. "If we don't develop more respectable opposition," Hamilton wrote an Idaho GOP leader in May, "the organization members who are opposed to Willkie will find themselves embarrassed by simply being 'aginers,' and damned by being classified as blind antagonists to him." Dewey continued to declare that he was unavailable for the nomination, and some party leaders were starting to believe him. Even Bricker's supporters acknowledged that he was a handsome mediocrity. "An honest Harding," said Alice Roosevelt Longworth. Senator Taft complained, "His speeches don't amount to anything," and said that Bricker's campaign lacked direction. Hamilton refused an offer to manage Bricker's presidential bid. "Frankly, Bricker's campaign has lagged so much and his speeches have been so innocuous," he wrote Ruth Hanna McCormick Simms, "that I don't know whether he can be pulled back into the picture or not." Hamilton wrote an Illinois party leader: "I am quite frankly alarmed about the Willkie situation. If Willkie goes along at the present pace, and if no one develops to oppose him, he will win several of the early primaries of '44, and those who oppose him will be forced to a position where the favorite son campaign will have to be waged against him. You and I both know that this is an artificial approach, and I am fearful that it will put the organization in such disrepute that it may be obliged to accept him again, or suffer severe consequences in failing to do so."

"Despite the wishful thinking of the organizational leaders throughout the country," Hamilton wrote in late June, "Willkie continues to gain ground. I have every reason to believe that he has made considerable headway in the Southern states and in New England." Mrs. Simms advised Hamilton that Willkie would run strongly in Illinois "unless he is opposed with an organized effort."[8]

On June 27, however, Willkie fell from first place in the Gallup poll of rank-and-file Republicans, a position he had maintained since the Philadelphia Convention and which had given credibility to his claim that he was the people's choice. Now, however, the numbers showed that Dewey held the edge–37 to 28 per cent, with General Douglas MacArthur receiving 15 per cent and Bricker 10. Willkie's camp made the argument that he was still the stronger candidate in a general election, but a followup Gallup survey indicated that Dewey ran four points stronger against FDR. A *Pathfinder* magazine poll of Republican legislators in thirty-eight states gave Dewey 29 per cent to Willkie's 25 and Bricker's 18 per cent.

When asked in Ohio if he would challenge Bricker on his home court, Willkie said, "I have not decided whether I will be a candidate and therefore, I cannot answer that question. Ham Fish is against me. Gerald L. K. Smith is against me, and I understand Landon is against me. If this keeps up I may be nominated in spite of myself." Following his press conference, Willkie opened the door and caught up with several reporters. "Say, add Colonel McCormick of the *Chicago Tribune* to that list."

Gently scolded by William Allen White for putting Landon in the same category with reactionaries, Willkie replied: "I stand corrected. I offer in extenuation, however, that my friends should not expect me to be a christian always—the turning of the other cheek gets a little tiresome. I don't mind the blows so much as the annoyance. Landon came east and at every port he told newspaper men off-the-record that my standing in the midwest was such that I would be hung if I ever appeared in that section. . . . I know that I should let all this float by. I made the remark in Ohio, half jocularly. I admit that in cold print it didn't sound that way. I am resolved to be a good boy and I think I have held rather rigidly to the rule of never attacking a man personally until he first attacks me."

"I got a good giggle out of the Landon wisecrack," the Kansas newspaperman answered. "In my case I should have done exactly as you are doing. But my case is different than yours. I am an irresponsible editor and I could fade from the picture without affecting the situation. But you can't." A month later, White wrote Willkie: "Roosevelt has lost the ball; I doubt if he can ever get it again. Bricker will only fumble it. Dewey doesn't dare to grab it at this time. Stassen is handicapped by his job; so is MacArthur. You are the only American of either party who can step out and take the moral, intellectual, and political leadership of this country. It must be done with dignity, but at the same time without a mealymouthed humility."[9]

In August of 1943, Willkie took a working vacation in Rushville and issued a declaration of purpose for his candidacy. "Outdated policies must go," he insisted, urging the GOP to eliminate "isolationism, ultra-nationalism and destructive criticism" from its platform and adopt one based on "liberal progressive ideas." Willkie said, "The Republican party must point the way to an affirmative America—America as she can be under enlightened and liberal leadership, at home united, prosperous and socially advancing; abroad, respected as a practical worker for world peace and economic development and the leader of the gathering forces of enlightenment and independence." He held a series of meetings in Indiana with Cake,

Weeks, Baker, and other political associates, mapping his schedule for the busy autumn months.

Samuel Grafton, liberal columnist of the New York *Post,* spent two days with Willkie in Indiana. Although progressive journals were skeptical about Willkie's conversion to liberalism, Grafton left Rushville convinced that it was genuine. "It's wrong to talk about making a labor union man Secretary of Labor as a boost to the labor movement," Willkie said, leaning on a fence at his farm. "That's no boost to the labor movement. If I found a capable labor union official, I'd make him Secretary of War or Attorney General, if he were a good lawyer. Let him do a bang-up job and sell the labor movement to the country that way. Let the country realize that labor fellows are fellows like other fellows, capable Americans, like men in other fields. That's the big way to help Americans to learn to live together."

Discussing civil rights, Willkie said he wanted to name a black to his Cabinet or the Supreme Court. "If I am elected, and I do not do this," he told Grafton, "I want you to write a piece saying that on such-and-such a day, in Rushville, Indiana, Wendell Willkie made such-and-such a statement, and that Wendell Willkie is a liar."

In his living room, Willkie talked about his *One World* philosophy with homespun eloquence. "I tell you that if a man is not, deep in his belly, in favor of the closest possible relations with Britain and Russia, then it does not matter what else he is. This is the touchstone to a man's entire position in politics today. Only occasionally does it happen that one issue arises which is so controlling that every other issue is subsidiary to it, and this is it. But it is not enough for a man merely to repeat the right words about world collaboration. He has to be on fire with it. He has to feel, in his belly, that this is the door which will open outward to an expansion of American activity and prosperity. You cannot be wrong on this issue and right on any other."

Grafton soon reported, "There are two fixed poles in Mr. Willkie's political life today, an interest in civil liberties and an interest in international collaboration. It seems to me highly unlikely that he can ever be shaken from his adherence to both. Would he accept political oblivion, if he had to, as the price for sticking to these concepts? I am certain, as of this moment, that he would."[10]

Willkie was already paying a price for going against the grain. Republican National Chairman Spangler did not invite him to participate in the GOP's conference on postwar foreign policy in early September at Mackinac Island. Dewey, Taft, Vandenberg, and Warren were among the leaders of the conference. "It seems perfectly fantastic to me," Vandenberg wrote in his diary, "that we should attempt to pre-commit America in respect to a peace which as yet is totally in the dark. I have no sympathy whatever with our Republican pollyannas who want to compete with Henry Wallace." The Michigan senator told Thomas Lamont, "I am hunting for the middle ground between those extremists at one end of the line who would cheerfully give America away and those extremists at the other end of the line who would attempt a total isolation which has come to be an impossibility." Dewey announced that he favored a postwar alliance with the Soviet Union, Britain, and China as well as American membership in an international organization. Taft, calling Dewey's suggestion foolish, said the New York governor had "swallowed whole the proposals espoused by Walter Lippmann." Later, however, Dewey wrote Taft, "You and I were on the same side in practically every argument." The Ohio senator was counting on Dewey in the effort to block Willkie. "The chief stumbling block to a united policy," Taft told Dewey, "is your friend in New York."[11]

At Mackinac Island, the Republicans adopted a resolution supporting "responsible participation by the United States in a postwar cooperative organization among sovereign nations to prevent military aggression and to attain permanent peace with organized justice in a free world." On September 19, Willkie wrote William Allen White: "I think Mackinac was a step forward. I believe it would have been better if it were a little more specific but, when one measures against what we could have gotten a few years ago, it seems absolutely amazing."[12]

Willkie's second presidential campaign, like his first, was launched in a national magazine. In 1940 his "We the People" article in *Fortune* had set him on the path to nomination in Philadelphia. Three years later Gardner Cowles gave him an even more impressive send-off in a special issue of *Look* magazine devoted almost entirely to Willkie. "Our purpose in carrying this article and in fact in publishing this issue," *Look* general manager Harlan Logan wrote Willkie, "is to advance the likelihood of your gaining the Republican nomination." Cowles quit the Office of War Information to become a senior strategist of Willkie's campaign. Willkie got to edit the articles about him as well as write responses to five questions for which he was paid $1,500. Renowned artist John Falter painted the cover portrait of Willkie wearing a dark business suit and standing against a backdrop of Indiana farmland and blue skies. At Willkie's suggestion, *Look* changed the cover line from "How to Beat Roosevelt" to "How the Republican Party Can Win in 1944."[13]

Cowles promoted the October 5 issue with a national advertising campaign that suggested Willkie might be "Another Lincoln," who could "bind up the nation's wounds" and achieve "a just and lasting peace among ourselves and with all nations." Sending his Willkie issue to thousands of Republican officials, Cowles wrote in a cover letter, "The editors of *Look* feel that what the Republican Party does in 1944 is of vital importance to the welfare of the country." The magazine included a photo album of Willkie's life, reports on his diplomatic missions by five well-known foreign correspondents, and a fictional preview of how Willkie captured the 1944 nomination in a repeat of the "Miracle of Philadelphia."

In the main article, Willkie stated that he would fight for the nomination and a liberal platform. "If the Republican party intends to drive heart and soul for liberal objectives," he wrote, "I shall give it my complete and undeviating service, whether as the convention's nominee or as a worker in the ranks."

From Washington, Krock wrote, "The politicians here were more than ever disposed to concede, after reading the *Look* article, that Mr. Willkie will be a formidable contender for the Republican 1944 nomination; [he] knows where his fences are weak and is setting out to repair them."

Senator McNary, whose 1940 presidential hopes had been dashed by the Willkie blitz, complained to Hamilton about the *Look* promotion for its Willkie issue, ruefully noting that no GOP contender of modest means could hope to compete with $400,000 worth of political advertising from a national magazine. McNary said that Willkie was running well ahead of the GOP field in Oregon. "You fellows better get a candidate," the Senate Minority Leader told Hamilton, "or you can bet Willkie will be nominated."[14]

Hamilton was, in fact, taking charge of a "Stop Willkie" movement funded by Joseph Pew of Pennsylvania and Edgar Monsanto Queeny, Missouri chemical millionaire, who had been a prominent Willkie supporter in 1940. During the autumn of 1943, Hamilton campaigned against Willkie in twenty states, encouraging the organization of favorite-son delegations to block his effort in the primaries. In closed-door sessions with Republican officials, Hamilton denounced Willkie as inept, untrustworthy, and a political turncoat. Fred Baker reported from Seattle, "He is absolutely devastating when he gets a hotel room full of people together and starts letting fly."

In a letter to a Republican leader, Hamilton made his case against Willkie: "He cannot command the support of the Republican organization that is necessary for any candidate to have, if he is to win, for they do not feel that he is a Republican. His philosophies are too nearly those of Mr. Roosevelt to present the clear-cut issues which will be needed, if we are to convince the country of our honesty, and finally he is brash in his conduct, in his statements, and the race will be too close to be thrown away by any more 'to hell with Chicago' speeches."

Willkie's rivals were beginning to emerge. Even though Dewey was renouncing any presidential ambitions, the New York governor was working behind the scenes to get the nomination. Thomas J. Curran, Dewey's longtime ally and president of the National Republican Club, struck at Willkie, saying that the voters "will see no advantage in shifting from a Democrat who knows he is bigger than his party to a Republican who thinks he is bigger than his party." Herbert E. Brownell, Dewey's campaign manager, recalled in 1981 that Willkie had been viewed all along as their most serious threat to the nomination. In October Ruth Hanna McCormick Simms cautioned Dewey, "The strategy of the national campaign is not being considered as seriously as I think it should be." Dewey replied that it was the "measured judgment" of Brownell, John Foster Dulles, and his other advisers that Willkie was losing strength. "This thing is going very well, I believe," Dewey told her. "Willkie is being too political."[15]

Harold Stassen, who had resigned the Minnesota governorship and gone on active duty with the Navy in the South Pacific, announced from the war zone that he would be available for the nomination if called. His midwestern supporters made preparations to enter his name in the primaries, although the Cowles brothers were advising Stassen to keep out of the race or risk splitting the progressive vote. The once cordial relationship between Willkie and Stassen had strained, partly because of the Minnesota Republican's negative review of *One World* in the New York *Times* but mostly because of their conflicting ambitions.

Senator Vandenberg was pushing General Douglas MacArthur for the nomination and, in the process, managed to get the War Department to rescind an order prohibiting members of the armed services from seeking political office. "I feel emphatically that our primary obligation to the general is to protect him against any untoward political activities that would in any way embarrass his present status," Vandenberg wrote privately. "I believe that his nomination must essentially be a spontaneous draft—certainly without the appearance of any connivance on his part."[16]

Ernest K. Lindley, writing in *Newsweek,* said that "MacArthur has become the rallying point for extreme reactionary and isolationist leaders in the Republican party." At Hamilton's farm on the Philadelphia Main Line, Vandenberg, Pew, Robert Wood, and Hamilton Fish organized the MacArthur draft movement. The isolationist press moguls—Colonel Robert McCormick, William Randolph Hearst, Frank Gannett, Roy Howard, and Cissy and Joseph Patterson (of the Washington *Times-Herald* and New York *Daily News*)—used their news columns to support MacArthur's candidacy and depict him as a true hero. MacArthur confided to his intimates that he expected to be the GOP nominee in 1944, and when war correspondents reported his interest in the White House, the general issued no denials.[17]

In early October, Willkie campaigned in California, one of his strongest states. A poll of California GOP leaders taken that month by the San Francisco Central Committee showed him leading Governors Warren and Dewey by a comfortable margin. Dewey's men had written off California, but Brownell made several trips to Sacramento urging Warren to enter the primary as a favorite son and deny Willkie the state's fifty delegates. Hamilton also made the trek to Sacramento for the same purpose, and Warren seemed receptive to the idea. Bartley Crum, Willkie's state chairman, argued that Willkie should not be forced out of the primary if Warren decided to run. "Only wishful thinking at its most dangerous worst can advocate that your fate in California should be left in his hands," another California friend told Willkie. "In fact, I am convinced he is certainly opposed to you and will work actively against you." Willkie, though, was hesitant to challenge a popular governor in his own state and pressed Warren for a commitment that at least half the delegation would be favorably disposed to his candidacy.[18]

Speaking before California's GOP Central Committee, Willkie paid tribute to FDR and criticized his own party's negative record on social reform. "You have to give the devil his due," he roared. "The social reforms of the New Deal are here to stay, and if you had been half as smart as President Roosevelt, the Republicans would have advocated the legislation that brought the New Deal to power. If you continue to campaign on the basis of 'free enterprise' or against bureaucracy, regimentation, price ceilings, and federal centralization of power, you won't get anywhere."

By this time, few could doubt Willkie's liberal credentials. "The administration does not have to move much farther right or Willkie much farther left to reverse their relative position in 1940," I. F. Stone wrote in the *Nation.* "Willkie is playing a daring game. He believes that long ago he made himself unacceptable to Old Guard Republican leaders and that his only hope is to strike out boldly for a popularity that will force them to support his candidacy in 1944. He has cut loose from party moorings, turned his back on the country-club set, and invaded Roosevelt territory."[19]

Harold Ickes, the New Deal's old curmudgeon, who had led the Democratic attack on Willkie in 1940, had become captivated by the Republican's free-swinging liberalism. "He can either force the President to give real leadership to the people," Ickes wrote in his diary, "or he can furnish that leadership himself. . . . I wish that he were of the right temperament to give the kind of leadership we need. I think that if Willkie could get back into the Democratic party, he might have a better chance than as a Republican."

Robert E. Sherwood, FDR's speech writer and political adviser, recalled several years later, "It was my belief in 1943 and early in 1944 that if Willkie were to win the Republican nomination, Roosevelt would not run for a fourth term. I had no tangible basis for this belief, and it was a doubly hypothetical surmise because it was evident to Roosevelt that Willkie had no chance whatever of being nominated. Greatly as the Old Guard lords of the Republican machine hated Roosevelt, they had come to hate Willkie even more, and, be it said to his eternal credit, Willkie went out of his way to court their hatred by scorning their support."[20]

Willkie made little effort to mask his contempt for the Republican right. When Queeny of Missouri, head of the Monsanto Chemical Corporation and a prominent contributor and supporter in 1940, threatened to break off their friendship if Willkie did not moderate his views, he shot back: "I should count myself of little worth if I allowed either petty criticisms or personal attacks to influence my course of action. Even your letter, indicating as it does the loss of a friendship, which I have valued highly, will not deflect me from a course which I consider for the best interest of my country."

"I have never been awed by great wealth such as yours," Willkie wrote Queeny, "nor afraid of defending a Communist such as Schneiderman if I thought his cause was just. I wear my sovereignty under my own hat."

Early in the fall, Queeny sent Willkie a list of nine hostile questions that had been prepared with the assistance of Hoover and Hamilton and were signed by the state's 1940 GOP Convention delegates. "Do you believe," read one question, "it is desirable for America to permit flooding our country with alien individuals and alien ideas?" Another asked whether the United States "should become a member of a world supranational state." They demanded to know if Willkie would support the Republican ticket in the event he did not get the nomination. When he offered to reply to each of the questions at an off-the-record meeting with Missouri Republicans, the group demanded that it be opened to the public. "They aren't going to put Willkie on the spot," he snorted. "Even I ought to have the privilege of selecting the time and place of my own public discussion." The dispute was publicized in the Missouri press and got enough national attention to force Willkie to agree to their terms. The meeting was scheduled on October 15 in St. Louis.

Gardner Cowles urged Willkie to show restraint in St. Louis, because he could not afford to make more enemies in the GOP. "I hope you will take the time to think out, with the most scrupulous care, how you want to answer those questions," the publisher counseled. "I think the wrong answers could almost ruin you for the nomination. I think the right answers might make it obvious to everyone in the party almost immediately that you are actually the only possible nominee. . . . Remember, we have to get the nomination first; that nomination isn't going to be worth anything if the Republican Party is so split we cannot put it together for a winning election."[21]

Willkie exploded when he learned that the Missouri group was selling $50 box seats for his appearance and immediately plunked down $600 and rented the hall so that admission would be free. In his speech, Willkie ignored the loaded questions and made a tough attack on the Roosevelt administration's foreign policy and accused FDR of managing the news to manipulate public opinion. When he finished, Willkie received an ovation from the more than three thousand people who had come to hear him.

The next day Willkie appeared at a private luncheon of St. Louis industrialists and was introduced by Queeny as "America's leading ingrate." Willkie responded, "I don't know whether you're going to support me or not, and I don't give a damn. You're a bunch of political liabilities who don't know what's going on anyway."

Following this confrontation, Willkie's popularity shot up in the polls. On October 25, the Gallup poll showed him within four points of Dewey nationally and running ahead in New England, the South, the Rocky Mountain states, and the Pacific Coast states. "Willkie is now so far in front," *Life* magazine said on November 15, "that the contest within the party is between Willkie and Stop Willkie forces."[22]

While Henry Luce was still supporting Willkie, he was less committed than he had been in 1940 because of growing doubts about his friend's chances and his outspoken liberalism. "The fault is not that [Willkie] is too idealistic, but, rather, that his idealism is not quite on the right beam," Luce wrote one of his Washington correspondents. "His crusade is not correctly lined up with the historical realities." The *Time* publisher's wife, Congresswoman Clare Boothe Luce, said years later that she urged Willkie "to stop drinking, lose forty pounds and adopt a more realistic understanding of the Communists' announced plan to conquer the world." Her personal favorite was General MacArthur, but Henry Luce continued to back Willkie. In October Luce went to Capitol Hill and asked Senator McNary, whom he had once featured in a highly favorable *Life* cover article, to endorse his former running mate. Luce came away empty-handed, and McNary told friends it was his impression that the publisher expected to be Willkie's Secretary of State, a post which Luce had long coveted. In December, Luce told John Cowles that he was having second thoughts about serving on Willkie's small steering committee. "He said that while *Time* and *Life* would try to give Wendell all the breaks and emphasize the good things and minimize the bad things," Cowles recalled, "it was a little embarrassing for him to be a member of even an informal committee." Luce designated Roy Larsen, president of Time Inc., as his representative on Willkie's committee.[23]

"Willkie is, at this date, my personal preference for the Republican nomination," Luce wrote in a memorandum to his senior editors. "But the political position with which I have less sympathy than any other is the one which says: 'If the Republicans don't nominate Willkie, I'll vote for Roosevelt.'" Luce said that there were other Republicans who were capable of serving equally well in the presidency and that a problem with the Willkie-or-FDR people was that they wanted "change–without change."[24]

Willkie's candidacy was actively opposed by the party machines in the largest states–New York, Pennsylvania, Ohio, and Illinois–as well as his native Indiana. "There is little sentiment out this way in his favor," Landon wrote Hamilton from Kansas. "Outside of Nebraska, I don't know where he has any strength in any other midwestern state." Hamilton told Wisconsin's state chairman, "West of the Mississippi, Willkie has no initial strength of any consequence, except in Oregon. I'd bet my life today that he doesn't get 50 votes in that section of the country." Gardner Cowles told Willkie that he was losing ground with Republican businessmen and party activists. "The vast majority of them favor Dewey because they think he is safe and think you are not," said Cowles. "If you are beaten for the nomination, the thing that will beat you is that too many Republicans regard you as a carbon copy of Roosevelt."[25]

Under the circumstances, Willkie considered running as an independent. Marquis Childs reported in the St. Louis *Post-Dispatch* on December 11, 1943, that Willkie had "thoroughly explored the possibility of forming a third political party."[26] Intrigued by the wildcard option, Willkie found that the legal and technical difficulties in getting on the ballot in forty-eight states were too much to overcome in less than a year's time. So he abandoned his talk of a third force and concentrated on the Republican primaries.

By the middle of December, Dewey had extended his lead over Willkie to eleven points among Republican voters and held the edge in every region of the country except New England. "Willkie is fading fast–too fast," Dewey wrote Mrs. Simms. "He will probably have a revival. Bricker is doing better. . . . I think probably everybody will decide that they should wait until the convention and make up their minds." The New York governor told Simms that Colonel McCormick's threat to oppose Willkie in the Illinois primary was "a perfectly disastrous prospect. Our fat friend would get a brand-new lease on life."[27] As it turned out, McCormick did not run.

Though Willkie called himself a Republican, he was seeking the nomination as an outsider. "The greatest joy in life is to keep one's thoughts uncontrolled by formulas," he said. "I won't be dropped into a mould. I want to be a free spirit. If I wasn't one, I would still be sitting on a cracker box in Indiana."[28]

CHAPTER EIGHTEEN

ROSES IN THE SNOW

In January of 1944, Wendell L. Willkie met with a dozen key supporters in New York's old Ambassador Hotel. Many of them were convinced that he could not win renomination and were suggesting withdrawal. Though Willkie knew he was fighting an uphill battle, he was determined to prove himself in the primaries. Willkie told the group he would be running in New Hampshire, Wisconsin, Nebraska, Maryland, and Oregon. He pulled out of California with Governor Warren's pledge that half of the fifty delegates would be Willkie supporters. A heavy favorite in New Hampshire, Willkie was counting on an impressive victory there to demonstrate his popular appeal. In Wisconsin, however, Willkie was trailing Dewey by twenty points in the Gallup poll. To remain a national candidate, Willkie felt that he needed to show strength in the Republican heartland and could not sidestep Wisconsin. Willkie assured the group that an all-out campaign through the midwestern state would result in a victory. "If you friends will put up $25,000 to help me finance a campaign in the Wisconsin primary," Willkie said, "I will promise to withdraw from the 1944 race if I do not win a majority of the Wisconsin delegates."[1]

John W. Hanes agreed to raise the funds for Willkie's primary campaign, and Gardner Cowles offered to accompany Willkie into the state. On January 22, John Cowles wrote Willkie, "Winning Wisconsin is going to be an extremely tough job, but it is almost essential in order to win the nomination."[2]

"I am in complete accord with you," Willkie answered, "that winning Wisconsin is not going to be an easy job and I agree 100 percent that we must do some real campaigning in there. As a matter of fact, tentative plans call for me to be in there at least a week and maybe more just prior to the primary."[3]

When the Republican National Committee met in Chicago to select the site for the 1944 convention, Willkie made a strong pitch for New York. Hanes put together a financial package that doubled Chicago's bid and made available Madison Square Garden as the convention hall. Willkie's men contended that Chicago should not be chosen because it was the center of isolationism and its GOP politics were dominated by Colonel McCormick of the *Tribune,* Willkie's most persistent critic. The Office of Defense Mobilization had recommended Chicago to both major parties as a convention city because it would put less of a strain on the nation's railroads. "If they lose the fight against Chicago," Hamilton privately observed, "they have taken a licking on an issue of their own choosing. That will do Willkie no good. If they succeed in defeating Chicago and send the convention elsewhere . . . the party will be put in the position of refusing to cooperate with a reasonable request made in behalf of the war effort."[4]

By an overwhelming vote, the GOP national committee chose Chicago. Willkie's supporters claimed a partial victory, however, when an Associated Press poll of the national committee showed Willkie tied with Dewey as their favorite presidential hopeful. Willkie headquarters cited the poll as evidence that Dewey's momentum had slowed and Willkie's campaign was on the upswing. The Gallup poll dispelled those claims. On January 31, Dewey led Willkie by nineteen points among Republican voters and MacArthur was in third place, just five points behind Willkie.[5]

Willkie was swinging for the fences. On February 2, he delivered the first major speech of his comeback bid in New York *Times* Hall. Blasting the Administration's economic policies, Willkie said that unless tough measures were taken in Washington, the government would face a $300 billion debt after the war. Willkie called for doubling what the Administration was asking in taxes to $16 billion in order that the war effort could be funded on a pay-as-you-go basis. "We have been following a fiscal primrose path," he said. "It is time for us to face up. We must actually materially lower the American standard of living during the war. We must tax to the limit every dollar, corporate and individual, that is capable of bearing a tax. That limit is reached only when the war effort itself is threatened. All else must be sacrificed." Willkie said that once the war had ended, income taxes should be slashed, especially among middle- and lower-income families, to stimulate the economy.

"So-called political experts tell you that the American people will never stand for a tough tax program," Willkie declared. "I do not agree with those so-called experts. Give the people an understanding of those issues involved and they will do their duty by their country however incredibly painful it may be."[6]

Republican conservatives who denounced FDR's deficits turned their fire on Willkie for daring to suggest increasing taxes in an election year. President Roosevelt confided at a news conference that he wished he had Willkie's nerve. Historian Henry Steele Commager congratulated Willkie on what he called a farsighted, courageous, and statesmanlike address and said that he wished other Republicans had the courage to follow his leadership.[7]

"Wendell Willkie has a habit of crawling so far out on a limb," said the *New Republic,* "that his support does not seem to be connected with the Republican tree trunk at all. His bold tactics are the exact opposite of those employed by most of the politicians in his party." Arthur Krock, writing in the New York *Times,* said that political reaction to Willkie's speech provided "dismal confirmation that the elected of the people firmly believe a display of this type of courage and candor by a presidential candidate, even in wartime, is politically fatal."[8]

On its editorial page, the New York *Times* said Willkie's speech "strengthened the conviction" that he was "head and shoulders above any other man in his right and title to the Republican nomination."

Following the speech, Willkie took off on his first cross-country campaign swing of the year. Darryl F. Zanuck advised him to speak from notes rather than a prepared text. "You speak magnificently when you are guided by notes, or when you have your subjects catalogued for guiding purposes," said the Hollywood producer. "When you read, you somehow lose the full, wonderful drive that you normally and naturally possess." Zanuck said Willkie's earlier appearance at the Hollywood Bowl "seemed unnatural and rather artificial" when he used a text, "but the minute you tossed the papers aside, you electrified the crowd." He counseled Willkie to speak more slowly for newsreels and radio, noting that he talked "one-fourth faster" than FDR. "You should slow down your tempo and extend the pauses between phrases. This is a trick that we even have to remind our very best stars of." Willkie acknowledged that Zanuck was right in his criticism and promised to take the advice. Though he tried to speak slower and with more emphasis, he kept reading from a manuscript, which weakened his delivery.[9]

Willkie rumbled west in a private Pullman car that was so ancient that the Union Pacific refused to connect it behind the streamlined *City of San Francisco*. Instead, it was hitched to the *Overland Limited*. Willkie had meals in the dining car with other passengers. On this trip, he was accompanied by just four reporters compared to the fifty who traveled on his campaign train in 1940. Ralph Cake and Press Secretary Lem Jones were his traveling staff.

In Salt Lake City he reiterated his call for higher taxes. "Someone must tell the American people the truth," he said, "that's just the kind of fellow I am." In Twin Falls, Idaho, he debunked the "myth" that FDR was indispensable as a world leader. In Boise the three hundred tickets for his luncheon were sold out in twenty minutes. Idaho's governor, C. A. Bottolfsen, said that Willkie had "captivated" his audience and "greatly strengthened" his position in Idaho.

From the back of his railroad car, Willkie shouted to a small crowd in Baker, Oregon, "Confidentially, I am going to be nominated." Willkie said in Seattle that his differences with congressional Republicans were no greater than FDR's with congressional Democrats. "The Democratic party is in power," he said. "Its leader has the prestige of the presidency, yet repeatedly and on consequential measures, he has been unable to get his party to go along with him." His Lincoln Day address in Tacoma's Masonic Temple drew a standing-room crowd of four thousand Washington Republicans. Willkie charged that FDR promoted disunity by "making political friends of some economic groups and political enemies of others." He rasped, "We need a new leader. A leader who does not hold in his mind bitter or triumphant memories of past conflicts. A leader who does not think of the nation as made up of groups of people who can be played against each other to insure his continuing power. A leader with malice toward none."

On February 14, in Portland, Oregon, Willkie formally declared his candidacy for the 1944 presidential nomination. "I hope to seek the nomination at the Republican National Convention," he stated. "Everybody knows that anyway." At his side was Portland savings and loan executive Ralph H. Cake, Oregon's GOP national committeeman, chosen by Willkie as his national chairman and campaign manager. The silver-haired Cake, a Harvard-educated lawyer, would later play a major role in the 1952 nomination of Dwight D. Eisenhower.[10] Senator McNary had advised Cake against taking on the Willkie campaign, but it was the national committeeman's first chance at winning the big one and he grabbed it. "Willkie improved his position by his western trip," Oregan State Senator Coe A. McKenna wrote Hamilton. "He will carry Oregon in the primaries."

Willkie flew to Sacramento and completed the deal with Governor Warren in which he was promised half the California delegation. After a four-hour session with the governor, Willkie pronounced him "very agreeable." His opponents were pleased about his decision. "I think everyone will be relieved that he isn't" running in California, wrote Hamilton, "for certainly it would have required an active campaign on the part of the adherents to Governor Warren."[11]

Returning to Portland, Willkie rejoined the train and headed east through Montana, Wyoming, Minnesota, Iowa, and Illinois. At Great Falls, Montana, he donned a feathered warbonnet in a pose reminiscent of Calvin Coolidge and was inducted into the Blackfoot Indian tribe as "Flying Eagle." When Colonel McCormick took himself out of the Illinois primary, Willkie decided not to run there either. Back in New York, Willkie seemed greatly encouraged by his foray into the West.

In January, he had published an article in the New York *Times Magazine* entitled "Don't Stir Distrust of Russia," in which he berated Republican and Democratic politicians for seeking ethnic votes through anti-Russian propaganda. "We cannot impress upon Mr. Stalin the justice and wisdom of our ideas by using his country as a domestic political football," he wrote. Alluding to the Soviet Union's postwar ambitions, he wrote, "Of course, one of the most pressing questions in everybody's mind is what Russia intends to do about the political integrity of small states around her borders—Finland, Poland, the Baltic and Balkan states." The United States, he argued, should persuade the Soviets not to keep those occupied territories.

Willkie's candidacy received an unanticipated boost when he was denounced by *Pravda,* the official Soviet newspaper. *Pravda* attacked Willkie as a "political gambler," whose views were "hostile" to Russia, running for the presidency by "playing strange tricks." The Soviet newspaper linked Willkie with the British Government and the Vatican as an enemy of Russia. "I am at least in pretty good company," Willkie said. "The British government, the Vatican, and Wendell Willkie–that's pretty good company for an Indiana boy."

Several days after the *Pravda* blast, Willkie asked Sir Archibald Clark Kerr, British ambassador to Russia, to tell Stalin that if the attacks persisted, they might well make him President. Stalin later told the British diplomat that *Pravda* had been guilty of overkill. While taking issue with Willkie's postwar comments, Stalin expressed regret that the Soviet press had created an international incident. The Soviet leader told Kerr that he would cable an apology to Willkie, joking that he might say, "I like you but don't want you to be president."[12]

The State Department sent word to Willkie that Stalin might even make a public apology. Gardner Cowles told Willkie it would be better if Stalin kept silent. "There is just so much anti-Russian feeling in some branches of the Republican party," he wrote. "I would just as soon not have Stalin publicly commend you right now." Willkie solved that ticklish problem by reiterating his plea for an independent Poland. This time, though, the Kremlin did not respond.[13]

New Hampshire was Willkie's first primary test and he spent a day campaigning in the Granite State. On March 14, he won a solid if not spectacular victory, capturing six of the eleven delegates, with Dewey gaining two, and three uncommitted. "Unless Willkie makes a better showing in Wisconsin than he did in New Hampshire," Hamilton wrote A. L. Shultz, "I think the gentleman is going to hear taps blown over his political grave very shortly." To another GOP leader, Hamilton added, "The Willkie crowd in the east have tried to make the best of the New Hampshire primary, but I can't help but feel that in their hearts they must be disappointed. I personally had always given Willkie nine of the eleven delegates there, and surely they must have been counting on that many. To obtain only six in a state where they had been particularly active for the last three years is in my opinion a defeat rather than a victory."

Willkie's win in New Hampshire did not slow his downhill slide in the polls. In mid-March, the Gallup poll gave Dewey a 64 to 27 per cent lead over him among the party's rank and file. "Willkie is fading fast," wrote Alf M. Landon. "I don't see where he will have much more than 100 votes on the first ballot."[14]

Willkie was putting all his poker chips on Wisconsin, possibly the most isolationist state in the union. "Here the Republican opposition to Willkie is bitter, actually hatred of the man at times," a Milwaukee *Journal* political writer reported in a memo to John Cowles. "Let us be entirely frank–Wisconsin has its pro-German bloc–those people hate the ground Willkie walks on." Despite the state's progressive tradition, Wisconsin was not as liberal as its reputation. Only two years later Joseph McCarthy would oust Senator Robert M. La Follette, Jr., in a bitter Republican primary fight. Four years earlier Dewey had swept the primary, and he retained the backing of county leaders. The Gallup poll showed Dewey with 40 per cent and Willkie 20 per cent of Wisconsin's GOP. "Wisconsin is one of the most difficult states for me to make such a test," Willkie conceded. "I have no illusions as to the difficulty of that test."[15]

Even so, Willkie put together an impressive Wisconsin organization and delegate slate, headed by Vernon W. Thomson, the youthful speaker of the assembly and future governor. Nearly every newspaper in the state, including the prestigious Milwaukee *Journal,* was supporting his candidacy. Thomson had originally been for Dewey but switched to Willkie when the New York governor told him he would not seek the nomination. Though FDR had carried Wisconsin in 1940, Willkie had run ahead of the state's Republican ticket and thought he could regain much of that following. Acknowledging that it was make-or-break time, Willkie took the *Twentieth Century* from New York to the Midwest for two full weeks of campaigning.

As the train headed west, Willkie talked with several reporters in the drawing room of his private car and admitted that he nearly dropped from the race several weeks earlier because of negative reaction to his call for higher taxes. "You think I haven't a chance for the nomination, do you?" he asked Marquis Childs. "Well, don't count me out yet."

"Sometimes I wonder why I put so much into this," Willkie said. "Two weeks ago, I drew up a statement stepping out. I had thought about it very carefully. I am very happy in my law practice. I like the kind of life I have. I don't need public office. It's a terrible grind. It means sacrificing so much. Then, that day, I got a number of letters from people who believe in the things I stand for, and therefore they have faith in me. I tore that statement up. I decided to carry on the fight."[16]

For the next thirteen days, Willkie campaigned across snow-covered Wisconsin with stubborn defiance. Never before had a national political figure of his stature invested so much energy and time in a single primary. "Willkie has conducted throughout the state," wrote Willard Shelton in the *Nation,* "one of the most fantastic presidential campaigns in American history. He has hit the towns and countryside with the personal zeal of the old-time circuit rider on the glory trail."[17] Thomas L. Stokes, Scripps-Howard political columnist, who had followed Willkie's 1940 campaign, said, "There's something a bit like the glamorous Broadway star going back to the five-a-day in the provincial theaters in Wendell Willkie's attempted comeback on this Wisconsin circuit. Or, perhaps like the major league pitcher, back in the minors, ostensibly to cure that ailing left wing so the old hop will come back on the ball."

Marquis Childs was struck by the impact of the war on the electorate. "Going out into the country on a political tour you begin to realize what it means to take ten or eleven million young people out of circulation," he wrote. Most of Willkie's audiences, he noted, were made up of gray-haired men and women. "They sit quietly. They seem to listen intently," said Childs, "and they show almost no response of any kind."

Willkie got off to a bumpy start. In Richland Center he rambled through a long farm speech. "Willkie's speech was flat," Vernon Thomson recalled years later. "Most of the farmers sitting there didn't seem enthused."[18]

In Oshkosh he showed emotion and roused his audience with an attack on Dewey and his cohorts who thought it "clever to be silent" and "smart politics to manipulate the nomination." An older man approached Willkie and advised him that if he wanted to carry Wisconsin, he should pledge an immediate end to the war. In Fond du Lac Willkie described this conversation and shouted, "If that is the price, then don't elect me. I am for totally defeating our enemies. I want not less done about winning the war, but more."

In Ripon, where the Republican party had been organized nearly a century earlier, Willkie spoke in the auditorium of Ripon College on

"The Functions of a Political Party." He declared, "A political party can never stand still. Those leaders of a party who insist on applying old formulas to present problems merely because those formulas worked in the past are damaging the party and will eventually destroy it. For they are standing still while the world around them moves."

True political leaders, argued Willkie, had a duty to risk defeat rather than compromise on questions of principle. "In times of crisis," he said, "the American people have always been more concerned with issues than with personalities. A political party, therefore, which aspires to lead the country in time of crisis must face the issues and provide solutions for them. At such time, trimmers and dodgers lead their party to destruction."[19] Childs predicted that Willkie's Ripon speech "may well become one of the vital documents in our political history." He wrote, "In a moment of bitterness and dissension, of cynicism and indifference, Willkie has with simple clarity, defined the dilemma of the Republican Party. And more than that, he has defined the political crisis of our time." Henry Steele Commager told Willkie that future historians would remember his speech as an important statement on the role of political parties. "You were absolutely right," said Commager, "in recalling the origin and early history of that party and in insisting that the party face real instead of sham issues."[20]

To many observers, it appeared that Willkie was making inroads. "I would certainly not make a prediction of any kind," Wisconsin GOP Chairman Thomas E. Coleman reported to Hamilton on March 18. "The Willkie group is putting on the best campaign, due, of course, to the fact that they have a candidate on the ground." Hamilton replied, "It seems to me that Willkie is stabbing the soft underbelly of the Republican party in going into Wisconsin." Hamilton wrote A. L. Shultz, "It seems to me it wouldn't hurt to cushion the possibility of a Willkie victory there with something in your column . . . that if Willkie wins, it won't mean much because the ticket is split four ways and Willkie is the only one who has been in the state to campaign."[21]

Willkie opened fire on his opponents. He slammed Dewey in Kenosha. "I almost despise those who remain silent more than those who speak out in open opposition," he said. Willkie was embittered over Stassen's entry into the primary. The thirty-six-year-old former

Minnesota governor was serving as Admiral William F. "Bull" Halsey's chief of staff in the South Pacific. Before Stassen left for the war, Willkie had specifically asked him about Wisconsin, and the Minnesotan had assured him that he would not be running and promised the support of his organization. Soon, however, Stassen changed his mind and notified Secretary of the Navy Frank Knox that he would accept the nomination but not actively seek it. "I went into the service in the last war," Willkie acidly commented. "I was deeply worried and thought I ought to fight. I had no other objective until the war was over except to devote myself entirely to that cause knowing that I could not possibly comprehend the problems at home or do anything about those outside issues until the war was over."[22]

Showing his old verve, Willkie lashed out at his conservative critics. In Janesville he repudiated Republican National Chairman Spangler for suggesting that the party might benefit from the Administration's wartime Irish and Polish policies. In Appleton he denounced Colonel McCormick, whose Chicago *Tribune* had been attacking him daily in its southern Wisconsin circulation area. "Any Republican candidate of the school of thought of the Chicago *Tribune* will be overwhelmingly defeated. In the industrial centers, there is open resentment against the school of thought of narrow nationalism, economic toryism and opposition to social advances." Willkie referred to isolationists as "cowardly, yielding people who didn't want to fight for what is right."

In La Crosse Willkie thundered, "If I have no other reason to ask for your good will, I am entitled to at least some of your support for the enemies I have made. I have the most valuable list of enemies of any public or quasi-public figure in America." In Green Bay, an isolationist stronghold, he defended his early backing of lend-lease. "I never will be prouder of anything in my life," he said. At one stop, he responded to the charge made by political extremists that he was attempting to bring the United States under the authority of an international superstate. "That is so foolish," he asserted. "Certainly no one would expect Wendell Willkie to give away the substance of the nation. I did not get where I am by being a nut."

The seven 1942 Dodges in Willkie's motorcade drove more than fifteen hundred miles through the snowy Wisconsin countryside. Heading into northern Wisconsin, he slogged two hundred miles through a blizzard. It took five hours for Willkie to make the hundred-mile trip from Wisconsin Rapids to Eau Claire. In parts of the state, he traveled across the snow in a horse-drawn sleigh. Willkie invariably ran behind schedule. When one of the cars in his procession ran over a boy's dog, Willkie stopped to console the youth and bought him a black cocker spaniel. En route to Madison, he stopped the motorcade at a country auction and climbed on a farm wagon to make a brief talk. Such impulsive gestures frustrated his staff, for he often left audiences waiting for more than an hour. "Lateness in meeting speaking engagements detracted greatly from effectiveness of Willkie program," Madison publisher Don Anderson wired Lem Jones.

Throughout his comeback bid, Mrs. Willkie was at his side, smartly dressed and nearly always cheerful. When her husband's hair got windblown, she put her hand on his head and attempted to smooth it. In Milwaukee she listened straight-faced as a local GOP leader introduced her as "one who bears the aroma of her native Hoosier State." Willkie responded, "I've heard Indiana described in many ways, but I have not heretofore thought of the sweet smells that come from there." Even though Edith had been through a national campaign before, she still resented the intrusions on her private life. When photographers asked her to pose with Willkie, one of them asked if she minded. "I'll always mind," she replied.

In the final week of his Wisconsin campaign, Willkie attracted overflow crowds. Speaking in a Milwaukee arena where Dewey had addressed one thousand people in 1940, Willkie drew more than four thousand. When the pro-Dewey county chairman snubbed him in Sheboygan and refused to make available his party headquarters, Willkie's supporters rented the city armory and packed it on a rainy night with a friendly crowd of five thousand. In Waukesha, a previously indifferent county chairman, impressed by Willkie's drawing power, asked to introduce the chairman of the rally. Willkie estimated that he appeared before more than seventy thousand Wisconsin voters in his two-week blitz. "Everyone was impressed by the huge crowds," Thomson said. An aide told Willkie, "If this is any indication, you should win big." "Yes," replied the candidate, "if they vote for me."

State Chairman Coleman wrote Hamilton on March 24, "It seems generally acknowledged that wherever Willkie has delivered a written speech on the radio it has been quite unsatisfactory and has been received with no warmth or enthusiasm by the listeners. His biggest and best meeting was in Sheboygan. Interestingly enough, Sheboygan is quite a German stronghold. He had 5,000 people there for an evening meeting. It is difficult to understand why the results of his appearances are so spotty. It seems that the normal thing is that he does very well in some localities and very badly in others."[23]

Willkie's opponents were staying away. Dewey sent a telegram asking his supporters to withdraw as candidates for delegate, but his slate remained on the ballot, headed by Secretary of State Fred R. Zimmerman, a former governor and America First isolationist. "Draft Dewey" billboards were plastered in all parts of the state, and more than 200,000 Dewey brochures were mailed to the state's voters. Stassen, too, was making an expensive direct-mail effort. Campaigning for Stassen, Minnesota Senator Joseph Ball went after the German vote in claiming that the former governor was committed to the postwar territorial integrity of Germany. Eighty-one-year-old Wisconsin Governor Walter Goodland endorsed Stassen. General MacArthur's candidacy was promoted in the *Progressive,* political organ of the La Follette family. Former Governor Philip F. La Follette was then serving on MacArthur's staff in the Southwest Pacific.

Ending his Wisconsin campaign in Superior, Willkie noted that he had been the only presidential candidate who had cared enough to come into the state. Willkie urged the state's voters not "to buy a pig in a poke" and took a parting shot at Dewey for his failure to "discuss issues or take a stand." Heartened by his reception in the closing days of his Wisconsin drive, Willkie told Cowles he thought he had a fifty-fifty chance. "He was upbeat all the time and full of enthusiasm," said Thomson. Willkie's traveling press corps, most of them veteran political observers, gave him the edge. State Senator Bernard Gettelman, a Dewey backer, predicted that Willkie would capture a majority of Wisconsin's twenty-four delegates. Democratic State Chairman Thomas King estimated a minimum of fifteen Willkie delegates. Cowles, who had been at Willkie's side for ten days, was much more cautious.[24]

Three days before the primary, Coleman reported a private poll to Hamilton which indicated Dewey was the likely winner and Willkie might get shut out in the race for delegates. "Such a result seems quite impossible," added Coleman, "considering the time that Willkie spent here."

Tired and hoarse, Willkie rested for a day in Minneapolis with the Cowles brothers and then moved into Nebraska for the next primary. John Cowles told Willkie that Roy Dunn, Minnesota's GOP National Committeeman, would be helpful in breaking loose some of Stassen's own delegation for their cause.[25]

On the night of April 4, Willkie listened to the returns from Wisconsin in his suite at the Norfolk Hotel in Norfolk, Nebraska. With returns from fifty of the more than three thousand precincts reporting in, Willkie sensed that his candidacy was doomed. "Well, that looks like it," he said. "We said it would be all or nothing and it looks like nothing." When someone suggested that the early returns were inconclusive, Willkie smiled and shook his head. By midnight, it was official. Dewey had won seventeen delegates, Stassen four, MacArthur three, and Willkie none. "I'm glad I made the fight," he said. "I'd do the same thing if I had it to do over again."

Willkie asked Cowles whether Wisconsin had voted for isolationism or against him personally. In Willkie's judgment, it was partly both. "Willkie flew into a violent rage," said Cowles, "when I reminded him of his pledge to all of us that he would withdraw if he failed to win a majority of the Wisconsin delegation. He talked about bolting to Roosevelt. He talked about possibly repudiating Dewey. Finally, after consuming a good deal of Scotch, we went to bed about 4 A.M. and I still had no commitment from Willkie that he would withdraw."

At breakfast later in the morning, Cowles did not bring up Willkie's political future. The defeated candidate indicated that he planned to go through with the day's schedule. In a news conference, he told reporters, "Off the record, it looks like Dewey on the first ballot." He addressed an open-air rally in West Point and a luncheon in Fremont. He admitted that he felt "a bit heartbroken." That night he delivered a foreign policy speech in Omaha's shabby, barnlike Municipal Auditorium.

As he finished his text, Willkie interjected, "Now, my fellow Americans, I have something quite personal that I want to say on this occasion, something that perhaps is of not much importance—but it involves what I have been trying to do—the things I have been fighting for." Wisconsin's verdict, he said, was "naturally disappointing." Then, he declared, "It is obvious now that I cannot be nominated. I therefore am asking my friends to desist from any activity toward that end and not to present my name at the convention."

Leaving the auditorium, Willkie would make no further comment about the GOP race. Edith, carrying a bouquet of several dozen red roses, told reporters that anything "Wendell" did was "1,000 percent alright" with her.

On the train back to New York, he played gin rummy and read *The Count of Monte Cristo,* which had been among his favorite books since boyhood. When he arrived, the switchboards at his law office and at his Grand Central Station headquarters were both jammed with calls from friends and well-wishers. His mail room was filled with bundles of condolence messages from throughout the country.[26]

"The part you still have to play in American life," wrote Walter Lippmann, "will be greater, not less than that which you have already played. It often happens that those who cannot exercise power come thereby to exercise greater influence." Henry Steele Commager expressed regret at Willkie's withdrawal and wrote, "I think your Wisconsin campaign was in every way admirable and splendid." William L. Shirer added: "Your defeat in the Wisconsin primaries at first seemed to me a terrible blow not only to you, but to all of us who had hoped that the people of the Middle West at last understood the destiny of this country. On second thought I am inclined to believe that in making the fight you did, you cleared up the fundamental issues facing this country." From Oregon, Charles A. Sprague wrote: "The night your withdrawal was announced, I had a group of Young Republicans in my campaign office in Portland. They were truly heartsick over the news. I know that men in the service felt the same way. What concerns me is, if we blast the faith of our younger members of our party, what hope will we have for the future?"[27]

Willkie took the defeat hard. At a luncheon with the editors of *Newsweek,* he talked about why his campaign had come apart. "He was no happy warrior," recalled Raymond Moley. "He showed traces of bitterness toward what he called the machine and Old Guard Republicans and especially toward the then ascendant Dewey, whom he branded as opportunistic and incapable of statesmanship." When Moley asked what happened to him in Wisconsin, Willkie grumbled, "The damn county committees were against me."[28]

Thomas E. Coleman, Wisconsin's GOP chairman, had a somewhat different view. "I do not believe that the Willkie defeat was primarily an indication that the state of Wisconsin is isolationist," he wrote Hamilton. "In fact, I believe that the election could have occurred in any of a great number of states with the same result. Of course, in our communities where the population is quite heavily German and where they have kept up their German customs, there is no question that Willkie's vote was almost nil. . . . Furthermore, he talked about so many things that he did not become the symbol of any one thing to any large group of people. I heard the attitude expressed by many people that if there was going to be a change in presidents, there was no use taking a man just like the man we have, and that hurt him a great deal."[29]

Roy A. Roberts, managing editor of the Kansas City *Star,* who had been a Willkie adviser in 1940, said, "Willkie at heart is a genuine liberal, more so even than President Roosevelt. He sought to pitch his place in politics to the left of Roosevelt" at a time when the GOP was on "a definite swing to the right." Political scholar Wilfred E. Binkley observed, "Willkie's difficulty in 1944 was the fact that both on domestic and foreign policy, he was still the Wilsonian Democrat. His plea for real economic enterprise and the freeing of individual opportunity from the menace of monopolistic and government restraints was but the New Freedom of Woodrow Wilson whose disciple he never ceased to be."[30]

Willkie insisted that he had no regrets. "I've had three great satisfactions in my life—the nomination, the book, and this campaign," he told the *New Yorker*. "Somehow, I feel damned proud."[31]

CHAPTER NINETEEN

BREAKING AWAY

During the weeks following his Wisconsin defeat, Wendell L. Willkie made it clear that he did not consider it his last hurrah. "Frankly, I haven't decided what I am going to do," he wrote Charles A. Sprague. "I'm terribly troubled, but whatever I do, I am going to do on the basis of my conscience, irrespective of any personal consequence. I'm sure we will find ourselves together in many future battles. Let's not be discouraged. I'm sure in the long run our viewpoint will prevail."

"I know most people assume that one situated as I am must be depressed," he wrote South Carolina writer Josephine Pinckney. "As a matter of fact, I am on top of the wave. And I didn't dip my colors in falling. You probably don't realize how much satisfaction there is in that. For you have not had to live under the crushing pressures of political expediency."

Closing his campaign headquarters, Willkie announced that he was resuming law practice, but most of his friends were skeptical. "He was no more capable of retiring into the practice of law," said Barnes, "than he was of becoming a dirt farmer." Soon after the primary, Willkie sent letters to twenty leading political writers with copies of Turner Catledge's New York *Times* report that Wisconsin's Progressive party had split with the New Deal and joined forces with Republican isolationists. "All these things I took into account in my fight in Wisconsin," Willkie wrote. "The whole problem may be solved if the country understands the situation. And the situation can be corrected only by vigorous, forthright leadership in the Republican Party. It cannot be glossed over or solved by mere general words.

"Naturally," Willkie added, "as a Republican, I would prefer to work within the Republican Party. But I will be damned if I am going to sit by while the peace of the world is wrecked again as it was in the Twenties."[1]

Willkie had been unhappy with *Time*'s coverage of the primary, especially the magazine's analysis of his defeat that had said, "Wisconsin had clearly voted no confidence in global good will and a foreign policy of generalities." At a dinner with Luce, Willkie could not keep his temper. "His face became a bowl of fury," Luce said later. "He half rose and I really thought this giant of a man was going to reach across my sister and sock me." Willkie growled, "Harry, you may be the world's best editor, but you are certainly the world's worst politician."

Several days later Willkie wrote his friend, "I thought the article misstated the facts about the Wisconsin primary and therefore drew erroneous conclusions. Naturally, being human and in view of your many expressions of friendship for me, I thought it appropriate to call your attention to what I, at least, thought an undeserved blow at a time when the blows were coming rather thick. I know also that Mr. Hull and his office had been following the same line in reprisal for my sharp criticism of the conduct of the State Department."

"But forget it," he concluded. "I am the first to recognize your complete right to express any opinion you have in publications which you own. I certainly maintain my own right to express my opinions. I do hope you have more luck in shaping the Republican Party than I have had."[2]

When Frank Knox died in late April, it was widely reported that FDR wanted to name Willkie as Secretary of the Navy. A popular theory was that Roosevelt wanted to bring him into the Administration as a buildup for the vice-presidential nomination. It was well known that Democratic leaders were pressing for the removal of Henry Wallace from the national ticket, and if Willkie accepted a Cabinet portfolio, some political writers were suggesting that it would make him more acceptable to Democratic delegates. Willkie had turned thumbs down on earlier attempts to bring him into a high-level government post, and his attitude had not changed.

"As to the Secretaryship of the Navy and other similar suggestions," he wrote Marquis Childs on May 10, "obviously no one from the outside becoming Secretary of the Navy at this time, no matter how great his administrative skill or wide his knowledge, could possibly master the multiple ramifications of the Navy Department or the Navy and its activities short of several months.

"As a matter of fact, with an impending invasion, a new man of conscience and not a mere front would probably be a nuisance. The only objective the administration could possibly have (even if it is considering such a move which I seriously doubt) in offering me the position would be for the political benefits. I, of course, have no way of measuring how many, or if any, people believe in me. If, however, I have only one follower, I certainly owe him the obligation not to use the faith of that relationship for purely political purposes or to permit the administration or the Republican Party to use it for such purposes.

"If I had a notion that I was the only one qualified to serve as Secretary of the Navy, or in any other position," Willkie wrote, "I would, of course, accept if offered. Or if I really thought that such action on my part would unify the people, I would, of course, accept. Not believing either of those things, I would, of course, not accept. By the same token, the many suggestions that are made to me that I should in advance agree to accept some important position in government under the anticipated Republican administration of Mr. Dewey or support him in the hope of some position, leave me equally cold."[3]

In the end, Roosevelt did not make the offer which Willkie almost certainly would have refused. Although they had not met for nearly two years, they were in frequent contact through intermediaries. Willkie was in no hurry to make an endorsement in the 1944 election. "I think you are wise to adopt a rule of silence at the present time," advised Sprague. "You will find the emissaries of the nominee rapping at your door with palm branches in their hands after the convention. It might be well to let them cool their heels for a time."

John D. M. Hamilton wrote privately, "If Willkie comes out against the Republican candidate, he will be in the position of a political spoilsport and he will influence practically no one. The most dangerous thing he could do in my opinion is to simply keep quiet."

Which was exactly what Willkie was doing. Both FDR and Dewey were anxious to have his support. Elmo Roper, the respected pollster, estimated that Willkie still had a devoted following of between five and six million voters and suggested that his endorsement could be a factor in the November election. Willkie would not take the decision lightly.[4]

He submitted a proposed platform to the Republican National Convention, but it was ignored by the conservative resolutions committee. So Willkie had his platform published in the *Herald Tribune,* Boston *Herald,* Minneapolis *Star-Journal* and *Tribune,* Des Moines *Register* and *Tribune,* Portland *Oregonian,* San Francisco *Chronicle,* and New York *Times.* Willkie called for more comprehensive coverage under Social Security, declaring that "protection against old age, illness and economic misfortune must be a right for everyone." He advocated civil rights laws for fair employment, open housing, and voting rights and dismissed states rights as an argument against social progress. He urged the repeal of the Smith-Connally Act banning strikes and asked both labor and business to become more socially responsible. To promote international trade, he called for a reduction of tariffs. To stimulate the postwar economy, he recommended tax incentives for business. In foreign policy, he said that the Administration's conduct had produced "dislike, distrust, and loss for the United States without achieving the intended political aims." Republicans, said Willkie, should "frame and pursue a foreign policy that will recapture America's lost leadership." The platform committee shunned Willkie and sought the foreign policy views of Dewey, Bricker, and Vandenberg.

The party that had nominated him for the presidency four years earlier was treating him as a heretic. GOP National Chairman Spangler invited Hoover to address the convention but not Willkie. Dewey blocked efforts to make him a delegate-at-large from New York. In a calculated insult, Spangler offered Willkie a box seat in Chicago Stadium to watch the convention with "honored guests." Willkie chose to stay in New York.

Willkie launched a final effort to stop Dewey's nomination. The Cowles brothers and Luce were promoting the youthful Stassen. In the preconvention issue of *Life,* the former Minnesota governor received more than generous profile treatment as the "perfect Republican candidate for 1944." Willkie, however, disliked Stassen even more than he did Dewey. He wrote Helen Rogers Reid: "I would like to go along with him [John Cowles] on his Stassen idea. I can't, particularly in light of Joe Ball's speeches for Stassen in Wisconsin and Nebraska. For he demanded a United Nations declaration against any dismemberment of Germany or violation of her territorial rights. I do not happen to be wise enough to know just what should be done about Germany, but I am smart enough to know the effect on German-American voters in Wisconsin and Nebraska of such chatter."

His preference, Willkie told his political allies, was Governor Leverett Saltonstall of Massachusetts. And Willkie convinced Luce and several other friends to make a last-ditch attempt for the Massachusetts Republican. "Naturally," Luce recalled, "Willkie's hope could be–it was his only hope–that if the convention deadlocked, he might have a chance." Governor Saltonstall met with Willkie's group but declined to make the race. Sam Pryor telephoned Willkie that there was enough anti-Dewey sentiment that it might be possible to deny the New Yorker the nomination if they combined forces with Bricker and promised the Ohio governor second spot on a Willkie ticket. "I can't do it," Willkie replied, acknowledging at last that it was too late.[5]

Fearful of a floor fight over the platform, Dewey and Senator Taft had members of the drafting committee pledged to secrecy until it was read from the podium. Willkie telephoned Arthur Krock and asked if he might obtain a copy of the foreign policy plank. "Can't you get it yourself?" asked Krock. "No," said Willkie, "you see the Republican is a very private party."

Krock got a copy from Senator Warren Austin on the condition that Willkie would not break the embargo. The New York *Times* columnist called Willkie and told him Austin's ground rule. "Go ahead," said Willkie, which Krock took to be his acceptance of the condition. As Krock read the plank, which called for "international cooperation" but rejected U.S. membership in a "world state," Willkie groaned his displeasure. The next day Krock was embarrassed when Willkie called a news conference and repudiated the plank as too vague on U.S. participation in a United Nations organization.[6]

"There must be no playing with phoney phrases," said Willkie. "We should speak in words forthright, clear and strong." He did not, though, have the delegates to make a successful challenge from the floor at Chicago Stadium and did not really try. The platform was adopted by an overwhelming vote. Dewey took the nomination on the first ballot and tapped Bricker as his running mate after California's Warren turned down the vice-presidential nomination. "Hearty congratulations to you on your nomination," Willkie wired his longtime rival. "You have one of the great opportunities of history."

Willkie pointedly was not endorsing Dewey. His closest political associates were urging him to declare his support of the ticket in a gesture of unity. Shortly after the convention, Luce invited Willkie to his Waldorf Towers apartment for dinner with Herbert Brownell, Dewey's campaign manager and the newly installed Republican National Chairman. "Willkie came in, looking more than ever like a huge woolly bear—but a bear in a bad, dangerous mood," Luce said later. "It was a painful hour. Willkie behaved atrociously—grumbling, growling and saying everything he could think of against Dewey."

Predicting that Dewey would be defeated by FDR, Willkie told Brownell that he would make a third presidential bid in 1948 and offered to make him campaign manager. "My whole theme that night," recalled Brownell in 1981, "was to appeal to his selfish interest. I told him that he wouldn't get the party's support in 1948 if he didn't support the ticket. The more I made this argument to Willkie, the more it seemed to appeal to him." Willkie did not, however, make a commitment.[7]

"In my judgment," Willkie wrote John Cowles, "the President will be overwhelmingly re-elected."[8]

Ever since FDR and Willkie began their wartime collaboration on lend-lease, there had been speculation in the public prints about the maverick Republican joining the Democratic ticket in 1944. Public opinion polls indicated that Willkie's prestige had grown as a result of his Wisconsin defeat. Drew Pearson wrote that the "only vice-presidential running mate who could add votes to FDR is his old political opponent, Wendell Willkie." A Democratic official said, "With Willkie on the ticket, we could close up the headquarters and not even raise a campaign fund." Roosevelt, when asked about the possibility, said that he could not take the lead because it would look like a deal but would welcome Willkie's nomination from the convention floor. FDR sounded out his 1940 opponent about his availability.

Early in July, Secretary Ickes telephoned Willkie and said he was coming to New York to meet with him at the President's request. Willkie, Ickes, and Gardner Cowles met for dinner at the Ambassador Hotel. The old New Dealer said, "I've been sent up by the President and he wants to know if you would accept if he nominated you for vice president on the Democratic ticket." By the time that Ickes left, Willkie had not given a definite answer. Though interested in the vice-presidency, Willkie was aware that FDR had given many Democrats similar proposals in the past and left them disappointed once they confirmed their ambitions for the job. "Wendell left it open," recalled Cowles. "I told him that he couldn't do it. He'd have turned on all those friends who supported the hell out of him in 1940." Cowles also made the argument that it would have the unmistakable aroma of a political deal and "that wouldn't sit well with the country."[9]

Some months earlier, Roosevelt had told his son James to drop the trial balloon with Democratic leaders that he might invite Willkie to run with him in 1944. Walter Trohan reported in the Chicago *Tribune* that Justice Frankfurter was plugging hard for a Roosevelt-Willkie unity ticket. Although party regulars were skeptical about any such proposal, it was clear that FDR liked and admired his 1940 opponent. Robert Sherwood recalled, "Once I heard Hopkins make some slurring remark about Willkie, and Roosevelt slapped him with as sharp a reproof as I ever heard him utter. He said, 'Don't you ever say anything like that around here again. Don't even *think* it. You of all people ought to know that we might not have had Lend Lease or Selective Service or a lot of other things if it hadn't been for Wendell Willkie. He was a godsend to this country when we needed him most.' "

Though, remarkably, there were no leaks about the Willkie-Ickes meeting, the Republican maverick's name frequently surfaced in press speculation about FDR's running mate.

Willkie refused to discuss the matter with other close friends and political associates and left no written record of his thoughts. Cowles said he was doubtful that the Democratic convention would ratify his nomination even if FDR proposed it. It appears that the talks between Willkie and the Administration broke down before the convention opened on July 19. Two days earlier FDR wrote George W. Norris, "I don't think there is any possible danger of Willkie, though feelers were put out about a week ago."

On the evening of July 11, the President discussed the vice-presidency with Democratic politicians Robert E. Hannegan, Edward

J. Flynn, and Frank C. Walker, all of whom said that Wallace should be dumped. FDR, agreeing to select a new running mate, mentioned Justice William O. Douglas, but the bosses were less than enthusiastic. Hannegan recommended Senator Harry S. Truman of Missouri, and Roosevelt gave his approval.[10]

At the convention, Senator Robert F. Wagner of New York sparked a "Draft Willkie" movement. Edward Loughlin, head of New York's Tammany Hall, former North Carolina Governor O. Max Gardner, and Wisconsin Congressman Howard McMurray were all pushing for Willkie. So, too, was the indefatigable Drew Pearson. On the second day of the convention, Pearson put Loughlin in touch with Leo T. Crowley, FDR's floor manager. The Tammany Hall chief said he was anxious to second Willkie's nomination–Senator Wagner planned to give the nominating speech–and reported that support was growing for the maverick's candidacy. Acknowledging Willkie's strength, Crowley replied that the White House and party hierarchy were determined to put across Truman.

"Crowley poured cold water on the idea of your being on the ticket," Pearson wrote to Willkie. "He admitted that he had talked to the President about it and the President had said that if there should be a spontaneous move in the convention, he, FDR, would be favorably disposed. However, Crowley went on to say that the President since that time had given definite instructions that Truman was to be his man. Crowley also made it plain that he was working 100 percent for Truman's nomination and that any proposal of the name of Wendell Willkie might throw a monkey wrench into the machinery."

Senator Wagner, in a final appeal, telephoned FDR's secretary, Grace Tully, and asked her to have the President return his call. When there was no answer from the White House, Wagner folded the Willkie candidacy. Vice-President Wallace went to Chicago Stadium and fought for renomination. On the first ballot, Wallace held the lead, but Truman clinched the prize on the second when the big-city machines and southern conservatives combined to give him a majority. "I feel very definitely that Roosevelt made the mistake of his life," Pearson told Willkie. "If we had a nonpartisan Democratic-Republican ticket, the liberal forces of the country would be insured 100 percent victory and we would have broken down the artificial barriers in both parties–even made way for a party regrouping."[11]

Willkie was already working on his concept of a liberal third force. In the late spring, he had approached David Dubinsky, president of the International Ladies Garment Workers Union, about plans to launch a national third party–not for the 1944 campaign but for the postwar years. Both the Republican and Democratic parties had shifted to the right, Willkie noted, and he predicted that conservatives would dominate the Democratic party once FDR was gone from the scene. "He made it plain," said Dubinsky, "that he was more than eager to volunteer to lead a liberal coalition under a third-party banner."

Dubinsky and Alex Rose of the Millinery Workers told Willkie that he should first establish a political power base and offered him the Liberal party nomination for mayor of New York City in 1945. Mayor La Guardia was winding up his third term, and it was generally assumed that he would not seek a fourth. "We advised Willkie that, if he declared his candidacy for Mayor early in 1945, the Republican Party in New York City would not dare deny him its endorsement," said Dubinsky. "Even if the party leaders tried to blackmail him, he would win the nomination hands down. We assured him that he could count on our backing as well. That would mean he would be running on a Republican-Liberal coalition ticket, which couldn't lose."

Willkie sensed that his election as New York's mayor would be a springboard for his national third party. Dubinsky and Rose were elated by Willkie's enthusiasm. "As we drank coffee and brandy at the end of the long evening," recalled Dubinsky, "we were all inspired with the belief that we had made a historic decision–a decision that would surprise not only the city but the whole country."

With the city hall elections more than a year away, Willkie took few friends into his confidence about his plans. When he sought William L. Shirer's counsel, the CBS correspondent said that Willkie would be a formidable candidate in any contest. Willkie discussed his idea of a national third party with former Pennsylvania Governor Gifford Pinchot, who had been an organizer of the 1912 "Bull Moose" Progressive party. Pinchot, encouraging him to attempt "a new setup in American politics," later told FDR about Willkie's goal. The President was visibly excited by the prospect of a new party.

"It was Willkie's idea," Roosevelt told Judge Samuel Rosenman, his closest associate. "Willkie has just been beaten by the conservatives in his own party who lined up in back of Dewey. Now there is no doubt that the reactionaries in our own party are out for my scalp, too—as you can see by what's going on in the South. I think the time has come for the Democratic party to get rid of its reactionary elements in the South, and to attract to it the liberals in the Republican party. Willkie is the leader of those liberals. He talked to Pinchot about a coalition of the liberals in both parties, leaving the conservatives in each party to join together as they see fit. I agree with him one hundred percent and the time is now—right after the election. We ought to have two real parties—one liberal and the other conservative. As it is now, each party is split by dissenters."

FDR explained that he was thinking about "long-range politics," not the 1944 elections but said the new party could be ready in four years. "From the liberals of both parties," said Roosevelt, "Willkie and I together can form a new, really liberal party in America."

Roosevelt asked his longtime aide to hold a secret meeting with Willkie. On July 5, Judge Rosenman and Willkie conferred for more than two hours in a private suite at the St. Regis Hotel. Willkie was so apprehensive about news leaks that he stepped into the bedroom when the waiter brought lunch. Rosenman told Willkie that the President, too, was interested in the creation of a progressive third party. "He wants to team up with you," the judge said, "for he is sure that the two of you can do it together. And he thinks the right time to start is immediately after the election."

"You tell the President," said Willkie, "that I'm ready to devote almost full time to this."[12]

Once the campaign had ended, Willkie said that he would look forward to discussing the plan with FDR. They should not meet until then because it would "give rise to many conjectures." Willkie and Rosenman talked at length about some of the groups and personalities who might form the core of the new party. The President was so fascinated by Rosenman's report that he wrote Willkie on July 13 and suggested an earlier meeting. "What I want to tell you is that I want to see you when I come back [from a western tour]," FDR wrote, "but not on anything in relation to the present campaign. I want to talk with you about the future, even the somewhat distant future, and in regard to the foreign-relations problems of the immediate future."

"The subjects concerning which you suggest we have a talk on your return from the West are, as you know, subjects in which I am intensely interested," Willkie replied. "I am fearful, however, that any talk between us before the campaign is over might well be the subject of misinterpretation and misunderstanding. And I do not believe, however much you or I might wish or plan otherwise, that we could possibly have such a talk without the fact becoming known.

"Therefore, if it is agreeable to you, I would prefer postponement of any such talk until after the November elections.

"I hope you will understand that I make this suggestion because you in a great way, and I in a small one, have the trust and confidence of people who might see in the most innocent meeting between us at this time, some betrayal of the principles which each of us hold so deeply."[13]

Willkie never mailed the letter. He was furious when gossip columnist Leonard Lyons reported that FDR was trying to set up a meeting with him, suspecting that the White House planted the item for political profit. Yet Willkie had shown the letter to Henry Luce and Arnold Beichman, political correspondent for *PM*. "Smart s.o.b., isn't he?" Willkie asked Beichman. He let Beichman make a typewritten copy of FDR's letter with the understanding that he would not be identified as the source. When other reporters asked about the invitation, Willkie replied with a terse "No comment."

The President further strained his relationship with Willkie by denying at a press conference that he had extended an invitation. Willkie, who had asked former Ohio Governor James M. Cox to serve as the go-between, told him that he was no longer interested in talking with Roosevelt. In an August 21 letter, FDR apologized to Willkie for the leak and retracted his denial. "I am awfully sorry that there was a leak on a silly thing like this–but I still hope that at your convenience–and there is no immediate hurry–you will stop in and see me if you are in Washington or run up to Hyde Park if you prefer."[14] Within three days, FDR's second letter was published in the newspapers, and Willkie snapped, "I've been lied to for the last time."

In a public statement, Willkie said he "would much prefer that no such conference occur until after the election. But if the President of the United States wishes to see me sooner, I shall of course comply."

Roosevelt persisted in his efforts to meet with Willkie. Senior Administration officials said that FDR hoped to send Willkie to Europe as his personal representative with authority to set up civilian control of Germany after his election. FDR told his son Elliott that he would support Willkie for secretary-general of the proposed United Nations organization. That summer, delegates from the United States, Great Britain, Russia, and China had gathered at Dumbarton Oaks and sketched an outline for the United Nations charter. Finally, the President sent word that he would like to have Willkie come up to Hyde Park on Labor Day weekend. Willkie was scheduled to be in Rushville but said that he would be willing to talk on his return.[15]

Willkie's Republican friends were worried that he might join the Administration. "You need have no fears about my accepting any position from either Franklin Roosevelt or Thomas Dewey," he wrote Gardner Cowles on August 15. "I am so fed up on pragmatic politicians that there is no inducement that would prompt me to serve under either of them in any capacity."[16]

The Dewey camp was troubled by reports that Willkie might endorse Roosevelt. Russell Davenport and Bartley Crum, two of his closest political associates, were campaigning for FDR. Governor Dewey tried and failed to reach Willkie by telephone. He politely declined an invitation to meet with Dewey in Albany.

On August 21, Willkie conferred with Dewey's foreign policy adviser, John Foster Dulles. Richard H. Rovere said that Willkie blamed Dulles more than Dewey for his defeat in 1944. "It pleased Willkie to think of Dewey as a person of no consequence whatever—as, in fact, a product of Dulles' imagination. This conceit possessed him so that he elaborated it into a theory of history that made John Foster, Benjamin Harrison's Secretary of State and Dulles' grandfather, the author of the original sin. Foster had inflamed his grandson with the desire to be Secretary of State. To satisfy this desire, Dulles had first to create a President. He settled on Dewey, became Dewey's leading patron, and financed the early Dewey campaigns. In the summer and early fall of 1944, Willkie could believe that the worst consequences of John Foster and his grandson were about to be realized."

Dulles gave Willkie assurances that Dewey shared his commitment to a United Nations organization. Willkie was not, however, ready to give the New York governor his blessing. By remaining aloof, he hoped to extract further concessions. Turning down Bruce Bliven's offer to write the special Dewey supplement for the *New Republic,* Willkie said, "I would have a lot of fun doing what you suggest, but I am not the one to do it." He did, though, provide lots of ammunition for reporters writing critical pieces about the GOP nominee. He got Arnold Beichman interested in the isolationist activities of Dewey's campaign treasurer, James S. Kemper. He virtually ghosted Drew Pearson's column charging that Hoover had surfaced as a leading Dewey strategist. When Dewey berated Hamilton Fish for making anti-Semitic slurs, Willkie told reporters that the governor lacked the courage to speak out against the congressman's isolationist record.[17]

"I know in view of the formulas and codes of politics, it must be quite difficult for some to understand what I am trying to do," he wrote Krock on August 28. "In my mind, at least, it is quite simple. I have some very definite convictions about both our foreign and domestic policy. I happen to think of both Mr. Roosevelt and Mr. Dewey as what I call pragmatic politicians. If one states it kindly, one says they seek to articulate the opinion of the masses. If one says it unkindly, one says that they follow the polls and engage in vote-catching. . . . I am greatly interested in creating a body of public opinion which will force either or both of them to go in the direction in which I believe they should."[18]

Keeping up the pressure, Willkie wrote two articles for *Collier's* late in the summer which were published in September. The first, "Cowardice at Chicago," was critical of both parties for "double talk, weasel words and evasion" in their platforms. Willkie called for more forthright language from the candidates on postwar security, breaking up the Old World's colonial empires, and the establishment of an international political organization. His second article, "Citizens of Negro Blood," was an eloquent plea for racial equality. Willkie termed the 1944 platforms "tragically inadequate" in dealing with racial discrimination and proposed that FDR issue an executive order ending segregation in the armed services. He also called for a federal antilynching law and repeal of the poll tax. These articles and his earlier newspaper series were later published by Simon and Schuster in a small book, *An American Program.* In the foreword, Willkie wrote, "our attitude on racial minorities and on our international obligations will constitute a test of our sincerity at home and abroad and of our ability to bring about, with other nations, a world of peace and security."[19]

Willkie was thinking seriously about becoming a newspaper publisher. Earlier in the year, he had tried but failed to purchase the Indianapolis *Star*. By the summer, he was negotiating to buy the Chicago *Daily News,* one of the most distinguished newspapers in America, which had been owned by his friend Colonel Frank Knox. When Knox died in the spring, the trustees of his estate wanted to sell the newspaper to another progressive Republican of national stature. Perhaps more than anyone else, Willkie filled both requirements. When he said that he would move to Chicago and take over the daily management of the newspaper, the trustees took the *Daily News* off the block until Willkie had a chance to meet with them. They arranged a meeting in July, which Willkie was forced to postpone until September.

By that time, he was gravely ill. Late in August, while traveling by train to Indiana, he had struggled in opening the door in the dining car. Soon after his arrival in Rushville, he suffered a heart attack. Mary Sleeth, who ran his farms, persuaded him to see a doctor. Willkie refused, though, when the physician tried to get him to a hospital. "I've got too many things to do and say," he told Sleeth, "to be written off as an old man with a bum heart."[20]

He looked pale and gaunt when Lem Jones met him at Penn Station. Willkie was so weak that he had to be helped off the train by Jones and a porter. His press secretary wanted to call an ambulance, but Willkie demanded a cab so that he could go home. When he reached his apartment, Willkie was in terrible pain and asked for sedatives. He was then rushed by ambulance to Lenox Hill Hospital.

The prognosis was not encouraging. His once strong physique had turned frail. He had a coronary thrombosis. For years, Willkie had been careless about his health. He chain-smoked Camels, refused to be concerned about his diet, and never exercised. All these factors had taken a toll. Willkie did not want the public to know of his condition. On his instructions, the hospital press spokesman reported that he was being treated for a stomach disorder and physical exhaustion. "I have a case of colitis," he wrote Hanes on October 2. "The doctor would like for me to get as much rest as possible, and freedom of mind."

Willkie had not lost his zest for the political wars. "If for any reason you desire to make a political attack on me," he wrote Hanes, who was bitter that he had not endorsed Dewey, "won't you please wait two or three weeks when I will be out of the hospital and well, at which time I will be in a position to take care of myself."

On September 27, he wrote Governor Saltonstall: "I hope you do not get yourself so closely tied up with the recent nonsense Dewey has been talking that you sink with him if he sinks. Of course, as a Republican governor, you will want to support him formally but for God's sake don't sacrifice your principles. Much more is at stake even than your own political future. And the only way that fellows like you and me can really contribute to our party's welfare at this time is by a certain aloofness which may force the candidate to take the right course, if anything can do so."

Willkie and Walter White had planned to write a book together on the struggle for racial equality. From his hospital bed, Willkie wrote his old friend that he hoped to "escape" in a few days. "Then let's get together for a couple of cocktails to discuss the book, though God alone knows when either you or I will ever get the time to write a book." Referring to another of White's book projects, Willkie added, "Whatever you are writing in seclusion, for my sake please give them hell."

For a time, he appeared to be on his way to recovery. Near the end of September, his doctors said Willkie would soon be released. Friends made available a house in Florida for his convalescence period, but Willkie decided that he wanted to spend the next few months in Rushville. In his hospital room, Willkie edited the galleys of *An American Program,* corresponded with friends, and received a few visitors. On Saturday, September 30, he saw Roscoe Drummond, Washington bureau chief of the *Christian Science Monitor*. Willkie telephoned Drummond at his New York hotel and gave him instructions on how to get to his room by a side door and avoid nurses who might object.

"He was looking rested, robust, and buoyant," Drummond recalled. "He was eager to talk of everything and his energy filled the little hospital room to overflowing. All the New York Sunday newspapers were strewn on the floor where he had tossed them after reading and a dozen of the latest books were piled helter-skelter on a little table by his elbow. The sum of our conversation was that he had seen nothing thus far in Mr. Dewey's commitments to justify his calling on those who thought as he did to vote for him, and he had certainly not reconciled himself to back the President he had tried to defeat four years earlier. It was a hard decision for Mr. Willkie, because he was not one to 'take a walk,' to declare a 'plague on both your houses.' "[21]

From his hospital bed, Willkie wrote Drummond: "I enjoyed our talk this morning very much. Frankly, I cannot answer your ultimate question [whom he would endorse] yet because I have not finally decided. . . . It is a delicate subject and though I constantly try to find a method of expression about it, to date I have failed completely."

On October 4, Willkie caught a streptococcic throat infection, and his condition suddenly worsened. His lungs became congested and his fever rose to 104°F. Penicillin injections helped lower his temperature, but he remained critically ill. On Saturday, October 7, the hospital disclosed to the public that Willkie was in critical condition. That evening he suffered three more heart attacks, and since coming to the hospital, he had survived thirteen such attacks. But not the fourteenth. At two-twenty on Sunday morning, he died after the final heart attack. Lem Jones, his voice breaking, spoke to reporters in the lobby. "It's all over," said Jones. "He went very fast."

Willkie's sudden death at the age of fifty-two came as an abrupt jolt to most of his countrymen. In New York's Pennsylvania Station, the Red Caps paid tribute to Willkie as "the most courageous champion in recent times of all minority groups." In a London pub he had visited in 1941, his photograph was draped with black crepe, and one of the regulars toasted him: "We're sorry he's gone. He was a proper gent–very easy to mix with." Secretary of War Henry L. Stimson offered a hero's burial in Arlington National Cemetery, but Edith Willkie decided he would be buried at Rushville.

His body was placed in the center aisle of the Fifth Avenue Presbyterian Church, and sixty thousand people lined up to pay their last respects. During the New York services, a crowd of thirty-five thousand gathered outside the church and listened to the funeral over loudspeakers. Eleanor Roosevelt observed in her column that the large number of blacks in the crowd was a fitting tribute to Willkie's leadership in civil rights. The flag-draped coffin made the journey to the Midwest by train.

On a gentle slope in Rushville's East Hill Cemetery, Willkie was buried in a grave marked by a twelve-foot granite cross and an open book carved in stone with quotations from *One World*. "If men ask where is his monument, let them but look around at a world, one in integrity like his own," eulogized Reverend George A. Frantz, "one in a passionate dedication to freedom like that which consumed him."

And with that, Wendell L. Willkie was laid to rest—back home in Indiana. Though he never became President, he had won something much more important, a lasting place in American history. Along with Henry Clay, William Jennings Bryan, and Hubert Humphrey, he was the also-ran who would be long remembered. "He was a born leader," wrote historian Allan Nevins, "and he stepped to leadership at just the moment when the world needed him." Shortly before his death, Willkie told a friend, "If I could write my own epitaph and if I had to choose between saying, 'Here lies an unimportant President,' or, 'Here lies one who contributed to saving freedom at a moment of great peril,' I would prefer the latter."[22]

ACKNOWLEDGMENTS

I am indebted to the late Edith Willkie, who made available her husband's private papers for this biography. The Willkie manuscripts have been annotated and are carefully preserved in the Lilly Library at Indiana University. I owe a considerable debt to Saundra Taylor and Kathy E. Wyss of the Lilly Library for guiding me through this vast collection of Willkie material, which until recently had been closed to scholars.

John Broderick and his staff at the Manuscript Division, Library of Congress, were enormously helpful as was Sally Marks of the diplomatic records branch of the National Archives. William Emerson of the Franklin D. Roosevelt Library and Tom Thalken of the Herbert Hoover Library pointed me to useful materials regarding Willkie's relationships with those two presidents. Charlotte McNary Limerick gave me access to her father's private correspondence during the weeks when he was Willkie's vice-presidential running mate. Richard L. Strout of the *Christian Science Monitor* generously shared his files and correspondence from his 1940 campaign coverage. Richard Norton Smith, author of a splendid biography of Thomas E. Dewey, lent me his notebooks and other primary source material on Willkie's chief Republican rival of the forties. Senator Robert A. Taft, Jr., kindly gave me access to his father's papers at the Library of Congress. Richard Kluger, author of a forthcoming study of the New York *Herald Tribune,* provided helpful insights about Willkie's close friend Irita Van Doren, as did Mrs. Van Doren's daughter, Barbara Klaw.

Among those who gave me assistance by sharing their experiences with Willkie were Joseph Alsop, Betty Barnes, Ray Bliss, Herbert Brownell, Ralph H. Cake, Marquis Childs, Thomas Corcoran, Gardner Cowles, Marcia Davenport, Willard Edwards, James A. Farley, George H. Gallup, Charles A. Halleck, John D. M. Hamilton, John W. Hanes, Palmer Hoyt, Edwin F. Jaeckle, John S. Knight, Alf M. Landon, Henry Cabot Lodge, Kenneth McCormick, Warren Moscow, Elliott and James Roosevelt, Oren Root, Harold E. Stassen, Richard L. Strout, Robert A. Taft, Jr., Vernon Thomson, and F. Clifton White.

Barbara Newcombe, Mary Hushens, and Carolyn Hardnett of the Chicago *Tribune*'s library staff were unfailingly helpful in locating dusty old files on Willkie and his era. So, too, were Joe DiMarino, Joe Gradel, Bill Matheuss, and Mary Holland of the Philadelphia *Inquirer*'s library.

I am very grateful to Robert J. Donovan and Lou Cannon for reading the manuscript and making many helpful suggestions. My editor, Lisa Drew, and her associates Anne Hukill, Sarah Parsons, and Katherine Precht were thoughtful and perceptive in their comments, generous with their time, and fun to work with. Fred Wiemer's copyediting was invaluable. My agent, Gerard C. McCauley, gave me the encouragement to undertake this biography and made it happen. I am indebted to James Squires, F. Richard Ciccone, Dennis Gosselin, and Ray Coffey of the Chicago *Tribune,* who enabled me to have time to complete this long project. As always, I am indebted to Susan and Erin Neal for their patience and support.

BIBLIOGRAPHICAL ESSAY

Wendell L. Willkie has been described by leading historians as perhaps the "most undocumented of our public men." In 1952, Professor Allan Nevins of Columbia University lamented, "He kept no diary; he had no Boswell to record his conversations; he wrote few letters of a personal or revelatory nature." Within the last few years, however, Willkie's papers have been made available to scholars, as have the private letters of his most important contemporaries. The State Department only recently declassified its documents pertaining to his wartime diplomatic missions for FDR, which are open to researchers at the National Archives. The largest and most comprehensive collection are Willkie's private papers in the Lilly Library at Indiana University. Unhappily, there is only fragmentary material from his youth and his business career as chief of Commonwealth and Southern. Starting with his initial efforts to gain the 1940 Republican presidential nomination, Willkie's political career is well documented in his own correspondence and the writings of his associates. His speeches and published articles from 1930 until his death in 1944 were helpful in providing insights into his developing political philosophy. Another useful collection housed in the Lilly Library are the papers of Oren Root's Associated Willkie Clubs of America. The Franklin D. Roosevelt Library at Hyde Park has valuable information on Willkie's battle with the New Deal over the TVA, the 1940 presidential campaign, and includes the correspondence between FDR and Willkie, which illuminates their wartime cooperation and the convergence of their political views.

The manuscript division of the Library of Congress has Willkie's original and heavily marked-up manuscript for *One World* and extensive collections of Willkie material in the papers of Irita Van Doren and Joseph Barnes. Other relevant collections include those of Charles L. McNary, John D. M. Hamilton, Robert A. Taft, William Allen White, Felix Frankfurter, Harold L. Ickes, and Raymond Clapper. The Frankfurter and Ickes diaries were especially valuable. The Thomas E. Dewey papers at the University of Rochester shed new light on the relationship between the bitter GOP rivals. The Herbert Hoover Library at West Branch, Iowa, has the former president's correspondence with and about Willkie. Charlotte McNary Limerick made available her father's correspondence with his family during his weeks as Willkie's running mate in 1940.

Even though Willkie never got around to writing his autobiography, no fewer than eight of his top campaign aides recorded their reminiscences of his 1940 campaign. Marcia Davenport's *Too Strong for Fantasy* (New York: Scribner's, 1967) and Oren Root's *Persons and Persuasions* (New York: W. W. Norton, 1974) are firsthand accounts of how the Willkie movement was launched by key participants. Joseph W. Martin's *My First Fifty Years in Politics* (New York: McGraw-Hill, 1960), written in collaboration with Robert J. Donovan, is especially valuable for its treatment of the general election. Charles A. Halleck's oral history interview at Indiana University and the unpublished recollections of John D. M. Hamilton at the Library of Congress were useful and informative. Henry Cabot Lodge's *The Storm Has Many Eyes* (New York: W. W. Norton, 1974), Gerard Lambert's *All Out of Step* (Garden City, N.Y.: Doubleday, 1956), and Paul C. Smith's *Personal File* (New York: Appleton-Century-Crofts, 1964) were also helpful.

Of earlier Willkie biographies, the most authoritative is Ellsworth Barnard's *Wendell Willkie: Fighter for Freedom* (Marquette, Mich.: Northern Mich. U. Press, 1966). Joseph F. Barnes's *Willkie* (New York: Simon & Schuster, 1952) is an engaging and sympathetic portrait written by a longtime friend. Donald Bruce Johnson's *The Republican Party and Wendell Willkie* (Urbana, Ill.: U. of Ill. Press, 1960) is a blandly written, thoroughly documented study of Willkie's political rise and fall. Mary Earhart Dillon's *Wendell Willkie* (Philadelphia: J. B. Lippincott, 1952) is a negative assessment that is flawed by the author's reliance on questionable sources. Muriel Rukeyser's *One Life* (New York: Simon & Schuster, 1957) is a distinguished poet's free verse tribute to Willkie. Nelson Sparks's *One Man* (New York: Raynor, 1943) is a political hatchet job funded by Willkie's right-wing critics and reads as if it might have been written by Victor Lasky. *Wendell Willkie of Elwood* (Elwood, Ind.: National, 1940) by Herman O. Makey is a campaign biography that contains useful background on Willkie's youth in Indiana. *This Is Wendell Willkie* (New York: Dodd, Mead, 1940) is a compilation of Willkie's important speeches and published articles up to his nomination and includes a first-rate introduction by Stanley Walker, one of the legendary newspapermen of the "front page" era. Alden Hatch's *Young Willkie* (New York: Harcourt, Brace, 1944) was written with the subject's cooperation and is highly readable, but it must be used with caution because some of the stories are apocryphal.

Willkie's *One World* (New York: Simon & Schuster, 1943) is his enormously readable memoir of his 1942 world-encircling trip as FDR's special envoy to Russia, China, and the Middle East. His other book, *An American Program* (New York: Simon & Schuster, 1944) is critical of the Republican and Democratic parties for their reluctance to tackle civil rights and other tough social issues. In this little volume, Willkie described his vision of America in the postwar era.

Never Again: A President Runs for a Third Term by Herbert S. Parmet and Marie B. Hecht (New York: Macmillan, 1968) is a compelling and scholarly account of the 1940 presidential campaign. Warren Moscow's *Roosevelt and Willkie* (Englewood Cliffs, N.J.: Prentice-Hall, 1968) is valuable for its background on the Willkie boom in the spring of 1940, and the GOP convention. "The FDR Tapes" in the February/March 1982 issue of *American Heritage* is the best source on the President's strategy and tactics in the 1940 campaign against Willkie. Samuel Rosenman's *Working with Roosevelt* (New York: Harper, 1952) and Robert E. Sherwood's *Roosevelt and Hopkins* (New York: Harper, 1948) are reminiscences by two of FDR's top aides in the third-term campaign. James MacGregor Burns's *Roosevelt: The Lion and the Fox* (New York: Harcourt, Brace, 1956) and *Roosevelt: The Soldier of Freedom* (New York: Harcourt, 1970) are indispensable to any student of the period and as definitive as any treatment of FDR. William Leuchtenberg's *Franklin D. Roosevelt and the New Deal, 1932–1940* (New York: Harper, 1963) and Arthur M. Schlesinger, Jr.'s *The Politics of Upheaval* (Boston: Houghton Mifflin, 1960) are important studies of the period. Schlesinger's *The Imperial Presidency* (Boston: Houghton Mifflin, 1973) provides useful background on the 1940 destroyer-bases exchange with Great Britain. Wayne S. Cole's *Roosevelt and the Isolationists* (Lincoln: U. of Neb., 1983) includes a comprehensive chapter on the campaign of 1940.

Of the remembrances by FDR's associates, the following were helpful for insights into Willkie: *The Price of Vision: The Diary of Henry A. Wallace, 1942–1946,* edited by John Morton Blum (Boston: Houghton Mifflin, 1973); *Go East, Young Man: The Early Years* by William O. Douglas (New York: Random House, 1974); *The Journals of David E. Lilienthal,* 6 vols. (New York: Harper, 1964–76); *From the Diaries of Felix Frankfurter,* edited by Joseph P. Lash (New York: W. W. Norton, 1975); *Navigating the Rapids: From the Papers of Adolf A. Berle,* edited by Beatrice Bishop Berle and Travis Beal Jacobs (New York: Harcourt, Brace, 1973); *The Secret Diary of Harold L. Ickes,* 3 vols. (New York: Simon & Schuster, 1953–54); *The Memoirs of Cordell Hull,* 2 vols. (New York: Macmillan, 1948); *Special Envoy to Churchill and Stalin* by Averell Harriman and Elie Abel (New York: Random House, 1975); *On Active Service in Peace and War* by Henry L. Stimson and McGeorge Bundy (New York: Harper, 1948); *Jim Farley's Story* by James A. Farley (New York: McGraw-Hill, 1948); *You're the Boss* by Edward J. Flynn (New York: Viking, 1947); *White House Witness, 1942–1945* by Jonathan Daniels (Garden City, N.Y.: Doubleday, 1975); *The Roosevelt I Knew* by Frances Perkins (New York: Viking, 1946); *FDR, My Boss* by Grace Tully (New York: Charles Scribner's, 1949); *This I Remember* by Eleanor Roosevelt (New York: Harper, 1949); *My Parents: A Differing View* by James Roosevelt (Chicago: Playboy Press, 1976); *Affectionately, FDR* by James Roosevelt and Sidney Shalett (New York: Harcourt, Brace, 1959); *A Rendezvous with Destiny: The Roosevelts of the White House* by Elliott Roosevelt (New York: G. P. Putnam's, 1975); and the *Diaries of Edward R. Stettinius, Jr.,* edited by

Thomas M. Campbell and George C. Herring (New York: New Viewpoints, 1975).

A number of the journalists who followed Willkie's career have produced their memoirs, which include some revealing Willkie anecdotes and observations on his time. Roscoe Drummond's recollections in Isabel Leighton's *The Aspirin Age* (New York: Simon & Schuster, 1949) are especially helpful. Marquis Childs's *I Write from Washington* (New York: Harper, 1942) and *Witness to Power* (New York: McGraw-Hill, 1975); Arthur Krock's *Memoirs: Sixty Years on the Firing Line* (New York: Funk & Wagnalls, 1968) and *The Consent of the Governed and Other Deceits* (Boston: Little, Brown, 1971); Turner Catledge's *My Life and the Times* (New York: Harper, 1971); Bill Lawrence's *Six Presidents, Too Many Wars* (New York: Saturday Review Press, 1972); Carey McWilliams' *The Education of Carey McWilliams* (New York: Simon & Schuster, 1978); Drew Pearson's *Diaries, 1949–1959,* edited by Tyler Abell (New York: Holt, Rinehart & Winston, 1974); Walter Winchell's *Winchell Exclusive* (Englewood Cliffs, N.J.: Prentice-Hall, 1975); Samuel Grafton's *An American Diary* (Garden City, N.Y.: Doubleday, 1943); Raymond Moley's *Twenty-Seven Masters of Politics* (New York: Funk & Wagnalls, 1949); Richard H. Rovere's *The American Establishment* (New York: Harcourt, Brace, 1962); Raymond Clapper's *Watching the World, 1934–1944* (New York: McGraw-Hill, 1944); Burton Heath's *Yankee Reporter* (New York: Funk & Wagnalls, 1940); Guy J. Forgue's *Letters of H. L. Mencken* (New York: Alfred A. Knopf, 1961); Carl Bode's *The New Mencken Letters* (New York: Dial, 1977); and Nicholas Roosevelt's *Front Row Seat* (Norman: U. of Okla. Press, 1953) were all useful in providing background on Willkie, FDR, and their era. The Willkie-Luce connection is detailed in Robert T. Elson's *The World of Time Inc. 1923–1941* (New York: Atheneum, 1968) and *The World of Time Inc. 1941–1960* (New York: Atheneum, 1973) and is covered to a lesser extent in W. A. Swanberg's *Luce and His Empire* (New York: Charles Scribner's, 1972), Stephen Shadegg's *Clare Boothe Luce* (New York: Simon & Schuster, 1970), and David Halberstam's *The Powers that Be* (New York: Alfred A. Knopf, 1979). Ronald Steel's *Walter Lippmann and the American Century* (Boston: Little, Brown, 1980) and Marion Sanders's *Dorothy Thompson: A Legend in Her Time* (Boston: Houghton Mifflin, 1973) are useful biographies of prominent journalists who were Willkie's friends and occasional advisers.

There is an abundance of literature on the Republican party in the 1940s, of which the most important works are Richard Norton Smith's *Thomas E. Dewey and His Times* (New York: Simon & Schuster, 1982); James A. Patterson's *Mr. Republican: A Biography of Robert A. Taft* (Boston: Houghton Mifflin, 1972); David Burner's *Herbert Hoover: A Public Life* (New York: Alfred A. Knopf, 1979); Joan Hoff Wilson's *Herbert Hoover: Forgotten Progressive* (Boston: Little, Brown, 1975); Gary Dean Best's *Herbert Hoover: The Post-Presidential Years, 1933–64* (Stanford, Calif.: Hoover Inst. Press, 1982); Donald McCoy's *Landon of Kansas* (Lincoln: U. of Neb. Press, 1966); C. David Tompkins's *Senator Arthur H. Vandenberg: The Evolution of a Modern Republican* (E. Lansing: Mich. State U. Press, 1970); Arthur H. Vandenberg, Jr.'s *The Private Papers of Senator Vandenberg* (Boston: Houghton Mifflin, 1952); George H. Mayer's *The Republican Party, 1854–1966* (New York: Oxford U. Press, 1967); and Malcolm Moos's *The Republicans* (New York: Random House, 1956).

John Morton Blum's *V Was for Victory: Politics and American Culture During World War II* (New York: Harcourt, Brace, 1976) is an excellent history of the home front. Other worthwhile accounts include Geoffrey Perrett's *Days of Sadness, Years of Triumph* (New York: Coward, McCann, 1973); Kenneth S. Davis's *Experience of War: The United States in World War II* (Garden City, N.Y.: Doubleday, 1965); Robert A. Divine's *Second Chance: The Triumph of Internationalism in America During World War II* (New York: Atheneum, 1967); William Manchester's *The Glory and the Dream* (Boston: Little, Brown, 1973); Cabell Phillips's *The 1940s: Decade of Triumph and Trouble* (New York: Macmillan, 1975); and Samuel Eliot Morison's *Oxford History of the American People* (New York: Oxford U. Press, 1965). Joseph Lash's *Roosevelt and Churchill* (New York: W. W. Norton, 1976); Herbert Feis's *Churchill, Roosevelt, and Stalin* (Princeton, N.J.: Princeton U. Press, 1957); Robert Dallek's *FDR and American Foreign Policy* (New York: Oxford U. Press, 1979); Barbara Tuchman's *Stilwell and the American Experience in China* (New York: Macmillan, 1971); William Manchester's *American Caesar* (Boston: Little, Brown, 1978); and William Roger Louis's *Imperialism at Bay* (New York: Oxford U. Press, 1978) shed light on Willkie's wartime role.

The New York *Times,* Chicago *Tribune,* and Philadelphia *Inquirer* have preserved their extensive files of Willkie clippings and the New York *Herald Tribune*'s Willkie files are available in the Joseph Barnes papers in the Library of Congress. The National Archives film and recorded sound division has a wealth of Willkie material, including much newsreel footage of the 1940 convention and campaign and Willkie's wartime activities.

REFERENCES

CHAPTER ONE ELWOOD

On Willkie's formative years, Dorothy Dunbar Bromley's "The Education of Wendell Willkie," which appeared in the October 1940 *Harper's* is enormously helpful, along with Janet Flanner's "Rushville's Renowned Son-in-Law," *New Yorker,* October 12, 1940. Marcia Winn's series on Willkie's early life, Chicago *Tribune,* July 1–8, 1940, included numerous interviews with Willkie family and friends. Herman O. Makey's *Wendell Willkie of Elwood* and Alden Hatch's *Young Willkie* were also sources for this chapter. *Life* magazine's August 12, 1940 profile of Elwood is also useful. In the summer of 1979, the author visited Elwood.

CHAPTER TWO REBEL WITH A CAUSE

In addition to the sources cited in the previous chapter, the Indiana *Daily Student,* Indiana University archives, and Ellsworth Barnard's *Wendell Willkie: Fighter for Freedom* provided the background for this chapter. Gardner Cowles described Willkie's experience in Puerto Rico during a May 11, 1978 interview.

CHAPTER THREE ADVENTURES OF A YOUNG MAN

1. Barnard, *Wendell Wilkie,* p. 49; Barnes, *Willkie,* p. 29.
2. Barnard, p. 51.
3. WLW letter to *Harper's,* April 1944.
4. Barnard, *Wendell Willkie,* p. 54.
5. WLW letter to *Harper's,* April 1944.

6. Akron *Beacon-Journal,* June 28, 1940.
7. WLW to Newton D. Baker, April 1924, Baker MSS, Library of Congress.
8. WLW column in Birmingham *Age-Herald,* reprinted in *U.S. News,* September 8, 1944.
9. Ibid.
10. See Robert K. Murray, *The 103rd Ballot* (New York: 1976) for background on the 1924 Democratic convention; and also David M. Chalmers, *Hooded Americanism* (Garden City, N.Y.: Doubleday, 1965), pp. 175–82, for history of the Klan's political influence in Ohio.
11. Akron *Beacon-Journal,* July 11, 1924, July 17, 1924.
12. Akron *Beacon-Journal,* July 7, 1940.
13. John S. Knight, letter to author, January 17, 1978.
14. Barnard, *Wendell Willkie,* p. 47.
15. Ibid., p. 74.
16. Knight letter.
17. WLW to Hugh S. Johnson, quoted in *Saturday Evening Post,* June 22, 1940, p. 114.

CHAPTER FOUR COMMONWEALTH AND SOUTHERN

1. Interview with David E. Lilienthal, May 10, 1977.
2. Geoffrey Hellman, "Eleven Years with the Wendell Willkies," *New Yorker,* July 13, 1940, p. 19.
3. WLW letter to *Harper's,* April 1944.
4. Alva Johnston, "The Man Who Talked Back," *Saturday Evening Post,* February 25, 1939, p. 34.
5. Toledo *Blade,* March 5, 1940.
6. WLW, Birmingham *Age-Herald* column, in *U.S. News.*
7. Profile of Commonwealth and Southern, with sidebar on WLW, *Fortune,* May 1937.
8. WLW testimony before House Military Affairs Committee, April 14, 1933, WLW MSS.
9. Lilienthal, *Journals,* vol. 1, pp. 711–13.
10. Franklin D. Roosevelt to WLW, January 8, 1935, FDR Library. WLW to Edith Willkie, quoted in Barnes, *Willkie,* p. 77.
11. Lilienthal, *Journals,* vol. 1, pp. 46–47.

CHAPTER FIVE NEW DEAL CRITIC

1. Lilienthal, *Journals,* vol. 2, p. 425.
2. George W. Norris to FDR, November 13, 1936, FDR Library.
3. WLW to FDR, May 21, 1936, WLW MSS.
4. Lilienthal, *Journals,* vol. 1, pp. 64–65.
5. WLW to FDR, November 23, 1937, WLW MSS.
6. Edward Weeks to WLW, WLW MSS.
7. WLW, "Political Power," *Atlantic Monthly,* August 1937.
8. WLW to David E. Lilienthal, December 10, 1938, WLW MSS.
9. Douglas, *Go East, Young Man,* pp. 282–83.
10. Ibid., p. 283.
   "Indiana Advocate," *Time,* July 31, 1939, pp. 42–45.

CHAPTER SIX A LOVE IN SHADOW

1. Ruth Sheldon, "Edith Wilk Willkie," *Scribner's Commentator,* September 1940, p. 9.
2. Janet Flanner, "Rushville's Renowned Son-in-Law," *New Yorker,* October 12, 1940.
3. WLW to Mrs. Robert Hall, December 17, 1937.
4. Interview with William L. Shirer, October 16, 1981.
5. Rebecca West, "Wendell Willkie: Where Is He Going?" *Picture Post,* October 24, 1942.
6. de Roussy de Sales quoted in Dillon, *Wendell Willkie,* p. 293.
7. Harold L. Ickes, diaries, April 10, 1943, Ickes MSS.
   Cowles interview.
8. Shirer interview.
   Ickes diaries, April 10, 1943, Ickes MSS.
9. Cowles interview.
   Malcolm Cowley, *And I Worked At the Writer's Trade* (New York: Viking, 1978), p. 63; Hiram Haydn, *Words and Faces* (New York: Harcourt, Brace, 1974), p. 165.
10. Interview with Marcia Davenport, August 17, 1981.
11. Interview with Kenneth McCormick, September 1982.
12. Interview with John K. Hutchens, August 27, 1982.
13. WLW to Irita Van Doren, August 15, 1938, Van Doren MSS.
14. WLW to Van Doren, undated.

15. WLW to Van Doren, undated.
16. Interview with Richard Kluger, September 8, 1982.
Sanders, *Dorothy Thompson,* p. 254.
17. WLW to Van Doren, undated.
18. Barnes, *Willkie,* p. 156.
19. Confidential sources.
20. Interview with Barbara Klaw, December 12, 1978.
Interview with Joseph Alsop, September 1, 1981.
21. Davenport interview.
22. Davenport interview.
Jane Dick, *Volunteers and the Making of Presidents* (New York: Dodd, Mead, 1980), p. 25.
23. Lilienthal, *Journals,* vol. 6, pp. 71–72.
24. Ickes diaries, February 8, 1941, Ickes MSS.
25. Interview with Marquis Childs, September 22, 1978.
26. WLW to Van Doren, April 19, 1940, Van Doren MSS.

CHAPTER SEVEN THE LONG SHOT

1. Transcript of "Town Meeting of the Air," January 6, 1938, WLW MSS.
2. Johnston, "The Man Who Talked Back," p. 11.
3. WLW to Roy Nesbitt, January 11, 1938.
4. Parmet and Hecht, *Never Again,* pp. 50–53.
Mary Gilson to WLW, January 7, 1938.
Edward R. Stettinius, Jr., to WLW, January 11, 1938.
Herbert Bayard Swope to WLW, January 10, 1938.
5. WLW to Felix Frankfurter, March 3, 1938.
Frankfurter to WLW, March 4, 1938, Barnes MSS.
6. Elson, *Time Inc. 1923–41,* p. 416.
Arthur Krock, New York *Times,* February 22, 1939.
7. G. Vernor Rogers, letter to the editor, New York *Herald Tribune,* March 3, 1939.
8. WLW to J. G. Baldwin, March 7, 1939.
WLW to Evva Skelton Tomb, April 7, 1939.
9. David Lawrence column, May 22, 1939, WLW MSS.
WLW to David Lawrence, June 12, 1938, Barnes MSS.
10. Nathan Miller quoted in Barnes, *Willkie,* p. 159.
11. *Time,* July 31, 1939, p. 45.

12. S. F. Porter, "Mr. Willkie's Man Davenport," *This Week*, August 18, 1940, p. 7.
M. Davenport, *Too Strong for Fantasy*, p. 259.
13. Elson, *Time Inc. 1923–41*, pp. 416–18.
John K. Jessup quoted from his preface to Russell Davenport, *The Dignity of Man* (New York: Harper, 1955).
14. M. Davenport, *Too Strong for Fantasy*, pp. 114–18.
15. Ibid., pp. 261–63.
16. Dick, *Volunteers*, p. 23.
17. Shaddegg, *Clare Boothe Luce*, p. 117.
Wilfred Sheed, *Clare Boothe Luce* (New York: E. P. Dutton, 1982), p. 85.
18. Moscow, *Roosevelt and Willkie*, p. 53.
M. Davenport, *Too Strong for Fantasy*, p. 265.
Dick, *Volunteers*, pp. 23–24.
19. Parmet and Hecht, *Never Again*, pp. 68–69.
20. Dillon, *Wendell Willkie*, p. 124.
21. Moscow, *Roosevelt and Willkie*, p. 50.
22. WLW quoted in Parmet and Hecht, *Never Again*, p. 72.
23. WLW to Arthur Krock, December 1, 1939.
24. WLW to Gardner Cowles, April 3, 1940.

CHAPTER EIGHT HATS IN THE RING

1. New York *Sun*, January 16, 1940.
2. Arthur H. Vandenberg, diary, November 27, 1938, Vandenberg MSS.; see also Dean Acheson, *Sketches from Life of Men I Have Known* (New York: Harper, 1960), pp. 125, 145–46; Rovere, *American Establishment*, pp. 182–87; and Tompkins, *Senator Arthur H. Vandenberg*, pp. 159–83.
3. Smith, *Thomas E. Dewey*, pp. 285–301.
4. Patterson, *Mr. Republican*, pp. 205–22.
5. Ickes, *Secret Diary*, June 25, 1939, vol. 2, p. 656–57.
Charles L. McNary to Kern Crandall, January 25, 1940, McNary MSS.
6. Richard L. Neuberger, "McNary's Chances," *Life*, May 13, 1940, p. 14.
Marie B. Hecht, *Beyond the Presidency* (New York: Macmillan, 1976), pp. 137–38.
Burner, *Herbert Hoover*, p. 332.
Wilson, *Herbert Hoover*, pp. 221–23.

CHAPTER NINE THE FIRES OF SPRING

1. Russell Davenport to WLW, February 18, 1940, WLW MSS.
2. WLW to Davenport, February 20, 1940, WLW MSS.
3. WLW, "We the People," *Fortune,* May 1940.
4. Gardner Cowles to WLW, April 1, 1940.
   Frank Knox to WLW, March 23, 1940.
5. Oren Root to WLW, April 9, 1940.
   Interview with Oren Root, August 10, 1981.
   Root, *Persons and Persuasions,* pp. 18–49.
6. Russell Davenport to Raymond Clapper, April 6, 1940. Clapper MSS.
7. Janet Flanner, "Rushville's Renowned Son-in-Law," *New Yorker,* October 12, 1940.
   Cowles interview.
8. Henry R. Luce to *Time* editors, quoted in Elson, *Time Inc. 1923–1941,* p. 422.
9. Halleck interview, Indiana University oral history project.
10. Sinclair Weeks, memorandum on WLW's nomination, Hamilton MSS.
11. WLW interview in Philadelphia *Bulletin,* April 16, 1940.
12. Lambert, *All Out of Step,* p. 257.
13. Herbert Hoover to Walter Newton, May 11, 1940, postpresidential correspondence, Hoover Library.
14. WLW quoted in *Time,* June 24, 1940, p. 18.

CHAPTER TEN "WE WANT WILLKIE"

1. McCoy, *Landon of Kansas,* p. 438.
2. Lasadas Fargo, *The Game of The Foxes* (New York: David McKay, 1971), pp. 480–82.
   Parmet and Hecht, *Never Again,* pp. 137–39.
3. "Story of Wendell Willkie," *Time,* June 24, 1940, pp. 16–19.
   "Willkie Would Win," *U.S. News,* June 28, 1940, pp. 16–17.
   Saturday Evening Post, June 22, 1940.
4. Halleck oral history.
5. Catledge, *My Life and the Times,* pp. 120–21.
   Damon Runyon column, New York *Daily Mirror,* June 26, 1940, p. 10.
6. Krock, *Memoirs,* pp. 192–95.
   Catledge, *My Life and the Times,* p. 121.

7. Interview with Edwin F. Jaeckle, November 1981.
8. Interview with Richard L. Strout, September 1981.
9. Interview with Ralph H. Cake, August 24, 1971.
10. Charles L. McNary to Ella Stolz, June 25, 1940, McNary MSS.
McNary to Cornelia McNary, June 27, 1940.
11. Vandenberg, *Private Papers,* pp. 5–6.
12. Alf M. Landon to Arthur Capper, June 5, 1940, Landon MSS.
13. Halleck oral history.
14. Charles A. Sprague to Sigfrid Unander, June 25, 1940, Sprague MSS., Oregon State Archives.
15. Halleck oral history.
16. James P. Selvage, oral history, Hoover Library.
Herbert Hoover to George Sokolsky, August 5, 1940.
Dorothy Emerson affidavit, July 3, 1947, postpresidential file, Hoover Library.
17. Pryor quoted in Johnson, *The Republican Party and Wendell Willkie,* p. 92.
18. Halleck oral history.
19. *Editorial Research Reports* survey, July 2, 1940.
20. New York *Herald Tribune,* June 27, 1940, p. 1.
21. Interview with Alf M. Landon, June 21, 1976.
22. Halleck oral history.
23. Vandenberg, *Private Papers,* pp. 5–7.
Herbert Clark to Herbert Hoover, July 1940, postpresidential file, Hoover Library.
24. John Cowles to C. Nelson Sparks, December 4, 1943, WLW MSS.
25. Thomas E. Dewey to James A. Patterson, October 20, 1969, Dewey MSS.
26. Martin, *Fifty Years in Politics,* pp. 153–59.
27. John D. M. Hamilton, Hamilton MSS., Library of Congress.
28. H. L. Mencken to Doris Fleeson, July 3, 1940, quoted in Bode, *The New Mencken Letters,* p. 463.
29. Cake interview.
30. Charles L. McNary to Ella Stolz, June 28, 1940.
McNary to Cornelia McNary, June 29, 1940.
31. Martin, *Fifty Years in Politics,* p. 160.
32. Ickes, *Secret Diary,* June 29–30, 1940, vol. 3, p. 220–23.
33. Farley, *Jim Farley's Story,* p. 244.

34. Charles L. McNary to Carl E. Wimberly, June 28, 1940.
Vandenberg, *Private Papers,* p. 7.
35. Hans Thomsen quoted in Fargo, *Game of the Foxes,* p. 482.
36. Cowles interview.
37. Luce quoted in Elson, *Time Inc. 1923–1941,* p. 427.
38. *Editorial Research Reports* survey, July 2, 1940.

CHAPTER ELEVEN LIMELIGHT

1. Alf M. Landon to WLW, July 9, 1940.
Sherwood, *Roosevelt and Hopkins,* p. 174.
Winchell, *Winchell Exclusive,* p. 126.
Catledge, *My Life and the Times,* p. 122.
2. Halleck oral history.
3. Moley, *Twenty-Seven Masters of Politics,* pp. 49–50.
4. Martin, *Fifty Years in Politics,* pp. 103–7.
5. Ibid.
6. Root interview.
R. N. Smith, *Dewey,* p. 326.
7. Charles L. McNary to Cornelia McNary, July 9, 1940.
8. Paul Smith, *Personal File* (New York: Appleton-Century-Crofts, 1964), pp. 255–56.
9. Interview with John W. Hanes, October 9, 1981.
10. Cowles interview.
Lambert, *All Out of Step,* pp. 259–60.
Ruth McCormick Simms to Thomas E. Dewey, July 16, 1940.
11. Herbert Hoover to Walter Brown, July 26, 1940.
Interview with Elliott Roosevelt, February 1982.
12. Herbert Hoover to Gardner Cowles, August 16, 1940.
13. Joseph Persico, *The Imperial Rockefeller* (New York: Simon & Schuster, 1982), p. 32.
14. Richard L. Strout to Erwin D. Canham, August 22, 1940.
15. Martin, *Fifty Years in Politics,* pp. 109–10.
Interview with Palmer Hoyt, September 8, 1974.
16. Pryor quoted in Parmet and Hecht, *Never Again,* p. 211.
Cowles interview.
Walter Lippmann to WLW, July 30, 1940, quoted in Steel, *Walter Lippmann,* pp. 386–87.
17. Richard L. Strout to Erwin D. Canham, August 22, 1940.

18. Ibid.
19. M. Davenport, *Too Strong for Fantasy*, p. 275.
Halleck oral history.
Martin, *Fifty Years in Politics*, pp. 112–13.
Hanes interview.
Edward J. Flynn, quoted in Moley, *Twenty-Seven Masters of Politics*, p. 50.
20. Richard L. Strout to Erwin D. Canham, August 22, 1940.
21. Lawrence, *Six Presidents*, pp. 39–41.
22. Alsop interview.
Barnes, *Willkie*, pp. 201–3.
23. W. A. White to FDR, August 11, 1936, FDR Library.
24. R. N. Smith, *Dewey*, p. 329.
25. Schlesinger, *The Imperial Presidency*, p. 107.

CHAPTER TWELVE THE CAMPAIGN OF 1940

1. Marquis Childs, "The Education of Wendell Willkie," in Milton Crane, ed., *The Roosevelt Era* (New York: Boni & Gaer, 1947), p. 477.
2. Ruth Sheldon, "Edith Wilk Willkie," *Scribner's Commentator*, September 1940, p. 21.
3. Dillon, *Wendell Willkie*, pp. 187–88.
4. Daniels, *White House Witness*, p. 119.
5. Raymond Clapper 1940 correspondence, n.d., Clapper MSS.
Douglas, *Go East, Young Man*, p. 339.
R. J. C. Butow, "The FDR Tapes," *American Heritage*, February/March 1982, pp. 20–22.
6. Halleck oral history.
Interview with Henry Cabot Lodge, August 1981.
Time, November 4, 1940.
7. John D. M. Hamilton, "Willkie's First Trip," Hamilton MSS.
Lawrence, *Six Presidents*, p. 41.
Robert A. Taft to Thomas E. Dewey, September 17, 1940, Taft MSS, Library of Congress.
Clapper, *Watching the World*, pp. 159–61.
8. Lawrence, *Six Presidents*, p. 43.
9. M. Davenport, *Too Strong for Fantasy*, p. 277.
Barnes, *Willkie*, p. 197.
Hamilton, "Willkie's First Trip."

10. Lambert, *All Out of Step,* p. 260.
George Sokolsky to Herbert Hoover, August 24, 1940, Hoover MSS.
A. L. Shultz to John D. M. Hamilton, September 15, 1940, Hamilton MSS.
M. Davenport, *Too Strong for Fantasy,* p. 276.
Luce letter to Davenport quoted in Elson, *Time Inc. 1923–1941,* pp. 437–38.
Ibid., p. 442.
11. Walter Lippmann to WLW, July 30, 1940.
Luce quoted in Elson, *Time Inc. 1923–1941,* p. 436.
Clapper, *Watching the World,* p. 161.
12. Childs, "The Education of Wendell Willkie," p. 475.
13. Hamilton, "An Offer of the Chairmanship," Hamilton MSS.
Martin, *Fifty Years in Politics,* p. 126.
14. Butow, "The FDR Tapes," pp. 18–19.
15. P. Smith, *Personal File,* pp. 263–65.
16. Walter Lippmann to Henry Luce, September 30, 1940, quoted in Steel, *Walter Lippmann,* p. 387.
Sanders, *Dorothy Thompson,* pp. 265–70.
Robert A. Taft to Horace Taft, July 6, 1940.
17. Rovere, *American Establishment,* p. 194.
Root interview.
18. Burns, *Roosevelt: The Lion and the Fox,* pp. 445–46.
Ickes, *Secret Diary,* October 19, 1940, vol. 3, pp. 351–52.
19. Lash, *Roosevelt and Churchill,* pp. 237, 246–47.
20. Fargo, *Game of the Foxes,* pp. 482–93.
Joseph Goebbels, *The Goebbels Diaries,* December 14, 1942, p. 276.
21. Joe Louis, *Joe Louis: My Story* (New York: Harcourt, Brace, 1978), pp. 158–59.
22. Lawrence, *Six Presidents,* p. 43.
23. Catledge, *My Life and the Times,* p. 121.
Charles L. McNary to Ella Stolz, September 25, 1940.
McNary to Cornelia McNary, October 4, 1940.
Halleck oral history.
Interview with Carlton Savage, February 4, 1982.
McNary to Cornelia McNary, September 17, 1940.
McNary to Ella Stolz, October 14, 1940.
24. Edward Willkie quoted in Barnard, *Wendell Willkie,* p. 258.
Rosenman, *Working with Roosevelt,* p. 242.
Sherwood, *Roosevelt and Hopkins,* p. 191.

25. Ibid., p. 190.
26. Herbert Hoover to Charles Evans Hughes, October 17, 1940, Hoover MSS., also quoted in Merlo Pusey, *Charles Evans Hughes* (New York: Macmillan, 1951), pp. 785–86.
27. Michael Beschloss, *Kennedy and Roosevelt* (New York: W. W. Norton, 1980), pp. 15–17, 215–19.
William Stephenson, *A Man Called Intrepid* (New York: Harcourt, Brace, 1976), pp. 161–62.
28. Melvyn Dubofsky and Warren Van Tine, *John L. Lewis* (New York: Quadrangle, 1977), pp. 357–66.
Perkins, *The Roosevelt I Knew,* pp. 116–17.
Hamilton, "John L. Lewis Broadcast in the Campaign of 1940," Hamilton MSS.
Childs, "The Education of Wendell Willkie," in *The Roosevelt Era,* pp. 471–72.
Interview with George H. Gallup, October 13, 1976.
29. Lodge interview.
Martin, *Fifty Years in Politics,* pp. 119–20.
Lambert, *All Out of Step,* p. 260.
Charles L. McNary to Cornelia McNary, October 20, 1940.
30. Raymond Clapper to Henry Luce, October 8, 1940.
H. L. Mencken to Elizabeth Peck Hanes, October 15, 1940.
Root, *Persons and Persuasions,* p. 48.
31. *Time*'s November 11, 1940 election special issue and the November 7 New York *Times* provided detailed accounts of WLW on election night.
32. WLW to FDR, November 6, 1940, President's personal file [PPF], FDR Library.
N. Roosevelt, *Front Row Seat,* p. 244.
Henry L. Stimson to WLW, November 10, 1940, WLW MSS.
33. Cake interview.
Martin, *Fifty Years in Politics,* p. 120.
Flynn, *You're the Boss,* pp. 168–69.
34. Herbert Hoover notes on November 16, 1940 meeting with WLW, postpresidential file, Hoover Library.
WLW to Mark Sullivan, November 24, 1940.
WLW to Mark Sullivan, November 25, 1940.
35. Lambert, *All Out of Step,* p. 260.
36. J. Roosevelt, *My Parents,* p. 164.

CHAPTER 13 THE POLITICS OF WAR

1. Lodge interview.
   Cowles interview.
   Blum, *V Was for Victory,* p. 265.
2. Excerpts from letters to WLW quoted in New York *Times,* November 17, 1940.
   WLW campaign correspondence.
   Hubert Work to David Lawrence, December 2, 1940, WLW MSS.
   David Lawrence to WLW, December 4, 1940.
3. Hamilton memorandum on his resignation as executive director, Hamilton MSS.
4. WLW to Donald Thornburgh, December 18, 1940.
   WLW to David Sarnoff, January 4, 1941.
5. Childs, "The Education of Wendell Willkie," in *The Roosevelt Era,* p. 479.
   Shirer interview.
   William H. Lawrence to WLW, April 5, 1943.
6. WLW to Irita Van Doren, November 21, 1940.
   WLW to Van Doren, November 26, 1940.
7. Felix Frankfurter, private diary, January 16, 1941, Frankfurter MSS, Library of Congress.
8. WLW to Robert S. Allen, January 17, 1941.
9. Stephenson, *A Man Called Intrepid,* p. 169.
   Frankfurter diary, January 16, 1941.
10. WLW to Allen, January 17, 1941.
11. Martin, *Fifty Years in Politics,* pp. 128–29.
12. Arthur Capper to Alf M. Landon, January 23, 1941.
13. John D. M. Hamilton to James Winne, May 16, 1941.
14. Frankfurter diary, January 16, 1941.
15. J. Roosevelt and Shalett, *Affectionately, FDR,* p. 325.
    Grace Tully, *FDR, My Boss,* p. 58.
    Perkins, *The Roosevelt I Knew,* p. 117.
16. Alsop interview.
    Lawrence, *Six Presidents,* p. 61.
    Krock, *The Consent of the Governed,* p. 58.
17. Lash, *Roosevelt and Churchill,* p. 280.
    Sherwood, *Roosevelt and Hopkins,* pp. 2–3.
18. Perkins, *The Roosevelt I Knew,* pp. 117–18.
19. Ickes diaries, February 8, 1941, Ickes MSS.

20. Eleanor Roosevelt, *This I Remember*, p. 222.
21. Childs, "The Education of Wendell Willkie," in *The Roosevelt Era*, p. 478.
22. WLW to Robert S. Allen, January 17, 1941.
23. Anthony Eden quoted on WLW in Frankfurter diary, March 17, 1943, Lash, *From the Diaries of Felix Frankfurter*, p. 219.
24. WLW response to Curran published in New York *Times*, January 31, 1941.
25. Winston S. Churchill, *The Grand Alliance* (Boston: Houghton Mifflin, 1950), p. 25.
    Lash, *Roosevelt and Churchill*, p. 281.
26. Rebecca West to author.
    WLW to Irita Van Doren, January 29, 1941.
    WLW to Van Doren, February 5, 1941.
27. Churchill, *Grand Alliance*, p. 25.
28. U.S. consul in Manchester (Tait) to Secretary of State, NADR, February 4, 1941.
29. Secretary of State to U.S. minister in Dublin, January 21, 1941, NADR.
30. U.S. minister in Dublin to the Secretary of State, February 4, 1941, NADR.
31. WLW told the anecdote about his conversation with the King and Queen in his March 25, 1941 speech in Montreal, Willkie MSS.
32. Harry Hopkins to FDR, January 1941, Hopkins confidential file, NADR; also quoted in Sherwood, *Roosevelt and Hopkins*, p. 243.
33. Cordell Hull to WLW, January 30, 1941, NADR.
    U.S. minister in London to Secretary of State, January 31, 1941, NADR.
34. Mark Sullivan, "Willkie's Odyssey," Philadelphia *Inquirer*, February 8, 1941, p. 1.
    Perkins, *The Roosevelt I Knew*, pp. 118–19.
35. Dillon, *Wendell Willkie*, pp. 239–40.
36. John Cowles telephone interview with Raymond Clapper, February 10, 1941, Clapper MSS., Library of Congress.
37. Arthur Krock to WLW, February 9, 1941.
38. WLW testimony before Senate Foreign Relations Committee, excerpts published in New York *Times*, February 12, 1941.
39. William Allen White to Judge William A. Smith, quoted in Barnes, *Willkie*, pp. 254–55.

40. Ernest K. Lindley, "Willkie's Increasing Stature," Washington *Post,* February 23, 1941.
41. Clapper, *Watching the World,* p. 166.
42. Martin, *Fifty Years in Politics,* p. 121.
43. Childs, "The Education of Wendell Willkie" in *The Roosevelt Years,* p. 469.
44. Ickes, *Secret Diary,* February 8, 1941, vol. 3, p. 427.
Perkins, *The Roosevelt I Knew,* p. 119.
45. Churchill to FDR, draft of reply to WLW, May 19, 1941, FDR Library.
46. FDR to John G. Winant for Churchill, May 19, 1941, NADR.
47. Winston Churchill to WLW, quoted in Lash, *Roosevelt and Churchill,* p. 319.
48. The U.S. consul general in Toronto to the Secretary of State, March 26, 1941.
49. WLW, "Americans, Stop Being Afraid," *Collier's,* May 10, 1941.
50. WLW interview in *Look,* November 4, 1941.
51. FDR to WLW, August 25, 1941, PPF FDR Library.
52. David Niles to FDR, October 27, 1941, PPF.
FDR to Edwin M. Watson, October 28, 1941, PPF.
53. FDR to WLW, December 5, 1941, PPF.
54. McNary to Ella Stolz, December 12, 1941, McNary MSS.
55. WLW to FDR, December 10, 1941, WLW MSS.

CHAPTER 14 THE HOME FRONT

1. Barnard, *Wendell Willkie,* pp. 323–25.
Sherwood, *Roosevelt and Hopkins,* p. 475.
2. WLW interview in *Look,* April 7, 1942.
Burns, *FDR: Soldier of Freedom,* p. 274.
3. Farley, *Jim Farley's Story,* p. 346.
4. FDR to WLW, February 21, 1942, FDR Library.
5. Martin, *Fifty Years in Politics,* p. 131.
Cowles interview.
6. WLW to Drew Pearson, June 26, 1942.
7. Interview with Warren Moscow, February 1982.
Warren Moscow, *Politics in the Empire State* (New York: Alfred A. Knopf, 1948), pp. 79–80.
8. Thomas E. Dewey to Annie L. T. Dewey, April 6, 1942.

9. Martin, *Fifty Years in Politics,* p. 131.
10. WLW interview in *Look,* April 7, 1942.
11. WLW lists choices for governor, New York *Times,* April 4, 1942.
12. WLW to Pearson, June 26, 1942, and July 2, 1942.
13. Gardner Cowles to WLW, May 21, 1942.
WLW to Cowles, May 25, 1942.
14. British ambassador in Washington to Foreign Office, June 4, 1942, quoted in H. G. Nicholas, ed., *Despatches from Washington* (Chicago: U. of Chicago Press, 1981), p. 42.
15. Drew Pearson and Robert S. Allen column, Philadelphia *Record,* June 23, 1942.
16. N. Roosevelt, *Front Row Seat,* p. 244.
Henry Cabot Lodge to WLW, April 29, 1943.
Transcript of WLW-Forrest Davis telephone conversation, NADR.
WLW to Joseph Barnes, April 26, 1943.
WLW to Elliott Bell, December 1, 1942.
Frankfurter diary, January 16, 1941, Frankfurter MSS., Library of Congress.
17. Freda Kirchwey, "The Willkie Boom," *Nation,* July 4, 1942.
Bartley Crum quoted in Barnard, *Wendell Willkie,* p. 569.
"The People's Choice," *Time,* June 29, 1942.
18. WLW to Benjamin Teitel, June 23, 1942.
19. Dorothy G. Hays to Lem Jones, June 21, 1942, Willkie MSS.
20. Lem Jones quoted in Barnard, *Wendell Willkie,* p. 332.
21. Cowles interview.
Thomas E. Dewey to Annie Dewey, July 29, 1942.

CHAPTER 15 SPECIAL ENVOY

1. WLW quoted from press conference at U.S. embassy, Ankara, September 7, 1942, NADR.
2. Barnes, *Willkie,* p. 289.
3. FDR to George C. Marshall, July 31, 1942, President's personal file, FDR Library.
4. Forrest Davis interview with WLW, NADR.
Cowles interview.
Burns, *FDR: Soldier of Freedom,* p. 276.
5. Milton S. Eisenhower, *The President Is Calling* (Garden City, N.Y.: Doubleday, 1975), pp. 148–49.
6. FDR to Chiang Kai-shek, August 21, 1942, FDR Library.

26. U.S. ambassador in the Soviet Union (Standley) to the Secretary of State, September 23 and 25, 1942, NADR.
27. WLW-Forrest Davis transcript, NADR.
28. Pearson, *Diaries,* p. 387.
29. WLW, *One World,* pp. 80–84.
U.S. ambassador in the Soviet Union (Standley) to the Secretary of State, September 26, 1942, NADR.
30. FDR press conference 849, October 6, 1942, vol. 20, p. 131, FDR Library.
Wallace, *Diary,* November 4, 1942, p. 129.
31. Winston Churchill quoted in Chicago *Tribune,* September 30, 1942.
Clement Attlee quoted in Chicago *Tribune,* September 28, 1942.
Nicholas, ed., *Despatches from Washington,* p. 89.
32. Pearson column, Philadelphia *Record,* December 11, 1942.
Barnes, *Willkie,* pp. 301–3.
See also "What Foreign Correspondents Think of Willkie," *Look,* October 5, 1943, pp. 32–34.
33. "Willkie Helps Bridge Russian-American Gap" by Ralph Parker, New York *Times,* September 27, 1942.
34. Cowles interview.
35. WLW-Davis transcript, NADR.
WLW, *One World,* p. 15.
36. "Willkie Speaks Out," *New Republic,* October 19, 1942, pp. 482–83.
Winston Churchill quoted in New York *Times,* November 11, 1942.
Wallace, *Diary,* pp. 207 and 211, May 22, 1943.
37. U.S. ambassador in China (Gauss) to Secretary of State, October 8, 1942.
38. Tuchman, *Stilwell,* pp. 331–38.
John S. Service memorandum to U.S. ambassador in Chungking, November 14, 1942, NADR.
39. Blum, *V Was for Victory,* p. 268.
40. John Paton Davies, *Dragon by the Tail* (New York: W. W. Norton, 1972), p. 235.
Davenport to WLW, undated memorandum on China trip, WLW MSS.
41. WLW, *One World,* pp. 130–33.
Theodore H. White and Annalee Jacoby, *Thunder Out of China,* (New York: William Sloane, 1946), p. 125.
42. WLW, *One World,* p. 134.

7. Alexander Werth, *The Year of Stalingrad* (New York: Alfred Knopf, 1947), p. 261.
8. WLW, *One World*, p. 3.
9. Ibid., pp. 4–12.
10. Frank Gervasi, "Willkie at the Front," *Collier's*, October 24, 1942
Churchill to WLW, quoted in WLW to Joseph Barnes, December 8, 1942.
11. WLW, *One World*, p. 15.
12. The U.S. minister in Egypt (Kirk) to the Secretary of State, September 17, 1942, NADR.
WLW, *One World*, p. 3.
13. U.S. minister in Turkey (Steinhardt) to the Secretary of State, September 11, 1942, NADR.
14. Cowles interview.
Brock, U.S. minister in Turkey (Steinhardt) to Secretary of State, *Look*, October 5, 1943, p. 32.
15. The U.S. consul in Lebanon (Gwynn) to the Secretary of State, September 18 and September 21, 1942, NADR.
16. Charles de Gaulle to FDR, October 26, 1942, quoted in Milton Viorst, *Hostile Allies: FDR and Charles de Gaulle* (New York: Macmillan, 1965), p. 106.
J. Edgar Hoover to Adolf Berle, December 19, 1942, NADR.
17. WLW, *One World*, pp. 23–24.
18. Cowles interview.
19. U.S. consul general in Jerusalem (Pinkerton) to the Secretary of State, September 21, 1942, NADR.
WLW, *One World*, pp. 26–27.
20. Wallace, *Diary*, pp. 124–25.
21. WLW, "Nine Months Later," Willkie MSS.
22. U.S. chargé d'affaires in Iraq to the Secretary of State, September 14 and 23, 1942.
The Assistant Secretary of State (Alling) to WLW, December 11, 1942, NADR.
23. U.S. consul general in Iran to the Secretary of State, September 18, 22, and 24, 1942, NADR.
24. "What Foreign Correspondents Think of Willkie," *Look*, October 5, 1943, p. 32.
25. U.S. ambassador in the Soviet Union (Standley) to the Secretary of State, September 22, 1942, NADR.

43. Pearson, *Diaries,* p. 388.
Davies, *Dragon by the Tail,* p. 255.
44. Ibid., p. 256.
45. Cowles interview.
WLW to Joseph Barnes, December 11, 1942.
46. Cowles interview.
Tuchman, *Stilwell,* p. 335.
47. Ibid., pp. 333–34.
48. WLW, *One World,* pp. 137–38.
49. Barnes, *Willkie,* p. 307.
50. Dillon, *Wendell Willkie,* p. 288.
51. WLW draft notes for conversation with FDR, October 14, 1942, Willkie MSS.
Acheson quoted in Ickes diaries, November 1, 1942, Ickes MSS., Library of Congress.
52. "Report to the American People," October 26, 1942, WLW MSS.
53. Clare Boothe Luce to WLW, October 27, 1942, WLW MSS.
William Allen White column, Philadelphia *Bulletin,* October 29, 1942.
54. WLW, *One World,* pp. 175–76.
Stimson and Bundy, *On Active Service,* pp. 543–44.
55. Barnes, *Willkie,* p. 313.
56. WLW to Mrs. Raymond Clapper, January 2, 1943.
57. Reviews: New York *Herald Tribune Books,* April 11, 1943; *New Yorker,* April 17, 1943, p. 79; *New Republic,* April 19, 1943, p. 513; *Commonweal,* April 30, 1943, p. 45.
58. Barnes, *Willkie,* p. 316.

CHAPTER 16 THE GOOD FIGHT

1. Carol King, "The Willkie I Knew," *New Masses,* October 24, 1944, pp. 10–11.
2. Ibid.
3. Barnes, *Willkie,* p. 318.
WLW, "Fair Trial," *New Republic,* March 18, 1940, pp. 370–72.
4. WLW to Bartley Crum, December 3, 1941.
5. King, "The Willkie I Knew," p. 10.
6. WLW brief, *Schneiderman* v. *U.S.*, Barnes MSS.

7. Frankfurter diary, March 13, 1943, Frankfurter MSS., Library of Congress.
8. WLW, "The Case for the Minorities," *Saturday Evening Post,* June 27, 1942, p. 14.
9. Cleveland Amory, *The Last Resorts* (Westport, Conn.: Greenwood, 1973), p. 145.
10. R. J. C. Butow, "The FDR Tapes," *American Heritage,* February/March 1982, p. 24.
11. WLW, *American Program,* p. 49.
12. WLW speech before NAACP convention, July 19, 1942, Willkie MSS.
13. Walter White, *A Man Called White* (New York: Arno, 1969), pp. 200–2.
14. WLW interview in *Look,* October 5, 1943.
15. Walter White to George Gallup, May 29, 1944, WLW MSS.
Elmo Roper to Russell Davenport, July 26, 1943, WLW MSS.
16. Russell Davenport, "The Ordeal of Wendell Willkie," *Atlantic Monthly,* November 1945, p. 69.
McWilliams, *Education of Carey McWilliams,* p. 114.

CHAPTER 17 STARTING OVER

1. Cowles interview.
Nicholas, ed., *Despatches from Washington,* p. 42.
2. John D. M. Hamilton to Roy Dunn, November 18, 1942, Hamilton MSS.
Luce quoted in Elson, *The World of Time Inc., 1941–1960,* p. 71.
3. Frederick E. Baker to Ralph H. Cake, November 16, 1942, WLW MSS.
4. Martin, *Fifty Years in Politics,* p. 134.
5. Indianapolis *Star,* February 28, 1943, p. 1.
6. Homer E. Capehart to WLW, February 13, 1943.
John Cowles to WLW, February 11, 1943.
WLW to John Cowles, March 25, 1943.
7. Moley, *Twenty-Seven Masters of Politics,* pp. 52–53.
8. Elson, *Time Inc. 1941–1960,* p. 71.
John D. M. Hamilton to Ezra Whitla, May 25, 1943.
John D. M. Hamilton to Ruth Simms, June 21, 1943.
John D. M. Hamilton to Werner Schroeder, June 11, 1943.
Ruth Simms to John D. M. Hamilton, June 17, 1943.

9. WLW to William Allen White, June 14, 1943.
William Allen White to WLW, July 8 and 20, 1943.
10. "I'd Rather Be Right" by Samuel Grafton, New York *Post,* October 16, 1944.
11. Vandenberg, *Private Papers,* p. 56.
Robert A. Taft to Thomas E. Dewey, July 27, 1942, Taft MSS.
12. WLW to William Allen White, September 19, 1943.
13. WLW interview, *Look,* October 5, 1943.
Harlan Logan to WLW, May 27, 1943.
14. Arthur Krock, "Willkie Plan of Attack," New York *Times,* September 22, 1943.
John D. M. Hamilton notes on conference with Charles L. McNary, October 19, 1943, Hamilton MSS.
15. John D. M. Hamilton to C. D. Hicks, December 31, 1943.
Ruth Simms to Thomas E. Dewey, October 25, 1943.
Dewey to Simms, November 19, 1943.
16. Vandenberg, *Private Papers,* p. 78.
17. Manchester, *American Caesar,* p. 357–63.
18. Bruce Johnstone to WLW, November 8, 1943.
Bartley Crum to Charles Blyth, December 2, 1943, WLW MSS.
Drew Pearson, Philadelphia *Record,* October 16, 1943.
19. I. F. Stone, "Willkie and FDR," *Nation,* October 24, 1942, p. 403.
20. Ickes, diaries, October 25, 1942, Ickes MSS.
Sherwood, *Roosevelt and Hopkins,* pp. 830–31.
21. WLW to Edgar M. Queeny, June 12, 1942, and October 6, 1943.
Queeny questions for WLW published in New York *Times,* September 12, 1943.
Gardner Cowles to WLW, September 24, 1943.
22. *Life,* November 15, 1943, p. 30.
23. Luce quoted in Elson, *Time Inc. 1941–1960,* p. 71.
Shaddegg, *Clare Boothe Luce,* p. 193.
Hamilton on McNary-Luce meeting, October 1943, Hamilton MSS.
John Cowles to Sinclair Weeks, December 21, 1943, WLW MSS.
24. Elson, *Time Inc. 1941–1960,* p. 80.
25. Alf M. Landon to John D. M. Hamilton, September 15, 1943.
John D. M. Hamilton to Thomas Coleman, December 13, 1943.
Gardner Cowles to WLW, January 21, 1944.
26. Willkie's exploration of an independent candidacy was disclosed by Marquis Childs, St. Louis *Post-Dispatch,* December 11, 1943, p. 1.

27. Thomas E. Dewey to Ruth Hanna McCormick Simms, December 23, 1943.
28. WLW quoted by Wilfred E. Binkley, "Wendell Willkie: The Party's Embarrassing Conscience," in J. T. Salter, ed., *Public Men In and Out of Office* (Chapel Hill: U. of N.C. Press, 1946), p. 53.

CHAPTER 18 ROSES IN THE SNOW

1. Interviews with Hanes and Cowles.
   Gardner Cowles to John W. Hanes, January 21, 1965, Hanes personal files.
2. John Cowles to WLW, January 22, 1944.
3. WLW to John Cowles, January 27, 1944.
4. John D. M. Hamilton to Harold W. Mason, January 6, 1944.
5. George H. Gallup, *The Gallup Poll* (New York: Random House, 1972), vol. 1, pp. 428–29.
6. WLW speech, February 2, 1944, WLW MSS.
7. Henry Steele Commager to WLW, February 4, 1944.
8. "Willkie Dares Again," *New Republic*, February 14, 1944, p. 197.
   New York *Times*, February 3, 1944.
9. Darryl F. Zanuck to WLW, October 7, 1943; see also Zanuck to WLW, October 27, 1943 and January 19, 1944, WLW MSS.
10. Cake profile, *Time*, February 28, 1944, p. 24.
11. Coe McKenna to John D. M. Hamilton, March 1, 1944.
    John D. M. Hamilton to Walter Tooze, January 24, 1944, Hamilton MSS.
12. WLW, "Don't Stir Mistrust of Russia," New York *Times Magazine*, January 2, 1944, pp. 3–4.
    U.S. ambassador in the Soviet Union (Harriman) to FDR, February 7, 1944, NADR.
13. Gardner Cowles to WLW, January 1944, WLW MSS.
14. John D. M. Hamilton to A. L. Shultz, March 16, 1944.
    Hamilton to Henry A. Bubb, March 16, 1944.
    Alf M. Landon to John D. M. Hamilton, March 1, 1944.
15. Memo to John Cowles on Wisconsin political situation, December 21, 1943.
    WLW to John Cowles, January 27, 1944.
16. Marquis Childs, New York *Post*, April 7, 1944.
17. Willard Shelton, "Willkie Against the Gods," *Nation*, April 8, 1944, p. 412–13.

18. Interview with Vernon Thomson, 1981.
19. WLW speech, "The Function of a Political Party," March 20, 1944, WLW MSS.
20. Childs column, Washington *Post*, March 22, 1944, p. 11.
Henry Steele Commager to WLW, April 17, 1944.
21. Thomas E. Coleman to John D. M. Hamilton, March 18, 1944.
Hamilton to Coleman, March 21, 1944.
Hamilton to A. L. Shultz, March 23, 1944.
22. WLW attacks Harold Stassen, New York *Herald Tribune*, March 22, 1944.
23. Thomson interview.
Thomas E. Coleman to John D. M. Hamilton, March 24, 1944.
24. Cowles interview.
Thomson interview.
25. Thomas E. Coleman to John D. M. Hamilton, April 1, 1944.
John Cowles to WLW, April 2, 1944.
26. Cowles interview.
"Proud," *New Yorker*, April 22, 1944, p. 21.
27. Walter Lippmann to WLW, April 10, 1944, WLW MSS.
Henry Steele Commager to WLW, April 17, 1944.
William L. Shirer to WLW, April 10, 1944.
Charles A. Sprague to WLW, May 22, 1944.
28. Moley, *Twenty-Seven Masters of Politics*, p. 54.
29. Thomas E. Coleman to John D. M. Hamilton, April 20, 1944.
30. Binkley, "Wendell Willkie: The Party's Embarrassing Conscience," in *Public Men In and Out of Office*, pp. 68–69.
31. "Proud," p. 21.

CHAPTER 19 BREAKING AWAY

1. WLW to Charles A. Sprague, June 1, 1944.
WLW to Josephine Pinckney, May 1, 1944.
Barnes, *Willkie*, p. 362.
WLW to Marquis Childs, May 10, 1944.
2. Elson, *Time Inc. 1941–1960*, p. 82.
WLW to Henry R. Luce, April 18, 1944, WLW MSS.
3. WLW to Marquis Childs, May 10, 1944.
4. Charles A. Sprague to WLW, May 22, 1944.
John D. M. Hamilton to James M. Bailey, April 10, 1944.
Elmo Roper, New York *Herald Tribune*, October 14, 1944.

5. Elson, *Time Inc. 1941–1960,* p. 85.
Barnard, *Wendell Willkie,* p. 476.
6. Arthur Krock, *Memoirs,* p. 196.
7. Elson, *Time Inc. 1941–1960,* pp. 88–89.
Interview with Herbert Brownell, September 10, 1981.
8. WLW to John Cowles, July 8, 1944.
9. Cowles interview.
10. FDR to George W. Norris, July 19, 1944, FDR Library.
Burns, *Roosevelt: Soldier of Freedom,* pp. 503–6.
11. Drew Pearson to WLW, August 1, 1944.
12. David Dubinsky and A. H. Raskin, *A Life with Labor* (New York: Simon & Schuster, 1977), pp. 285–87.
Shirer interview.
Rosenman, *Working with Roosevelt,* pp. 463–70.
13. FDR to WLW, July 13, 1944, FDR Library.
WLW to FDR, never mailed, in WLW MSS.
14. FDR to WLW, August 21, 1944, FDR Library.
15. Elliott Roosevelt interview.
Bartley Crum to Joseph Barnes, February 25, 1952, Barnes MSS.
16. WLW to Gardner Cowles, August 15, 1944.
17. Rovere, *American Establishment,* p. 196.
WLW to Bruce Bliven, June 29, 1944.
Arnold Beichman, "Willkie: Fact and Myth," *New Leader,* April 20, 1953, p. 21.
18. WLW to Arthur Krock, August 28, 1944.
19. WLW, "Cowardice at Chicago," and "Citizens of Negro Blood," *Collier's,* September 7, 1944, and October 7, 1944.
20. Barnes, *Willkie,* p. 384.
Barnard, *Wendell Willkie,* p. 493.
21. WLW to John W. Hanes, October 2, 1944.
WLW to Leverett Saltonstall, September 27, 1944.
Walter White, *Man Called White,* p. 205.
Roscoe Drummond, "Wendell Willkie: A Study in Courage," in *Aspirin Age,* p. 467.
22. Ibid., p. 445.

INDEX

M

B
Willkie
Neal
Dark horse : a biography of
Wendell Willkie